# Contents

List of Tables     ix

List of Figures     xi

One: **Introduction and Background**     1

Two: **The Family**     19

Three: **The Developmental Cycle in Domestic Groups**     47

Four: **Descent and Descent Groups**     69

Five: **Alliance Theory; Part I: Theory**     105

Six: **Alliance Theory; Part II: Applications**     129

Seven: **Mathematical Models of Marriage Systems**     151

Eight: **Methods for the Analysis of Kinship Terminology**     165

Nine: **Linguistic Models for Kinship Semantics**     191

Ten: **Iroquois Systems of Kinship Terminology**     219

Eleven: **Omaha- and Miwok-Type Terminologies**     247

Twelve: **Information Theory and Social Organization**     279

Thirteen: **Conclusions**     311

**Bibliography**     319

**Index**     343

discussing the relevant literature in cognitive psychology, decision theory, statistical learning theory, and related areas which anthropology students can no longer assume are irrelevant to the study of social organization.

Generally the text falls into two interrelated sections: a review of the substantive areas, and a critical discussion of recent methodological innovation. Following an introductory course in anthropology the book may be used in either a one-semester course for juniors or seniors or, with supplementary readings, in a graduate-level seminar on social organization.

Both authors would like to express their thanks to the many people who made this book possible. Buchler would like to express a deep intellectual and personal debt to Professor George P. Murdock for introducing him to the field of social organization and to Professor Claude Lévi-Strauss, Professor Louis Faron, and Professor Hugo Nutini for their encouragement during the past five years. Selby would like to express an enduring debt to Professor A. Kimball Romney, who made the study of social organization exciting and vital for all his students, to Professor Roy G. D'Andrade for his constant stimulation, to Professor Duane Metzger for his encouragement, to Professor Nevitt Sanford, and to Professor Bernard Siegel, who made it possible for him to study, and bore with him, for the past six years.

We are also deeply indebted to Professors Richard N. Adams, Hugo G. Nutini, Alan Beals, John Hotchkiss, and Nicholas A. Hopkins for their comments on various chapters, and to two of our students, Richard A. Thompson and Ricardo Falla, S.J., for many helpful suggestions and criticisms. We are indebted to Lucy G. Selby for her analysis of the trobriand, which falls in Chapter Two.

This book is dedicated to our parents, wives, and children as an expression of the fact that, on the affective level, descent and affinity are not contrastive.

I. R. B.
H. A. S.

# Preface

Since the publication of Lowie's (1948) review of the field of social organization numerous articles and monographs have been published on various special topics that are usually assigned to the category of kinship and social organization. Although many of these publications synthesize particular areas and others present significant methodological and theoretical innovations, there has been no general stocktaking of current developments in the anthropological approach to social organization for very nearly two decades. The need for a work of this sort was called to our attention by students on both the undergraduate and graduate level who had grown weary of searching for back numbers of various journals, and who felt the need of a source book where reference to the various interests and controversies that they were being exposed to for the first time could be traced down. This book is designed, therefore, to introduce students of social anthropology and related fields to the contemporary scene in the study of social organization and, at the same time, to present a partial historical review of modern developments in the field. We also hope that the text may prove helpful to anthropologists working in other areas who may be interested in reviewing current developments and who have neither the time nor the inclination to track down the original sources.

This text should be considered a stocktaking of the field, rather than a completely comprehensive view, although we have attempted to review and evaluate in some detail the writing of British social anthropologists, American formalists, and French structuralists. No other text, currently on the market, makes this effort.

The demands of reviewing the literature have precluded developing new and demanding approaches in the area of mathematical applications, or of

First Printing

Library of Congress catalog card number: 68-18473

THE MACMILLAN COMPANY, NEW YORK
COLLIER-MACMILLAN CANADA, LTD., TORONTO, ONTARIO

Printed in the United States of America

**Ira R. Buchler** and **Henry A. Selby**

Department of Anthropology, University of Texas

# Kinship and Social Organization

An Introduction to Theory and Method

**The Macmillan Company**, New York

**Collier-Macmillan Limited**, London

# List of Tables

2–1. Proportion of Female-Headed Households in Twenty
     Communities     25
2–2. Matrix of Relational Types     27
2–3. Interaction Codings     30
2–4. Table of Relationships     32
3–1. Spouse-Seeking and Economic Status     50
3–2. Spouse-Seeking and Relative Wealth of Household     51
3–3. Spouse-Seeking and Economic Status in Absolute Terms     51
3–4. Household Size Under Four Conditions     54
3–5. Distribution of Household Types, Yalcuc, Mexico (Tzotzil)     56
3–6. Number of Family Types by Age of Women, Rural Village,
     Peru     58
3–7. Numerical Composition of the *bilek* Family     63
3–8. Genealogical Composition of the *bilek* Family     64
3–9. The *bilek* Family     64
4–1. Marriage, Bride Wealth, and Other Variables: A Comparison
     of Three Societies     84
4–2. Scale of Priorities for Exchange     97
5–1. Ordering of Three Types of Social Structure     117
6–1. Diagram of Terminological Spaces in Dravidian Kinship     137
6–2. Marriage and Section Assignment (Aranda)     142
7–1. Natchez Marriage and Descent Rules     157
7–2. The Ideal Marriage Relations and the Actual Marriages
     Among the Purum     161
8–1. Discriminant Variables     187
10–1. A Scalogram Analysis of Iroquois Terminological Systems     222

11–1. A Scalogram Analysis of Omaha Terminological Systems   254

11–2. Purum Categories of Descent and Alliance   268

12–1. Representation of Aranda Section System   288

12–2. Kin Types and Descent Rules   290

12–3. Information Measures   291

12–4. An Illustration of Gradual Uncertainty-Reduction: Kariera Kin Classes   292

12–5. An Illustration of Gradual Uncertainty-Reduction: Kariera Sections   292

12–6. Kariera Kinship Model   294

12–7. An Illustration of Gradual Uncertainty-Reduction: Aranda Kin Classes   295

12–8. An Illustration of Gradual Uncertainty-Reduction: Aranda Sections   296

12–9. Information Measures: Australian Section Systems   297

12–10. Sections and Moieties in Murngin   297

12–11. Efficiency Scale: Australian Section Systems   298

12–12. Efficiency Scale: Section Systems   299

12–13. The Minimum Mean Semantic Information Quantity (*Hsem*) for Kinship Terms in Six Cultures   301

12–14. A Folk Taxonomic Hierarchy of Nuer Spirits of the Above and Spirits of the Below   304

# List of Figures

2–1. Leach's Diagram, Drawn for a Female Ego                                40
2–2. Trobriand Kin Terms for a Female Ego                                   41
2–3. Trobriand Kin Terms for a Male Ego                                     42
5–1. Diametric Structure of Winnebago Village                              108
5–2. Concentric Structure of Winnebago Village                             108
5–3. Representation of the Relational and Positional Properties
     of the Dualistic/Triadic Elements of the Social Structure of (1)
     Winnebago, (2) Bororo, (3) Indonesian Society                         109
5–4. Idealized, Simplified Representation of a System of Asym-
     metric Exchange                                                       115
5–5. Matrilateral Cross-Cousin Marriage                                    121
6–1. Simplified Representation of Bilateral Cross-Cousin Marriage
     in Kariera                                                            144
6–2. Asymmetrical Intermarriage in an Eight-section System                 146
6–3. Alternating Marriage and Murngin Section System                       147
7–1. The Optimal Lines for Symmetric Exchange                              154
7–2. The Instability ($g > p$) of the Asymmetric Case                      155
7–3. The Ideal Marriage Relations Among the Clans of the Purum             160
7–4. The Ideal Marriage Relations Among the Kachin                         160
8–1. A Componential Representation of American-English Con-
     sanguineal Core Terms                                                 184
8–2. Analysis of American Kinship System                                   188
9–1. Key Diagram of a Perfect Tree                                         193
9–2. A "True" Tree                                                         194
9–3. A "True" Paradigm                                                     194
9–4. Key Diagram of a Perfect Paradigm, with Perfect Taxonomy              195

9–5. A Perfect Paradigm                                                    198
9–6. A Componential Representation of American-English Con-
     sanguineal Core Terms                                                 198
9–7. A Venn Diagram for a Pair of Referential Kin Terms                    200
9–8. An Imperfect Tree and True Paradigm                                   202
9–9. Ortho-space                                                           203
9–10. Nonortho-space Type I                                                203
9–11. Nonortho-space Type II                                               204
9–12. Logical Partitions for a Three-item Set                              205
9–13. A Typological Ordering                                               208
9–14. A Partial Taxonomic Diagram of One Dialect of American-
      English Kinship Terminology                                          210
9–15. Completely Connected Path Rules for a Three-level Taxonomy           213
9–16. A Completely Connected Graph for Taxonomic Orderings                 213
9–17. A Partial Tree Graph of American-English Kinship Termi-
      nology                                                               215
9–18. Partial Tree Graphs with Referential Synonyms                        215
11–1. The Subvarieties of "Omaha-Type" Systems of Terminology
      on the Basis of Generation Skewing in the Consanguineal
      Domain                                                               261
12–1. Representation of Kariera Section System (after Radcliffe-
      Brown)                                                               284
12–2. Representation of Kariera Section System (after Lawrence)            285
12–3. Representation of Kariera Section System (after Dumont)              285
12–4. Representation of Aranda Section System (after Radcliffe-
      Brown)                                                               286
12–5. Representation of Aranda Section System (after Lawrence)             287
12–6. Aranda Section System: Alternation of Intermarriage in
      Alternate Generations                                                287
12–7. Aranda Section System: Transition from Kariera to Aranda             288

**Kinship and Social Organization**

An Introduction to Theory and Method

# Chapter One
# Introduction and Background

We can date the beginning of the scientific study of kinship systems to about 100 years ago. Lewis Henry Morgan had completed *Systems of Consanguinity and Affinity of the Human Family*, although six years were to elapse before its publication in 1870. It was a monumental work, one of the very few in the history of science that have been virtually without predecessor. As Lowie has stated (Lowie, 1937, p. 62), "Morgan's unique distinction lies in literally creating the study of kinship systems as a branch of comparative sociology." In *Systems*, Morgan amassed an enormous amount of data on kinship terminologies, "formulated a bold and original theory to explain the various kinds of kinship systems he had discovered, . . . [and] . . . worked out a classification of kinship systems that is at least as good as any we have today" (White, 1959, p. 10). Since Morgan's work, increasing numbers of scholars each decade have written about kinship and social organization, especially in the years after World War II. The tradition of study in the area of kinship systems is comparatively long for a social science, and the continuity of effort has been productive, sufficiently so to enable us to declare the study of kinship and social organization the most highly developed area of social anthropology.

This present book is a partial stock-taking of some of the more recent work that has taken place, particularly since World War II. This chapter serves, in the main, to introduce the reader to the issues that are to be presented for discussion, particularly in the following five chapters. No attempt is made here to write the intellectual history of a centenary discipline. Others have accomplished this at least in part (Fortes, 1951; Eggan, 1937; Beattie, 1964; Murdock, 1949, 1951; Firth, 1951; Hallowell, 1960; Linton, 1936; Lowie, 1920, 1937, 1948; Romney, 1961; Davenport, 1963; Befu, 1965; and

Tax, 1937). An attempt is here made, rather, to sketch the relevant background to the specific issues that are taken up later. Under the general heading, "The Family," we discuss some problems concerned with biology and kinship, and the extensionist hypothesis. We also consider the growth of the notion of "componential definitions" in kinship. Under the general heading, "Group Formation and Descent Theory," we examine the history of the idea of descent and the role played by descent theory in the context of evolution and also the relation between descent groups and the forms of kinship terminology, and the development of universal sociological principles in the study of descent. Under the general heading, "Alliance Theory," we discuss briefly the work of the French sociological school, in particular, Durkheim, Mauss, and Lévi-Strauss in the creation of an orientation to social structure that is of great contemporary interest.

## THE FAMILY

Morgan had written *Systems* at a time when interest in the evolution of human society was very strong. In 1861, for example, *Das Mutterrecht* (Mother-right) of J. J. Bachofen had been published, and classical scholars, particularly in Germany, had instituted the search for the origins of the literature and social institutions of Greece and Rome, which they pursued with excessive zeal. In literature and history the cult of *Quellenforschungen* spilled over into anthropology and led to the construction of large-scale schemes for the interpretation of human history in terms of a series of cultural stages whereby man advanced from a state of primitive savagery to the status of a Victorian bourgeois gentleman; technology, religion, and social organization were envisaged as marching in more or less parallel columns to the summit of Victorian civilization.

Morgan also contributed to this exercise in what Radcliffe-Brown has called "conjectural history." In *Ancient Society* (1877), Morgan postulated a series of nine steps within three stages whereby all mankind had evolved from primitive savagery through barbarism to civilization. So far as social organization was concerned, evolutionists such as Bachofen (1861), Morgan (1877), Kohler (1884), Lubbock (1892), Frazer (1910), Ward (1921), Rivers (1924), and Briffault (1927) assumed a beginning state of human social organization, which came to be called "primitive promiscuity," signaled, in Morgan's (1877) scheme, by a Hawaiian type of kinship nomenclature. On a priori grounds development was seen to proceed through a period of mother-right, to father-right, with unlinear institutions withering away finally to an approximation of the patriarchal bourgeois family.

The family as such was largely bypassed in early studies on social organization—or perhaps better—was so taken for granted that there was no need felt to view it as an object of study. Evolutionary considerations, or the explanation of widely distributed clusters of customs such as wife-stealing

(McLennan), avoidance behavior (Tylor), and the clan (Morgan), were regarded as both more problematic and more productive.

From the many studies conducted by amateurs and professionals in Australia at the end of the last century (see Malinowski, 1913; Frazer, 1910, Vol. IV for bibliography) grew the notion that the key to primitive social organization had been found in this most "primitive" of known societies. The status of the family as an object of study can be seen in statements that the Australians did not have families at all. Howitt (1906, p. 157), for example, declared,

The social unit is not the individual, but the group; the former merely takes the relationships of his group, which are of group to group.

Suggestions of "group marriage" among Australians are to be found repeatedly in the literature (Fison, 1880), indicating to some that the family as a social form was a relatively late development. As Westermarck remarked, specifically in relation to Fison's work (Westermarck, 1891, p. 56),

As to the South Australians, Mr. Fison's statements have caused not a little confusion. On his authority several writers assert that among the Australian savages groups of males are actually found united to groups of females.

Westermarck went on to attack the notion of "primitive promiscuity" and "group marriage" and, through a mass of documentation and analysis of the reports, demolished the contention from the ethnographic sources. He had not been the first to reject it, Tylor, for example, (1891, p. 288ff.) had never advocated it (Lowie, 1937, p. 99).

## BIOLOGY AND KINSHIP

Implicit in the notion of group marriage and the replacement of the family by larger social units was the proposition that primitive man was ignorant of the facts of biological procreation, and therefore incapable of formulating any Ego-centered kinship system. Hawaiian systems, which differentiate only by sex, generation, and relative age, were said to have arisen out of this condition of ignorance, and to have "survived" as refractory nuclei of archaic conditions when they were found in more "advanced" technologies. Van Gennep (1906), attacking this notion, established a fundamental distinction between *parenté sociale*, and *parenté physique*, and this distinction has stood up (though at times ignored) until the present (see Barnes, 1964). Malinowski (1913) in his study of the family among the Australian aborigines took up Van Gennep's distinction and developed it into his own terminology of a necessary opposition between physical and social parenthood. This required a redefinition of the whole notion of consanguinity, upon which Morgan (1870) had based his original researches. Morgan had stated that kinship was based upon folk knowledge of biological consanguinity. Malinowski, under the influence of Durkheim, pointed out that consanguinity was a cultural conceptualization, part of the set of collective representations of any society. He stated (1913, p. 179),

... consanguinity ... is the set of relations involved by the collective ideas under which facts of procreation are viewed in a given society.

And again, more clearly (1913, p. 182),

Consanguinity (as a sociological concept) is therefore not the physiological bond of common blood, it is the social acknowledgement and interpretation of it.

Malinowski challenged the notion that the native Australians in a social sense "had no fathers." He brought out example after example to show that this was clear nonsense, and that in fact the Australians not only were perfectly aware of the distinction between physical and cultural paternity but that strong affective ties existed between father and son, and not between a group of "fathers" and a group of "sons." And this in turn refuted the notion that kinship was biologically determined, inasmuch as there was clear evidence that the Australians had no notion of the facts of physiological paternity. In Chapter Two, this topic is taken up again in the light of an attempt by Ernest Gellner (1957) to construct an "ideal language for kinship," utilizing the biological "facts" of consanguinity. We find discussion of these ideas continued in the 1950s and 1960s.

## THE EXTENSIONIST HYPOTHESIS

Morgan (1870) attempted, as mentioned earlier, a typology of kinship terminologies. To his mind two major criterial distinctions had to be made between kinds of kinship terms, and these he labelled *classificatory* and *descriptive*. Classificatory terms are those which subsumed a relatively large number of biological kin types, whereas descriptive terms subsumed relatively small numbers of types—preferably having unique referents. Unfortunately he went on to impose this scheme upon whole terminological systems. Fitting the typological scheme to his evolutionary framework, he proceeded to state that more "primitive" systems were classificatory, whereas more "civilized" systems were descriptive. Problems of how to analyze degrees of extension, or how to discover the semantic criteria by which people made important distinctions between kinsmen were ignored in his evolutionary scheme.

Two major orientations to the problem of the nature of kinship extensions have been formulated. The first of these, the *social learning* approach, is linked with the names of Evans-Pritchard (1929, 1932), Brenda Seligman (1929), Malinowski (1927, 1930), and Radcliffe-Brown (1924). In this view the explanation for the extension of kinship terms belongs in the domain of developmental psychology. In essence these theories state that the way in which the behavior is learned constitutes the explanation of the behavior itself. The second approach to kinship terminological extensions can be called the *semantic* approach, or perhaps better the *linguistic* approach. This orientation to kinship terminologies is linked with the names of Kroeber (1909), Unwin (1929), Hocart (1937), Davis and Warner (1937), and the latter-day structural linguistic approach (Lounsbury 1964a, 1965, and Romney, 1965).

The social learning approach attempts to establish the behavioral and psychological processes that bring about the extension of kin terms from genealogically close relatives to those who are genealogically distant. It is worth noting that the manner in which the problem is stated implies the conceptual framework of its own solution. Kinship terms that range beyond one biological kin type are "extended"; that is, their root meaning is somehow to be located before the extension takes place, and the problem is to discover the underlying processes.

Evans-Pritchard stated the hypothesis as follows (1929, p. 191),

Through the sentiments which a child builds up around those who associate most intimately with it—its mother, father, brothers and sisters in the ordinary patrilocal family—it acquires a large number of attitudes towards the extra-family world, e.g. towards authority, towards the opposite sex and so on. Many of these attitudes are towards persons, especially towards relatives, and we know that the patterns of behavior which a man observes towards his kin are due in the first place to an extension of his intra-family sentiments to include these people. Owing to the deep attachment of a child to its parents it takes over their disposition towards its relatives. It imitates its parents and looks at its relationships through their eyes. These dispositions become observable to it both as socially prescribed behavior-patterns and also as the real feelings of its parents towards these people and such feelings are often revealed in the confidence of home life as sometimes very different from the attitude which is expected in public.

There can be no doubt that children do learn the extended meaning of their kinship terminology: children learn languages. However, the short leap from a theory about social learning to a semantic theory is logically indefensible. The denotative meaning of a kinship term is susceptible to structural analysis; how learning takes place is a *psychological* problem, existing completely apart from the semantic analysis. They are related problems, but the relation is exceedingly complex, and we still lack a set of procedures that would enable us to go from the structural analysis of denotative meaning, through social learning to the analysis of connotative meaning. Evans-Pritchard fell into the trap called the *genetic fallacy*, i.e., the essence of an entity is isomorphic with the process by which it arrived at its present state. Malinowski took the argument further, and when inquiring about the nature of the clan, stated (1930), "I myself have witnessed the 'origins of the clan' in Melanesia, and I think that even from this one experiment I can draw a universally valid conclusion. The clan originates in the mind of every new generation by the progressive extension of affective ties."

The extensionist hypothesis had the support of all the "inner circle" (Malinowski, 1930) of British anthropologists. The combined stature of Seligman, Evans-Pritchard, and Malinowski was sufficient to lend it wide acceptance. But it did not represent the only way of looking at kinship terminologies or the only solution to the problem of extensions. Kroeber had stated the "linguistic" position in a 1909 article entitled "Classificatory Systems of Relationship." In this article he viewed kinship systems as "linguistic patterns of logic" (Kroeber, 1952, p. 172), and examined seven California and five other North American Indian terminologies in order to determine the nature of the criteria used in the classification of kinsmen. By comparing the principles of classification of kin terms in his sample of twelve, Kroeber discovered that eight "inherent distinctions" (Murdock, 1949, p. 136) were being made in the formulation of kin type ranges, or the assignment of relatives to classes labelled by kin terms. *Generation* was recognized, i.e., relatives of different generations tended to be distinguished. *Affinity, collaterality, sex of relative, bifurcation, sex of speaker, relative age,* and *decedence* were the others. (See Murdock, 1949, p. 136ff. for full discussion.) These were the criteria that partitioned the genealogical code. [Lowie (1929) added the ninth, *polarity*.]

Historically, Kroeber's paper is important because it exploded the notion of a simple classificatory/descriptive typology of kinship systems. Kinship systems were seen to make use of a limited number of coding principles in mapping kin types onto kin terms. Unfortunately, however, the message of the paper, that kinship systems are deserving of study in and of themselves, and not simply because they are the royal road to historical reconstruction or comparative sociology, was lost because of an unfortunate choice of words at the conclusion of the paper. To Kroeber, kinship terms and kinship systems were susceptible to linguistic analysis, and psycholinguistic processes alone could "explain" kinship terminologies. He stated (1909, p. 83), "Terms of relationship reflect psychology not sociology. They are determined primarily by language, and can be utilized for sociological inferences only with extreme caution." Later he regretted his phraseology, explaining (1952, p. 172), "I should have said that kinship systems are linguistic patterns of logic, and that their uncritical or unrestrained use as if they were uncontaminated reflectors of past or present institutions was unsound and dangerous. They certainly possess an interest in themselves and they do present problems of the relation of language and thought and of both to psychology. Instead of logic, however I spoke of 'psychology' . . . . It would have been right to say, that, as part of language, kin term systems reflect unconscious logic and conceptual patterning *as well as* social institutions."

At the time of the elaboration of the extensionist hypothesis, other objections were also made. Although at the time the connection was not made, the objectors' line of reasoning can be seen to be based on considerations not unlike those of Kroeber. Some (like Hogbin, 1930) objected that the extensionist hypothesis was much too simple minded and would not account for the sentimental evidence. But others (like Hocart and Unwin) objected very strongly to the acceptance of the term *extensions*, which implied an orientation to a "problem" that restricted the answer to only one kind of answer. Their criticisms still stand and are echoed in Chapter Two in our comments on the Lounsbury-Leach controversy on Trobriand. Unwin (1929, p. 164) criticized the rationale behind the extensionist position on the grounds that the basis of the analysis was wrongly conceived. He disliked the use of English glosses for kin categories of different ranges, and despite a stern rebuke from Malinowski (1930), declared (1930, p. 76), "We badly need a large collection of native terminologies, collected on a frame of reference which excludes direct translation by our own kinship terms. Until this has been done, discussion of their meaning would appear to be premature." So, in 1929, componential definitions and the ethnogenealogical method (Conklin, 1964, and see Chapter Eight) were being called for. The minority objection was overborne by the combined weight of the establishment, however, and the extensionist hypothesis proved extremely durable, so much as to form a basic part of Murdock's sociological analysis, and Lounsbury's formal analysis.

Hocart (1937) also objected strenuously to the frame of reference implied by social learning theory, and foreshadowed in more explicit terms than Unwin the approach now called *componential analysis*. Hocart was distinctly interested in the correlation of kin terminology to sociological, or behavioral, data and saw clearly the implicit fallacies of the extensionist definitions. He is worth quoting at length (1937, p. 545),

The person most commonly called *tama* in Melanesia, the one most in evidence is a man's father. He is the man who will be named if you asked, "Who is your *tama*?" So *tama* has been duly set down as "father." The same has been done with other kinship terms in Melanesia and elsewhere. It was soon noticed however that other men besides the father are called *tama*. By all rules the first translation should have been dropped, and a new one found to cover all the different *tama*'s and thus express the essence of *tama*-ship. Unfortunately no single word can do so and it has remained in the literature of the South Seas as "father," with the proviso that is "extended" to cover father's brother, father's father's brother's sons, and so on. Ever since we have been racking our brains to explain how Melanesians call their uncles, even remote cousins "fathers."

The effect on theory has been disastrous. The order in which we have learned the *uses* of *tama* and similar words has been confused with the order of development in actual history. Because we first took it to mean father, we slip unwittingly into the assumption that it meant father originally.

Hocart went on (1937, p. 546) to define *tama* as "all males of the previous generation on the father's side" and to suggest a form of notation for the expression of kin terms—such that a matrilateral cross-uncle (MB/FZH) in a "Kariera" system (see Chapters Four, Five, and Twelve) could be represented as 1 Op/Ego, expressing the fact that the classification included all males "one generation up on the opposite side."

For the first systematic attempt to construct a metalanguage for the analysis of kinship we turn to Davis and Warner (1937). Noting that as of that date (1937, p. 291)

... the history of kinship theory reveals that its main tradition beginning with ... Morgan, and extending to the present day ... has been interested not much in kinship *per se* as in kinship as an index of something else. Morgan's interest in evolution has given place to an interest in social organization, so that the attention in kinship is now focused upon relations between kinship and other aspects of social structure, but the fact remains that until today the central stream of thought on the subject has essayed internal analysis only when forced to it by the insistent criticism of alleged external correlations.

Davis and Warner constructed a notational system utilizing five "structural units of the biological level." They recognized (in biological parlance) the criterial properties of (1) ascending and descending generations, (2) sibling-ship, (3) relative age, (4) same sex-opposite sex, and (5) affinity. In their formal language it was possible to express all of Kroeber's categories (or "inherent distinctions"), and the range of a kin term using three algebraic strings. The system is extremely cumbersome, particularly because Davis and Warner wished to give the fullest possible specifications of the kinship terms, and not the minimum information that, combined with a set of rules (expansion or reduction), would generate the content (range of biological kin types) of the kin term. They wished to operationalize the notions of "classificatory" and "descriptive" by the creation of a third type, "isolating," and to scale the degree to which whole systems could be said to "classify" or "isolate" on a continuum. In this sense the experiment was a failure. However, it did point out the great need for both the examination of kinship terms, per se, and of the categories of classification that are implicit in kinship terminologies. In order to accomplish this, a calculus and theory of trans-formations, or mappings had to be constructed and applied to semantic systems. This was not accomplished until structural semantics had reached a mature stage of conceptualization. Much of the latter part of the book (Chapters Seven, Nine, and Ten) is concerned with these developments.

## GROUP FORMATION AND DESCENT THEORY

Early work in the study of group formation and descent theory was bedevilled by the hypothesis of unilineal evolution. The importance of descent groups in the structure of society had been recognized from an early date because of the studies and influence of the ancient historians, who attempted to block out the early history and social development of the Roman *gens*.

[See Fustel de Coulanges (1864) for bibliography.] Bachofen (1861) called attention to the problems involved in the study of matrilineal institutions, and set out the evolutionary hypothesis that matrilineal institutions were the outgrowth of primitive promiscuity, and that patrilineates evolved from matrilineal institutions. This hypothesis was picked up and developed on a global scale by Morgan (1870), McLennan (1886), Tylor (1889), and Frazer (1910), with McLennan and Frazer both arguing the possibility of either matriarchal or patriarchal priority and Morgan and Tylor championing the priority of the matriarchate. (See Lowie, 1937, pp. 39–85 for summary and bibliography.)

Modern theory of descent and descent groups can be traced to the work of Rivers (1915, 1924) primarily, and Lowie (1919, 1920). Rivers established a set of definitions, while Lowie exploded the notion that contemporary ethnographic evidence supported the "conjectural history" of lineal institutions of the evolutionists. Rivers (1924, pp. 85ff.) dissected the terms, *matriarchate* and *patriarchate*, distinguishing three constructs, descent, inheritance, and succession. He said that the term *descent* applied to the membership of a group, and to this only. "We speak of descent as patrilineal when a child belongs to the social group of his father, and as matrilineal when he belongs to the social group of his mother, . . . Descent can also be used of the process by which a person becomes a member of a class" (1924, p. 86). *Inheritance* was defined as (1924, p. 87) "the process (of) . . . the transmission of property"; *succession* as ". . . the transmission of office." Rivers noted that in his usage the term *descent* could be applicable only when the structure of the group was unilateral, and earlier (1915, p. 851) had stated that "the term (descent) is most appropriate when the community is divided into distinct social groups." In other words, so far as Rivers was concerned, a concretistic and sociological approach to the analysis of descent systems was the single appropriate approach. Implicit in his formulation was the notion that reported descent groups were exclusive, bounded, and sociologically important in that they determined group activity. He did not make use of the notion, as Scheffler (1966, p. 542) has noted, that descent categories also refer to "kinds of genealogical continua connecting person with their ancestors," nor that descent ideologies could exist apart from their realization and application in social activities.

Lowie (1919, 1920), on the other hand, attacked the evolutionists' notion that there was a unitary custom complex such as the matriarchate, showing that its constituent components (matrilineal descent, matrilocal residence, matrilineal inheritance, matrilineal succession, and the avunculate, or investment of authority in the mother's brother) were cross-culturally distributed in such a way as to indicate that they were independent one of the other. Residence and the avunculate were, in particular, refractory to unitary hypotheses. He turned to the next problem: if there is no evidence that the matriarchate preceded the patriarchate and if the matriarchate does not in fact exist, then what is the utility of the notion of descent and descent groups in sociological research? Lowie's answer was to search for correlations with other institutions, particularly in the area of kinship terminology. With unilineal institutions (*sibs* in Lowie's terminology), one was apt to find what he later termed (1928, p. 266) *bifurcate merging terminology*, whereby father was merged with father's brother, but was distinguished from mother's brother, and likewise, mother's sister was merged with mother, and was distinguished from father's sister. In the presence of sibs (and exogamy), father and father's brother would be members of the same unilineal group, and therefore share in the same social identity. So with mother and mother's sister who because they belong to the same group (not father's) would tend to be terminologically merged. This was borne out at a high level of reliability by Murdock (1949, p. 164). Lowie further noted that the cross-parallel distinction was characteristic of unilineal groups, and from this he suggested that moiety organization was the earliest (i.e., most widely distributed) form of the sib. Cross cousins were merged and differentiated from parallel cousins; therefore cross cousins belonged to one group, and parallels to another.

In the 1920s, then, the modern study of descent systems was well under way. In 1913, of course, Radcliffe-Brown had published his now classic articles on the social organization of the Australian tribes, wherein the notion of descent was highly developed. The continuing search for the correlates of descent organization (particularly in the area of kinship terminology), eventuated in Murdock's (1949) demonstration that (1) lineal organizations were associated with bifurcate merging terminology, (2) matrilineal institutions tended to be associated with terminological mergings in matrilines, other than own (specifically, FZD = FZ; BD = MBD); (3) patrilineal institutions, likewise, were associated with terminological mergings in patrilines other than own (MBD = MZ; FZD = ZD); and (4) in the presence of exogamous moieties terms for WBW tended to be the same as those for female parallel cousins, inasmuch as my parallel cousins married WB, or at least were of the same group as those that did.

Murdock discovered in his analysis that descent groups were the most important of the three determinants (descent, marriage, residence) of kinship terminology (Murdock, 1949, pp. 180–181).

That the relative efficacy of marriage forms is lower than that of descent or kin group affiliation is suggested by the markedly higher values of coefficients of association and indices of reliability in tests of the theorems concerned with the latter . . . than in those dealing with the former . . . . Since patrilineal descent and non-sororal polygyny tend to produce different types of kinship terminology, i.e., bifurcate merging and bifurcate collateral respectively, the distribution of these types when both factors are present should shed light on their relative efficacy. A special tabulation of the incidence of such terms for aunts and nieces, omitting cases of double descent, reveals that bifurcate merging occurs approximately 50 per cent more often . . . . Since sororal polygyny exerts an influence on kinship terms identical with that of unilinear descent, the cases in which only one of the two factors is present provide another opportunity for comparison . . . . Here bifurcate merging terminology is found associated with sororal polygyny in slightly less than half of all instances of bilateral descent, whereas it is associated with unilinear descent in slightly more than half the cases where sororal polygyny is absent . . . . *All of the above facts point in the same direction, i.e., toward the superior relative efficacy of rules of descent when compared with forms of marriage.* (Italics ours.)

Murdock's book (1949) has so laid the ghost of the controversy over the relationship between kinship terminology and other aspects of social structure (the behavioral hypothesis), that we tend to forget that the hypothesis was a subject of lively interest for many years.

On the negative side (those who denied that there was any necessary correlation between behavior and kinship terminology) were Kroeber (1909), Gifford (1940), and Opler (1937). On the positive side (those who maintained that there *is* a correlation between behavior and kinship terminology) were ranged Radcliffe-Brown (1935a, 1935b), Lowie (1920, 1948), and the vast majority of their students. Kroeber, as will be recalled, attempted to establish that kinship terms were linguistic entities, susceptible to semantic analysis but that, as well, they were subject to the vicissitudes of history, the effect of diffusion, and the principles of historical linguistics. Therefore, at best, correlations with sociological phenomena were unlikely to be productive. Gifford (1940) characterized the search for correlations as a "will-o'the-wisp" and stated (1940, p. 193), "Always there are exceptions which must be explained by 'additional factors.'" In line with Kroeber, he went on, "As . . . (linguistic phenomena) . . . (kinship terms) belong to and reflect primarily, the basic pattern of social structure, and as such they constitute an archaic and highly refractory nucleus which yields unevenly here and there to influences from the secondary pattern of social structure."

On ethnographic grounds Opler (1937) objected to the behavioral hypothesis. One good example was taken from his notes on Jicarilla Apache (1937a, p. 212). In Jicarilla male and female cousins are classified together, subsumed under the same kin term. Yet, for a girl (female speaking), sharply contrastive behavior is adopted towards female in comparison with male cousins. Towards female cousins, a female speaker acts in a sibling-like way; towards male cousins she adopts a pattern of extreme avoidance. Other behavioral discriminations, which are not mirrored in the kin classifications, are adduced to make the point that appropriate kinship behavior is learned through the total cultural apparatus: myth, cautionary tale, direct education, and the inculcation of a belief cluster that attributes grave dangers to association with the male cousin.

Generally speaking, however, anthropologists held to the hope that kinship terminology was consistent with behavioral pattern, and constituted the appropriate path to the understanding of social interaction.

Radcliffe-Brown repeatedly (1935a, 1935b) asserted that the correlation existed. His statements were based on the consideration of his own field experiences in Australia and the Andamans, and from a reading of the literature. In 1930 he stated (1930, p. 427), ". . . it can be shown that there is a very thorough functional correlation between the kinship terminology of any tribe and the social organization of that tribe as it is at present." Radcliffe-Brown (1935a, 1935b) declared (1935, p. 531) that ". . . we can expect to find, in the majority of human societies, a fairly close correlation between the terminological classification of kindred or relatives and the social classification. The former is revealed in the kinship terminology, the latter in social usages of all kinds, not only in institutions such as clans, or special forms of marriage, but specifically in the attitudes and behavior of relatives to one another . . . . For me, this assumption . . . was originally a deduction from a more fundamental working hypothesis, viz., that any social system . . . must normally possess a certain degree of functional consistency."

Thus for Radcliffe-Brown the behavioral hypothesis was derived deductively from his a priori notions about the homeostatic nature of social systems, and was "tested" in single ethnographic cases, or over whole areas where the ethnography was adequate. Not until Murdock created and made use of the Cross-Cultural Files could adequate sampling and control procedures be utilized in comparative designs and a true test of the behavioral hypothesis be made. Chapters Six and Seven of Murdock's *Social Structure* both vindicated Radcliffe-Brown and Lowie's contention that the behavioral hypothesis was accurate, and showed that the determinants of kinship terminologies were complex and interacting. Murdock (1949, p. 126) states,

No single factor or simple hypothesis can account for all observable effects. From this it follows that different determinants must often exert their pressure in opposite directions. What operates is therefore a sort of parallelogram of forces, and the phenomena which ensue represent, not the effects of particular forces but the resultant of them all . . . .

Since multiple factors are nearly always operative [in determining kinship terminologies], perfect statistical correlations between any particular kinship determinant and the terminological features that it tends to produce should never be expected, even if the hypothesis is entirely sound.

So far as descent and descent theory are concerned, Murdock showed that the relative efficacy of descent groups in determining the form of kinship terminology was greater than either marriage rules, or residential forms (Murdock, 1949, pp. 180–182). By 1949, then, it had been shown, first, that the behavioral hypothesis was correct, and, second, that there was a rank ordering of the hypothesized determinants of kinship terminologies: (1) descent rules (2) marriage rules (3) residence rules. Alternate theories of the determinants of kinship terminologies are taken up in our discussion of Omaha systems in Chapter Ten.

At the same time as Murdock was using correlational analysis with the Cross-Cultural Files, Radcliffe-Brown and his students were approaching the subject of the efficacy of descent and descent theory from a different angle. We discuss Radcliffe-Brown's point of view at length in Chapter Four; here we will seek merely to lay the groundwork for the subsequent treatment. Rivers (1915, 1924) had failed to distinguish between "principles of descent" and concrete descent groups. Interested in historical reconstruction, he saw descent principles and groups from the evolutionary-historical point of view, and not as interacting variables. Radcliffe-Brown and his students (notably Tax, 1937) were concerned with developing the underlying principles of descent groups, as well as establishing propositions, or sets of rules, which could serve as shorthand statements of a general kind about the relation between kinship terminology and behavior. Tax (1955, p. 22) described his rules and principles as follows:

These rules and principles are purely empirical—the result of observation and analysis—and however they may be explained, they must be recognized as, at the least, important tendencies in human nature and society. If they are rather to be considered "cultural", then they are among the most widespread of cultural traits. At any rate, it is proposed here to use these rules and principles in explaining the genesis, the continuous regenesis, and the reasons-for-being of both the terminological usages and the social customs that usually accompany them.

We can briefly summarize the rules and principles, noting that when a rule states that $X$ "will be called" $Y$, it is to be inferred that forms of social behavior are also implied. (Tax, 1955, p. 19 fn.) There are eight rules and four principles: (1) the Rule of Uniform Descent states that the children of a single kinship category will be called by a single term; (2) the Rule of Uniform Reciprocals states that all the members of a kinship category consistently reciprocate with all the members of another single category provided one member does; (3) the Rule of Uniform Siblings states that "if the male of a pair of siblings is called $A$, and the female is $B$, then whenever a man is called $A$, his sister must be called $B$"; (4) the Rule of Uniform Mates states that all the members of the class of kinsmen designated by a spouse term will be called *spouses* by Ego; (5) the Rule of Uniform Ascent asserts that parents of a single kin category are merged by Ego; (6) the Rule of Equivalence states that "two people who call a third person by the same term should be siblings to each other"; (7) people toward whom Ego behaves identically or similarly will be called by the same term, people toward whom Ego behaves differently will be called by a different term, and people who behave toward each other in the same way call each other by the same term; and (8) that where there exists no reason to the contrary, people will reciprocate behaviorally.

Tax further summarizes four principles of Radcliffe-Brown: (1) the Principle of Equivalence of Siblings, whereby universally siblings are considered as a unit (from outside the sibling group), except in the presence of the principle of sex differentiation; (2) the Principle of Sex Differentiation, whereby "people of opposite sex tend to be more differentiated than people of the same sex" (Tax, 1955, p. 21); (3) the Generation Principle whereby "persons of one generation tend to respect those of the generation above"; and (4) the Sex Principle, whereby people respect those of opposite sex.

Thus Radcliffe-Brown's students attempted to summarize the behavioral and terminological universals of comparative sociology. They were later elaborated by Radcliffe-Brown in his *Introduction to African Systems of Kinship and Marriage* (1950), and it is this exposition that we utilize for discussion in Chapter Four. To anticipate slightly, it will be shown that these "rules" and "principles" are devoid of semantic and sociological significance. The rules are entirely *ad hoc*, mere verbal summaries, as Lowie calls them. They describe some data in some kinship systems, but nowhere is any attempt made (nor can it be) to indicate the scope of the rules, nor the conditions under which they may obtain. The application of the principles shows them to be tautological. An Omaha system, for example, is seen to recognize certain principles in its mergings, and the mergings are the validation of the efficacy of the principle. The reasoning is entirely circular. However, one of Radcliffe-Brown's teachings, which was never codified in any manner, did yield results of great value. He insisted upon the close examination of kinship terminology and behavior in single societies, and upon the method of what Eggan (1954) has called the method of "controlled comparison." Kinship data on North American tribes were organized and analyzed with care and precision, and a happy absence of abstract theorizing. McAllister's work (1935, 1937) on Kiowa Apache; Eggan's on Cheyenne and Arapaho (1937), and the Western pueblos (1950); Tax' study (1937) of Fox; Gilbert's (1937) on Eastern Cherokee; and Opler's (1937) on Chiricahua Apache were all tightly organized. The failure on the theoretical level, their simplistic organization in terms of "principles" (see Tax, 1955, p. 254) was the inevitable result of an attempt to translate one aspect or level of terminology (the structural semantic) to another (the sociological) without admitting the contingency that is inevitably involved in the translation process. (See Chapter Two, and comments on the Leach-Lounsbury controversy.)

Briefly then, descent theory, once it broke through an early preoccupation with evolution, found its basis in River's (1915, 1924) formulations. It was seen early by Lowie and others to be a determining factor in the morphology of kinship terminologies, as subsequently demonstrated by Murdock. In the hands of Radcliffe-Brown, however, it became a conceptual scheme, which, however much it led to empirical studies of clarity and accuracy, led also to a focus on concrete relations on the one hand, and tautological reifications on the other. Its influence can be seen throughout this book, not only in Chapter Four, but also in the treatment on "Alliance Theory," and in the discussion of lineal systems (Chapter Ten) and section systems (Chapter Eleven).

## ALLIANCE THEORY

Schneider (1965a) and Dumont (1953a, 1966) have made a convenient distinction between descent theory and alliance theory. By emphasizing the differences, they have, perhaps, obscured the fact that the two are largely complementary. Descent theory is more highly developed in the empirical study of what Lévi-Strauss has called Crow-Omaha systems, whereas alliance theory has made its greatest strides in the study of bounded systems, or elementary structures, where it has been able to attain to a greater degree of abstraction and generality than descent theory. In this section we examine the antecedents of alliance theory, and thereby complete our survey of the background to the more basic substantive issues in this book.

Alliance theory owes its genesis to Durkheim, its advancement to Marcel Mauss, and its realization to Claude Lévi-Strauss. It was Durkheim (1947, first ed. 1893) who first developed in an explicit fashion the notion of "organic solidarity," which subsequently played a large part in the theory of *elementary structures* of Lévi-Strauss. So far as Durkheim was concerned, social evolution (that is to say, the development of complexity in social relations) was associated with, or signalled by a change in penal methods and judicial process in the "moral order." Simple, homogeneous societies were characterized by repressive sanction. The collectivity punished members directly, out of a sense of moral outrage, for any offense against the common conscience. The common conscience was based upon the "essential social similitudes," which corresponded to the "mechanical solidarity" that arose from the unity-in-totality of the social organism. (See Durkheim, 1947, pp. 70ff.) As society became more complex the essential social similitudes were replaced by a social order based on the integration of articulated differences. This in turn was co-ordinate with the development of a moral, "restitutive sanction" based not upon sense of moral outrage, but rather upon the necessity to maintain the differentiated social organism in some state of homeostasis, or harmony. With social development, says Durkheim (1947, p. 131),

Society becomes more capable of collective movement, at the same time that each of its elements has more freedom of movement. This solidarity resembles that which we observe among the higher animals. Each organ, in effect, has its special physiognomy, its autonomy. And, moreover, the unity of the organism is as great as the individuation of its parts is more marked. Because of this analogy we propose to call the solidarity which is due to the division of labor, organic.

Loosely speaking, then (we shall have occasion to examine the theoretical and methodological significance of these concepts subsequently), Durkheim set up two ideal types of society: at one pole the collectivity based on collective representations, and the "association of similitudes," and at the other the articulation and organization of diversity associated with the division of labor. The first type of society is characterized by "mechanical solidarity" and the second by "organic solidarity." How the solidarity is achieved is not a focus of interest; it exists and that suffices—it exists because it has to exist. The metaphor of the human body, of homeostasis, is introduced analogically to "account" for the existence of solidarity.

Marcel Mauss, Durkheim's nephew and collaborator, discovered the basic integrative mechanism—exchange. In *Essai sur le Don* (1923–4), Mauss examined the sociology of exchange in Polynesia, North America, and Asia. But rather than some ethnographic recapitulation à la Frazer, he provided a novel approach and conceptual framework. In discussing exchange, Mauss observed that he was not in the realm of economics, but rather that his discussion concerned a social fact that permeated primitive life; so much so that he was led to call exchange a total social fact (*fait social total*), and to refer to this omnipresent, central focus of social relations as *prestations totales*, that is the exchange not only of the products of social activity (technology, economics, ritual) but also all values that make up the content of the exchange (myths, dances, magical formulae, ornaments, and so forth). And, as Lévi-Strauss points out (Lévi-Strauss, 1950, p. xxxiv), in so doing he lifted us out of the anecdotal, or moralistic discussion of primitive society by creating a set of utilities and a matrix in which the utilities were susceptible to formal analysis. As a result culturally disparate customs that had appeared to be irreducible—out of the assumption of cultural relativism—became reducible to a fundamental, that is to say, general form (Lévi-Strauss, 1950, p. xxxiv).

Les types deviennent donc définissables par ces caractères intrinsèques et comparables entre eux puisque ces caractères ne se situent pas dans un ordre qualitatif, mais dans le nombre et arrangement d'éléments.[1]

Mauss brought to our notice that the elements of presentation were part of a system, and that the locus of analysis need not be the vastly diverse elements (themselves incomparable), but rather the arrangement of the elements in system of complementary relations.[2]

Mauss could not take the final step, however, in motivating his theoretical scheme. Like Durkheim, when confronted by the problem of why exchange relations were central, omnipresent, and constant in form, he resorted to a mysticism, which constituted a major obstacle to the development of a true supra-empirical theory until Lévi-Strauss took the final step of clarification. Instead of seizing upon the relevance of the *underlying ordering of elements* into systems, Mauss returns to the empirical level. Having arrived at the important conception that exchange is the common denominator of a vast number of social activities, which in themselves appear to be irreducibly heterogeneous, Mauss failed to see that explanation did not lie at the level of the facts. In order to account for the continuing cycle of prestations, he

[1] And so the types became definable in terms of these intrinsic characteristics, and mutually comparable because these characteristics are not qualitative, but are rather an ordered arrangement of elements. (Our translation.)

[2] Here we see a typical expression of what Leach has called *la pensée Lévi-Straussienne*.

postulated that there was an inner (animate) force in the *object* of the exchange, which forever seeks reciprocity and balance. The Polynesians, for example, had a native term *hau* to describe this force, and Mauss assumed it to be present in all exchange relations (Mauss, 1950, pp. 161, 170). He omitted to notice, even though he recorded it (Lévi-Strauss, 1950, p. *xl*) that Papuans, and Melanesians ". . . have only one word to designate purchase and sale, borrowing and lending. Antithetical operations are expressed by the same word." Not until Lévi-Strauss (1949) reconceptualized the notion of exchange was it seen that there was no need to account for exchanges by some third factor. The value of exchange lies in itself: *exchange per se has a positive value*. To borrow a vocabulary from Barth (1966, p. 13), the motivation of the system does not lie at the transactional level; there is more (or less, if you will) to the exchange relationship than is expressed by $A^x \rightleftarrows B^y$, if for $A$, $x \leq y$, and for $B$, $x \leq y$, ($A$ and $B$ being parties to the exchange; $x$, $y$ the utilities). There is a constant on both sides of the equation that is the *positive value that attaches to exchange* itself. Postulation of such a constant enables us to leave the complexities and incomparabilities of the empirical level, and concern ourselves with the underlying regularities in the arrangement of elements into systems. To look ahead slightly, one can quickly see the productivity of this point of view in the comparative study of marriage systems, if women are to be viewed as objects in a cycle of prestations. One need not concern oneself with the problematic aspects of cultural relativism, but rather with the comparison of ordered relations and the construction of types and the study of systems of transformations and mappings, (the study of various forms of homomorphisms). Knowing that (Lévi-Strauss, 1963b, p. 2)

. . . exchange in human society is a universal means of ensuring the interlocking of its constituent parts and . . . this exchange can operate at different levels among which the most important are food, goods, services and women,

it becomes possible to examine marriage systems within a single frame of reference—stripped of their cultural uniqueness.

As Nutini (1967) has shown, this orientation to relations rather than terms, which had been foreshadowed by Boas in the previous century, is much more consonant with the kind of theory that typifies modern science than the consitutent analysis of concrete entities on the empirical plane. It was facilitated by the development of structural linguistics and modern algebra; the importance of which was recognized by Lévi-Strauss in 1945, and made explicitly a part of the theoretical scheme in his *Elementary Structures* (1949).

These issues are taken up in some detail in Chapters Five and Six. Here only a sketchy outline of the background has been given.

# Chapter

# Two

# **The**

# **Family**

The first problem we shall take up in this exposition of the major substantive and methodological issues in the study of kinship and social organization concerns the family  Why the family—rather than residence rules, kinship terminology, principles of marriage and exchange, or some other topic? Many texts begin with either  a definition of the family or a proposition that the family is universal. Murdock (1949) opens his discussion of social structure by stating,

The family is a social group characterized by common residence, economic cooperation and reproduction. It includes adults of both sexes, at least two of whom maintain a socially approved sexual relationship, and one or more children, own or adopted, of the sexually cohabiting adults.

Similarly, Bohannon (1963), after giving passing reference to "kinsmen" and "kinship terms," takes up the family. In this chapter we will be more explicit about why we should choose the family, rather than some other unit of analysis, and will review the theoretical assumptions that have compelled analysts to consider the study of the family to be a high-priority matter.

One compelling reason is the matter of analytic priority. The family unit in its various forms and manifestations must be reckoned with in discussion of residence, kinship terminology, marriage, and virtually every other topic that is traditionally reviewed in treating kinship and social organization. How is it possible to discuss the distribution of affective relations within the family or lineage, or the problem of "kinship extensions" without a grasp of the underlying principles of family organization and of the family types that are partial and incomplete expressions of these principles?

[19]

Second, there is considerable confusion in the literature over the family, most of which is subterranean, and has to do with our inability to account for data that has come forward since Murdock (1949). We would hold that new data has required us to refine our definitions and conceptualizations of the basic concepts of household and family. The first part of this chapter introduces the new data in a very truncated form, and attempts to point out the scope and purpose of definitions of the family.

But there is a second problem in tampering with definitions as they now stand. Current notions of the family (and its implied universality) have engendered a body of theory about kinship terminology that is basic to the modern methodologies and progress that have been made over the last decade in the area of transformational and componential analysis. The underlying assumption (as we shall see later) of transformational analysis is the extensionist hypothesis. And the extensionist hypothesis requires that kinship terms be genealogical referents. The semantic domain to which they belong must be genealogical. Leach and Needham have categorically asserted that this is not the case, that kinship terms are not genealogical in their reference, but rather sociological, and therefore they require a different sort of analysis than that which Americans (such as Murdock (1949), Lounsbury (1956, 1964a, 1965), Goodenough (1956a, 1964, 1965a), Romney (1965), and so on) have subjected them to. To many American formalists kinship terminologies are based upon the nuclear family, which is universal, and the notational transformations that take place in a generative analysis are analogous to the psychological process of stimulus generalization whereby terms are extended from the primary meanings (kernels, or nuclear forms) to secondary, or extended meanings.

What we show, later in this chapter, is that all kinship systems are cognitively based upon a relational set which we can describe by using the traditional terms *descent, affinity,* and *consanguinity* (and the sociological distinction of "sex"). However, the fact that all speakers can make distinctions based on these criteria does not necessarily imply that empirically and sociologically the full set of relations is to be found "on the ground." Counter to Lounsbury (1965), there is a logical leap from statements about analytic techniques such as componential and transformational analysis (based on linguistic, i.e., structural semantic theory), to sociological statements that are based upon empirical observation and investigation. The success of transformational and componential accounts assures us that analysis based on genealogical criteria is accurate, predictive, and generalized, more so than any other technique (we examine an excellent example in the Trobriand discussion). This success does not assure us, however, that kinship systems are uniquely and best analyzed as genealogical codes; it is simply that we have not developed techniques as adequate for the display of other kinds of dimensions in the analysis of kinship.

indicating that at the grandparental level MD, PD, and CD were also found, but only on the paternal side. We can thereby indicate the range of family types in the following matrix, utilizing the category names that have become standard in the literature.

Table 2–2.  Matrix of Relational Types

| Conventional nomenclature | Relational types | | | | | | |
| --- | --- | --- | --- | --- | --- | --- | --- |
| | PD | MD | CD | W+ | H+ | GP[a] | GM[a] |
| Matrifocal | − | + | − | − | − | − | − |
| Matrifocal extended | − | + | − | − | − | − | + |
| Nuclear | + | + | + | − | − | − | − |
| Patrilineal extended | + | + | + | − | − | + | − |
| Famille souche | + | + | + | − | − | + | − |
| Matrilineal extended | + | + | + | − | − | − | + |
| Polygynous | + | + | + | + | − | − | − |
| Polyandrous | + | + | + | − | + | − | − |
| Patrilineally extended polygynous | + | + | + | + | − | + | − |
| Matrilineally extended polygynous | + | + | + | + | − | − | + |
| Patrilineally extended polyandrous | + | + | + | − | + | + | − |
| Matrilineally extended polyandrous | + | + | + | − | + | − | + |
| Polygynous-polyandrous | + | + | + | + | + | − | − |
| Patrilineally extended polygynous-polyandrous | + | + | + | + | + | + | − |
| Matrilineally extended polygynous-polyandrous | + | + | + | + | + | − | + |
| Kibbutz | − | − | − | − | − | − | − |

[a]The assumption is made here that if polygyny or polyandry is found at the parental level, it will also be found at the grandparental level. No separate entry at the grandparental level has been made to accommodate anomalous cases.

Some comments on Table 2–2 are called for. No distinction is made between the *famille souche* (Le Play, 1884, pp. 29–40) and a patrilineal extended family type (based on the patrilocal extended household, translated into a family type). We included it as a separate entry simply because it has been commented upon in the literature recently (Levy in Coale *et al.*, 1965, p. 48).[4] Structurally there is no difference between these two types in the

[4] Levy (*loc. cit.*) describes the *famille souche* as follows: "Ideally speaking the membership of a *famille souche* proliferates vertically along generational lines as does a lineally extended family but not horizontally along sibling lines. All siblings, regardless of sex, except one marry out and give up membership in their family of orientation. One is selected to remain a member and continue the family line."

matrix. Informants will, however, recognize a difference. Judging from the descriptions of Le Play and others (Arensberg and Kimball, 1940; Park, 1962), it could appear that on the ethnoscientific level a distinction would be made between them. Typically we do not distinguish between the patrilineal extended family made up of two nuclear families of different generations, and those composed of more than two families. When we speak of the patrilineal extended family we include the possibility that a male head of the family may be living with the families of procreation of more than one of his sons. In the case of the *famille souche*, this is not so. The heir of the family land is a single individual. Upon receiving his inheritance, his social status changes, and he marries. Therefore, in the *famille souche* we never have more than the family of procreation of *one* male child. Our incapacity to distinguish between these two sorts of families in the matrix is not unique—it is an artifact of the typological method as it has been applied in the past to family typologies. We merely seek to point it out.

Breaking family types down into a matrix of constituent relations is more than an exercise in analysis. It implies a frame of reference that is of great utility in the understanding of issues such as the durability of the family, or the stability of role occupants; the relation between structure and relational content both within family type, and between the family and the wider kinship network; and the relation between structure and demographic variables.

But there is an objection to this procedure that should be anticipated. The family is a low-level theoretical construct with virtually no explanatory or predictive value. It therefore seems likely that a truly productive approach to family and domestic organization will primarily be concerned with the processes that underlie these forms, with defining thresholds and invariants, rather than with refining typological distinctions. Here, the typological approach has been followed more as a device for reviewing the background to the study of the family, than as an attempt to advance another typological scheme.

## STABILITY OF ROLE OCCUPANCY

In the nonnuclear cases in our typology, one characteristic seems to stand out. In both the Nayar case and the matrifocal case anomaly appears to center upon the paternal-conjugal dyad. As was suggested earlier, our concern must be directed at the transference of rights between groups linked by the conjugal dyad. It seems that correlates to the anomalous structural features are to be found in the degree to which rights *in uxorem* (over a woman *qua* wife), and rights *in genetricem* (over a woman *qua* bearer of children, or over the progeny of a union) are transferred from the family of orientation of the woman to the man or his group with whom she coresides. In the Nayar case both kinds of rights are transferred, but these rights are only briefly activated upon the death of the role incumbent. In Nayar sexual services are not available at any time from a woman because she is a party to the marriage ceremony. Rather they are services formed in the context of a series of continuing prestations from the women of one matrilineal sub-caste, to the men of another. A man has no rights over the children of his wife, except for the requirement that they (along with *all* the children whom-ever the social father [pater] might be) observe fifteen days ritual pollution on his death (Gough, 1959a, p. 358).

In the matrifocal case even fewer rights are transferred. As with Nayar, the proffering of sexual services is contingent upon the rendering of services for the woman and her household in the form of food or wage contributions. It is a prestation and not a right. No rights *in genetricem* are recognized.

In conjunction with Fallers' (1957) reformulation of Gluckman's (1950) hypothesis a cultural universal might be suggested. Whereas Gluckman (1950) proposed that divorce rates were correlated with degree of patriliny, Fallers related marriage stability to the degree to which women were absorbed into the man's lineage. He states in conclusion (1957, p. 121),

Where a woman, either through the complete transfer of her child-bearing proper-ties or by other means, is socially absorbed into her husband's lineage, patriliny tends to stabilize marriages; where a wife is not so absorbed and thus remains a member of the lineage into which she was born, patriliny tends to divide marriages by dividing the loyalties of spouses.

As Lévi-Strauss (1960b) has pointed out, it matters not at all whether we regard the exchange properties from the point of view of the male or from that of the female. From the female point of view we would state the con-clusion as follows: the degree to which the female or her group retains rights *in genetricem* and *in uxorem* will be positively correlated with the degree of instability in the marriage. In fact, it seems probable that, on a cross-cultural basis, an intensity order or rank ordering of ordinal or greater than ordinal strength of the transference of these rights would enable us to provide a somewhat more contextually relevant basis for formulating a typology of family forms than is available at present.

## RELATIONAL CONTENT

The dyadic frame of reference for the discussion of the family is also of great utility in the analysis of the content of relations within the family, and between the family and the wider kinship network. The dyadic frame of refer-ence has been implicit in the social-psychological analysis of relational content, such as has been commonplace with psychologists and sociologists for decades, but rare in anthropology, despite the fact that it has proved provocative and productive when utilized. Francesca Cancian (1963, 1964) has developed, for example, a method that would be extremely productive were it to be applied cross-culturally.[5]

Cancian (1964) has utilized a modified version of the Bales scoring system for interaction (Longbaugh, 1963), by which it is possible to score interaction rates and content through observation of small groups. Her study took place in the *municipio* (township) of Zinacantan in Chiapas, Mexico, among Tzotzil-speaking Indians. She spent four days and four nights with each of ten families in a nonrandom sample and coded interaction for nine hours during that period in each family. Table 2–3 of interaction codings is given as follows:

**Table 2–3.   Interaction Codings**

| Behavior | Category assignment |
| --- | --- |
| Child to mother (child whines) | Seeks affect |
| Mother to child, "What do you want?" | Gives affect, seeks information |
| Child to mother, "I want my seat." | Gives information |
| Mother to child, "Here it is, take it." | Gives information, dominates |
| Child to mother (child takes seat) | Accepts dominance |

(After Cancian, 1966, p. 260)

From her data Cancian was able to make a number of propositions, two of which are nonintuitive and of interest for comparative purposes. First, it appeared that all the members of a family display the same level of affect towards each other, although the level varied from family to family. So far, then, as it is possible to measure affectivity of relational content, it would appear that in this community of ideally patrilineally extended households, measurement of the affectivity level of one dyad is predictive of the level of all other dyads within the household group, and by extension within the family. Second, it was found that the amount of dominance-submission measured between dyads was stable within the same household, and by implication for the family at large.[6] This is an example of the kind of

---

[5] Zelditch's now classic (1955) study of role differentiation in the nuclear family should be mentioned. In a study of 55 societies father and mother roles were scored for degree of relative "instrumentalism" and "expressiveness" (the terms are Parsonian). Father role was always found to be more instrumental than mother.

[6] Statistical tests were not available for the final analysis, but an initial (if improper) use of Chi square indicated that the first proposition was significant at the .001 level, and the second at the .02 level of chance occurrence (Cancian, 1964).

"internal" analysis that is possible if one examines the constituent structures comprising the various family types, rather than do what anthropologists are prone to do, namely take the nuclear family as the sociological building block, and the relational content within the family for granted.

With the dyadic frame of reference we can also consider relations between dyads included in the family type for any culture, and dyads that link family roles to roles outside this structure. Possibly the best-known hypothesis in all of anthropology (in this conjunction) arises out of Radcliffe-Brown's (1924) treatment of the mother's brother in South Africa. Radcliffe-Brown noted that a special relationship seemed to obtain between the mother's brother and sister's son in a widely separated number of societies, principally in Africa and Oceania. He states that the father and his relatives in strongly patriarchal societies "must be obeyed and respected (even worshipped, in the original sense of the word)," ". . . the father punishes the children . . . [while] the mother is tender and indulgent to her child, and her relatives are expected to be the same, and so also the maternal spirits" (1965, p. 28). In other words, when a society is "disbalanced," in the sense that the relational content of the paternal and maternal dyad is distinguishable, we can expect to find correlates in the relational content of other dyads that extend beyond those included in the nuclear, or the culturally defined family. The "disbalance" in Radcliffe-Brown's view is related to the system of descent. Patriarchal relations are found with patrilineal descent, and matriarchal with matrilineal.

Lévi-Strauss (1963a) has shown that the matter is neither that simple, nor theoretically that restricted. In his view, the avunculate (the set of the following dyads: paternal, maternal, and avuncular [i.e., ego-MoBr]) constitute the logically elementary atom of kinship which "is the sole building block of more complex systems" (1963a, p. 48). He points out that Radcliffe-Brown's formulation is deficient in that it omits to consider a number of exceptions to the hypothesized connection between descent and relational content. In the Trobriand case, the reverse correlation (matriarchal relations and matrilineal descent) holds, but fails to include or consider one of the most striking aspects of the Trobriand system, namely the brother-sister avoidance. Among the Cherkess of the Caucasus (a patriarchal type), the correlation holds as well, but again a most striking characteristic of the relational system is the extreme closeness between siblings. Consider the husband-wife relation. In Trobriand it is characterized by intimacy, warmth, tenderness, and reciprocity. Among the Cherkess, however, the relation is characterized by extreme avoidance. The analysis of relational content even when reduced to simplest form appears highly variable. But it remains so only if we consider the dyads serially. If we examine the range of variation in terms of the *relation* between sets of relations, order is quickly established. "It is not enough to study the correlation of attitudes between father/son, and uncle/sister's son. This correlation is only one aspect of a global system containing four types of relationship, which are organically linked, namely, *brother/sister*, *husband/wife*, *father/son*, and *mother's brother/sister's son*. The two groups in our example illustrate a law which can be formulated as follows: In both groups, the relation between maternal uncle and nephew is to the relation between brother and sister as the relation between father and son is to that between husband and wife" (Lévi-Strauss, 1963a, p. 42). At each generational level there is one positive, warm relationship, and one negative, distant relationship. Thus, if the husband-wife relationship is warm and positive, the brother-sister relationship will be negative, and vice versa. A woman can be in a close relationship to *either* her brother or her husband, but not both. The same is true for intergenerational relations (father-son and nephew-uncle). Thus we can derive a table of relationships (Table 2–4) for Lévi-Strauss' five cited societies, a plus indicating a warm relationship, and a minus a distant one.

### Table 2–4. Table of Relationships

| Role dyads | Societies | | | | |
|---|---|---|---|---|---|
| | Trobriand | Siuai | Cherkess | Tonga | Lake Kutubutu |
| Uncle-nephew | − | + | − | + | − |
| Brother-sister | − | + | + | − | + |
| Father-son | + | − | + | − | + |
| Husband-wife | + | − | − | + | − |

(Adapted from Lévi-Strauss, 1963a, p. 45.)

The kind of analysis shown in Table 2–4 is not to be confused with Cancian's. On the face of it they are diametrically opposed, but one must maintain the distinctions in levels of analysis. Both are interesting examples of the utility of dyadic analysis. Cancian is maintaining that, given a cultural system or a social structure, however much variance may exist on the behavioral level between replicated structures (Zinacantecan families, in this case), in fact one can predict in each case the degree of intracultural variance from a knowledge of the relational content of one dyad. This is not the same as saying that there is a limited repertoire of possible structures in comparative analysis. To bowdlerize Cancian's statement, we could say that in any culture there are loving families and cold families, and that inspection of the relational content on one dyad will enable an observer to infer the content of the other dyads.

If we combine the theoretical insights of both, we see that we can develop heuristic devices as well as a frame of reference for analysis. We have systematic relations between dyads, as well as systematic, but limited, possibilities for combination of role-relation types (in terms of oppositions) across cultures. Such systematic relations bounded within a structural universe are precisely those which, like kinship terminology, have always provided us with our best opportunities for controlled comparison, and formalization. We have established a universe of discourse and laid down the assumptions under which analysis can proceed. There is no reason why progress in the analysis of family organization cannot make one of those saltations that the study of kinship did, when the structuralists took the materials of kinship terminology from the hands of the historicists (such as Rivers, 1914), and developed comparative and formalist methodologies of their own.

## THE FAMILY AND KINSHIP TERMINOLOGIES

The next step in our discussion of the family is to examine the relationship between the elementary units of kinship and the wider network of kinship relations. We confine our attention to two major problems. We discuss the semantic content of *biological kin types*, under the heading "Biology and Kinship," and conclude the chapter with an extended treatment of the extensionist hypothesis, and the issues that have been raised by the success of relatively recent methodologies such as transformational and componential analysis.

### BIOLOGY AND KINSHIP

The first issue can be phrased as a question, "To what extent can we state that biological kin types are constructs that are based on 'biological facts?'" The resolution of this problem is quite simple, and probably would not be raised except for an attempt by Ernest Gellner (1957, 1960, 1963) to construct an ideal language for kinship based upon the "biological facts of life," rather than upon sociological constructs. Anthropologists are in unwonted agreement that Gellner's insistence upon the biological nature of biological kin types is entirely misplaced (see Needham, 1960a; Barnes, 1961, 1964; Schneider, 1964, 1965a; and Buchler, 1966a).

Gellner (1957) has attempted to construct an unambiguous, semantically invariant language (ideal language) for the discussion of kinship. He has contended that it would be possible to construct a system of designations for any bounded population merely by assigning names to individuals based on their biological parentage. Thus, if a mother were to bear the name GEL the son would bear the name GELM and subscripts or numerals could be introduced to distinguish siblings. Such a notational scheme would enable the ethnographer to dispense with the metalanguage of kinship constructs. He could systematically determine the patterns of the incest taboo (certain names do not occur), patterns of marriage (only certain names are compossible), as well as the nature of kin terms (specifiable name forms are categorized together), and would be able to relate marriage types to demographic data (certain name types are associated with population growth, decrease, and so forth). *The problem is whether "father" or "mother" or "son" or "daughter" is a biological or a sociological conception.* Gellner assumes that it is biological, and anthropologists agree that it decidedly is not. Barnes (1961, 1964) and Buchler (1966a) have been the two more emphatic exponents of the cultural, or social, definition of biological relatedness. They examine the relation between the "father" and his progeny. Anthropologists have been making the distinction between *pater* or "social father" and *genitor* "he who is believed to have actually fathered the child" for many years now (Malinowski, 1963, orig. 1913). Until Gellner, however, they did not see the need to distinguish between these two and the *genetic father*, i.e., the person who in Barnes' (1961, p. 297) words "supplies the spermatazoon that impregnates the ovum that eventually becomes the child." And the fact is that this person may be or may not be culturally relevant. He may be known, or he may not be. And an anthropologist may do all the detective work he wishes and may never be able to find out who this person was. This condition may arise because of casual sexual relations (if the mother does not know who the "father" [i.e., genetic father] might be, but can assign only probabilities among a population with which she has enjoyed sexual contact in the preceding period), but also because assigning fatherhood, be it genetic or social, is a cultural matter. Barnes (1964) points to some Scandinavian examples of modern societies that utilize legal conventions to assign paternity, i.e., genetic fatherhood. And if a culture that has access to "scientific" data for assigning fatherhood must fall back on a cultural rule, then what of cultures where genetics is unknown. In some Australian societies,

indigenous theories of procreation have no place for (the genetic father), and attribute the onset of gestation to action by a spirit. One group, the Muribata, recognize another social role, the "firestick father," the individual who, they believe, directs the spirit to the mother. But the "firestick father" is neither believed to be a genitor, nor is necessarily identical with the genetic father. The distinction between the genetic father and the "firestick father" is shown by the fact that the "firestick father" is sometimes a woman" (Barnes, 1964, taken from Malinowski, 1913).

Therefore, insofar as Gellner's scheme requires that the "facts of the physical world" determine the assignments of names in the construction of the ideal language, it would appear that such a formulation will prove impossible simply because it is impossible for any population anywhere to determine the correct name assignment. The data simply are not known; and an ethnographer who attempted to determine reliably and exhaustively what the data were would spend many unfruitful months in the field and never be able to know what degree of accuracy his informants' statements contained.

And to cap the argument, Buchler (1966a) has shown that in at least one society (the Cayman Islands) the identity of the genetrix may pose problems as well. Common sense would indicate that the facts of gestation are exceedingly difficult to hide, and therefore one can be fairly sure who one's mother was, and accurately report it. But, in the Cayman Islands (British West Indies), a girl who stays on in her parents' house becomes "sister" to her own children, and they in turn refer to their mother's parents as their parents. In this case the genetic mother becomes "sister" and the "genetic" grandparents become "parents." This becomes of importance in the consideration of incestuous behavior. In the Cayman Islands (as everywhere in the world) sexual relations between a father and his daughter are considered taboo. Yet a man was having incestuous relations with his daughter, or so was thought by a number of informants. Still, there was not complete agreement on the matter. Informants stated that although some of the daughter's siblings (or half-siblings, more correctly) were children of the incestuous father, yet clearly this child was not (the implication being that if the man was having incestuous relations with the child, a fortiori she could not be his child). Which brings up a familiar cultural practice: that of redefinition. As Firth (1930) has shown, when a man marries a close (taboo) relative there occurs "a readjustment of kinship attitudes and corresponding terminology. Joking relations become formal respect relations, people with whom a reciprocal relationship of mutual assistance and support existed become strangers—and their terminological assignment changes as well." In short, as Buchler states (1966a, p. 23),

The cognitive aspects of incest, then, belong to the domain of semiology: the relationships of signs (terms) to each other (syntax), to the social objects which they signify (semantics) and to their users (pragmatics).

It would appear, then, that Gellner's scheme, for all its desirability, is not possible, nor even relevant to the purpose of anthropologists. Kinship statuses are culturally, and not biologically, defined. And, although the primary kin types (F, M, H, W, S, D, B, Z) appear to be based upon the "facts" of biology, in fact they are susceptible *only* to cultural definition. *Biological kin type* is a misnomer, and it would be more proper (if more awkward) to call these notational symbols, *sociological constructs, based in part upon biological considerations.*

## THE EXTENSIONIST HYPOTHESIS AND THE FAMILY

Earlier in this discussion we showed that the nuclear family is not universal, and that neither is the family itself by the terms of Murdock's (1949, p. 1) definition. This decision is not without its implications for the study of kinship, and in this section and the following we take up the implications of the restricted distribution of the nuclear family for the study of kinship.

It has been maintained that kinship systems are based on the nuclear family. This implies that, in the absence of the nuclear family, kinship terminologies as we understand them could not exist in the form that we know them to exist in all societies. First, we analyze how this position seems to have arisen, and then criticize the notion that a kinship system cannot exist in the absence of the nuclear family.

Since the time of L. H. Morgan, the utility of "primary kin types" for the analysis of kinship terms has been recognized. The primary kin types are "father," "mother," "husband," "wife," "brother," "sister," "son," and "daughter." Progress in the study of kinship systems would have been impossible without the conceptualization of a system of points, onto which it is possible to map the range of kin terms. Using these primary kin types singly and in combination, it is possible to list *denotata* (or range) of any kinship term. It is also true that these eight primary kin types denote all dyadic relations of the nuclear family, from every actor's point of view. And for this reason it has been felt that the set of relations thus summed must be common, in sociological terms, to all societies. But this is misplaced concreteness, involving the reification of a method of analysis, extrapolating from analytic method to the domain of sociology. It might seem (as to Lounsbury, 1965, pp. 181–184) that the few exceptions to the universally present nuclear family are of nugatory importance. But, if we, by logical fiat, rule these exceptions out of discourse, we are brought to the absurd position of saying that in the West Indies and in parts of Latin America there are no families among large segments of the lower classes, merely households. And further, we are forced to state (if we make the further assumption that the family is the elementary atom of kinship), that in the West Indies they do not have a "true" kinship system. But, in our view there is no need to maintain the irreconcilability of the centrality of the family to the analysis of kinship, and the utility of primary kin terms.

The fact that a father is unidentified does not mean that a child cannot know the meaning of kin terms that refer to patrilateral relatives. The primary kin types which are used in the analysis of the denotative meaning of these terms have cognitive not sociological referents.

It seems to be an anomaly that the correlation between the universal utility of the biological kin types and the existence of the nuclear family does not hold. But, in fact, we do not have to posit the universality of the nuclear family to account for the universality of kinship systems. We merely have to assume that on the cultural (or cognitive) level, the concepts of affinity, descent, and consanguinity coexist with the recognition of sexual differences. It is but one short step from this statement to asserting that the minimal group in which these relations are all present is the nuclear family, and there- fore, the nuclear family must exist—but it is precisely that step that must not be taken. This brings us directly to a discussion of the extensionist hypothesis—a hypothesis based upon the assumption that genealogical relations are primary, basic, and necessary in the elaboration of kinship terminologies.

The essentials of the extensionist hypothesis were stated in its clearest form by Malinowski (1929, pp. 525–526; 1932, 3rd ed., pp. 442–443):

I have intentionally and carefully distinguished this from so-called classificatory kinship ties; for the mixing up of the individual and the "classificatory" relation, kept apart by the natives in law, custom and idea, has been a most misleading and dangerous cause of error in anthropology, vitiating both observation and theory on social organization and kinship . . . The child is taught by its elders to extend the term *inagu* to her (mother's sister), and his extension is made natural and plausible to the child by the considerable similarity between its relations to mother and mother's sister. But there can be no doubt that the use of the word remains always what it is, an extension and a metaphor.

Murdock (1949, p. 132) has discussed the phenomenon of merging of relatives into terminological classes on the principle of stimulus generalization, "Generalization is the mechanism by which any response, learned in connection with a particular stimulus or pattern of stimuli, tends also to be evoked by other stimulus situations in proportion to their similarity to the original one."

It is assumed that the "primary" meaning of a kinship term is that of the relative closest to Ego, and that the relatives of the same terminological class, but more distant genealogically, are members of the class by virtue of the *extension* of the term from closest to more distant kin.

Murdock's (1949) use of the notion *stimulus* and *response* implies that a part of the environment and a part of behavior are called stimulus (eliciting, discriminating, and so on), and response only if the dynamic laws relating them show smooth and reproducible curves (laws generating isomorphic results over a large but finite set of cultures: Skinner, 1957; Chomsky, 1964). But in Murdock's usage, the notion *stimulus* loses all objectivity. Stimuli are driven back into the organism; they are no longer a part of the outside physical world. For the identification of stimuli in social anthropology is not merely a matter of identifying components of the natural world; these components are always mapped into a cultural grid that is internalized by native speakers, and the identification process presupposes the grid's prior decoding. It is in this sense that Murdock's talk of stimulus situations disguises a retreat to mentalistic psychology (cf. Chomsky, 1964, p. 553). Murdock's use of response masks similar problems that students of ethnoscience have been explicitly concerned with in their attempts to enumerate meaningful units of verbal and nonverbal behavior within the context of particular cultures.

Recent studies of the acquisition of syntax (e.g. Mehler, 1963; Fodor, 1966; McNeill, 1966) and of the syntax of kinship reckoning (Chapters Ten and Eleven) suggest that any analysis of the processes underlying the learning of systems of social classification that ignores the problem of determining what the internal structure of an information-processing (hypothesis-forming) system must be to enable a child to arrive at an array of cultural syntaxes from the available data in the available time, is unlikely to lead to significant results (c.f. Chomsky, 1964, p. 578). Murdock's use of the notion "generalization" manages to blur almost everything of interest in this process.

If we think of a semantic space made up of the universe of all primary kin types or primitives (e.g., F, M, Z, B, D, S, H, W), plus all secondary relatives (or biological kin types, e.g., FB, FZ, MB, MZ, HB, HZ, and so forth; there are 33 of them), plus all tertiary relatives (MBD, MBS, MZD, and so forth; utilizing in each case three biological kin types and arbitrarily cut the universe at that), we will have a space that is to be partitioned into those classes of relatives which are grouped together under one kin term. For example, for American-English terminology we will have one set of relatives that are grouped together under the term *uncle*. These relatives are FB, MB, FZH, MZH, for some speakers. In our analysis we will attempt to find the criteria, or components, that partition the space such that these four relatives, and only these four relatives, fall into one class together. By trial and error, we find that three criteria will discriminate this class of relatives. These are: sex (which has two values, male and female) coded for "male sex"; generation (i.e., own generation: 0, son's generation: −1, father's generation: +1, grandfather's generation: +2, and grandson's generation: −2) will be coded for value +1; and collaterality (i.e., whether the relative in question [here "uncle"] is in direct line through my parent or my children [zero-degree collateral], or whether he stands related to my line through sibling links.)[7] By coding our criteria in this manner we formulate a set of attributes that defines relatives who are called *uncle* and only those relatives called uncle. In plain language we would say that *uncle* "means" first degree collateral male of ascending generation plus one.

The point is that we have used "genealogical" criteria to partition the space that contains genealogical elements. Had there existed a kin term that was distinguished by other criteria (as, say, would a hypothetical term such as "sugar daddy"), then we would have to introduce a criterial attribute, "rich—generous/not rich—not generous," in order to partition the set and permit the inclusion within a class of all those relatives called "sugar daddy." We would be introducing a sociological criterion, and the analysis could not be said to be carried out with "genealogical" partitions in a genealogical space.

---

[7] Lounsbury has defined degree of collaterality as follows (1956, p. 168): "'Degree of collaterality' between a pair of consanguineal kinsmen is equal to the number of generations up a descent line of the higher generation member of the pair, or of either if of the same generation, up to their common ancestor. It is thus a reciprocal constant: the degree of collaterality of the first with respect to the second is equal to that of the second with respect to the first, regardless of which is taken as Ego. Degree of collaterality, thus defined, is the primary dimension of our English kinship system. Lineal kinsmen (ancestors and descendants), as well as one's self, are of zero-degree collaterality; uncles and aunts, brothers and sisters, and nephews and nieces, as we use these kinship terms in English, are of first degree collaterality, while cousins are of second and higher degrees of collaterality."

## A CRITICAL CASE—THE TROBRIAND

All these issues are crystallized in the discussion that has been generated by Leach's (1958) paper on Trobriand kinship. We shall here refer the reader to the sources, and discuss in some detail Leach's analysis of Trobriand kinship, which is carried out as an exercise in the utility of sociological criteria for the analysis of kinship terminologies.

Leach (1958, p. 143) has stated that his "general standpoint is that kinship terms are category words by means of which the individual is taught to recognize the significant groupings in the social structure into which he is born; ... The genealogical analysis of Malinowski leads to a maze of anomalies." Lounsbury (1965, p. 147) argues that Leach overlooks or regards as erroneous the following points: "... the fundamental importance of the nuclear family and of the roles within it, ... the origin of kinship meanings within the nuclear family and the extension of these out from that point of origin along specified paths of connection, and ... the basis for such extension that is provided by genealogy and by family law, i.e., by the recognition of legal rights that are *ascribed* in terms of relationships found in the nuclear family, and of various relative products of these." We can show here that Lounsbury's analysis based on these principles correctly describes the Trobriand system, whereas Leach's analysis does not. Despite the fact that Leach's comments on the economic system of the Trobriands are perceptive and interesting, his preoccupation with these aspects of life and with "residence" and "domicile" lead him to formulate a system that will not predict kin terms accurately and which is not internally consistent.

To add to the complexity of both Leach and Lounsbury's arguments is the confusion in the actual assignment of kin terms to relatives: that is, Leach and Lounsbury do not even agree which relative is to be called what. Leach includes father's mother's brother in the *tama* category, which would seem to be in accord with Malinowski's statement (1929, p. 515), "*Tama* (gu)— Father, father's brother, father's clansman; father's sister's son," since father's mother's brother would be a clansman of father's. Lounsbury amends Malinowski and says that *tama* includes (1965, p. 148), "F; FB; [FZS]; [MZH]; father's clansman (of same or lower generation)." Presumably here Lounsbury feels that because every other relative of the second ascending generation is classified as *tabu*, he is justified in removing this "ambiguity." ("Ambiguities have been removed and reciprocals filled out," 1965, p. 185.) He calls FMB *tabu*, which then fits his own definition of *tabu* as "Grandparent" or "Grandchild."

Lounsbury also omits father's brother's children from his analysis, because "the parallel cousins on the father's side are not included under the sibling categories (*tuwa, bwada, luta*) in Malinowski's table of relationship terms (1929, pp. 515–516; 1932, p. 434), nor are these positions filled on the genealogical diagram which follows the table. We are left to conclude that these omissions were not fortuitous and that one's father's brother's children, in

Trobriand ideology, are not relatives." Lounsbury further points out that Malinowski says (1929, p. 101), "A boy and a girl who are the children of two brothers stand in no special relation to each other." Inasmuch as it is difficult to be sure what *special* means here, filling in these relationships seems reasonable: other writers, Leach included, have assumed that the Trobriand system would conform to the usual description of a Crow-type system and that therefore all parallel cousins are to be considered siblings. However, Lounsbury stresses that he is trying to make sense of Malinowski's data as presented; and he writes a restricted half-sibling rule, indicating that patri-lateral parallel cousins are in the null class (Figure 2–1).

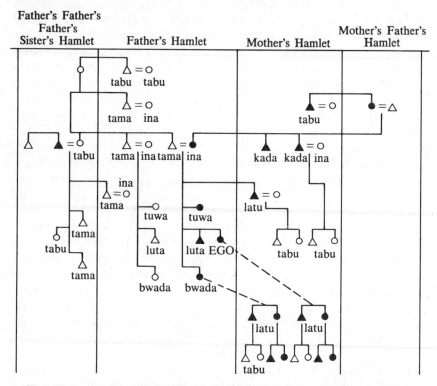

Figure 2–1.  Leach's Diagram, Drawn for a Female Ego (Leach, 1958, p. 130).[8]

The fact that Leach includes, perhaps inadvertently, father's brother's children in his chart (1958, p. 130) unfortunately invalidates one of his definitions from the start. He says (1958, p. 132), "*Kada, tuwa, bwada* are not here primarily 'mother's brother,' 'elder brother,' 'younger brother' but rather 'the domiciled males of my own sub-clan hamlet' categorized by age

[8] Sex of siblings has been reversed in Figure 2–1, in order to show younger and older sibling terms.

and generation." But father's brother's children are not domiciled in Ego's own subclan, but rather in father's brother's wife's brother's subclan hamlet (unless father's brother's wife and father's wife are sisters). Thus, Leach's definition of *kada*, *tuwa*, and *bwada* does not make sense of the data he presents (Figures 2–2 and 2–3).

More serious are the inconsistencies within others of Leach's definitions. Leach says (1958, p. 132) that "*Luta* is not simply 'sister' but 'alien girls resident in my father's hamlet.' The phonemically very similar word *latu* represents a corresponding category, namely, 'alien children resident in my own sub-clan hamlet.'" And later, he continues (p. 133), "The verbal similarity between the two terms perhaps reflects (the) . . . similarity of valuations. Malinowski's statements, taken as a whole, imply that while a boy can safely have love affairs with any of his *latu* and most of his neighboring *luta*, he can decently marry neither." Aside from the obviously absurd reasoning that two words that contain the same phonemes are semantically related, these definitions are misleading. A man's children live within his household from the time of birth to the age of puberty, for a boy, and until marriage, for a girl. Marguerite Robinson (1962, pp. 128–133) points out that a father among the Trobriands manages his daughter's marriage, and has the ultimate right to approve that marriage. A man's father brings an important gift to the parents of his son's bride; he pays for his son's marriage, which takes place within his house. A father protects his daughter with magic (Robinson, 1962, p. 141) and hands down important garden magic to his son. In what sense then are a male ego's children "alien," except for the fact that they are not members of their father's subclan and will not live with their father after marriage? It seems clear that except for subclan affiliation, which is reckoned genealogically, the "alien" label makes little sense here; therefore the line of reasoning that says that *latu* represents alien children is misleading.

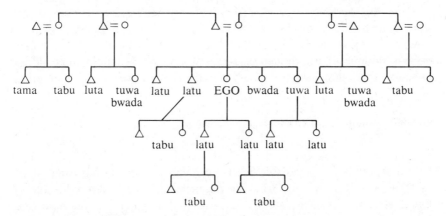

*Figure 2–2. Trobriand Kin Terms for a Female Ego (adapted from Fathauer, 1962, p. 262).*

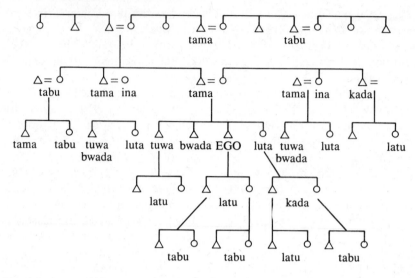

*Figure 2–3.   Trobriand Kin Terms for a Male Ego (adapted from Fathauer, 1962, p. 261).*

When we turn to a female ego, Leach's definitions make even less sense. Changing the sex terms, *luta* according to Leach would mean "brother, and alien boys resident in my father's hamlet"; this application of "alien" could be reasonably held, because the only people outside of one's own brother who are called *luta* are one's father's brother's children, who (if they exist at all as relatives) do not belong either to one's father's or to one's own sub-clan. On the other hand, *latu*, in Leach's terms, would be "alien children resident in my own sub-clan hamlet." But this term is applied to a female ego's own children and to her sister's children, who are members of female ego's subclan, but who will reside, with their mother, in their respective mothers' husbands' mothers' brothers' subclan hamlets, until marriage, at which time the male children will be resident in female ego's subclan hamlet. It seems then that distinctions based on concepts of "alienation" or on differences of "domicile" or "residence" do not work: "own children and children of same sex siblings" would be both a simpler and more accurate definition of *latu*.

Leach bases his definition of *tabu* on several factors: relative age and social distance, potential hostility as a result of *urigubu* payment, and so forth. "*Tabu* now appears as a general term, undifferentiated as to age or sex, comprising the whole broad category of potentially hostile "outsiders." The only individuals in the *urigubu*-receiving hamlets who are not categorized as *tabu* are the male *tama* who are domiciled in (and later residents of) Ego's father's hamlet" (1958, p. 132). Although these statements hold true for a male ego (the people labeled *tabu* in his two "home hamlets" are two generations removed from ego), they do not for a female ego. A female ego's brother's children and her mother's brother's children are called *tabu*, although both are resident in her own subclan hamlet, which is an *urigubu-giving*, not an *urigubu-receiving*, hamlet. In order to suggest that *tabu* implies hostility because of both payment and receiving of *urigubu*, the female before marriage would have to feel hostile toward her own subclan hamlet and toward the hamlet of her potential husband as well, and would therefore call the members of these hamlets *tabu*, which she might, if her potential husband's mother's brother's hamlet was unknown to her. However, because her brother's children and her mother's brother's children are *tabu* and therefore lawful marriage prospects, we can see from the diagram that she calls at least one potential husband's mother *Ina* and his father *Kada*. The simplest explanation again is one based on genealogical reckoning: female ego's brother's children are the reciprocal of father's sister, who is called *tabu*.

There appear to be errors and confusion in Leach's system when he uses such criteria as residence, potential hostility, and "alien-not alien" to describe kin categories. It can further be seen that when Leach is correct in his descriptions, he is using the genealogical method. For instance, he says (1958, p. 132), "*Tama* . . . is seen to refer to 'a domiciled male of my father's subclan hamlet.'" This looks at first like a sociological statement, but in reality it is not. The subclan hamlet as defined by Leach is a collection of men who belong to the same matrilineage, and who therefore live near and work the land owned by this matrilineage (1958, p. 124) "I and is owned by the matrilineal sub-clans. The married males of the sub-clan . . . live, each in his own domestic household, in a village, or section of a village, situated on or near the sub-clan land." Leach explains further (1958, p. 124), ". . . a Trobriand male is, from the start, domiciled in his own sub-clan hamlet, but his residence varies." Thus, "a domiciled male of my father's subclan hamlet" simply means, a male member of my father's matrilineal subclan. Another instance in which Leach would be right, if he had not included brother's children among his kin types, would be his definition of *kada*, *tuwa*, and *bwada*. He says these terms refer to "the domiciled males of my own sub-clan hamlet, categorized by age and generation"; in other words, men, or for a female ego, women, of my own matrilineal subclan. The concept of "domicile" adds nothing here, inasmuch as it means member of a certain subclan; thus the reasoning is entirely genealogical and as such is correct.

It is perhaps anticlimactic to mention that Lounsbury (1965) has shown that an analysis based entirely upon genealogical considerations is 100 per cent accurate in making the proper kin-class assignments. Further, Lounsbury states that his analysis is based upon the extensionist hypothesis and that, because the analysis succeeds, the assumptions behind the analysis must be correct. The extensionist hypothesis might appear to be demonstrated, the genealogical method might appear not to be misconceived. The probability of misconception, in this one case, is extremely low, but as Lounsbury points out (1965, p. 182), ". . . the Trobriand case is only one case of many where similar results have been recently obtained. These include some of ethnography's most puzzling cases, as well as several where the documentation provides much more data than we have for Trobriand and where it is consequently possible to check the predictions of the theory on a much more extensive scale than was possible in the present case . . . . With this many cases, and with this much data accounted for, the probability that the results could be due to chance is infinitesimal."

But there is a serious *non sequitur* here. Lounsbury has performed a linguistic analysis, utilizing the techniques and assumptions that underlie structural semantics. He wrote, in effect, an accurate syntactical account of Trobriand kinship. But his success in this matter does not rule out the productivity nor the viability of other kinds of analysis. As Hammel (1965a, pp. 65–6) has written of his own transformational account of Comanche kinship terminology,

The frame of reference and language of description imposed on the terminology examined here are genealogical. The general approach of this investigation, like that of others in the field of componential analysis, is that the minimal specification of necessarily associated characteristics on some descriptive grid constitutes the "meaning" of the items of data analyzed. Thus, to say that "lineal male relative of the second ascending generation" describes the necessary and sufficient conditions in our own culture for the inclusion of some person in the set, "grandfather," is to define "grandfather" solely by those characteristics. Considerations of affect, of decrepitude, of dandling on the knee, are not taken into account. Such an approach, however, does not insist that the genealogical characteristics constitute the only possible definition of "grandfather," but only that they provide an explicit and cross-culturally valid grid for the specification of a kind of denotation. The use of a genealogical grid in such analyses rests on the logical properties of its components and on the fact that it can be universally applied, if the statements of its components are sufficiently primitive. It is not necessary to insist that genealogical reckoning *must* lie at the base of status terminologies of kinship; it is sufficient to recognize that the two are usually in good accord.

Given the terms and methodologies of this approach (in particular transformational analysis), an elegant and generalizable solution to terminological sets can be formulated. Given a sociological approach to terminological sets (no matter how ingenious), the analysis fails simply out of the contingencies involved in correlating one level of analysis with another, correlating the sociological and the terminological.[9]

The test-comparison between Leach and Lounsbury is unfair in the sense that Lounsbury stacked the deck before the game started. He has bounded his universe very tightly (under the proper assumptions of transformational analysis) by restricting his perspective to a set of kinship terms, defined

[9] Murdock's (1949) correlational analysis is the best example of the degree of contingency involved.

beforehand in terms of biological kin types. Leach made no such restriction —he was concerned with the fit of two kinds of data, on two different levels. Whereas Lounsbury might expect mechanical (i.e., structural and non-contingent) relations to emerge in his solution, Leach could not. Therefore if we are to choose one method over the other, on the sole grounds that the method that admits of less contingency will necessarily "win," then what we have shown here is that the winner's circle is occupied before the race begins, and by Lounsbury.

Schneider (1965a, 1967) points out, with reference to componential and transformational accounts, that it is misleading to imply that *kinship terminology* is being analyzed. He states (1965a, p. 304),

It is, to be precise, the semantic domain defined by the control question insofar as that semantic domain is internally differentiated by something like kinship terms. It is *not* an analysis of terms for kinsmen. It is *not* an analysis of kinship terms. It is an analysis of the way in which kin types are classed by kinship terms.

The "control question" or framework of elicitation, by which the data is collected, determines that polysemy is eliminated. Thus when Lounsbury states that one necessarily must infer from the predictive accuracy of his method that the extensionist hypothesis holds as it stands, he too is switching levels of analysis, and stating a *non sequitur*. Operationally we may eliminate polysemy, but other kinds of analysis based on mixed strategies or pure sociological strategies are admissible, and if the results do not jibe with linguistic-structural analyses, then so much the better—we have learned more.

If we then consider the logical status of the extensionist hypothesis as well as the discussion over whether kinship terms *really are* sociological constructs, or genealogical constructs, we find that the issue is a false one, so long as it is phrased in terms of a mutually exclusive antithesis. Kinship terms are polysememic; they are category words that can (at this point in time) be most easily handled within the framework of transformational or componential analysis. If one is interested in mapping kinship terms onto economic exchange, and a network of affective *types* (phrased in dyadic terms), then sociological analysis will be of great utility. But if one is interested in the internal consistency of a corpus of linguistic data, mapped for the purposes of simplicity and elegance onto biological kin types, then transformational or componential analysis would be the best discovery device. The assumptions underlying the methodologies are method-specific— they do not permit us to make general statements about the nature (in its entirety) of the phenomena under observation. Transformational (or componential) analysis neither requires nor proves the extensionist hypothesis.

In this chapter we attempted to introduce the reader to some of the current issues in the study of the family. We examined the utility of dyadic analysis in study of family relations and in the construction of typology. Next we examined the sociological basis of genealogical constructs based upon biological kin types. And finally we looked at the viability of the extensionist hypothesis in the light of some recent methods of kinship analysis. Throughout this chapter we have treated the family as though it were a stable, quasi-static sociological unit. This is an analytic convenience, and we dispense with it in the next chapter, where the dynamics of the diachronic development of domestic and family cycles is studied.

With Murdock (1949), we assume that in every society there is a relational set that can be mapped onto the criteria of descent, affinity, and consanguinity.[2] It is identifiable by the informants because it is the minimum social unit that (1) cooperates in production and distribution, (2) is so age-graded as to allocate responsibility for the education and safety of children to the senior age-grades, and (3) engages in exchanges of women with other like units.

The criteria that establish the shape of the family are culturally derived as compared to the criteria for households that were derived by the ethnographer. The ethnographer translates these culture-specific criteria through the medium of genealogical symbols based on descent, affinity, and consanguinity. By analytic fiat then, a statement of the form: "The family in X culture should include at least three servants" is not admissible. The shape of the family exists solely in the minds of the informants, and the ethnographer merely translates the results of his rigorous and culture-specific methodology to establish what the family form of X culture may be.

We introduce these operational distinctions in the definition of *family* and *household* because they appear to be at least one way of avoiding the traditional ambiguities in the definition of family and household. Consider the following statement (Evans-Pritchard, 1951, p. 3),

The Nuer speak of a man's homestead as his *gol*, the primary meaning of which word is the heap of smouldering cattle-dung in the centre of a byre and the hearth around it. In its narrowest social use the word means family, the occupants of the homestead, and it may also therefore have the further sense of household, since there may be other persons living there than members of the owner's family who count nevertheless, as we would say, as members of the family. Frequently the

---

guistic shape of questions in the local language. Second, one seeks the appropriate questions that can be asked in the culture. One asks an informant, for example, "What kind of a question could I ask about 'X'?" Third, one forms "substitution frames" on the basis of information gained in steps one and two. These frames are culturally relevant general questions, "which produce lists, either through single or reiterated employment of frames . . . such lists (being) constituted of items which are mutually exclusive in some environment (i.e., that environment defined by the occurrence of the frame) in which all are appropriate." (Metzger and Williams, 1966, p. 390.) Such a frame might be, for example, "What is the first kind of 'X'?" "X", in this case, would be a term that an informant had volunteered in response to a general orienting question, one that might be glossed, for example, "trees-and-plants." Substitutions might be made then by the replacement of "first" by successive ordinal numerals, and the replacement of "X" by other high-level, general, terms. The fourth step is to turn all the questions into assertions, and check the body of information with other informants, with whom the elicitation had not taken place. The fifth step is a summary of the data by domains and contrast sets, within contrast levels (or taxonomic levels).

[2] *Descent* refers to the relation created by the fact of biological parenthood. *Affinity* refers to the relation between groups that is created by the exchange of rights over women. *Consanguinity* refers to the relation that is created through multiple births (sibling-ship).

## HOUSEHOLD AND FAMILY

Human beings everywhere live in households. Men and women in all societies take joint responsibility for children, and this joint responsibility is generally reflected in the physical proximity of their living arrangements. Operationally households can be defined as "that set of relationships which describes the associations of an individual over a 24 hour period" (Adams, n. d.). Household is defined by activity. Only one set of relationships is activated throughout the 24-hour period, and consistently enacted, and that is the household.

There are two approaches to the analysis of household types. One may speak of "ideal" household types, and one can speak of "modal" or "statistically marginal" household types. A statement made by an American informant about the "ideal" household could be, "The ideal household should include 3 servants," or "One's household should not include one's mother-in-law." The criteria that define the household are *ad hoc* and vary from culture to culture. In a closed endogamous community, it might be that households can be defined genealogically—that is to say, the activity-relationships take place with people who are related to the point of reference in a genealogical way. The most developed analytic form for the examination of households (Romney, n. d.) makes this assumption. But this need not necessarily be the case.

In the statistical approach to the study of the household, one lays down a set of ground rules for the delineation of residential forms (such as the activity definition given earlier), and one runs surveys on the distribution of household types across the community. The relationship between the "ideal" household form, and the "modal" form, is problematic, and has to take into account the "domestic cycle" (see Chapter Three for full discussion of domestic cycle).

The major point is that the analysis of the household proceeds on an ethnological plane. The criteria by which the shape of the household is determined are the ethnographer's. They may or may not coincide with those suggested by informants; they have to be comprehensive enough to enable the analyst to include all households in his discussion.

The *family* on the other hand is an ethnoscientifically derived construct.[1]

---

[1] [Ethnoscience and ethnoscientific are used in a narrow sense here. We refer, specifically, to a set of procedures that have been designed to determine the structure of categories in the informant's own view, in a non-Western culture where the anthropologist does not have complete control of the local language. The best accounts of the procedure are to be found in a series of publications by Metzger and Williams (1962, 1963a, 1963b, 1966). Their technique seeks to establish the nature of native categorial systems by finding out what the appropriate questions are that can be asked in a culture, and what the interrogative sentences are that will generate all and only the constituents of any category. Roughly speaking, there are five steps to this analysis (Thompson, n. d.). First, one learns the lin-

## THE DECISION-ORIENTED APPROACH

A second approach to the study of domestic organization is neither statistical nor typological in its orientation, but rather seeks to probe decision processes within the framework of *ideal patterns* and *jural rules*. For example, whereas the statistical approach put questions to census data of the kind, "What is the distribution of household types in segment $X$ of society $Y$?", the jural approach (in a modified form) asks questions concerning the *strategies* of individual actors, along the line of, "With what group type should individual $X$ of $Y$ social characteristics be associated?" This approach seeks to examine the ethnographic model (Goodenough, 1961, 1964) of behavior, and seeks to include not only spatial distribution but the set of situational, motivational, and cognitive factors which precipitate a decision on the part of the actor to engage in such behavior. This approach requires more data and a wider perspective than the statistical, which is based to a much greater degree on a priori grounds, and can be thought of as part of the ethnography of decision-making in a society. Its correspondence to the statistical model depends upon the exclusion of unique cases, and an understanding of the entire universe of factors that are used by the analyst to account for behavior of his informants. Only in the rare case will the correspondence be perfect. An example can be given of the jural approach taken from field work in the Oaxaca Valley (Selby 1966, 1967), in the village of St. Tomas Mazaltepec, in an examination of postnuptial residence.

Although a statistical summary of residential forms displays an amazing disparity, the jural pattern of postnuptial residence in this village is virilocal. To an actor (and his family) postnuptial residence (which will permit access to the household resources by the coresident) poses problems in strategy, which are seen to be resolved appropriately only in the context of a number of situational factors. For a man there are two alternative patterns of postnuptial residence, virilocal and uxorilocal. Virilocal residence is the preferred form, not in the statistical sense that it is the "normal" form of residence (which it is), but in the sense that positive value attaches to it. Associated with residential choice are a bundle of activities, which are denoted by the Spanish term *"pedimiento."* *Pedimiento* refers to that set of activities undertaken by both families whereby the hand of the potential spouse is "sought"; arrangements are made for the wedding; and financial commitments are made by both sides in deciding how much of a contribution will be made by each side to the expenses of the wedding (chief of which is the outlay of up to U.S. $800.00 for the wedding feast or *fandango*). By arranging to seek the hand of the groom, and by arranging to pay the greater share of the expenses, the family of a potential bride can arrange an uxorilocal marriage.

As mentioned earlier, the jural or normative rule is virilocality, to which positive value is attached. Positive value is also attached (by actors) to the resources of the household, and each actor (actor in the sense of negotiating family) attempts to maximize the values of the transaction. A male gains an initial "profit" by arranging a virilocal marriage. The comparative "loss" on the part of the bride is made up by the fact that she marries into a household with greater resources than her household "of orientation." Thus jurally we have a pattern of what the anthropologist would call hypergamy, and the native actor an equivalent exchange.

Consider the opposite situation—that of uxorilocal marriage. Uxorilocal marriage is not evaluated neutrally, but a negative value is placed upon it (from the point of view of the male actor). Thus a proportionately greater degree of incentive must be injected into the transaction in order to make the exchange between the two families a fair or equal exchange. Thus in the case of uxorilocal marriage the differential will be proportionately greater than in the case of virilocal marriage.

Furthermore, the actor point of view must be considered, because we can conceptualize the notion of "incentive" much in the manner of "relative deprivation." Economic differential sufficient to provide adequate incentive (for uxorilocal marriage in this example, but by inference to virilocal marriage as well) will vary directly with the economic status of the "lower" party in the exchange. In this village as in most Middle American peasant-Indian villages, a yoke of oxen, a burro, a plough, and a little land is sufficient to provide a subsistence base for a family. Below that point (and particularly in the absence of the all-important yoke of oxen), one is considered to be a member of a class of persons /ši?t mo?ten/ which we can gloss as "poor people." Entry into the class of people who "have something" is highly desirable and therefore the actor will require less incentive than a person "with something" who also is entertaining a decision to reside uxorilocally. As the following tables indicate there is a general correspondence between the SES measures and the actor's decision-frame of reference. Remembering as well, that the SES figures are derived from census materials taken up to 20 years after the time of marriage, it is in some ways remarkable that any correlation emerges at all.

First, it is clear that, of the 84 households surveyed (Table 3-1), the family that sought the hand of the spouse was, in fact, richer than the family from whom the spouse was sought (Table 3-2).

Table 3–1.  Spouse-Seeking and Economic Status

|                        | Number | Per cent |
|------------------------|--------|----------|
| Seeking family richer  | 52     | 62       |
| Seeking family poorer  | 23     | 27       |
| Both families equal    | 6      | 7        |
| Doubtful cases         | 3      | 4        |

These figures can be broken down to yield only those households for which we have both economic data, and data on which spouse was sought, husband or wife.

Table 3-2.   Spouse-Seeking and Relative Wealth of Household

|  | Household wealthier | Household poorer |
|---|---|---|
| Husband sought by wife | 4 | 15 |
| Wife sought by husband | 36 | 13 |

$$X^2 = 15.5 : P > 0.001$$

NOTE. We have additional data on the upper left hand cell; in three of the cases the women were scored as less wealthy than the men, but in fact they were owners of a houseplot and house at the time of the *pedimiento*. Houses are low-priority items in the community of Mazaltepec, and were not used in the calculation of relative wealth.

A part indication (the fuller explication of which demands fuller data and the construction of a linear program) of the motivational structure underlying the "seek or be sought" strategy can be seen in Table 3–3. In the "mating game" one loses points (if male) for "being sought." The degree of added incentive that is needed by males in order for them to accept the "seeking" of a woman (which in turn implies matrineolocal residence) is charted modally in Table 3–3.

Table 3-3.   Spouse-Seeking and Economic Status in
Absolute Terms

| | Economic status of seeking family | |
|---|---|---|
| | (1) | (2) |
| Which spouse sought | Livestock[a] | Almud count[b] |
| Husband | $6,380.00 | 6.33 (N = 16) |
| Wife | $4,044.00 | 4.16 (N = 35) |

[a]Livestock value is calculated using conventional estimates: a yoke of oxen is calculated worth $2,500.00; a cow at $1,600.00; a young bullock at $800.00; a burro at $125.00; a sheep or goat at $75.00; and a full-grown pig at $400.00. These estimates are based on informant statements. They do not represent the relative evaluation of these types of animals, by informants themselves; the ordering of values is arbitrary and *ladinized* (i.e., Hispanicized and commercial, not native).

[b]An almud is a volume measure of corn. Land is measured by the amount of corn which it will accommodate. In this way the quality of the land can be accounted for (one sows more corn on better land, and less on poorer).

In "modal" terms, which can at best give a general picture, it seems clear that relatively greater incentive is presented to men, in order to induce them to "be sought," and by implication, reside matrineolocally. On the average the families of the woman who sought the hand of a man for their daughter were wealthier in livestock to the amount of $2,336.00 (close to the price of a yoke of oxen), and in land to the amount of 2.17 almudes of corn sown.

These tables give no more than a general idea of the kind of motivational structure, and the kinds of considerations that must be taken into account if one is to render an adequate account of residential forms and household formation.

The utility of the decision-oriented approach is that it obviates the dichotomy posed by jural accounts on the one hand, and statistical summaries on the other. In our view it is necessary (with Goodenough, 1964) to have recourse to principles that underlie behavior, as formulated by the native-speakers, and implicit in their behavior. This requires an "ethnoscientific" definition of the behavioral parameters, an approach that requires of the informants that they indicate the behavioral segments they regard as critical to ordering their behavior as well as the situational determinants of decisions in the context of the behavioral segment. For example, it appears that residence per se is not an appropriate frame of reference for analysis. It is subsumable under the more general domain of analysis of status differentiation and exchange. The critical observed behavior is not the physical translation of a member of one family to the behavioral environment of another, but rather the negotation of sexual, physical, and economic rights involved in the process of the *pedimiento*. The exchange model relates to the underlying principles of the exchange, which can be summed up as follows.

1. Each party to the exchange must contribute approximately equal values.
   A. Values shall be defined in the following way.
      a. A positive value shall be deemed to be attached to residential exchange according to the jural model.
      b. A positive and measurable value will be attached to resources under the control of each domestic unit.
      c. The value of resources attached to each person will be calculated in two ways.
         i. The differential evaluation of resources (which is different from the monetary evaluation of the same resources).
         ii. The position of each actor in terms of the three economic divisions that are cognitively salient in the accounts of the informants.[1]

## THE DIACHRONIC APPROACH

A final mode of analysis can be seen to be logically derivative from the combination of the jural and statistical approaches. It differs only in its

---

[1] The three classes are made up of two named states and a residual state. One can be a person (1) ŝiʔ t moʔ ten, (2) naʔ móʔ ten (have much property), or (3) residual class).

focus and emphasis upon the total process of development and change in domestic units. This dynamic, diachronic point of view was introduced by Fortes, implicit in his study of Tallensi (1945, 1949a), and explicitly in his account of Ashanti (1949b). Since that time it has become implicit in most analyses of household composition, and been explicitly developed in a number of cases (cf. Mitchell, 1956; Smith, R. T., 1956; Tait, 1956; Hammel, 1961). Built into many of these studies is the assumption that the concept "structure" is "most appropriately applied to those features of social events and organizations which are actually or ideally susceptible of quantitative description and analysis" (Fortes, 1949b, p. 57). This conception of the structural properties of social facts was formulated by Fortes to account for the apparent absence of "a fixed norm of domestic grouping" and the consequent inappropriateness of ethnological constructs such as patrilocal and matrilocal to Ashanti local organization (Fortes, 1949b, p. 61). Initially, three "types" of Ashanti domestic units were isolated: namely, (a) households grouped around a husband and wife, (b) households grouped around an effective minimal matrilineage, and (c) various combinations of types a and b (Fortes, 1949b, p. 69). However, statistical analysis illustrates that these (a, b, and c) are not distinct forms of organization. They are rather "variations of a single 'form' arising out of quantitative differences in the relations between the parts that make up the structure" (Fortes, 1949b, p. 75). That is, Fortes (1949b, p. 84) construes various "types" of Ashanti domestic groups as the product of an invariant set of structural principles operating in different social contexts and indexing various phases in the developmental cycle of domestic organization.

More recently, Fortes (1962, pp. 2, 5) has suggested that the development of the domestic group—the transition from one phase of the developmental cycle to another—is governed by the relationship of the domestic domain (the internal field) to the political-jural domain (the external field), and that the following developmental paradigm can be applied (*mutatis mutandis*) to the domestic organization of any society: (1) *The Phase of Expansion:* During this phase, offspring are economically, affectively, and jurally dependent on their parents. (2) *The Phase of Dispersion or Fission:* This phase lasts from the marriage of the oldest child to the marriage of the youngest child. (3) *The Phase of Replacement:* This phase terminates with the death of the parents and the replacement of the family founded by them with their children's families. This type of orientation borrows from the decision-oriented approach in that it takes the actor's point of view into account. Analysts attempt to utilize simple enumerative techniques on cross-sectional data, which will permit inference about structural states of household during the life span of an individual.

Built into such analyses, and usually not explicated, are the constraints imposed upon expansion, fission, reduction of the household by demographic factors, specifically birth rates and death rates, as well as age at marriage.

Ignoring of these factors and the necessary constraints they place upon the composition of the domestic group has misled ethnographers in the past, and has bedevilled typological classification based on statistical measures. Coale (1965) has worked out one such model which it will be useful to summarize at this point. Given a birth rate of 50 and a death rate of the same (per 1,000), and the assumption that each female marries at age 15, bears children for 30 years (the birth of each of which is calculated to take place at the age of 30), a number of simulations can be carried out that will generate the average household size for any population. Coale sets four conditions for his model. In the first condition a woman moves out of the household upon attaining marriageable age (fifteen). This would be a "nuclear" case. In the second a woman moves out of the household of her mother, if the mother is dead; if not she stays on until the mother dies. In the third condition, a foster parent is admitted, who is a woman of the same age as the mother, and the child stays on in the household until the foster parent is dead. In the fourth condition the daughter moves out at age 15 if the mother is dead, but if the mother is alive one sister will stay on until the mother dies.

The relative size of the household can be calculated and is reproduced in Table 3–4 (taken from Coale, 1965, p. 68).

Table 3–4.  Household Size Under Four Conditions

| Condition | Size of household: nuclear family equals 100 |
| --- | --- |
| 1. (Nuclear case) | 100 |
| 2. (Separate household when Mo dies) | 136 |
| 3. Fosterage permitted | 175 |
| 4. One daughter stays after marriage | 116 |

Remembering that the size is calculated in terms of females only, we double the number to get the number of individuals in the household.

As can be clearly seen from Table 3–4, the population of the family, given the high death and birth rates that are felt to be generally accurate for under-developed countries, is surprisingly small. The distribution of household types cannot be plotted, but it is clear that under these conditions the nuclear form will predominate. By implication then, in the "natural," i.e., demographic, course of things, the model family form (and by inference, domestic form) will be nuclear. In an examination of domestic groupings, viewed statistically in cross-sectional analysis, the parameters of death rate, birth rate, and age of birth of first child must be taken into account as well as the usual data on residential change, age at marriage, and so on. More, they must be entered into the account of domestic cycle if we are to achieve controlled comparison from society to society.

Interest in domestic cycle stems ultimately from the anthropologist's assumption that a social structure is an enduring or persisting entity, independent of the life span of any particular population. The fact of persistence and the associated diachronic focus impels the observer to look for those mechanisms of social reproduction which, in Fortes' words (1962, p. 2), "includes all those institutional mechanisms and customary activities and norms which serve to maintain replenish and transmit the social capital from generation to generation." Domestic cycle, then, is concerned with social learning, a subject which anthropologists (with the exception of Margaret Mead and Gregory Bateson) have been wont to ignore. There exists the attendant danger of the recapitulation or genetic fallacy. As Goody (1959), Needham (1962a), and Lévi-Strauss (1963a) have commented in regard to the "patrilineal complex" of Radcliffe-Brown (1924), the danger exists that one will take a social learning point of view in the examination of social structure, to the degree that one will mistake the development of cognition, along with affective associations, for the necessary point of departure for structural analyses. Such a view can lead to erroneous conclusions, just as it did with Malinowski where kinship terminological structure was viewed in this context (see Chapter Two), and with Leach's (1958) analysis of Trobriand (see Chapter Two for extended discussion).

American analysts have been wont to separate the social learning aspects of the analysis of domestic cycle from the statistical (see Hammel, 1961, and Miller, 1964, for example). Miller's (1964) example is instructive in this regard, and in reviewing his work among the Tzotzil Indians of the state of Chiapas, Mexico, we can give an illustration of the kind of work that has become embedded in the standard repertoire of field work tasks.

In a complete census of the village of Yalcuc (thirty-nine households), Miller noted the distribution of households (distinguished on the ground that they shared food). Analysis of the frequency of identical types (based on dyadic composition) yielded the results shown in Table 3–5. From an examination of the frequency distribution it appears that the normative form of household is the nuclear form (or in Miller's terms, "single elementary family"). "Seventy-seven per cent (thirty out of thirty-nine) of the households are composed of a single elementary family, and the remainder of various combinations of families" (Miller, 1964, p. 177). An examination of the cycle through which the household passes, however, shows that the pattern of residence is not neolocal, but in reality patrilocal.

Marriage in Yalcuc takes place for a male about the age 18–20. At this point he seeks the hand of his bride. If he is accepted they are married and he spends some time in his father-in-law's house performing groom service. The extent of this time is not defined, it is variable, and we are not given any indication of the nature nor the determinants of the variance. Then he returns to his father's household, and after a period (when his brothers begin to marry) he moves out, either to another site within the general area of his

### Table 3–5.  Distribution of Household Types
### Yalcuc, Mexico (Tzotzil)

| Household members | Frequency |
|---|---|
| Man and wife | 4 |
| Man, wife, children | 21 |
| Widower and children | 1 |
| Widow and children | 3 |
| Widow and grandchildren | 1 |
| Man, wife, and married son | 3 |
| Widow and married son | 2 |
| Brothers, wives, and children | 2 |
| Man, wife, married son, married daughter | 2 |
| Total | 39 |

(After Miller, 1964, p. 177)

father's household or he builds a new house for himself. In this way we can exemplify Fortes' (1958, pp. 4–5) three phases of household and family growth as follows. *Expansion* takes place as the children of the family grow to maturation. *Dispersion* takes place as the son brings in his wife for a period of a year or more, and spends time as well in his father-in-law's household. *Replacement* comes about with the establishment of a new cycle of growth, and the death of the father of the family.

At this point we can return to the data on household composition with an understanding of the kind of process in terms of which nonmodal or deviant cases are defined. In the case where married children of both sexes are living with their father, it appears that we do not have a case of (1) virilocal (2) groom service conjointly, but rather a case of "lucrilocality." That is residence choice arising out of the greater economic opportunity afforded by an exceptionally wealthy household head. The two joint fraternal households are a temporary expedient (temporary in the sense that the brothers maintain separate residences in town, and this joint household is on their land allotment), and is not symptomatic of a patterned deviation of any kind.

From this analysis Miller can distill four principles of residential alignment, which emerge from his analysis of cases in the framework provided by the developmental model, and which would not have been possible in the case that he had used merely the statistical model. The principles (Miller, 1964, p. 181) are

(1) The temptation of immediate fission by elopement are offset by the economic advantages of maintaining ties with both sets of parents, since by the system of alternating residence a new couple can remain semi-dependent for several years and then have help in building a house.

(2) The needs of parents for assistance in their old age and the prospects of in-heriting the house predispose the son who marries last to remain with his parents until their deaths.

(3) Unusual economic advantages, such as those offered by the wealthy and pro-ductive household (which contains married children of both sexes) may be the basis for maintaining an exceptionally large domestic group.

(4) Considerations of convenience may incline childless couples or part-time residents to establish joint households.

Thus by utilizing the developmental model, ethnographic insights that are quite impossible with the purely synchronic approach may be attained.

A second kind of analysis that gains immensely from the use of the devel-opmental model is comparative analyses embracing two or more communi-ties. We can exemplify the comparative approach by an examination of Hammel's (1961) work with two Peruvian communities.

Hammel classified families into six types, taking the age of each woman in the census and plotting the composition of the entire household for that age: (1) nuclear (woman and spouse with/without children, own or adopted, but no other), (2) more-than-nuclear superordinate (woman + spouse with/ without children + spouse of child, or grandchild), (3) more-than-nuclear (woman + spouse + adult with/without family), (4) more-than-nuclear subordinate (woman + spouse + parents [own or Hu's]), (5) less-than-nuclear nondependent (woman without spouse, with/without peer or children), and (6) less-than-nuclear dependent (woman without spouse + par-ents or grandparents). Then by plotting the distribution of types by decades (women's ages) he ascertains (given adequate sampling and the assumption that household composition has been stable over the period being examined) the probability that a person at any age point (reckoned by decades) will be a member of a household of a given type. For example, in the age range 15 to 65+ we can observe the following distribution of the population by house-hold type. For convenience we include only those women who have offered evidence of current or previous sexual relationship, (i.e., we omit, or control for, those women who have not profferred the opportunity of sexual cohabi-tation to a man, and therefore cannot be reckoned in with the population of women who have put themselves in the position of "potential spouse"). The frequencies and percentages shown in Table 3–6 emerge.

The same kind of analysis can be performed with other communities and the data scanned for comparative purposes, and hypotheses can be formed to account for significant variation in the two. In the slum, for example, a greater number of less-than-nuclear communities are found. This can be seen as a result of relatively greater economic marginality associated with slum-living. One needs as many wage earners as possible; it is more difficult to "afford" a coresident, nonworking wife. The comparatively greater lateral "spread" of slum families indicates this as well; it comes about as the result

Table 3–6. Number of Family Types by Age of Women, Rural Village Peru

| Age | Nuclear | | More-than-nuclear super-ordinate | | More-than-nuclear lateral | | More-than-nuclear subordinate | | Less-than-nuclear non-dependent | | Less-than-nuclear dependent | |
|---|---|---|---|---|---|---|---|---|---|---|---|---|
| | No. | Percentage | No. | Percentage | No. | Percentage | No. | Percentage | No. | Percentage | No. | Percentage |
| 15–24 | 7 | 37 | 0 | 0 | 2 | 7 | 7 | 37 | 0 | ... | 11 | 42 |
| 25–34 | 23 | 62 | 1 | 3 | 4 | 11 | 1 | 3 | 1 | 2 | 7 | 17 |
| 35–44 | 13 | 52 | 7 | 28 | 1 | 4 | 0 | ... | 2 | 8 | 2 | 8 |
| 45–54 | 13 | 42 | 10 | 32 | 1 | 3 | 1 | 3 | 5 | 16 | 1 | 3 |
| 55–64 | 6 | 38 | 6 | 38 | 0 | ... | 0 | ... | 4 | 25 | 0 | ... |
| 65+ | 3 | 19 | 5 | 31 | 0 | ... | 0 | ... | 8 | 50 | 0 | ... |

(Adopted from Hammel, 1961, p. 994).

of the coresidence of wage-earning contemporaries, as compared to the comparatively more frequent lineal (generational) extension of the village household.

Hammel's (1961) household analysis demonstrates the effectiveness of the developmental model in comparative research. Family cycles of development can be seen and compared. It permits the simultaneous consideration of hypotheses based on ecological and economic variables, which are very much more difficult to handle if one takes either "jural" accounts or non-developmental statistical summaries as one's point of departure.

## STOCHASTIC PROCESSES

An alternative approach to the developmental properties of domestic groups may be developed on a logical level and in different terms by (1) isolating variant forms of domestic organization, (2) specifying the rules or processes that govern transitions from one domestic form to another, and (3) deriving developmental cycles from these rules (cf. Otterbein, 1963b). An approach of this sort attempts to account for the probability that similar domestic forms may be the product of somewhat different, but complementary, developmental cycles. The purpose of this section is to present a general, stochastic model for computing transition probabilities between forms of domestic organization. We hope, therefore, to relate Fortes' emphasis on the importance of numerical data in the analysis of domestic organization to the analytic notion of logically derived developmental cycles. The mathematical machinery that we use in this chapter is generally referred to as a Markov chain.

*A Markov chain process* may be defined in the following manner (Kemeny, Snell, and Thompson 1962a, p. 171):

Let us assume that we are concerned with a sequence of "experiments" with certain general properties:

**i.** Each experiment has an outcome that is one of a finite number of possible outcomes, $a_1, a_2, \ldots, a_r$.

**ii.** On any given experiment, the probability of outcome $a_j$ depends at the most upon the outcome of the immediately preceding experiment.

**iii.** The probability of outcome $a_j$ on any given experiment is represented by numbers $p_{ij}$, given that outcome $a_i$ occurred on the preceding experiment.
   **a.** The outcomes $a_1, a_2, \ldots, a_r$ are called *states*, and
   **b.** The numbers $p_{ij}$ are called *transition probabilities*.

**iv.** If we assume that the process begins in some particular state, then we have enough information to determine the tree measure for the process and can calculate probabilities of statements relating to the over-all sequence of experiments. A process of the foregoing kind is called a *Markov chain process* (Kemeny, Snell, and Thompson 1962a, p. 171).

Let us illustrate the forms in which transition probabilities can be exhibited.

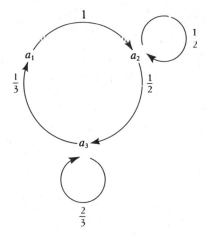

The square array of transition probabilities that corresponds to this diagram is the matrix.

$$P = \begin{array}{c} \\ a_1 \\ a_2 \\ a_3 \end{array} \begin{array}{ccc} a_1 & a_2 & a_3 \\ \left( \begin{array}{ccc} 0 & 1 & 0 \\ 0 & \frac{1}{2} & \frac{1}{2} \\ \frac{1}{3} & 0 & \frac{2}{3} \end{array} \right) \end{array}$$

**a.** An "impossible transition" is indicated by an entry of 0.
**b.** The sum of the elements of each row is always equal to 1 in any matrix

of transition probabilities as the elements of the $i$th row represent the probabilities for all possibilities when the process is in state $a_i$.

Why use Markov chains in the study of the developmental cycle in domestic groups? The answer is quite simple. Given a set of family forms, domestic groupings, or states in the Markov model, we would like to make probability statements of the form: If a domestic grouping is in state $i$ at the beginning of the developmental cycle—or *process*—what is the probability that after $n$ steps it will be in state $j$? This probability is denoted by $p_{ij}^{(n)}$; it does *not* refer to the $n$th power of the number $p_{ij}$. We are interested in assigning probabilities for all possible starting positions $i$ and all terminal positions $j$.

For a Markov chain with the transition probabilities indicated the foregoing diagram and starting position or state $a_1$—the conjugal dyad, what are the probabilities of the terminal positions $a_1$, $a_2$, and $a_3$, after $n$ steps, where $n = 3$? These probabilities are calculated from a *tree* and a *tree measure* (Kemeny, Snell, and Thompson, 1962a, p. 173) for

$$pa_1^{(n=3)} \rightarrow a_1, \qquad pa_1^{(n=3)} \rightarrow a_2, \qquad pa_1^{(n=3)} \rightarrow a_3,$$

by summing the weights assigned by the tree measure to all paths through our tree that end at terminal positions $a_1$, $a_2$, and $a_3$. Thus, in the matrix

$$p(n) = \begin{pmatrix} p_{11}^{(n)} & p_{12}^{(n)} & p_{13}^{(n)} \\ p_{21}^{(n)} & p_{22}^{(n)} & p_{23}^{(n)} \\ p_{31}^{(n)} & p_{32}^{(n)} & p_{33}^{(n)} \end{pmatrix}$$

the "upper" row vector[2] for the tree measure

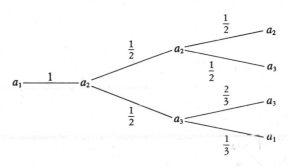

add up to 1.

$$P_{(3)} = \begin{array}{c} \\ a_1 \\ a_2 \\ a_3 \end{array} \begin{pmatrix} \overset{\displaystyle a_1}{\frac{1}{6}} & \overset{\displaystyle a_2}{\frac{1}{4}} & \overset{\displaystyle a_3}{\frac{7}{12}} \\ p_{21}^{(n)} & p_{22}^{(n)} & p_{23}^{(n)} \\ p_{31}^{(n)} & p_{32}^{(n)} & p_{33}^{(n)} \end{pmatrix}$$

[2] A row vector is an ordered collection of numbers written in a row.

For example, (1) $p_{11}^{(3)}(a_1 \rightarrow a_1) = 1 \cdot \frac{1}{2} \cdot \frac{1}{3} = \frac{1}{6}$; (2) $p_{12}^{(3)}(a_1 \rightarrow a_2) = 1 \cdot \frac{1}{2} \cdot \frac{1}{2} = \frac{1}{4}$; and (3) $p_{13}^{(3)}(a_1 \rightarrow a_3) = 1 \cdot \frac{1}{2} \cdot \frac{1}{2} + 1 \cdot \frac{1}{2} \cdot \frac{2}{3} = \frac{7}{12}$.

A matrix in which the *row sums* are all equal to 1 is called a *stochastic matrix*.

*Definition*. A stochastic matrix is a square matrix with nonnegative entries such that the sum of the entries in each row is 1 (Kemeny, Snell, and Thompson, 1962a, p. 217).

*Definition*. A row vector $p$ is called a *probability vector* if it has nonnegative components whose sum is 1 (Kemeny, Snell, and Thompson, 1962a, p. 218). Each row of a stochastic matrix is a probability vector.

The probabilities for the foregoing tree measure satisfy the equations

$$p_1^{(n)} = p_1^{(n-1)}p_{11} + p_2^{(n-1)}p_{21} + p_3^{(n-1)}p_{31},$$
$$p_2^{(n)} = p_1^{(n-1)}p_{12} + p_2^{(n-1)}p_{22} + p_3^{(n-1)}p_{32},$$
$$p_3^{(n)} = p_1^{(n-1)}p_{13} + p_2^{(n-1)}p_{23} + p_3^{(n-1)}p_{33}.$$

It is not hard to give intuitive meanings to these equations. The first one, for example, expresses the fact that the probability of being in state $a_1$ after $n$ steps is the sum of the probabilities of being at each of the three possible states after $n - 1$ steps and then moving to state $a_1$ on the $n$th step. The interpretation of the other equations is similar (Kemeny, Snell, and Thompson, 1962a, p. 218).

At this point it may be helpful to consider a recent application of Markov chains to the problem of cultural stability and change, with particular reference to the age grade system of the Shoa Galla (Hoffmann, 1965 and n. d.). The Galla system is of the Gada, or cycling type.

Age sets, in which membership endures for life, spend eight years successively in each grade, with a spectacular ceremony marking each transition. When there are five, a son belongs to a set bearing the same name as his father's, and is initiated into the first grade when his father retires from the fifth, i.e. exactly forty years later (Murdock, 1959, p. 326).

In the analysis of cultural processes that entail an intergenerational dimension, such as the developmental cycle in domestic groups, age grades, residence, occupational mobility, and so on, two types of models will transform a culture into some point in the future: deterministic models and stochastic models (Hoffmann, n. d., p. 1). A deterministic model specifies which of several alternative states will follow another one as the culture moves through time. Stochastic models specify the probabilities governing the transitions from state to state, rather than the exact alternative configurations that will develop at a particular future point. Hoffmann (1965 and n. d., pp. 5–8) has illustrated that, in dealing with intergenerational processes, we must often be content with the more oblique probabilistic information that is generated by stochastic models.

How might we go about recoding ethnographic data into the language of stochastic processes? Consider Hoffmann's (n. d., pp. 10–11) translation for age sets. The numerical properties of age sets—number of members, distribution of their ages—are referred to as vectors, as they describe an age set at a particular point in time. The history of an age set may be described by the changing values of the components of its vector. These components are called *states*. Hoffmann (n. d., p. 11) partitions age set vectors into three states: $s_1$ = ages 13 to 19; $s_2$ = ages 20 to 29; $s_3$ = age 30 or older. If, at any point in time, there are 100 males in an age set, distributed in the manner $s_1$: 25; $s_2$: 55; $s_3$: 20, then this information can be written in vector notation as $n$-tuples of numbers (0.25, 0.55, 0.20). We can easily translate this in terms of the developmental cycle in domestic groups by considering the numerical distribution of household types as a vector with the types as components or states of the vector. A vector of this sort is an initial probability vector as it describes the states at the beginning of an arbitrary time sequence (Hoffmann, n. d., p. 11).

In Hoffmann's (n. d., pp. 12–13) simulation of the Gada system, the array

*Sons:*

$$
\text{Fathers:} \quad
\begin{array}{c}
s_1 \\ s_2 \\ s_3
\end{array}
\begin{pmatrix}
10/65 & 25/65 & 30/65 \\
55/150 & 60/150 & 35/150 \\
5/25 & 15/25 & 5/25
\end{pmatrix}
$$

expresses the origin of $s_1$ sons from $s_1$ fathers (10), from $s_2$ fathers (55), from $s_3$ fathers (5), and so on. The product of the multiplication of a probability vector and a matrix of transition probabilities is another probability vector, which predicts the distribution of domestic forms, people among the states of an age set, or any other intergenerational process, at some future point in time. The matrix is now treated as a stochastic process that transforms a system from one point in time into the future, rather than as a passive information storage device (Hoffmann, n. d., p. 14). This multiplication is defined by:

$$(a, b) \begin{pmatrix} c & d \\ e & f \end{pmatrix} = (ac + be, ad + bf).$$

In Hoffmann's (n. d., p. 15) simulated model of a patrilineage cycling through age grades,

$$(0.25, 0.55, 0.20) \begin{pmatrix} 0.154 & 0.384 & 0.462 \\ 0.367 & 0.400 & 0.233 \\ 0.200 & 0.600 & 0.200 \end{pmatrix} = (0.28, 0.44, 0.28),$$

which means that the matrix predicts "that there will be a slightly higher proportion of sons in $s_3$ than there were fathers a generation ago, and that this extra population has drifted into $s_3$ from $s_2$. The history of this patri-lineage is becoming somewhat ominous" (Hoffmann, n. d., p. 15). If the initial vector is multiplied by the second power of the transition matrix—predicting the proportion of various people in the various states at a point in time two generations in the future—then the stability seems somewhat less ominous. The resultant vector is: (0.27, 0.46, 0.27).

The stability of the system, or equilibrium properties of the chain, are found by raising the transition probabilities to higher and higher values until it approaches a new matrix whose rows are identical. This vector is called the limiting vector for that Markov chain because it will not change when multiplied by the matrix of transition probabilities:

$$(a_1, a_2, a_3) \begin{pmatrix} p_{11} & p_{12} & p_{13} \\ p_{21} & p_{22} & p_{23} \\ p_{31} & p_{32} & p_{33} \end{pmatrix} (a_1, a_2, a_3).$$

Now that we have touched briefly upon certain basic properties of Markov chains, we are ready to consider a classic study of the developmental cycle in domestic groups within this frame of reference: Freeman's (1962) analysis of the family system of the Iban of Borneo.

An Iban long-house is a "village" consisting of a single terrace of attached houses (Freeman, 1962, p. 20). Iban use the word *bilek* to (1) describe the separate en-closed rooms of a long-house, and (2) refer to the family group which owns and occupies one apartment of a long-house (Freeman, 1962, p. 20). This family group is primarily defined by the criterion of local residence. The Iban *bilek* family may be characterized by two characteristics: numerically, it is a small group; genea-logically, it is a simple group (Freeman, 1962, p. 23).

This is well illustrated by Freeman's (1962, p. 23) tabulation of all *bilek* families for three long-houses (Table 3–7).

**Table 3–7. Numerical Composition of the *bilek* Family**

| Frequency | Number of persons in *bilek* family | | | | | | | | | | | | |
|---|---|---|---|---|---|---|---|---|---|---|---|---|---|
| | 2 | 3 | 4 | 5 | 6 | 7 | 8 | 9 | 10 | 11 | 12 | 13 | 14 |
| **Rumah Nyala** | ⋯ | 7 | 3 | 4 | 3 | 2 | 2 | 1 | 3 | ⋯ | ⋯ | ⋯ | ⋯ |
| **Rumah Sibat** | 3 | 2 | 7 | 4 | 9 | 4 | ⋯ | ⋯ | 3 | ⋯ | ⋯ | ⋯ | ⋯ |
| **Rumah Tungku** | 2 | 4 | 9 | 9 | 6 | 7 | 7 | 1 | 3 | ⋯ | 1 | ⋯ | 1 |
| **Totals** | 5 | 13 | 19 | 17 | 18 | 13 | 9 | 2 | 9 | ⋯ | 1 | ⋯ | 1 |

The variation in the size of *bilek* families

results from the fact that our sample includes *bilek* families at several different stages of development, from households consisting of a single married couple at one extreme to those which extend through four consecutive generations at the other (Freeman, 1962, p. 23).

The basic forms of domestic grouping—or states in a Markov chain process—are illustrated by Freeman's (1962, p. 24) classification of the genealogical composition of the *bilek* family (see Table 3–8).

#### Table 3–8. Genealogical Composition of the *bilek* Family

| Number of generations in *bilek* family | Frequency | Approximate percentage of sample | Main type of genealogical composition |
|:---:|:---:|:---:|---|
| 1 | 3 | 3 | Married couple, without children |
| 2 | 43 | 40 | Parents with children |
| 3 | 51 | 48 | Grandparents, child and spouse and grandchildren |
| 4 | 10 | 9 | Great-grandparent, child and spouse, grandchild and spouse and great-grandchildren |

The four main types of genealogical composition of the *bilek* family are, analytically, the primitive elements that are transformed and permuted by the processes that increase and decrease the personnel of a *bilek* family. These are (Table 3–9) (Freeman, 1962, p. 26)

#### Table 3–9. The *bilek* Family

| Processes whereby the personnel of a *bilek* family may be increased. | Processes whereby the personnel of a *bilek* family may be diminished. |
|---|---|
| 1. By the birth of a child | 1. By the death of a member |
| 2. By the adoption of a child from another *bilek* family | 2. By one of its members being adopted into another *bilek* family |
| 3. By an individual marrying into the *bilek* (possibly with children by a previous union) | 3. By an individual marrying out into another *bilek* (possibly with children by a previous union) |
| 4. By the return of an out-marrying member after divorce (possibly accompanied by children) | 4. By the return of an affine to his (or her) natal *bilek* after divorce (possibly accompanied by children) |
| 5. By amalgamation with another *bilek* family | 5. By partition: the secession of some members to set up a new and independent *bilek* family |

For purposes of analysis and computation, we collapse Freeman's types of genealogical composition to three types and "juggle" the percentages: $s_1$ = married couple, without children (5); $s_2$ = parents with children (40);

$s_3$ = grandparental types (55). This information may now be written in vector notation: (0.05, 0.40, 0.55).

According to the processes enumerated by Freeman whereby the personnel of a *bilek* family may be increased or diminished, it is clear that any individual domestic form may develop from a variety of antecedent states. Let us assume that the various domestic forms in $s_1$ develop from states that can be expressed by the partial matrix:

For $s_2$,

For $s_3$,

In our final step of data processing, the entries in the array are converted into decimals:

$$\begin{matrix} 0.50 & 0.33 & 0.17 \\ 0.44 & 0.33 & 0.23 \\ 0.11 & 0.44 & 0.45 \end{matrix}$$

In order to predict the distribution of households in each state at some future point in time, we multiply our initial probability vector by the matrix of transition probabilities. The product is another probability vector, which predicts the distribution of households among the states:

$$(0.05, 0.40, 0.55) \begin{pmatrix} 0.50 & 0.33 & 0.17 \\ 0.44 & 0.33 & 0.23 \\ 0.11 & 0.44 & 0.45 \end{pmatrix} = (0.29, 0.39, 0.35).$$

At this stage, the model predicts that there will be an extremely higher proportion of households in $s_1$ than there were at our initial time period and that this extra population has drifted from $s_3$ into $s_1$.

We now want to strengthen the mathematical machinery of the model so that it will be possible to predict to an unlimited number of time intervals (e.g., generations). As we raise the matrix of transition probabilities to higher and higher powers, it will approach a new matrix whose rows are identical. The limiting vector that is a product of this operation represents the equilibrium proportion for the Markov chain: it will not change when multiplied by the matrix of transition probabilities. As the theorem under discussion states that the limiting vector will remain invariant when multiplied by the transition matrix, the following matrix equation will hold

$$(a_1, a_2, a_3) \begin{pmatrix} 0.50 & 0.33 & 0.17 \\ 0.44 & 0.33 & 0.23 \\ 0.11 & 0.44 & 0.45 \end{pmatrix} (a_1, a_2, a_3),$$

which results in a system of three simultaneous equations:

$$0.50a_1 + 0.44a_2 + 0.11a_3 = a_1,$$
$$0.33a_1 + 0.33a_2 + 0.44a_3 = a_2,$$
$$0.17a_1 + 0.22a_2 + 0.45a_3 = a_3,$$

from which the limiting vector (0.38, 0.36, 0.26) is computed. Ultimately, the limiting vector will describe the proportion of domestic forms in each state, if the data is Markovian. Here we note a continual drift from $s_3$ into $s_1$, which is eventually stabilized.

The "model" developmental cycle, suggested by Freeman's (1962, p. 24) outline of the "main types of genealogical composition" of the Iban family, may also be formulated on a mechanical plane mapping the binary features for domestic forms—enumerated in Chapter Two—onto transformations. For example, Freeman's "diminished nuclear type" may be written

$$\begin{bmatrix} + & CD \\ - & PD \\ - & MD \end{bmatrix}.$$

This type is transformed into the "nuclear type with children" by the following rewrite rule

$$\begin{bmatrix} + & CD \\ - & PD \\ - & MD \end{bmatrix} \rightarrow \begin{bmatrix} + & CD \\ + & PD \\ + & MD \end{bmatrix}.$$

Principles of Iban filiation complicate the derivation of domestic forms on a mechanical level. Iban filiation is utrolateral (Freeman, 1962, p. 27):

a system of filiation in which an individual can possess membership of either his father's or his mother's birth group (i.e., the *bilek* family among the Iban), but not both at the same time.

A rule that transforms the nuclear type with children into a type (Freeman's Type III), which is defined by structural replication through one member of the conjugal dyad to include members of a generation higher, is written

$$
\begin{bmatrix}
+\ CD \\
+\ PD \\
+\ MD \\
-\ GPVGM
\end{bmatrix}
\rightarrow
\begin{bmatrix}
+\ CD \\
+\ PD \\
+\ MD \\
+\ GPVGM
\end{bmatrix},
$$

where $V$ is the connective for *exclusive disjunction* (*GP* or *GM* but not both).

The connective for exclusive disjunction ($V$) is introduced to account for a cardinal principle of Iban social organization (Freeman, 1962, p. 27):

In theory, each child is, by birth, eligible for membership of either his father's or his mother's *bilek* family, but the necessity of a single place of local residence means that, in practice, he becomes a member of only one of these two groups.

A *bilek* family that contains four generations is derived by the following rule

$$
\begin{bmatrix}
+\ CD \\
+\ PD \\
+\ MD \\
+\ GPVGM
\end{bmatrix}
\rightarrow
\begin{bmatrix}
+\ CD \\
+\ PD \\
+\ MD \\
+\ GPVGM \wedge \\
\ GPVGM
\end{bmatrix},
$$

where $\wedge$ is the connective "*and.*"

The important point of this exercise is not the predictions generated by a stochastic model within a particular empirical context: this is the interpretation of the calculus within the partially simulated context of Iban domestic organization. Of more general interest is the notion that it is the transition matrix that determines the future distribution of domestic forms, rather than the initial vector (Hoffmann, n. d., p. 20). This perspective opens up a variety of approaches and poses a series of questions relevant to process and change. Consider one example: residence rules. We may say that a given society is "matrilocal," typologize residential processes (Fischer, 1958), or consider the decision processes underlying residential choice (Goodenough, 1956b). But if we choose to say, by whatever measure, that a society is "patrilocal," it is of considerable importance to construct and examine a transition matrix in order to determine the stability of the patrilocal tendency, to compute a limiting vector that may well indicate a drift towards neolocal or matrilocal residence. An interpretation of either drift or stability might then be suggested by an analysis of the decision processes governing choice within the system. Here, then, is a new way of coming at the problem of process.

## CONCLUSION

In this chapter we have attempted to point out some of the difficulties implicit in the dynamics of household formation. Every social anthropologist encounters problems in the delineation of the physical and social spaces in any community, and we have sought to point out some of the more useful formulations and methodologies that bear upon this deceptively complex problem. Implicit in this discussion has been the notion of *residence*, and the ethnographic and theoretical difficulties inherent in (1) the mapping of residence, (2) the formulation of residence rules, and (3) the delineation of social spaces of importance for the description of primary groups in primitive society. We had tried to indicate our agreement with Goodenough (1956b) that we are more interested in strategies and motives, and underlying structures than with topological descriptions. The problem of residence, as it is generally posed, is a false one. The analytic and operational priority given to residence forms arises from the ethnographic situation—it seems to be a *natural* way of viewing the physical alignments in communities of the type that most anthropologists study. But, it is probably a red herring; even for typological purposes. Residential configurations are an end-result of a set of motives, incentives, and structural definitions, which, however much they may be unique to the particular community under study are reducible (hopefully, and in the long run), to (1) generalized sets of ground rules (cultural rules by which games are played) and (2) sets of strategies (activities that are possible alternatives by the terms of the ground rules, and are selected by the players to maximize values within the context of ground rules and their culture).

Most of the chapter has been devoted to an examination of ways of formulating ground rules in a generalizable form. Brief mention was made of the underlying strategies of players in the example from Mazaltepec (Selby, 1966) and Yalcuc (Miller, 1964). Much remains to be done in this area, both in the collection of data that will render native decisions comprehensible and amendable to formal analysis, as well as in the invention and elaboration of mathematical or formal techniques for the handling of this data.

# Chapter Four

# Descent and Descent Groups

Social anthropology has gained a tremendous amount of insight into the workings of social systems from the concept of descent. In the analysis of social structures, particularly in Africa, it has been found that descent principles order a great deal of behavior, and clarify institutionalized forms of interaction on both the domestic and the jural-political level. By *descent* we mean the criteria and processes by which group membership is determined by reference to one or both parents. We start with the concept of *filiation* (Fortes, 1959, p. 206), by which is meant "the fact of being the child of a specified parent." *Filiation* in all societies is, by definition, bilateral—a child is the descendant of his *pater*, and *mater*, social father and mother. *Pace* Leach (1957) (looking at the *internal* structure of a descent group), a person is entitled to claim kinship with his parents' kin group because he is the child of the parents. And every society recognizes the relationship of the child through ascendants of both sexes, regardless of the rule of group formation (patrilineal, matrilineal, and so on), and the family type characteristic of the society. Thus in the extreme, Nayar, as in the matrifocal cases (discussed in Chapter Two), patrilateral ties are recognized by the child, and legitimized by the society, despite the sociological unimportance, or absence of the father from the "family" grouping.

In the allocation of jural status to a child, societies differ in the way in which rights and duties are allocated. In the common, patrilineal, case, for example, a child is enrolled at birth into a group that consists of all those kinsmen who are agnatically related to him (i.e., through males). It is with this group that he will be most closely identified and associated, and to this group he will be most saliently oriented on occasions when he requires aid and assistance, or his participation in activity groups is obligatory (see

Murdock, 1949, p. 15). Descent groups are formed by the application of a descent principle, and the dichotomization of a person's kinsmen into those who are "of his group" and those who are not. This is not to say that relatives "not of his group" are not relatives, and not recognized as such by him. By reason of what Fortes (1953, 1959) has called "complementary filiation," a person continues to recognize the relatives of the "side" that is not selected by the social rules, though it is likely that his behavior towards these relatives will be different from behavior toward structurally similar relatives on the "selected" side.[1]

In this view of descent groups, and group formation in general, the "principle of descent" (to interpolate a Radcliffe-Brownian phrase) is recognized as prior, by both the analyst and the native informant. This assumption pervades "descent-group analysis" and has made for a great deal of contention and confusion. We will elaborate this point of view in order to show its implications for the study of social structure.

A person's primary loyalty is to his descent group, and from this group, in unilineal societies, he derives the greatest portion of his social identity. But the structure of relationships was prior to and extended beyond the individual member. A characteristic of a descent group was that not only had it a recognizable social identity and sociological visibility, it was *corporate.*

A corporation is generally held to display two characteristics. As Maine (1871, p. 181) has suggested, it displays perpetuity through time. It is not dependent on the lives of the constituents—it exists independently of them (see Fried, 1957, p. 18). In Radcliffe-Brown's (1935b, p. 34) terms, a corporation meant "a defined group . . . which maintains a continuity of possession," and this possession was an estate "a collection of rights (whether over persons or things) with the implied duties, the unity of which is constituted . . . by the fact that they . . . can be transmitted as a whole or in division . . ." Perpetuity and possession were the characteristics of a corporation. A corporate unilateral descent group can then be seen to be a group recruited by unilateral filiation, by virtue of which individuals are ascribed rights over persons and property and assigned duties as well. The generalized term for the collective membership of a corporate unilineal descent group was a *lineage.* According to the prevailing rule of descent, recruitment was said to be matrilineal or patrilineal.

Other characteristics could be assigned to lineages as well. They were exogamous; marriage within the lineage was prohibited. Women who

---

[1] Thus Fortes (1959, p. 207) points out that the patrilineal Tallensi will "joke" with a parent of either parent except in the case that the father's father is head of the descent group in which Ego is a member. In that case "joking"—the normative behavior in the domestic sphere—is ruled out by the interposition of the jural norms that prescribe different conduct toward the lineage head.

married into a patrilineage were then nonmembers, they retained their rights and duties in another corporation—that to which they had been assigned by birth. This led Murdock (1949, p. 66) to coin the expression "compromise kin group" to distinguish lineally organized aggregations of consanguineal kinsmen, from those residential aggregations of persons which included both consanguineals and affinals.

The lineage has the identity of a single individual when viewed "from out-side" or in relation to the jural-political sphere (Fortes, 1959). Thus on such occasions as the lineage was implicated in relations with outsiders, one member represented all members. Thus blood-money for the murder of individual *a* from lineage *A*, at the hand of individual *b* of lineage *B* was paid by one lineage to the other (from *B* to *A*). Cases of murder within the lineage were seen to be "private" affairs and were settled within the lineage. Likewise on the occasion of the marriage of individual *a*, the members of *A* paid bride price on his behalf to the members of *B*.

Finally, the corporate nature of the unilineal kin group could sometimes be seen not in the exercise of collective rights over property and persons but in the sporadic activities of the collectivity in acts of sacrifice, or "totem worship." It was as though the true nature of the lineage was latent, or dor-mant, in some cases and was activated only upon certain occasions.[2] Mayer (1949, p. 22), for example, suggests that the latent corporativeness of Gusii society can be seen not in the ownership of property, but rather in the duty of members to defend the property of the lineage against attack. It could be, then, as Fried (1957, p. 19) has suggested that the incautious ethnographer might not note the presence of a corporate group simply because he was not present to observe the occasion of the formation of an activity group.

In the codification or "apotheosis" (as some American commentators would have it) of unilineal principles, namely the INTRODUCTION by Rad-cliffe-Brown to *African Systems of Kinship and Marriage* (1950), we can see in full the utility and limitations of social analysis through the use of the construct of unilineal descent and descent groups. Out of the abundance of African data, Radcliffe-Brown has been able to derive a *lineage principle* which he sees as operating in a determinative fashion in almost every society (1950, p. 35). Out of the principle of the "unity and solidarity of the lineage" arises explanations of, for example, the merging of kin types, particularly across generations. In an Omaha system, for example, Ego uses the same term for females of his own and adjacent generations who are members of his mother's line. Males of own and adjacent generation are also merged into one term. The ignoring of the distinction of generation in these cases indicates the potent effect on behavior of the principle of the solidarity of lineage. But more in combination with another principle "the unity and

---

[2] Murdock has preferred the term "occasional kin group" to designate more accurately such aggregations; we will discuss this further in the section on cognatic systems.

solidarity of the sibling group," all terminological mergings could be explained, and the classificatory aspect of terminological systems was the outcome of the working of two universal principles.

Although Radcliffe-Brown was the "great codifier" and was earliest to state his theoretical predilection for unitary theory (the famous essay on the patriarchal complex was published in 1924), Evans-Pritchard was the first to put these theoretical notions to the test in the field in a series of ethnographies, which began with *The Nuer*, published in 1940. From this ethnography we get a clear, elegant picture of the social structure of a transhumant, Sudanic society, where the lineage principle dominated and determined social roles. The model was composed of a pyramid of structurally opposed groups, all based on agnatic principles. The Nuer became the exemplar of the segmentary society (Evans-Pritchard, 1940, p. 198); an individual belonged to a series of groups, all agnatically formed, arranged in pyramidal fashion on successively higher levels of inclusion. A Nuer belonged to (a) his minimal lineage, a group of agnatically related people, all descendants of a common ancestor from three to six generations removed in time, (b) his minor segment, which was made up of a number of minimal segments, once again descended from a common ancestor, (c) his major segment made up of a group of minor segments, (d) his maximal segment, (e) his clan and finally, (f) his tribe, which encompassed the nation of some 200,000 (Evans-Pritchard, 1940, p. 110) persons. Each segment was structurally opposed by a segment of similar order, such that in a conflict between two minimal segments of the same minor segment, only the actual members of the minimal units were involved. But should the conflict occur between members of opposed minor segments, then members of all the related minimal units would be brought into the conflict, and so on up to the tribal level where, in the case of conflict with a neighboring tribe such as the Dinka, the whole tribe would be involved.[3]

Lineages in Nuer are corporate in the sense that land is allocated to tribes, or sections of tribes, but ownership is expressed in terms of clans and lineages (Evans-Pritchard, 1940, p. 16). Localization takes place to some degree, in that the members of a cattle camp take their name from the "dominant" lineage in the camp, and relations between members of the same camp are phrased in the language of lineage.[4] In Fried's words (1957, p. 10), "At the very least it may be said that the framework of social behavior in the community is kinship, specifically agnatic kinship, genuine or fictitious."

Descent theorists feel generally that in every sphere of social life the *lineage principle* is primary and determining. *Domestic relations*, and the distribution of affective vs. authoritative relations are to a large degree determined by the presence of the lineage. In a "patrilineal society" the content of social relations between males is determined by relative status in the line.

[3] See Sahlins (1961) for interesting treatment.
[4] The ambiguity in this phrasing is intentional.

With father a male ego will have a dominant-submissive relation, as he will with father's father (if the latter is head of the lineage). In a matrilineal society (Richards, 1950), *the* problem is seen to be the conflict between the lineage principle, whereby the unity and solidarity of a group of related women has to be maintained, and the more general principle, whereby men have executive control in all societies everywhere. This central problem was susceptible to a number of solutions, and in fact, upon the basis of these solutions a typology of matriliny could be devised. *Marriage*, however much it may initially be seen as an alliance between two lineages, is viewed, in its internal aspects, as subsumable under the principles of analysis that govern the lineage. Affinal relationships are subsumed under the principle of "complementary filiation," whereby the individual is seen as affiliated in a "complementary" fashion (Fortes, 1959, *passim*) to his mother's agnates. Counter to the view of Lévi-Strauss (1949), Leach (1951, 1961b), and others who see in the exchange of women a powerful instrument making for the unity and organic solidarity of networks of groups, lineages are seen in this view to be related in terms of the principle of segmentation, and structural opposition. The purpose of marriage is not to further the solidary relations between groups, but rather the adjudication of rights over property and women from within. The *internal* view of social relations is always stressed to the detriment of a wider view.

*Property and economic activity* are seen not as the basis of social organization (see Worsley, 1955), but rather as derivative from the social organization. The lineage principle is prior, and economic and ecological relationships are secondary.

Religion and cult are also seen as by-products of the lineal social organization. Cosmological ideas are derived from the social structure (Evans-Pritchard, 1953a), and cult activities are arranged and carried out in terms of groupings made up on principles of kinship and political organization derived from the lineage. The prevalence of ancestor worship, and the fixity of the notion of the importance of genealogical continuity, prevalent in lineal societies, is seen as an expression of the workings of the social organization. *Morals* are based upon the lineage principle. In Fortes (1949a, p. 347) this aspect is stressed.

There is a wide variation in the conventions and customs governing sex relations, procreation, and child-rearing in these (patrilineal) societies. But there appear to be certain basic features common to all patrilineal societies in the form of the moral values attached to social relationships within the focal field of kinship. Incest taboos; the stress of sexual fidelity in marriage; the supremacy of husband-father; filial piety counteracting the suppressed antagonism between father and son, mother and daughter—these are some of the main features common to the schemes of moral values found in all patrilineal societies.

These values embody the fundamental moral axioms of society; and it is this that makes kinship, regarded as a mechanism for the ordering of social relationships within a given society one of the irreducible principles of social structure in such a society.

Problems of *jurisdiction* in the study of customary law were to be analyzed in terms of the lineage. Blood money was paid from lineage group to lineage group. Feud groups were determined by the principle of lineage segmentation, such that groups in conflict were always equal, and the field of conflict was either at the level of minimal unit, minor unit, major unit, and so on, depending on the structural distance between the combatants. Internal disputes were handled by the lineage, and in some cases murder of a lineage member was disregarded inasmuch as the murderer was deemed to have hurt himself, and therefore compensation to the third party was not required, because none was involved.

Putting the matter bluntly, then, we can see what an enormously powerful analytic device lineage theory was. Given the existence of corporate descent groups, the analysis was half done; the procedural focus was fashioned. Not only was the central construct of his analysis given, but his field of observation was determined as well. Ecology, economics, psychology, group formation, sociometrics, all were ruled out of the field by analytic *fiat*. One can see, as plainly, how this device could be of enormous utility in field work, inasmuch as no observer could possibly hope to use statistical analysis in the preliterate population that ran into the hundreds of thousands, and yet he could perform those wonders of synthetic analysis which were both necessary to a Colonial Office, and satisfying to the writer.

But, equally clearly, there are a number of problems in this kind of a formulation, of the ideal picture of a patrilineal organization. The first has to do with the adequacy of the construct for the explanation of the observed phenomena. The question can be put: granting that the Nuer are a pervasively patrilineal people, in whom the working of the lineage principle can be seen with great clarity, to what degree do the facts (observed social alignments and activities) accord with the formulation? This is a general problem that has to do with the adequacy of constructs.

First it would appear that the behavior of the Nuer does not correspond in detail to what Evans-Pritchard describes in ideal terms. None of Evans-Pritchard's theoretical statements about lineage, kinship, or political structure would lead us to predict that lineages are of little importance to the Nuer, that Nuer think generally in terms of local divisions and not of lineage relations but rather of relations between local groups. He reports that an attempt to discover lineage relations apart from their community relations (outside a ceremonial context) generally "led to misunderstanding in the opening stages of an inquiry" (Evans-Pritchard, 1940, p. 203). Certainly, with all that we know from Evans-Pritchard's extensive treatment of the importance of locality, and the expressions of the lineal principle in intergroup exchanges such as bridewealth, we would be hard put to predict the following statement with which his general analysis of kinship and local community concludes (Evans-Pritchard, 1951, p. 28):

I suggest that it is the clear, consistent and deeply rooted lineage structure of the Nuer which permits persons and families to move about and attach themselves so freely, for shorter or longer periods, to whatever community they choose by whatever cognatic or affinal tie they find it convenient to emphasize; and that it is on account of the firm values of the structure that this flux does not cause confusion or bring about social disintegration. It would seem it may be partly just because the agnatic principle is unchallenged in Nuer society that the tracing of descent through women is so prominent and matrilocality so prevalent. However much the actual configuration of kinship clusters may vary and change, the lineage structure is invariable and stable.

Schneider (1965a, p. 74) has referred to this passage as being another example of the "paradoxical obfuscation" for which Evans-Pritchard is so justly famed. But to us it appears that the *applicability* of the theory of relations is what is relevant and contestable. Evans-Pritchard seems to be inferring that the Nuer are perfectly aware of the patrilineal principles under which their society runs. These principles are so taken for granted that (1) they cannot consistently relate them to their own conduct, nor even their own identity and (2) all activity is so regulated by these principles that it becomes possible to tolerate inconsistency and incongruity simply because the principles themselves are the root, as it were, of the social psychology of Nuer social relations, and these principles remain undisturbed.

The question then can be asked, "How did the ethnographer find out that the lineage principle is so important, and such a determinative force?" (which of course begs that major prior question—what is the lineage principle?). It cannot be read out of the behavior of the Nuer, because they act, at times, as though social relations are based on nonunilineal or cognatic principles. It would appear, as well, that it cannot be read out of the vocabulary of behavior in terms of which the Nuer make decisions—if saliency of category is any measure of relative importance of conflicting principles—inasmuch as they seem to feel that locality, in whatever form it is taken up by the actor, has greater primacy in ordering his cognitive world and political decisions.

A second problem has to be dealt with. What is the nature of these principles that Radcliffe-Brown (1950, *passim*) makes reference to, and which we have alluded to in our analysis?

The principles of the solidarity and unity of the lineage, which are seen to underly the social structures, turn out upon examination not to be principles, or laws, but rather tautologies. The same data from which the hypothecated principle is derived is used to verify its existence and applicability. In the clear example of the working of the lineage principle, which brings about the terminological mergings characteristic of an Omaha system (Radcliffe-

Brown, 1953, p. 33), the argument is entirely circular. We account for the mergings by reference to the law of solidarity, and demonstrate the effect of the "law" by reference to the mergings. Small wonder that Murdock (1949, p. 121) has characterized the principles as "merely verbalizations reified into causal forces," while Lowie (1937, p. 224) has stated that such a law is "a trite statement of certain descriptive facts." Nowhere is the scope of the law or principle stated—a necessary prerequisite for any kind of scientific statement of relationships. If the law is universal (and Radcliffe-Brown appears to imply this), then how do we account for the fact that Crow-Omaha terminologies are only found in about one half of the systems that are characterized by unilineal descent groups. If the principle of the "unity and solidarity of the sibling group" accounts for terminological mergings as between siblings, how do we account for widespread "lineal" and "bifurcate collateral" terminologies? Nowhere is the scope of the law given, and we must reject the operation of these principles. Such principles are hardly theoretical in nature, if by theory we understand "a systematically related set of statements, including some law-like generalizations, that is empirically testable" (Rudner, 1966, p. 10). As Leach (1961, p. 301) has put it, more eloquently than we can,

The anthropologist with his wealth of detailed knowledge of the behavioural facts claims an intuitive understanding of the jural system which holds these behaviours in control. When he writes a structural analysis, it is this private intuition which he describes rather than the empirical facts of the case. The logical procedures involved are precisely those of a theologian who purports to be able to delineate the attributes of God by resorting to the argument from design.

This is not meant to reject out of hand the ethnographic work that has been done by British and American structuralists. It is one thing to condemn the underlying assumptions of their analysis, and yet another to condemn the extremely fine quality of the data, and the detailed accounts that we have as a result of it. Although much data is omitted from these accounts, and much desired data at that—any account is selective. What is being attacked here is a "model" of society, whereby social systems are seen to be in equilibrium, and the moral rules that make up the social system act as effective sanctions to keep it in equilibrium, so that the society may endure. This structuralist model is of limited utility—especially when we work with "non-African" societies, whether in Africa or elsewhere. It is not merely that this model does not apply to nonunilineal systems, but that it does not apply to unilineal systems either, as abundant and increasing data from New Guinea is showing us daily. In these societies the relation between structure and the empirical data is exceedingly tenuous, and it has been shown repeatedly that an analysis in the form of jural rules will belie the ethnographic reality in such a way as to render understanding difficult at any level. Two things, at least, become clear from even a cursory reading of the New Guinea work; first that native peoples of this region are "adept" at making up social rules and explicating them in a consistent, ideological fashion, and second they are adept at breaking their own rules and bending rules to fit the situation. And a third thing will become clear before this analysis is concluded—namely that if we are to render a sufficient account of the social structure of the New Guinea peoples, and a fortiori of any peoples, we must consider, not some hypostatized theory of the social order, considered by itself, but rather the interplay of eco-systems, economics, and psychology along with morals, and minimally ascertain the relationship between ideal behavior, and the element of choice and the frequency of choice.

Let us follow up this point by comparing four societies, all patrilineal, all sharing many of the same ideological principles, two of which are African (Tale, and Tiv), and two from the New Guinea Highlands (Chimbu and Mae Enga). (On the Tallensi see, Fortes, 1935, 1936, 1940, 1944, 1945, 1949a, 1953; Worsley, 1955; and Rattray, 1932. On Tiv, see Bohannon, 1952, 1953, 1954a, 1954b, 1958. On Chimbu, see Brown, 1962 and Brookfield and Brown, 1963. On Mae Enga, see Meggitt, 1965.)

These four societies are all patrilineal, that is they are "composed" of patrilineal descent groups, which are organized on segmentary principles. The descent groups vary in size and field of operation from society to society. In Tiv, we find linked maximal lineages associating 800,000 members in a single genealogy, and we find maximal lineages with a depth of 17 generations (Gibbs, 1965, p. 525). In Tallensi we find linked maximal lineages of about 10 generations depth (Fortes, 1945, p. 31) "organize" a population of some 300,000 Tallensi, whereas in Chimbu and Mae Enga the scale diminishes. The Chimbu, numbering about 55,000, are in reality reduced to political units of "tribal" size numbering 4,000 persons (Brookfield and Brown, 1963, p. 3), whereas the Mae Enga number some 60,000. In all of these societies smaller units are subsumed by larger in pyramid fashion, making up a diagrammatic tree in the classic segmentary fashion. In each society the minimal unit is the domestic compound formed of a man, his wives, his married sons and agnatic descendants.

These societies all share characteristic features which lead us to regard them as similar. In all of them residence is ideally patrivirilocal, descent is patrilineal, inheritance and succession are determined by recourse to the "principles" of agnatic descent. Marriage practices include bride price, and the four societies are polygynous. Each society prohibits marriage within an individual's patriline, and each society also gradates moral sanctions, obligations, and privileges on the segmentary principle.[5] If we were creating a typology we would have good reason to class these societies together as segmentary, patrilineal societies, on the model of the Nuer. However much the patrilineal ideology might be normative in Chimbu and Mae Enga, the

---

[5] I.e., moral sanctions diminish with structural distance; they are inversely related.

relation between the normative and the empirical data is highly problematic. We can briefly mention some of the clear differences between the African and the New Guinea models.[6] We will briefly discuss recruitment to descent groups, land tenure, fissioning, and some aspects of marriage.

1. *Recruitment.* All the societies under discussion are made up of agnatic, corporate descent groups. The criterion by which members are recruited for these groups is *birth.* One becomes a member of one's agnatic descent group by patrifiliation. One's social identity is established by being the child of one's father. Yet, the New Guinea groups, though paying lip service to this "rule," break it to the degree that they admit affines, cognates, and non-agnates into the local descent group, and more importantly after a relatively short interim period permit them full membership in the group. Thus Brown (1962, p. 61) mentions that although 80 per cent of the men working on any parcel of clan land holdings could be said to be agnates, there were very few men "who had not at some time in youth or adulthood resided with nonagnatic kin or affines." Residence, does not of itself confer full member-ship. In Tiv, for example, 17 per cent of the compound members sampled by the Bohannons were nonagnates, and could succeed to the headship of the compound by virtue of seniority, but there was no question as to their status. They could not be adopted into the line in contravention to the rule or charter posed by the genealogical convention. In Mae and Chimbu this is not the case. Interest in genealogy is comparatively slight, and the residual claims of a cognate, or affine can be converted by genealogical *fiat* to *de jure* claims for membership. Frequently in these societies, "big men" will recruit affines and cognates for the purposes of strengthening one clan, or one sub-phratry, and improving its position in the competition for land and resources. These members are given quasi-rights in the parish land. Sisters may be adopted by ambitious men, or one's wife's brother, and if they remain they come to be regarded as members of the parish, along with their descendants. Fostering, adoption, and mere attachment to a parish are found as well, and these members come to be able to claim full rights for their descendants. As Meggitt (1965, p. 44) has shown, they work harder in group enterprises than agnates do, perhaps in an attempt to validate their claims to full rights, but in time these rights are granted. In time (about two or three generations) the genealogies will be altered in the minds of the parish members, and the nonagnate blot on their claims will be eliminated. This (*pace* Bohannon, 1952) does not happen in African societies. Genealogies of the full agnatic line in Tiv, for example, *are* changed to fit the putative history of that line, but only when the incumbent is long dead, and the actual historical facts of the case have lost their details such that no one can remember the precise

---

[6] Note that we have taken for comparative purposes two New Guinea societies that would be ranked as "highly patrilineal" on intuitive grounds by most observers. In Meg-gitt's (1965, p. 279) ordering of 14 New Guinea societies on the variable of agnation, they both rank with the highest group.

historical relations between the segments that were formed at this apical point in the genealogy, and new relations have grown up since that time which require the validation of a changed genealogical charter. In the "African" *type* society, the principle of agnation determines to a much greater degree the allocation to rights and duties in the descent group.

We do not know how far Meggitt's (1965) analysis of the relationship between membership change, recruitment, and the situation of the clan with respect to population pressure on land resources will be found to be widely distributed, but in the case of the Mae Enga it seems that these variables are highly correlated.

Agnatic membership in many New Guinea societies may be a function of variables other than sex and filiation. Meggitt (1965) shows that a "declining" clan has more land than it "needs," and less people than it needs. It cannot keep up its defensive strength without members, and therefore is faced with the minimax problem of recruiting enough outsiders to farm its relatively ample lands, in order to stave off predators. Thus an index of the degree of nonagnatic membership would be the population-land equation. However, the main point is simply that, despite an agnatic ideology that is thoroughly "Fortesian," the two patrilineal societies cited from New Guinea do not seem to be bound by it in the manner of the African societies.

2. *Land tenure.* The abrogation of "agnatic principle" is reflected in practices associated with land tenure as well. Once again ideology is similar for all societies. Rights to land-use devolve upon a member out of his agnatic status. Descent groups are localized in all four cases, and the lineage (or clan) exercises ultimate dispository rights over land, the residual rights being always retained by the corporate unit, not by the individual or his immediate family. Yet, despite the clear ideological similarities between all groups, the New Guinea cases, once again show a much higher degree of flexibility. In Brookfield and Brown's (1963, p. 128) analysis of land transfers, for example, we can see that land grants deriving from a woman's rights in her natal group, from wife's matrilateral kin, through a woman of the natal subclan, and through ties through sisters are sufficiently strong to account for 56 per cent of the recorded land transfers ($N = 224$). And, commenting upon the "lack of structure" in Chimbu relations, the authors remark (1963, p. 129) that "This spread of affines and kinsmen who may be called upon for land loans accords with the lack of differentiation of kin and affines in Chimbu. There are no strong respect, avoidance or joking relationships; all kin and affines may act as helpful friends." The possibility of activating a line of descent, for the purposes of acquiring land-use rights can be seen as an index of the "loose structure" of the New Guinea groups, as compared with the African groups, even though the actual amount of land so leased is not large.[7] Thus in the matter of land tenure, we find a diminished degree

[7] Nineteen per cent of the land was in current or recent use by nonagnates in one sample.

of adhesion to the agnatic "rule" in the more loosely structured societies. Land can be borrowed in "African" societies too, and indeed the Tale turn to their mother's brother if relations become overly strained with their father. Land, however, that is granted by the mother's brother never jurally passes to the sister's son. No rent is paid on this land, for that would legitimize sister's son's claim on it, and the land always reverts to mother's brother and his lineage (Worsley, 1955, p. 55).

A third variable that has been widely discussed in the literature pertaining to divorce (Gluckman, 1950; Fallers, 1957; Schneider, 1953) has to do with the degree to which a woman is absorbed into the local descent group of which she becomes a "part-member" at marriage. In the "African" case (the majority of societies surveyed), a woman's natal group retains some partial rights over her, and no complete transfer of rights to the husband's lineage takes place at any time. For example, a woman, generally, does not take over her husband's taboos, nor his magical powers, nor is she subject to supernatural danger from the same quarters as her husband. These she retains as part of her social identity in *her* natal group. She is viewed as a "stranger," as the Tallensi say in her husband's house and compound, and belongs to her own agnatic group with which she maintains contact, and in which she has rights. This may be viewed as an index of the degree to which the principle of agnation is stronger than the principle of local association. In the New Guinea societies, on the other hand, a woman tends to be absorbed into her husband's group. Meggitt (1965, p. 245) states that a female throughout her life has the jural status of ward under the guardianship of a man, and in important matters she simply does not have any jural status apart from her husband: no title to land, nor to the crops of the land which she herself gardens. Divorce is predictably low.

3. *Fission.* Fission, in Barnes' (1962, p. 9) terms in most of the New Guinea societies is not a regular or "chronic" business, brought about by the death of the father, and the subsequent segmentation of group along lines clearly seen in the structural model. In New Guinea segmentation takes place in a "catastrophic" manner. The break, in Barnes' (1962, p. 9) terms, "when it comes, appears to come arbitrarily." This is partly due in the past to the rearrangements that take place as a result of war, but it seems true that "the sanctions that maintain the segmentary *status quo*, whether derived from economic or physical pressures, or from cult and dogma, are weaker in the Highlands (of New Guinea) than in Africa, and the incentives for change are stronger."

Typically in a chronically segmentary society, a set of full siblings splits off at the time of the social death of their father, and then as they grow older and acquire wives, and other resources, they split off from each other, remaining perhaps in the same compound but forming new "gateways" as in Tallensi. The process is neither so patterned, nor so visible in New Guinea societies, unless some "catastrophic" chain of events forcibly segments the

society. A clan-section can grow until it becomes almost as great as the rest of the clan together, at which point it may begin to wean itself away from the clan and set itself up as an equal and structurally opposed unit on the next step higher (from clan-section to full clan). But for the first two generations it will retain religious and social ties with its former clan-section members, and only gradually will the segmentation become effective.

4. *Marriage practices.* An index of the degree to which, despite agnatic ideology, the Highlands people are "implicated" with their cognatic kinsmen and affines can be seen in the distribution and collection of bride price. Whereas bride price is present in all the societies under scrutiny, in the New Guinea groups, cognates and affines are called upon for contribution to an individual's bride wealth, whereas in the African cases they are not.[8] We view this as an index of the degree to which marriage is seen from a personal, ego-centered point of view, such that a cognatic relative can be called upon to help an individual who is related to him, as against a lineage point of view, whereby it is seen to be an affair strictly between two agnatic groups, an exchange of goods and rights between groups.

The principles that were worked out in the past for the study of unilineal kin groups appear to be of utility in the study of the Highland groups (or at least some of them, for we were careful to choose for comparative purposes highly agnatic groups). But although the outlines of the structure appear to be similar, we have been able to see that there is a great deal of variation in the way these analytic constructs can be used to order the data. The New Guinea societies are more "loosely structured" to use Held's (1957) and Pouwer's (1960) expression. The degree of congruence between the normative and the normal is diminished. Perhaps it is as Goodenough (1955), Worsley (1955), Sahlins (1963a), Salisbury (1956), Barnes (1962), and Brown (1962) have suggested, that a flexible grouping has a selective advantage in the allocation of people to changing ecological situations. The "optative" (Firth, 1957) characteristic of the loosely structured groups permits alignment of kinsmen on an opportunistic basis, enabling groups to restructure themselves realistically in order to exploit the environment while retaining a social structural ideology that permits exchange, alliance, and cooperation.

We will return to the problems inherent in the notion of the intensity measure of lineage strength; at this point let us briefly take up some of the more important work that has been done in this area.

In an analysis and comparison of Lozi and Zulu marriage, Gluckman (1950, pp. 190–192) formulates three propositions that are central to the "marriage stability literature" (Fortes, 1959; Goody, 1959). These are (1) The general durability of marriage is a function of the kinship structure as a whole. Divorce rate is only one index of marriage stability (Gluckman, 1950, p. 190). (2) Divorce is rare and difficult in a society organized on the

---

[8] The Nuer are of course an exception to this "rule" for the African type case.

principle of what Gluckman (1950, p. 190) refers to as "marked father-right" and frequent and relatively easy to obtain in systems organized on other principles. (3) Goods transferred (bride wealth) and divorce rate are directly but not causally associated: both are "rooted" in the kinship structure. Rare divorce allows high marriage payment, rather than the converse of this statement (Gluckman, 1950, p. 192). Further, rare divorce, it is suggested, is associated with the levirate, sororate, rights to claim a betrothed girl, and so on. All are found in "father-right societies" (Gluckman 1950, p. 192).

All this turns out to be related, in Gluckman's hypotheses, to the transfer of rights *in genetricem* at marriage. In patrilineal systems, marriage payment transfers a woman's procreative power absolutely to her husband's agnatic lineage for her life. In matrilineal systems, a woman produces for her own matrilineal line: marriage payments do not transfer rights over her procreative powers (Gluckman, 1950, p. 192).

Leach (1961b, p. 115) has pointed out that Gluckman's hypotheses imply that any society can be located on a continuous scale. The scale steps or markers might be Marked Father Right; Moderate Father Right; Bilateral (cognatic); Moderate Matriliny; Extreme Matriliny. "The general thesis seems to be that as we move along this scale from Marked Father Right towards Extreme Matriliny the probability of frequent and easy divorce increases while the probability of quantitatively large bridewealth payments decreases, the causal factor being the type of descent structure" (Leach, 1961b, p. 115).

Central to discussions of marriage stability, alliance theory criticisms of Gluckman-type hypotheses, and, indeed, the whole nature of the concept of descent (Leach, 1961b, p. 121) is the construct "degree of lineality." Attempts have been made to derive ordinal measures of this construct and to construct typologies of corporate unilinear descent groups. The primitive state of such typologies, the failure to develop adequate measures of the most basic ethnological constructs, and the exclusion of rules of strategy and the differential effects which they produce on the level of group composition, are well exemplified by the studies of Fried (1957) and Lewis (1965). They illustrate some of the problems inherent in "testing" formulations that employ—on an empirical level—such constructs as "lineality of descent" and "strength of lineality" as independent variables.

Fried (1957, pp. 23–24) develops a typology of descent groups by defining two base criteria, that of unilineality and of corporateness. Three additional criteria provide the basis for a logical typology of descent groups (Fried, 1957, p. 24). Fried then applies these admittedly Procrustean categories to several empirical cases and suggests several additional criteria (Fried, 1957, p. 27). Unfortunately, the results provide no meaningful—i.e., ordinal or stronger than ordinal—measure of degree of lineality (Buchler, 1967a). I. M. Lewis (1965, p. 108) provides a somewhat more functionally, but not methodologically meaningful factorization of descent. A tabulation of positive entries, as Lewis (1965, p. 108) recognizes, does not provide an adequate measure of "patrilineal strength," and our efforts to derive an ordinal measure of patrilineality from Lewis' tabulations have been unsuccessful. But these negative results need not lead us to the conclusion "that to create a class labelled matrilineal (or patrilineal) societies is as irrelevant for our understanding of social structures as the creation of a class of blue butterflies is irrelevant for the understanding of the anatomical structure of lepidoptera" (Leach, 1961b, p. 4). An adequate test of Gluckman-type hypotheses depends on the development of, at the very least, an intensity measure of a class of systems. Such a measure may be formally adequate, although, in itself, contributing very little to our understanding of "social structures." We would suggest that underlying such constructs as "degree of lineality" are two or more dimensions and, consequently, empirical descent systems will not rank order on a Guttman scale. A relatively simple multidimensional scale with a meaningful metric and zero point has been suggested by Coleman (1957). Even if such a scale were developed, there would remain very basic ambiguities in the original propositions. Consider, for example, Leach's (1961b, pp. 114–123) comparison of three culturally similar "patrilineal societies": (1) "Ordinary Jinghpaw"; (2) Gauri Kachins; and (3) Lakher. The relevant facts may be summarized. (1) In all three societies there is a high evaluation of class hypogamy, while class hypergamy is deplored (Leach, 1961b, p. 116). "A young man is expected to marry a girl of higher social status than himself, and he must in all events avoid marrying a girl of lower status than himself" (Leach, 1961b, p. 116). This evaluation is stressed more by Lakher than by Kachin. As bride price varies according to rank status of a girl's patrilineage, class hypogamy has a cumulative economic value. (2) Associated with hypogamy in all three societies is a "feudal-type" political structure. In the typical case, a man's father-in-law is also his political overlord. (3) All three societies have patrilineal lineage structures; Lakher lineages are not ordinarily of the segmentary type (Leach, 1961b, p. 116). In matters of bride wealth, marriage, and "associated variables," the following variations occur (Leach, 1961b, pp. 117–118) (Table 4–1).

Leach (1961, p. 119) suggests a significant difference in the nature of the institution of marriage in these societies, rather than in the system of descent. In the case of the "Ordinary Jinghpaw," the transfer of jural control over the bride for her own patrilineage to her husband's patrilineage is absolute and final. The "strength" of the affinal tie "rests on the strength of the sibling relationship between the bride and her original patrilineage. In the case of a quarrel it is this sibling link rather than the marriage link that is presumed to give way" (Leach, 1961b, p. 119). In this sense, bride price and the levirate may be regarded as partial and incomplete expressions of the "strength of the affinal tie," and this tie, in turn, is a partial expression of a more basic structural principle.

### Table 4–1.  Marriage, Bride Wealth, and Other Variables: A Comparison of Three Societies

|  | Ordinary Jinghpaw | Gauri Kachins | Lakher |
|---|---|---|---|
| Formal religious rite | Yes | Yes | No |
| Marriage stability | Marriage is indissoluble | Divorce is possible although not common | Divorce is easy and frequent |
| Bride wealth transactions | Complicated and expensive | Same as Jinghpaw | Very expensive; extraordinarily complicated |
| Retention— by husband's agnatic lineage —of rights in wife | Levirate-type of widow inheritance | Bride's lineage may provide another girl in the event of an unsatisfactory marriage; but bride price may be returned | No |
| Political stratification | Minimal stratification | Class-stratified | Class-stratified |
| "Strength" of agnatic descent groups | "Marked father right" | "Less marked father right" | Minimal |

Conversely, with the Lakher, the husband's group "can be regarded as 'hiring' the procreative powers of the bride for the purpose of raising children of relatively high status" (Leach, 1961b, p. 119). Permanent rights are acquired in children; they are not acquired in the person of the bride. Further, rights in children acquired by the husband's group are not absolute: the bride's "patrilineage retains a kind of lien on her children (particularly her daughters) so that when these daughters in due course come to be 'hired out' in marriage her original patrilineage claims half the rent" (Leach, 1961b, p. 119). In terms of Leach's (1961b, p. 120) interpretation, the locus of the "structural fragility" inherent in the affinal tie is, on the one hand, located in the sibling link between the bride and her lineage brothers ("Ordinary Jinghpaw") and in the marriage relationship (Lakher) on the other.

The conclusions that Leach derives from this analysis are of considerable importance for social anthropology.

I suspect that, in the end, we may have to distinguish two entirely different categories of unilineal descent systems. There is the category into which most of the African lineage systems seem to fall and which would include the non-exogamous lineages of Islamic Western Asia. In this case the ongoing structure is defined by descent alone and marriage serves merely to create "a complex scheme of individuation" within that structure. In contrast, there is the category of those societies in which unilineal descent is linked with a strongly defined rule of "preferred marriage." In this latter case "complementary filiation" may come to form part of the permanent ongoing structure, but to understand how this comes about we need to consider economic and political factors as well as the kinship structure in isolation (Leach, 1961b, p. 123).

So, in the study of descent groups we have seen a progress from the period in which the formal characteristics of unilineal systems were elaborated, an enterprise that eventuated in *African systems of kinship and Marriage* followed by a period of abridgement, during which the ideal form of the unilineal descent group was twisted and deformed in the hope that it could be utilized in the understanding of all unilineal groups. Generalizations that may have held for African tribes of up to millions of people were found to be less useful in a social context where groupings were small and ecological conditions (often) much more difficult.

In the area of theory it was found that bilateral societies were being bypassed by students, and the assumption was growing that somehow bilateral societies did not have to be explained.

Radcliffe-Brown (1950, p. 14) felt that unilineal principles were everywhere to be found, that there were "few, if any, societies in which there is not some recognition of unilineal descent, either patrilineal (agnatic), or matrilineal, or both." It is not difficult to divine what he meant in this passage, although his usage of the term *descent* is paralyzing if we are to interpret any skewing in the sociological patterning of activities in a society as symptomatic of an underlying descent principle. In this chapter we have been using the term *descent* much like Rivers did (1924, p. 86), when he restricted its usage to designate the mode whereby an individual becomes eligible for membership in kin groups, and unilineal kin groups at that. Certainly there are many societies in the world that lack unilineal kin groups. Murdock (1960, p. 2) has estimated that at least "a third of the societies of the world are not unilineal, in the sense that they do not employ either patrilineal or matrilineal descent as a major organizing principle in the groupings of kinsmen." Radcliffe-Brown was doubtless thinking of quasi-unilineal "criteria" such as name patriliny, which is characteristic of our society, Mayan groups, and others. He was positing from this demonstrable skewing on the observed level of nomenclature, that unilineal traces could be seen in other practices, and by inference, in the mind of his informants. This is an interesting question, one that cannot be solved by intellectual ukase, but rather by empirical research. It is perfectly legitimate to inquire as to whether the informant "sees" the world through bilateral lenses, and acts in accordance with the observer's bilateral orientation, or whether, in fact, in all societies we find unilineal skewing towards one's patrilateral or matrilateral relatives. We could further ask whether bilaterality is "the outcome of statistical choice" (Leach, 1960, p. 124), the outcome of multiple activities, affective orientations, and ideological principles in some kind of Aristotelian harmony. Research that is presently being carried on by one of the writers indicates that such a point of view is of great relevance in the study of "skewed" bilateral systems, where a bilateral kinship terminology, and an absence of differentiation on the ideological level between patrilateral and matrilateral relatives, or between patrilineally or matrilineally related relatives, is combined with pronounced patrilocality, and the presence of patrilateral work groups. Preliminary results indicate that such a "harmony" does emerge from multiple choices, despite the skewing at the observed level. It also indicates that ecological change, migratory pressure, and acculturation are leading to a matrilateral bias in these societies, such that (by Radcliffe-Brown's view) within the next decade we shall be able to observe (at this deeper level) a matrilateral bias, or in his terms "recognition of matrilineal descent." [9]

Oversimplifying, then, there are two kinds of societies in the world: those with unilineal rules of descent (patrilineal, matrilineal, double) and those without such rules. Putting aside the very important problem as to the relevance of descent for the organization of sociological data (to return to it later), we will examine this residual category of societies.

In the past, before the work of Goodenough (1951, 1955) and Davenport (1959), it was assumed that the criterion of unilineality was of surpassing importance in the understanding of social groups. But, as they have pointed out, the typological criterion of unilineality is neither necessarily relevant, nor productive, and can be said to be pernicious to the degree that it obscures structural similarities between groups that differ on this criterion. As Goodenough (1961, p. 1343) has pointed out, the criterial distinction should be rewritten to distinguish two major types, *ancestor-based* groups where common descent (be it matrilineal, patrilineal, or ambilineal) associates an aggregation of kinsmen into a corporation, no matter how they reckon their connection, and ego-oriented, or personal kin groups, which consist of "people who have someone as a common relative (though they may have no one as a common ancestor)."

At the polar extreme from societies in which each member, or constituent group (such as the nuclear family) gains its social identity from its definition

---

[9] In a Valley Zapotec Village (Selby, 1966, 1967) a small sample of respondents ($N = 35$) were asked to choose between patrilateral and matrilateral relatives in a series of "ideal" questions that referred to interaction pattern and affective preference. Scores were weighted to account for the imbalances in number of relatives available for interaction, and out of a total of responses, the sample as a whole indicated no preference for one side over the other. A ($N = 31$) sample of younger people (mean age = 16) consistently chose the matrilateral over the patrilateral side. This result was interpreted to mean that the structure as a whole was changing as a result of increasing matrilocality arising out of the freeing of arable land, and the resulting attempt on the part of more adventurous penny capitalists to arrange uxorilocal marriages for their children. Other explanations (social psychological, for example) can be entertained and research is in progress. No final decision about the underlying causes of this skewing can be made at this point.

in terms of the ideology of descent, we have purely *personal kindreds* (to use the most useful term coined by Leach, 1950). Recognition of the personal kindred may well coexist with unilineal or nonunilineal descent groups. In Choiseul, for example (Scheffler, 1965), the ego-based kindred (*sinangge*) exists and is of social relevance, along side of *kapakapa*, which is an agnatic descent group core characterized, ideally, by coresidence. "The father's side is stronger," say the Choiseulese, "but we do not throw away the mother's side."

The personal kindred (people who have someone as a common relative) though not an observable group is more than a mere category of kinsmen. Activities can be organized by an enterprising person, or sibling set, on the basis of kin ties to consanguines, traced cognatically. The Iban war party (Freeman, 1961), for example, is formed on the basis of cognatic ties, although the structure of the group is impermanent. To paraphrase Peranio (1961) *descent lines* can be activated among a person's kindred in cognatic societies for the purposes of some important activity or association. Such activities may or may not include affines (Murdock, 1964, p. 131), though they usually do, and for the purposes of clarity it seems proper to introduce Blehr's (1963) term *"kith,"* for cognatic groups that include consanguineals and affinals, and *kindred* for groups that include consanguineals only. At this point we must say that the structure of activities in *ad hoc* groups formed on the basis of cognatic ties, in societies characterized by kindreds is variable. This may well be the result of ignorance, and perhaps correlates will be found of a stability and predictability we associate with unilineal societies. We might expect, for example, that generally, more proximal ties are activated, prior to more distant; that same-generational affinals are activated before adjacent generation; and that lines of activation are recursive, groups that are constituted for one activity set, tend to replicate in other activity sets. Blehr (1963, p. 273) has found that in the constitution of Faroese boat crews, that "some ties are activated more than others, and, furthermore, that these ties are of two different types; those between individuals of the same generation (e.g. brothers, brothers-in-law, and male first cousins) and those between adjacent generations (e.g. fathers and sons, uncles and nephews)." On comparing the relative strength of the ties he finds that (1963, p. 274) "the ties of mutual obligations between brothers-in-law are stronger than those between male first cousins, but are less than those between brothers." He finds as well that residence accounts to a large degree for the activation of transgenerational ties, household members being called upon with regularity and priority.

Personal, ego-based, kindreds vary in a number of respects. Firstly, they differ in the degree to which they extend the boundary of the group. The *range of the kindred* can be measured by "the extent to which an individual can precisely trace bilaterally his (or her) genealogical relationships" (Freeman, 1961, p. 207). Freeman (*ibid.*) has stated that the most commonly reported range is third cousinhood, which presumably means that some unstated percentage of informants were able to trace and name relatives four links (ascending and collateral in combination) distant from themselves.

Some (probably few) societies are reported to bound their ego-based kindreds. The Nuniamut Eskimo, for example (Pospisil and Laughlin, 1963) do not extend the range of their kinship terms indefinitely. Persons of greater genealogical removal than four links are disregarded.

A third characteristic that has been found to be of heuristic value in distinguishing kindred subtypes has arisen out of the work of Pehrson (1954, 1957) with Lapp bands. In some societies kinship ties are seen to center on one network of relations, in this case the sibling set. Goodenough (1962) has given such kindreds the label "nodal," and states that "nodal kindreds" (at least for Lakalai, and Könkämä Lapp) are firstly "organized on a kinship basis, (2) with all genealogical ties leading into a dominant sibling group, (3) with a strong emphasis on conjugal affiliation of peripheral sibling groups to the dominant sibling group, and (4) with segmentation tending to follow the lines of sibling groups" (Goodenough, 1962, p. 10; internal quotation marks omitted). *Sibling* has the extended meaning on Lakalai of parallel cousins and age mates from own sib, or finally, triads, who share one sibling in common.[10] Membership is established by residence, and ideally, each hamlet will be inhabited by one set of siblings, their spouses and descendants. Each hamlet takes its "character" from the set of siblings that make up its core, and sibs that do not have enough men to warrant their forming a sibling set will relate themselves to the core. For this reason the organization is called *nodal*.

Following Davenport (1959, pp. 564–565) we can characterize another type of kindred organization that is corporate as well, the *stem kindred*. In some societies (Davenport points to Kalinga, and Ifugao [*loc. cit.*] as examples), ego-based kindreds are found in conjunction with rules of inheritance which feed into one individual who is the principal hereditor of the corporate property. In each generation, an individual becomes the node about which the kindred is oriented, and "there will be a genealogical line of title holders at the end of which is the holder's personal kindred." In Europe this kind of organization was characteristic of Irish peasant groups, and other areas where the *famille souche* was and is found.[11] In such organizations the range of the kindred is relatively fixed, and persons drop out of sight at every generation; the collateral range is limited.

The functional differentiation between such kindreds and unilineal societies is difficult to draw in precise terms. Both nodal and stem kindreds are corporate, and organize relations around a core (either an individual or a sibling group). As we will show later, a different kind of analysis is required to delineate such differences as do exist between them.

Traditionally the term *kindred* was used to apply to noncorporate groups. It was a residual category, of utility in those societies where either unilineal

---

[10] If *A*, *B*, and *C* made up the triad, *A*'s link with *C* would be common siblingship with *B*.
[11] See Chapter Two.

descent groups were not present in any form, or to denote those relatives who were at once nonunilineally related, and perceived by Ego as constituting a source of social resources. Murdock (1949, pp. 56–57) states that in our own society the kindred contains "that group of near relatives who may be expected to be present and participant on important ceremonial occasions such as weddings, christenings, funerals, Thanksgiving and Christmas dinners, and 'family reunions.'" Kindreds are overlapping, because my first cousin may be someone else's second cousin, and a third person's uncle, and for that reason can rarely be activated as a group, or collectively, however much subgroups may be formed within the kindred for specialized activities (see foregoing example from Iban and Faroese). The difference between the kindred and between one's relatives consists in the informant's mind. The kindred constitutes a group to the degree that the informant indicates that he sees himself bounded by a relational *cordon sanitaire* made of cognatically related relatives. This is crucial to the definition of the kindred. If we were, for example, to hypothesize the existence of kindreds in all societies where lineal or other definitive forms of organization were absent, we would be failing to make the distinction between "relatives," the range of which is discovered by ethnogenealogical means (Conklin, 1964), and the set of all relatives which the informant feels to be of special significance for his security —the kindred. We would be denuding the term *kindred* of any special meaning, whatsoever, and removing the study of kindreds from the sociological domain of the study of group relations. [See, on this point, Mitchell, 1963, 1965; Murdock, 1964; and Appell, 1967. Appell [1967, p. 204 fn.], states "My position has been that it is more useful to restrict the concept of the kindred to an ego-centered social isolate that has the characteristics of a collectivity in that the members have identical rights and obligations with regard to a common kinsman and are conscious of this."] For this reason we must exclude, for example, the Nuer *mar* from consideration as a kindred, (Freeman, 1961; Evans-Pritchard, 1940, pp. 193–194, 228) on the basis of Evans-Pritchard's statement that "any person to whom a man can trace any genealogical link, whether through males or females, is *mar* to him. A man's *mar* are consequently all his father's kin, and all his mother's kin, and we call this cognatic category his kindred." By *kindred*, Evans-Pritchard is clearly referring to a category of people whom we can call *relatives*, and this category must be clearly distinguished from *groups* of cognatically related kinsmen who are seen by informants as potential resources, whether they are activated or not. As with the family, so with the kindred, we are brought back to the ethnoscientific level, or the level of ethnomodel, as the ultimate term of the definition. [See, again, Appell (1967), on this point.]

## ANCESTOR–BASED NONUNILINEAL KIN GROUPS

Personal, ego-based kin groups are *laterally* organized (Goodenough, 1961, p. 1343). By this we mean that the generational spread of ties is highly restricted and rarely if ever is relationship counted more than four ascending generations from Ego. Ancestor-based groups on the other hand are *lineally* organized. Membership in lineally organized groups springs from one's position vis-à-vis an ancestor. Unilineal groups stress one-sex ties (through males and/or females),[12] whereas nonunilineal groups make use of either. An individual in societies characterized by nonunilineal ancestor-based groups has available to him a number of *descent lines*, initially through his mother or father, and from that point on through any one of their ascendants per generation (Peranio, 1961). For purposes of analysis we refer to the lines that are "picked up" from generation to generation by any Ego as his *lines of activation*. Ego validates his membership in whatever group (or groups) he claims it, through demonstrated links of descent from a common ancestor via specified males and females. Goodenough distinguishes two major types of ancestor-based groups, restricted and unrestricted, the former containing some descendants and the latter excluding some.

Restricted descent groups may be mutually exclusive in membership, or they may be overlapping, whereas unrestricted descent groups are necessarily overlapping, the same person belonging to more than one at a time (1961, p. 1344).

Restricted descent groups that are not overlapping (i.e., are "mutually exclusive") include unilineal societies, and include as well those nonunilineal descent groups that are locally organized. In the case that membership is fixed, and the boundary to the group is defined, the group can be called in Firth's (1957) usage, "*definitive*." In some societies members can choose to reside with one group or another, in which case the variable of *optation* is introduced, further differentiating our types. There is no necessary disjunction between optative and definitive groups, for as Schneider (1965a) has pointed out, a group can be seen to have defined boundaries at any one point in time, presumably at the time the reading is taken of descent group composition, the members being for the moment committed to their choice.

A second dimension on which these nonunilineal groups have been compared is on the basis of the type of linearity that can be constructed out of the ethnographic account. In cases where ancestor-based groups are formed out of people who are related through *either* male or female ascendants *concurrently*, we refer to them as *ambilineal*.[13] In cases where choice is made

---

[12] To anticipate ourselves somewhat, the distinction between unilineally organized groups and cognatic or nonunilineally organized groups may be clarified in reference to a more fundamental opposition: ground rules/strategy rules. British social anthropologists working with unilineal or double unilineal descent groups in Africa, have been, for the most part, concerned with enumerating ground rules. Ethnographers working in Oceania and New Guinea have been concerned with the relationship between ground rules and strategic options. On a deeper level the distinction between these "types of system" refers to epistemological orientation rather than ethnographic fact.

[13] Latin *ambo* = both; members can activate lines of descent through both males and females.

between either the male or female ascendant, or in the case of residentially constituted groups, between the parents of the husband, or wife, we speak of *utrolateral* affiliation, pointing to the fact that *either* one side, *or* the other, must be settled upon; both cannot be. (Latin *uter* = which (of two); members must choose *between* the two sides.) Frequently in the literature ambilineal corporate groups have been called *ramages* (after Firth, 1957, p. 6). Murdock (1960, p. 11) has adopted this usage, adding that in the case that ramages are localized, we can profitably speak of *ambilocal clans*. Examples of these structures can be found in Murdock (1960, Introduction), Goodenough (1961), and in Davenport (1959).

The plain fact is that one could go on almost indefinitely, so long as one's stock of Latin roots held out, creating finer and finer distinctions between putative nonunilineal descent group types. As Firth has put it, introducing a relatively recent attempt to categorize these types (1963, p. 22):

Definition (of bilateral descent groups) is much more difficult than with unilineal groups—hence the cautious, non-committal appellation of "nonunilineal." Each of the major terms of the concept is still a matter for argument. In nearly every type of bilateral descent group the bilaterality is not complete. The notion of descent varies from a broad genealogical connexion to the narrower politico-jural aspects of genealogical relations, or even to the unilineal transmission of rights in this field. In the criteria by which a group is recognized, the emphasis carries from a structural conceptualization with little concrete manifestation to an operational viewpoint, looking at multiple interrelationships in corporate action. In the absence of clear agreement, every student has tended to impose his own illusion of order upon the material.

And the problem is *not* simply that there seems to be an infinite number of morphological "types" of cognatic or unilineal social structures. We have to answer the question, "What precisely are we talking about when we speak of a society as having a patrilineal or cognatic structure?" Two problems are implicit in this question. First is the classificatory (typological) problem. If anthropology is passing through its classificatory-descriptive stage, and if, as well, Leach is right when he suggests that constructs like "patrilineal," "matrilineal," and so forth have little explanatory value, then we must suggest some adequate method for first classification, and second discussion of underlying processes. This we attempt in the next section. And we attempt to derive an "etic" level analysis which will enable us to make "emic" statements by focusing upon on-the-ground behavior to the exclusion of moral (jural) rules. It should be remembered that this is a crude, beginning formulation. In the final section of this chapter an attempt is made to indicate the general line of inquiry that seems to be necessary if we are to include both the jural-moral focus, and the behavioral data (statistical trends). We attempt to show that if ethnography is the business of describing an internal and unobservable mechanism, then there are a number of methodologies (derived from game theory, linear programming, decision theory), which will simultaneously permit the admission of two kinds of data into analysis: jural rules (ground rules), and behavioral trends (strategies), from which we can infer the nature of the decisions that are being made within the framework of the social constraints imposed by the "rules" of behavior.

Let us recapitulate (at the risk of repetition). We appear to have two polar types of theoretic scheme represented in the literature on descent and descent groups. As we saw previously, Radcliffe-Brown and Fortes consider it axiomatic that asymmetric filiation is of prior and critical importance in the study of social grouping. From the social definition of asymmetric filiation a number of surface structure principles can be derived. In comparing the matrilineal with the patrilineal case, the latter tends to lower rates of divorce, higher status for males, a greater degree of "inclusion" of spouse, a "special relationship" with mother's brother, and so on. The construct, then, is useful in that it generates correlations. Leach (1961a), on the other hand, believes that no moral order is implied by the construct of asymmetric filiation (as Fortes and Radcliffe-Brown imply), but that jural rules are the outcome of multiple statistical (individual) choices. What Radcliffe-Brown and Fortes feel to be morally constraining in human behavior (jural rules), Leach sees to be not normative but "normal," in the same way that a suicide rate is not a moral injunction but a fact of social life.

Both of these formulations are defective for comparative research. The first arbitrarily seizes upon one aspect of social life (descent) and gives it an inflated importance that obscures the structure of elements in the system— a fact demonstrated by the inutility of classification in terms of descent criteria when we came to study nonunilineal descent systems. Second, it is an undefined, vague construct, which has neither referents on an ethnographic plane nor the logical status or heuristic value of either an ideal type nor a model. Third, this state of affairs induces the analyst, indeed forces him, into a pernicious form of "level-hopping" that obscures the argument almost entirely.

At the other extreme from the "moral order" point of view lies the view that we have perhaps unfairly attributed to Leach, that social structure is emergent—the result of multiple, individual choice. The problem is that statistics alone will not give us any notion of the underlying constraints upon behavior, nor any idea of the factors extrinsic to decisions, motives, or plans in any social network. Thus, for the ethnographer, statistical operations, however much they may explicate the complexity of relations on the ground and provide us with measures of central tendency, do not afford any insight into the motivational or value structure of action that would enable us to understand and predict decisions of actors. It is as though we were attempting to understand the story of Swan Lake from a newspaper photograph of the *corps de ballet*. A statistical statement is the precise antipode of a genetic statement, and does not allow us to recreate the observed structure in any other form than the data, nor will it give us any insight into the relational properties involved in the system that we are studying. In other words, it may be a model, but inasmuch as we do not know what it is a model of, and because we have no capacity to generate isomorphic models using a different set of semantic rules, its value is diminished.

Given the unsatisfactory nature of these two approaches, let us attempt, with no timidity, another approach, despite whatever misgivings we might have about the atrabilious murmurings of our trans-Atlantic colleagues about another brand of Yankee reductionism. First let us, after Goodenough (1964), distinguish between two levels of discourse, the ethnographic and the ethnological. On the ethnographic level we attempt to derive models that accurately and elegantly describe the culture we are observing. "Ethnology . . . requires us to construct models that pertain to all . . . systems, in terms of which the many different ethnographic models can be compared. What these more general models look like, insofar as they have an empirical base, depends on the kinds of models we construct in the particular cases of ethnography" (Goodenough 1964, p. 221). Let us consider the problem of group formation and activity on both the ethnographic and the ethnological level. But rather than hop from one to the other, let us attempt to formulate, in due course, a set of rewrite rules in a formal metalanguage that will enable us to get out of our present bind and generate new hypotheses with wider applicability than the present ones.

Before continuing let us take the analogy of kinship as a guide. At the ethnographic level of kinship study we have discovered a set of universally useful relations, which we characterize in a notational system, commonly referred to as biological kin types. Biological kin types constitute for kinship theory the basic "etic" level of discourse. Utilizing biological kin types, we can set down the *denotata* of kin terms, and for every kin term we can explicate both its denotative range ("designate" in Goodenough's terms), and through the intuitions and calculations of the method known as componential analysis characterize the "meaning" or *significatum* of each kin term.[14] Then, taking the components that make up the significata of kin terms in each ethnographic case we can compare (much like Kroeber, 1909) kinship systems and derive a set of types, or perform the ethnological task of classification.

In the examination and analysis of social groupings (in social anthropology), we make the initial assumption that kinship is of importance and relevance in examining group composition. This is a necessary assumption at this point, which, though not necessarily crippling, reduces the scope of our theory to a large degree, and should be done away with as soon as an "etic" level of discourse for social groupings can be devised that can handle groupings of nonkinsmen. Let us also orient our analysis about the twin concepts of "transaction theory" and the notion of social behavior as exchange, which we derive from Durkheim, Mauss, Lévi-Strauss, and Homans.

[14] The vocabulary used here is fully explicated in Chapter Eight.

Third, let us take as our starting point an assumed equilibrium state of social relations in an idealized group whereby exchanges are instantaneous and symmetrical, such that at any point in time there is no disbalance in the system; in the economic metaphor, everybody has perfect credit, and no one owes any debts. This will represent an entropic state, the *tabula rasa*, and point of departure for our analysis.

In our logical development of social systems, let us recall that exchanges include not only such material commodities as economic valuables, but also social norms. There is some ethnographic justification for this assumption. Scheffler (1965, p. 295), for example, reports that his sophisticated ethno-theorists on the island of Choiseul claim, "Our customs are not firm; we look only for that which will help us to live well, and the rest is just talk." He continues, "Just talk is a highly significant social process [The Choiseulese] were, in their own way, getting at the fact that norms or customs are not an independent system in themselves but are rather part of a larger system of social action. They exist not only as 'guides to behavior' but also, and in this instance perhaps even more so, as rhetorical elements in behavior" (Scheffler, 1965, p. 295). Ideals are utilized in social transaction for purposes of bettering one's position vis à vis alter; they are a significant component of individual strategy in social transactions.

For the initial step of our analysis let us construct a statistical model (purely as a heuristic exercise) under the assumption that every individual in our population (which for convenience is restricted to adults of the population) can enter freely into exchanges with every other subject in the population. Our table of observations will be made up of an $n \times n$ matrix, which displays the value of all transactions that have taken place between each individual and every other, summed over (for purposes of simplicity) successive dyads. In our pure state we note that there are no differentials between any dyad (*ex definitione*).

This pure state however is never attained, even metaphorically in any complex of social transactions "in the world." If we try to approximate the conditions of interpersonal behavior, we have to introduce, at a minimum, two disbalancing factors. First, we must realize that in all known systems of exchange, time is a utility. People everywhere "charge interest" on exchange transactions, as well as attribute differential valuation to the initiation of the exchange. Points are gained, as it were, for initiating a transaction. Thus as soon as we introduce a diachronic dimension to our model, we transform the situation from the pure state. A second transformation occurs when we introduce the notion of differential status. We can examine this biasing factor from two points of view. It emerges that transactions initiated from one point in the network are "worth less" than transactions from another. We can represent the disbalance (summed over dyads) in terms of biological kin types, and establish the degree of departure from the starting point, and we will speak of this differential in terms of status differential between the two points. The differentials are plotted in terms of biological kin types, such that distributions of differentials (susceptible to statistical analysis) can be calculated for each and every dyad.

Our purpose throughout this logical exercise is to establish in some neutral manner the structure and comparative content of relations in a social group, without introducing predisposing terms, such as *lineage, descent group, patrilines*, and so on. Control is instead maintained by mapping exchange differentials onto biological kin types. Biological kin types further provide us with our metalanguage for the formulation of rewrite rules, which will enable us to move from the generalized interaction analysis of the model to the area of kinship relations, i.e., the area stipulated at the beginning of our analysis to be the area of interest. From the statement of differential relations between Ego and alters (in terms of biological kin types), we can establish an empirical basis for the examination of kin-based social systems.

Before we become lost in an oversimple analogy, we shall take an example of one such analysis (Keesing, 1967). Among the Kwaio of Malaita (Solomon Islands), ceremonial exchange takes place in a readily visible manner in the form of marriage contributions. The form, amount, content, and timing of the exchange are culturally defined, and such exchanges play a significant part in the social life of the people. On the ethnographic level exists the cultural principle that the groom's cognates and affines should contribute in the order of the closeness of kinship. The closer a relative is, the more he is bound to make a contribution and the greater the contribution should be. Other principles exist (men should give more than women, people removed in age should give less than those close in age, people in debt to the groom should give more than those not in debt), but the basic principle is as stated. This situation is interesting, insofar as we have been attempting in this chapter to establish the basis by which we can state that some relatives are of greater importance to Ego than others, and specifically Murdock (1949) was quoted to the effect that the population of a descent group is defined independently of filiation by reference to observed "closeness of kinship." Our larger assumption, here, is that those persons with whom one interacts for the purposes of exchange (recalling that exchange is used in its widest sense) with high frequency are "closer" relatives than those with whom one interacts with low frequency. From an analysis of marriage contributions, Keesing (1967, pp. 11–12) constructs a scale of kinship distance, as follows.

Genealogical distance is defined bilaterally according to the minimum number of genealogical links connecting either parts to the apical ancestor. The Kwaio appear at first glimpse to be the very paradigm of the bilateral society, except that their behavior is affected by four other variables that modify the judgment of kinship distance.

1. Comembers as a descent group are more closely related than nonmembers at similar genealogical distance.

2. Persons who lived together in childhood (or the childhood of the junior member) are more closely related than persons at similar genealogical distance who did not.
3. Persons habitually living in the same settlement or proximate settlements in adulthood are more closely related than persons at similar genealogical distance who are living apart. That is, local group (settlement and neighborhood) comembership and resulting interaction frequently increase the closeness of kinship.
4. Agnates are more closely related than nonagnates at similar genealogical distance.

For the purposes of this exposition let us change the wording of 1 and 4 slightly in order to remove the constructs that we are attempting to define. In the case of 1, we shall not make the theoretic assumption about the nature of the grouping although we will assume that this grouping is culturally visible, such that the Kwaio informants can delineate the boundaries and provide us with membership lists of the groups in question. In the case of 4, we shall merely assume that agnatic relations can be expressed in an "etic" manner through the medium of biological kin types, thus stripping the phraseology of the connotation of descent group theory. Let us make the further assumption that this exchange situation is a reliable index of all exchange relationships in the society. Let us, as well, reduce these statements by the use of shorthand.

 i. Let the number of genealogical links be expressed by subscript $n$.
 ii. Let us express common group membership as $G$, and express the fact that Ego and alter are not of the same group as $\overline{G}$.
 iii. Let us express the fact that Ego and alter lived together as children by the symbol $S$, and in the case that they did not, by $\overline{S}$.[15]
 iv. Let us express the fact that Ego and alter are neighbors by the expression $N$, and if not, by $\overline{N}$.[16]
 v. Let us express the fact that Ego is linked to alter through males alone as $A$, and if not by $\overline{A}$.[17]

We make the further assumption that these represent an ordered set of priorities. Only these priorities are relevant to the calculation of kinship distance. Reverting to our model, note how transactional skewings have taken place. First exchange disbalances across the whole model appear as between Ego and a set of other points that are linked through biological kin types. An ordinal scale is involved such that $G$, $S$, $N$, and $A$ are rank-ordered. For this net of exchanges we have derived an ordered set of priorities that

[15] Mnemonic $S$ = (classificatory) sibling.
[16] Mnemonic $N$ = "neighbor."
[17] Mnemonic $A$ = agnate.

account for the cutting points in the distribution of exchange values for all members (taken individually) with all members (again taken singly). The ordinal scale can be expressed as shown in Table 4–2.

**Table 4–2. Scale of Priorities for Exchange**

1. $G_n > \overline{G}_n$
2. $S_n > \overline{S}_n$
3. $N_n > \overline{N}_n$    $(n = n)$
4. $A_n > \overline{A}_n$

Note what we have done. First we derived the domains of enquiry from formal ethnographic techniques, which gave us reliable data on cultural definitions of events in which exchanges took place, their context, their setting, the nature of the exchange, and the cultural evaluation of the exchanges themselves. We took this one set of exchange relationships to be analogous to all exchange relationships, in the absence of a theory of exchange and social organization, which told us where to look for relevant exchange situations. Next we plotted the events and derived an ordinal scale of "closeness of relative." By reference to a simple set of rewrite rules, composed of genealogical links, and culturally defined measures of residential distance we devised an "emic" level of comparison that included our four variables. These derivations are not statistical; they are principles abstracted from the statistical array, and found to be of explanatory value in the study of exchange relations in this society. We can validate these principles by analyzing informants' statements about strategies in other behavioral domains, examining the motivational structure and rationale given by people who wish to enhance their prestige by exceeding the norm with respect to gift giving. Given that Ego and alter made the same contribution, but that $E$ could be typed as $(G+, S+, N+, A+)$, whereas alter would be typed as $(G-, S+, N+, A+)$, assuming that the culture is homogeneous with respect to the underlying principles of behavior, we can derive that alter has made a significantly greater contribution than has Ego. No statistical examination would have told us this.

Given that we can translate and classify relatives through the medium of our analytic apparatus already developed for this purpose, we can then set about comparing societies on the inferred degree of asymmetry with respect to one class of relatives over another and, in our view, we are much more likely to find correlates on the social-psychological level, and by inference on the structural level, than we are with the ill-defined categories we are presently using—such polymorphous catch-alls as "patrilineal," "ambilineal," and so on.

A second virtue of this kind of analysis is that it is positive and not negative in its approach. There has been a tendency in the anthropological literature to assume that "unilineal" societies were some kind of norm, and that societies that could not be readily recognized as unilineal were somehow anomalous. This negativism was reflected in Davenport's coinage of "nonunilinear."

A third virtue of this method is that it gets to the ethnographic core of the matter, and thereby provides guidance and methodological insight to the practicing ethnographer—which cruder categories had failed to do. The question about the nature of society is not prejudged; categories are not forced upon the ethnographer as the earlier "Notes and Queries approach" (Freeman, 1961) has tended to do. It presupposes accurate description and the construction of ethnographic models, but gives promise of the capacity for generalization and comparison that had been lacking.

Fourth, it establishes ground rules for the analyst in his work of translating ethnographic data, and results to the ethnological level. The rewrite rules as they are now formulated are admittedly crude, but then they need not be more so until we have devised theories of primitive social organization, which transcend the field of kinship.

## GROUP IDEOLOGY AND COMPOSITION

Finally, let us backtrack a little and take another approach to the relation between group ideology and group composition, and the implications of the disjuncture between these two for the formulation of "cultural rules" (ethnography), classification, and typology, as well as methodology. (We shall consider the question, "What is the most appropriate, productive manner in which we can view social situations in the field in order to understand what is going on, and retain, at the same time a frame of reference that is amenable to comparative research?"

The relations between ideology and composition and the significance and interpretation of these relations underlie discussions that consider the relative utility of formal and contextual classifications of descent groups. This distinction is central to Sahlins' (1961) critique of Murdock's (1960) classification of cognatic systems, and is directly relevant to the political role of descent groups.

Many of the Polynesian and Melanesian descent groups that Murdock (1960) assimilates into his cognatic category are, in terms of political constitution (ideology), ideally strictly agnatic. A necessary relation between the alleged descent principle and actual group composition does not obtain, "The *de facto* constitution and the political constitution (agnatic ideology) may vary independently" (Sahlins, 1963a, p. 41). Descent, then, is compromised in practice when it becomes the organizing principle of territorial segments (Sahlins, 1963a, p. 42). If descent is "more or less a fiction" with regard to the composition of segments when it is brought into the political domain, then we would expect to find empirical instances for two classes of independent variation—same composition : different ideologies :: same ideologies : different composition. This is the case, for "Corporate political segments of approximately the same agnatic constitution may have contrasting ideologies of descent, may be agnatic or cognatic, patrilinear or non-unilinear" (Sahlins, 1963a, p. 42). Consider some examples cited by Sahlins (1963a):

1. *Nuer.* In a political context, the agnatic ideology of Nuer descent groups is unchallenged, although, on the ground, matrilocality and the tracing of descent through women are prevalent (Evans-Pritchard, 1951, p. 28). Seen from within, cognation, for social purposes, is construed as equal to agnation, but viewed "as a unit from the outside, and its corporate relations with other village communities, lineage values are dominant" (Evans-Pritchard, 1951, pp. 16–17). Similarly, for many New Guinea Highland societies, ideology is generally agnatic, although the nonagnatic membership of any subclan may range as high as 50 per cent (Sahlins, 1963a; Ryan, 1959; Glasse, 1959; Meggitt, 1958).
2. And on the other pole of ideology, Sahlins (1963a, p. 43) considers the cognatic district groups of the To'ambaita of northern Malaita (Hogbin, 1939), whose *de facto* composition tends to be agnatic, and the cognatic Nootka house group (Drucker, 1951) that shows a tendency towards patrilocal residence and patrilineal composition.

In terms of deep rather than surface structure, if we may employ this distinction, the essential issue that must be considered is one of choice, or optation, on the one hand, and ascribed constraints on the other. Traditionally, this distinction has been employed on two discrete epistemological levels: first, to distinctive features of individual systems; and second, to refer to the "genetic properties" of social structures in a general sense. On the level of individual systems, and in reference to composition rather than ideology, Barnes (1962, pp. 6–7) distinguishes bounded and unbounded, or low- and high-levels of affiliation. In Barnes' view, African polysegmentary systems such as the Tallensi are characterized by little or no optation within the descent system, whereas many New Guinea societies are characterized by a rather high degree of optation. Degree of optation, rather than ideology of descent, is significantly related to local group composition. Although extent and range of affiliations distinguishes "big men" and "rubbish men" (Sahlins, 1963b) in New Guinea societies, the constructs *choice* and *strategy* may be legitimately applied to groups as well as individuals (Barnes, 1962, p. 7).

In a somewhat more general context, Leach (1962, p. 131) suggests that the distinction between descent and filiation may be considered a special case of the distinction between minimal choice or representative action and maximal choice or individual action. "Any property-owning corporation necessarily includes within its constitution a principle of recruitment. 'Recruitment by descent,' that is to say automatic recruitment by virtue of status at birth, is unique in that all individual option is eliminated . . ." (Leach, 1962, p. 131). Degree of choice is further reflected in Leach's (1951) distinction between local lines or groupings, on the one hand, and descent lines on the other, as well as Lévi-Strauss' (1949, pp. 242–245; 1961, p. 17) initial distinction between true descent lines and their mirror images: "conceptual constructs existing not in the actual social setting, but in the mind of the people who live in it" (Lévi-Strauss, 1961, p. 17).

With reference to the genetic properties of social structure, Leach (1960) suggests that social structures, in certain instances, may be usefully construed as the "statistical outcome of multiple individual choices rather than a direct reflection of jural rules," which Murdock (1960, p. 9) generalizes to "the *non sequitur* that jural rules are best regarded as the outcome of a statistical trend in individual choice" (Sahlins, 1963b, p. 44). This outlook and its converse perspective—that jural rules are absolute sources of functional constraint rather than probabilistic formulations—are equally unacceptable. One arbitrarily assigns individual choice behavior a logically or historically anterior status; the other fails to reckon with the probabilistic foundations of jural behavior (Buchler, 1967a). Both arbitrarily—although often implicitly—restrict the domain of rule-governed behavior to systems of jural constraint.

Far more basic than the categorization of descent groups and the refinement of conceptual tools is the general distinction between game rules or ground rules, on the one hand, and rules for playing games intelligently on the other. This distinction underlies discussions of "degree of optation," as well as numerous other issues of theoretical and methodological significance. Leach (1962, p. 133), for one, has suggested the universality of rules of the latter sort, "*In all viable systems there must be an area where the individual is free to make choices so as to manipulate the system to his own advantage.*" (Leach's italics) And he continues (Leach, 1962, p. 134), to distinguish between "person-to-person relations"—which are defined by jural rules—and other types of structural relations, which are similar to strategy relations in the Theory of Games.

In a graph- and set-theoretic characterization of rule systems, Atkins and Curtis (1967, p. 3) draw a similar distinction between (1) ground rules that structure the basic framework within which decision-making occurs, and (2) rules that guide choices among the options this framework allows. In our view, the Atkins-Curtis formulation (cf. Berge, 1966, pp. 52–64; 220–226) clarifies some rather fundamental theoretical issues in social anthropology. If we accept the postulated relationship between cultural ground rules and rules that guide choices within the framework structured by the ground rules, then the logical or historical anterior status of one or the other—jural constraints or individual choice behavior—may be viewed as either an arbitrary theoretical position or a trivial methodological expedient. This relationship, which replicates the mechanical/statistical distinction, appears to be far more productive than the traditional rule-constrained/loose-structure, or individual-choice opposition, which implies either absolute conformity or relative randomization. It is therefore relevant to consider, in greater detail, the Atkins-Curtis (1967) formulation. The significance and generality of this formal characterization of cultural rules to the analysis of descent systems, in particular, as well as model construction in social anthropology, in a general sense, should be apparent.

Entailed in every rule-type statement is a recognition of certain possibilities: the domain of application $S$ of any rule or rule system is a range of possibilities implied by the rules. Within the *possibility set S*, rules may be regarded as creating partitions such as $S = P, \overline{P}$, or selecting subsets $P \subset S$ (Atkins and Curtis, 1967, p. 3). Following the Berge (1966, p. 220) definition of the mathematical structure of a game, we may consider an abstract set $X$, the elements of which are the positions of the game, such as "statuses," "categories," "situations," and so on. The elements of $X$, or in cultural applications, the positions of a game or game-analogue may be regarded as a subset $X$ of a Cartesian product set, $S = AB \ldots N$, "where $A, B, \ldots N$ are the finite number of discrete and finite-valued variables required to define the elements of $X$ and to distinguish them, one from another" (Atkins and Curtis, 1967, p. 5). The factors of the Cartesian product are the coordinates of this space, if the product set $S$ is regarded as $n$-dimensional space. "It is possible that $X = S$. However, if $S$ is non-orthogonal, we may have $X = S'$, where $S'$ is a proper subset of $S$ obtained by deleting from $S$ all logically impossible combinations of the values of its coordinates" (Atkins and Curtis, 1967, p. 5). A multivalued function $\Gamma$ (Berge, 1966, p. 220) is defined, which maps $X$ into itself and summarizes the *move-defining rules* of a game. This function denotes ordered pairs of positions $x, y \in x^2$ "for which the rules allow an immediate or one-step move from position $x$ to position $y$" (Atkins and Curtis, 1967, p. 6).

In order to account for stochastic-type path rules—the most significant type in cultural situations—in which any given one-step move depends on moves that have preceded it, Atkins and Curtis suggest that the function $\Gamma$ may be defined as a subset of $X^m$, rather than $X^2$, in which case move-defining rules operate on multistep paths to rule in certain *sequences of moves* and to rule out others.

In the case of a two-person game, the notion "turn of play" is handled by partitioning the set $X$ in three parts: the positions in which it is (1) $A$'s turn to move, (2) $B$'s turn to move, and (3) nobody's turn to move—i.e., "winning" positions. The notion "turn of play" is a situationally significant constraint that is rarely formalized by cultural analysts, who, for the most part, are primarily concerned with position-and-move-defining rules.

At this level, the formulations of the game theorist tend to summarize what is often a large number of separate position-, move-, or turn-defining rules exclusively in terms of their joint effect, neglecting the structure of these individual or "component" rules and the details of their interaction—just that part of the problem that tends to be of most interest to anthropologists (Atkins and Curtis, 1967, p. 7).

## CONCLUSION

This methodological position may be generalized to an ethnological level by briefly considering, once again, the cognatic/unilineal distinction. Leaving aside, for the time being, the problem of developing measures for these constructs, the cognatic/unilineal distinction, like the preferential/prescriptive opposition, is essentially an arbitrary distinction between strategy rules and ground rules. If we may decode some of Evans-Pritchard's summary characterizations of Nuer social organization in terms of strategy and ground rules, it is perfectly clear that Nuer utilize many of the strategic options allowed by the ground rules, although the ground rules are so tenaciously adhered to that one need not be particularly concerned with systematically enumerating the complete set of strategic options, the contexts governing their operation, and the relationship of these options to the rules that structure the basic framework within which decision making occurs. Such a position is, in a sense, the converse of decision theory, which is essentially concerned with the problem of arriving at a decision after all the relevant facts are known (Buchler and Nutini, 1968). Adequate ethnological theories are strictly dependent on ethnographic accounts, which are concerned with the cultural knowledge that a player has about the contexts in which decision making occurs, as well as the processes underlying the acquisition of this knowledge. And it is precisely at this point that recent studies of language acquisition and information processing, within the transformational framework, may provide a link between language and culture on a deeper and somewhat less trivial level than has usually been regarded. In the study of grammatical structure an exclusive interest in ground rules may result in an unwarranted formalism. In the approach of Radcliffe-Brown, Evans-Pritchard, and Fortes, with regard to the study of descent systems, the possibility of establishing correspondence rules that link theoretic constructs with behavioral systems is eliminated. This is due to an exclusive concern with the system of jural constraints which structure the basic cultural framework.

A more basic point follows closely. It is, so to speak, a concern with low-level, "descent-type" constructs, their formal properties, contextual entailments, and typological ordering that has inhibited the study of descent systems. This is clearly illustrated by our inability to develop, in an adequate manner, certain fundamental problems that are hinted at in this chapter. Rather than assigning descent systems to an arbitrary and superficial pigeonhole such as cognatic or unilineal, we must develop adequate measures for these constructs and consider the optimization problems and interlinked decision processes that are characteristic of classes of systems and the conceptual transformations that map one structure onto another. These processes operate at a level that might ultimately result in the disappearance of the study of descent systems as a distinct field of inquiry, just as Lévi-Strauss' (1949) study of marriage systems has demonstrated that marriage forms, as well as other social processes, may be regarded as partial and incomplete expressions of certain underlying principles of reciprocity that may be expressed in a wide variety of contexts and domains.

To give a highly simplified and schematic example in reference to our review of Leach's (1957) discussion of lineage strength and marriage stability, let us attempt to classify systems in reference to the interlinked decision processes of the parties to an exchange, rather than in terms of quasi-ordinal category names such as "strongly patrilineal," "weakly patrilineal," and so on.

We may regard an exchange situation as completely competitive in which the interests of men and women are directly opposed. If the pairs of valuations of the four possible outcomes—in a two-person, two-strategy, zero-sum game—are represented by four outcome or base points, the preference scale of women by points along a horizontal axis, and the preference scale of men by points along a vertical axis, then the situation may be represented by (cf. Braithwaite, 1963, p. 18):

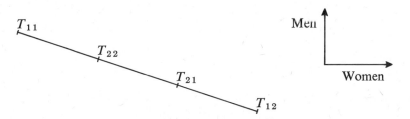

In the wholly competitive situation, women want their choice to result in a point as far to the right as possible, and men want their choice to result in one as high up as possible. Such a situation may provide a useful paradigm for the "Gauri-type" case that Leach (1961b) describes, distinguishing it from "Ordinary Jinghpaw-type" collaboration cases. The latter, and probably more interesting type of situation from the point of view of social anthropology, may be represented by plotting the four outcome points on a Cartesian plane (Braithwaite, 1963, pp. 12–13). *A* will wish that the jointly chosen outcome point is as far to the right as possible; *B*, as high as possible. If we may simplify in order to provide a concrete example in terms of the preceding section, let the husband's group = *A*, the wife's group = *B*; then I may represent the Lakher case; II, the "Ordinary Jinghpaw" case.

As soon as social anthropologists are prepared to consider, in a formal and systematic manner, the basic cultural, social, and psychological processes underlying the low-level constructs with which they appear to be obsessed,

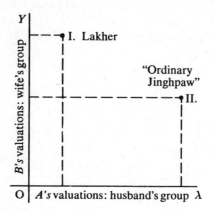

then they will be in a position to utilize the machinery of modern mathematics that has been developed to handle very similar types of problems.

# Chapter Five

# Alliance Theory: Part I— Theory

In the last chapter we discussed one way of modelling social action, generally referred to as descent theory. In this chapter we shall discuss another point of view, which has come to be called (after Dumont, 1957, 1966) *alliance theory*. At times these two orientations to the study of social structure have been treated as though they were mutually exclusive. In a later section on Dravidian and on Australian social systems we argue that the supposedly competing points of view are complementary in the main, overlapping at times, and rarely mutually exclusive or in opposition. Alliance theory has been most forcefully argued by Needham (1958b, 1960b, 1960c, 1961, 1962a, 1963, and in many other places) and Dumont (1950, 1953a, 1953b, 1957, 1966), but its parent is Claude Lévi-Strauss (1949, 1953, 1956, 1960a, 1965, 1966).

In Chapter One we discussed the antecedents of alliance theory. In the next two chapters we will discuss the implications of alliance theory for the construction of "models" of social structure, some of the problems that have arisen out of the "competition" between descent and alliance theory and finally empirical cases where an "alliance" point of view seems preferable to a "descent" point of view.

In Chapter One we pointed out that Lévi-Strauss had emphasized repeatedly that the exchange that Mauss had postulated to be the central perduring fact of social relations in primitive societies had, in and of itself, positive value. There was no need, then, to search for the underlying motivation of an exchange system, because the motivation was a part of the

[105]

transaction. Exchange per se has a positive value. We quoted Lévi-Strauss (1963b, p. 2) to the effect that,

... exchange in human society is a universal means of ensuring the interlocking of its constituent parts, and ... this exchange can operate at different levels among which the most important are food, goods, services and women.

There is, perhaps, more to this statement than might meet the unsuspecting eye. Before we undertake to discuss the more direct implications of this point of view (the alliance point of view) for the study of marriage systems, let us attempt to display the theoretical implications. And perhaps the best context for so doing is to follow a discussion by Lévi-Strauss and Maybury-Lewis about dual organizations (Lévi-Strauss, 1956, 1960a; Maybury-Lewis, 1960).

First a few words about the orientation taken by Lévi-Strauss to the subject of social structure. In his article "Social Structure," he outlines the prerequisites of any structure (1963a, pp. 279–280):

1. A structure exhibits the characteristics of a system. It is made up of several elements, none of which can undergo a change without effecting changes in all the other elements.
2. For any given model there should be the possibility of ordering a series of transformations resulting in a group of models of the same type.
3. It is possible to predict how the model will react if one or more of its elements are submitted to certain modifications.
4. The model should be constituted so as to make immediately intelligible all the observed facts.

We may add a fifth item (which, though implicit in the four enumerated is often overlooked, namely):

5. The model will be more than a summation of the observed facts: the relational information conveyed by the model will exceed that which is deducible from the empirical data.

Note first that the usage of the word *model* is vague, difficult, and misleading. The formal properties of the concept of "model" will be discussed shortly, but here suffice it to state that for Lévi-Strauss "structure" and "model" (in this context) seem to be interchangeable concepts, along with system; the semantic implication being one of emphasis, rather than formal distinction. With this brief, and overly simplistic foreword, we proceed to the analysis (à la Lévi-Strauss) of dual systems.

As has been known from the time of Curt Nimuendajú, the tribes of central and eastern Brazil have exhibited a classic dualistic structure. In the case of the Bororo, for example, the village arrangement purportedly gives us a mirror image of the social structure. "Briefly, the Bororo are organized into two exogamous matrimoieties, subdivided into four clans each. The circular Bororo village is divided into halves by an east-west axis; each half is occupied by one of two moieties, and the huts of the clans composing the moieties are arranged in a circle" (Nutini, 1965, pp. 713–714). The conscious model of the social structure, that is to say, the homemade model formulated by the natives themselves, corresponds to this account. But, we must not be misled by such constructions. Firstly the purpose of homemade models (conscious models) is not to explain the phenomena under consideration, but rather to perpetuate them, and for the scientist these models act as screens to obscure the underlying model, the unconscious model. It is as it is in linguistics. As Lévi-Strauss has commented;

First, structural linguistics shifts from the study of *conscious* linguistic phenomena to study of their *unconscious* infrastructure; second, it does not treat *terms* as independent entities, taking instead as its basis of analysis the *relations* between terms; third, it introduces the concept of *system*—Modern phonemics does not merely proclaim that phonemes are always part of a system; it *shows* concrete phonemic systems and elucidates their structure; finally structural linguistics aims at discovering *general laws*, either by induction or . . . by logical deduction, which would give them an absolute character (Lévi-Strauss, 1963a, pp. 33) [internal quotation marks omitted].

Set into the matrix of Bororo dualism, we find a triadic structure. Upon close inspection it appears that each of the clans contains within it three endogamous classes (upper, middle, lower), which in combination with the moiety arrangement produce a system of six marriage classes.[1] (For full discussion, see Lévi-Strauss, 1936, 1956.)

This triadism-in-dualism is an interesting phenomenon, and Lévi-Strauss finds parallels in structural problems in other areas of the world. For example Radin (1923) has stated of the Winnebago that informants of two different phratries report that there are two kinds of (homemade) models of the physical structure of the campsite.[2]

Informants from the upper phratry conceptualized the village in a form which we can describe as an encompassing circle, bisected by a diagonal, such that the lodges of the lower phratry occupied one half of the village site and the inhabitants of the upper phratry, the other. But, informants of the lower phratry conceptualized the physical layout in a concentric fashion, the inner circle representing all the lodges of the campsite, the outer circle bounding the cleared ground, out to the timber line. Lévi-Strauss refers to the first arrangement as the diametric structure (see Figure 5–1) and the second as the concentric structure (see Figure 5–2).

[1] We are using *class* here in a general and not technical sense.
[2] Later referred to as the "Winnebago discrepancy."

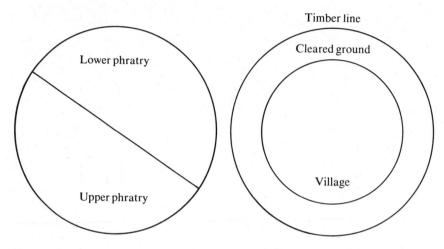

Figure 5–1. Diametric Structure of Winnebago Village (after Lévi-Strauss, 1963a, 134).

Figure 5–2. Concentric Structure of Winnebago Village (after Lévi-Strauss, 1963a, 135).

Diametric structures are widely distributed in association with dualistic systems. Concentric structures are also to be found, one such example being the village of Omarakana, so briefly sketched by Malinowski (1929, p. 10).

Associated with inner-outer bisection of the village was a set of symbolic oppositions: sacred/profane, raw/cooked, unmarried/married (i.e., sexual activity absent/present), male/female, and so on.

Thus we have three types of representations, the diametric, the concentric, and (c.f. the Bororo) the triadic. The question can then be put: is it possible to construct one model that underlies and displays these structural variations, and to adduce transformation rules that will generate the three seemingly discrete types? First Lévi-Strauss adds some further data that broadens the scope of the enquiry. In Indonesia the co-occurrence of dualism and triadism is often to be found. In "alliance parlance" we find moiety systems associated, for example, with unilateral cross-cousin marriage. Now this form of marriage indicates a triadic division, insofar as it presupposes three separate kinds of groups, (1) own group, (2) the group from which the males of own group take their wives, and (3) the group into which the women of own group are married.[3]

The question thus becomes one of general ethnological interest. How is it that in South America, North America, and Indonesia we find "classic

[3] We go into this in some detail later; suffice it to say here that matrilateral cross-cousin marriage (here "unilateral") creates a situation in which (given three groups $A$, $B$, and $C$) men of $B$ "take from" $A$ and "give to" $C$ (take women from $A$, and give women to $C$). A minimal representation of this form of social grouping, then, requires the creation of at least three groups in bride-giving/bride-receiving relations.

dualistic systems" in association with triadic elements. Is there an underlying model (or perhaps better here, "representation"), which will permit the simultaneous provenience of dualistic and triadic elements; a representation that will display the co-occurrence of both? Briefly, there is: we can concern ourselves simultaneously with (1) dualism/triadism and (2) diametric/concentric as they appear in the three cited cases in terms of three diagrams of identical form, indicating relational and positional properties that are identical in the (1) Winnebago, (2) Bororo, (3) Indonesian cases, even though the elements comprising the model (structure) are different. Take a diagrammatic representation as follows.

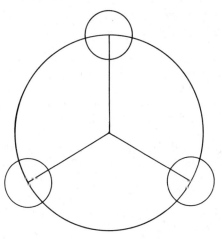

Figure 5–3. Representation of the Relational and Positional Properties of the Dualistic/Triadic Elements of the Social Structure of (1) Winnebago, (2) Bororo, (3) Indonesian Society (adapted from Lévi-Strauss, 1963a, p. 155).

The structure can be briefly described (Lévi-Strauss, 1963a, pp. 154–155). It consists of (1) a group of three small circles; (2) a triskelion (a tripod-like figure); and (3) a large circle.

In the Winnebago case the represented elements are as follows. The peripheral circle represents the physical boundaries of the camp, or the society. The three small circles represent the twelve clans divided into three groups, the two lower circles representing two groups of four clans each ("earth" and "water"), whereas the upper circle represents one group of four clans ("sky"). The triskelion represents the possibilities of marriage according to the exogamy rule of the moieties.

In the Indonesian case (dualistic system in conjunction with an implicitly triadic marriage system) the peripheral circle represents the social boundary of the system, whereas the three small circles represent the three intermarrying groups, and the triskelion, which in this case bisects the marriage groups, represents the separation of the sexes. This separation comes about, in a logical sense, as the result of the opposition between the marital destiny of males and females.[4]

The Bororo case is more complex. The peripheral circle represents the *non*exogamous moiety division, that is the social space within which marriage *does* take place. The three circles represent *groups of classes*, the upper circle, representing all the "uppers," the lower circles the "lowers" and "middles" between whom marriage does not take place. The triskelion, then, represents the trichotomization of exogamous prohibition, or the impossibility of marriage: uppers do not marry lowers, nor middles uppers, and so on.

To conclude we quote Lévi-Strauss (1963a, p. 161),

". . . it becomes clear that the most widespread opposition (that between binary and ternary structure) leads to symmetric and inverse applications in South America and Indonesia. In the Indonesian case, we have a system of moieties associated with generalized exchange,[5] that is, an asymmetric form of exogamy.

Ternary structure is thus used to define groups of affinal relatives, whereas binary structure expresses the two directions in which men and women, respectively, circulate. In other words, ternary structure refers to *classes*, binary structure to *relationships* between those classes. In South America, on the other hand (and apparently among all the Gê tribes), binary structure is used to define the groups, whereas ternary structure defines the two directions, not of the circulation of men and women this time, but the directions in which marriage is permitted or prohibited, to both sexes indiscriminately (because exchange is restricted according to a symmetric form of endogamy). In this case, then, binary structure refers to *classes* and ternary structure to *relationships*."

In this way then, the diametric/concentric, dualistic/triadic concurrence can be brought into concordance in terms of a model that includes them both. Anomalies, which had afflicted the student of dual organization since the time of Rivers who first noticed them, are handled simultaneously in terms of classes of phenomena on the one hand (dualistically distinguished) standing in ternary relations to each other.

This analysis has not gone unchallenged, however. Lévi-Strauss has been accused of facile manipulation of sociological data, of experimenting with a form of Euclidean cartography, of raising problems that didn't exist previously, and then disposing of them with an optical illusion of a quasi-Ptolemaic kind. For a reasoned summary of the counterarguments, we can turn to an article of Maybury-Lewis (1960).

First, according to Maybury-Lewis, we find that Lévi-Strauss makes no distinction between *organisation dualiste* (which we take to be the ensemble of social relations to be empirically noted in social systems in America north

---

[4] In a symmetric moiety system (bilateral cross-cousin marriage system), the destiny of each sex is the same. Any member of *A* finds a marriage in relation to *B* and vice versa. In an asymmetric system, the marital destinies are opposed, males of *B* take women from *A*, while the women of *B* are shunted out to *C*.

[5] Matrilateral cross-cousin marriage; see pp. 115–127.

and south), *système dualiste* (which we take to be the relational and positional properties of a model of such systems ranged in a comparative matrix), and *dualisme* (a summary term for the set of general statements that can be made in a less formalized manner about the sociological and cultural-symbolic properties of an ideal type of social organization). Levels are therefore crossed with abandon in a discussion of this kind, which "is the source of much confusion in his argument" (Maybury-Lewis, 1960, p. 18).

As for the Winnebago discrepancy, Maybury-Lewis feels that the informants are talking about different things; one set is describing the interior arrangements of the village, whereas the others are talking about the relationship of the village to its ecological background. The models can be superimposed to give a clear picture of the village in both aspects. And that is the answer to the opposition of diametric types versus concentric types. The dichotomy is a false one, and integration does away with it.

As for the Bororo, Lévi-Strauss' formal representation is devoid of sociological significance. The similarity (or symmetry) is *purely formal*. Again, the analysis of the Indonesian material is highly hypothetical. It is inaccurate (sociologically) to speak of "marital destiny" in asymmetrical systems. The important and central sociological fact of asymmetrical systems is that women circulate through the system in a unidirectional fashion, and therefore the distinction between asymmetrical systems (in which the marital destinies of the two sexes are opposed) and symmetrical systems (in which the marital destinies are identical) is supposititious, and again, devoid of sociological significance.

In fact an examination of the models shows (Maybury-Lewis, 1960, p. 35) that not only are the models constructed in such a way as to be sociologically misleading, but also the elements represented in the models are selected arbitrarily, and the features have "admittedly dissimilar functions" (Maybury-Lewis, 1960, p. 35).

Therefore, Maybury-Lewis concludes that social relations cannot be formally represented by models in the same way as mathematical relations can. Sociological models are not manipulatable in the sense that mathematical equations are. Conclusions drawn from such models, or from a comparison of such models without a simultaneous consideration of the data from which the models were constructed, run a serious risk of error.

This criticism comes up over and again, and the *modus operandi* implied by the construction of models and the stipulation of the scope of the construction have led to what must be one of the most long-winded, and spurious arguments in the history of social anthropology, largely because the word *model* has been used by various anthropologists to mean very different things.

We must be grateful to Maybury-Lewis not only for expressing the misgivings that most "empirically-minded" social anthropologists feel upon an examination of Lévi-Strauss' seemingly cavalier treatment and synthetic summation of the data on dual systems, but more, because he occasioned a reply from Lévi-Strauss, which goes far toward clarifying the latter's methodological stance.

The answer in sum is to be found in a single paragraph, which though widely quoted (see Schneider, 1965a, pp. 25–26) deserves restating (Lévi-Strauss, 1960a, p. 52).

. . . I suspect that Mr. M. L. remains, to some extent the prisoner of the naturalistic misconceptions which have so long pervaded the British school. He claims to be a structuralist, he even claims to defend structuralism against my reckless manner of handling it. But he is still a structuralist in Radcliffe-Brown's terms, namely, he believes the structure to lie at the level of empirical reality, and to be a part of it. Therefore, when he is presented a structural model which departs from empirical reality, he feels cheated in some devious way. To him, social structure is like a kind of jig-saw puzzle, and everything is achieved when one has discovered how the pieces fit together. But, if the pieces have been arbitrarily cut, there is no structure at all. On the other hand, if, as is sometimes done, the pieces were automatically cut in different shapes by a mechanical saw, the movements of which are regularly modified by a cam-shaft, the structure of the puzzle exists, not at the empirical level (since there are many ways of recognizing the pieces which fit together): its key lies in the mathematical formula expressing the shape of the cams and their speed of rotation; something very remote from the puzzle as it appears to the player, although it "explains" the puzzle in the one and only intelligible way.

As for the distinction between dualistic organization, dualistic system, and dualism, Lévi-Strauss (1960a, p. 46) was "avowedly trying to override these classical distinctions, with the aim of finding out if they could not be dealt with as open—and to some extent conflicting—*expressions of a reality to be looked for at a deeper level.*" (Italics ours.) Sociological divisions and symbolic correlates meet at a deeper level of analysis, and to maintain the distinction in the face of a successful attempt to synthesize them seems to be missing the point purposely.

And as for the problem of the sociological reality of the Winnebago representation via a triskelion, peripheral circle, and three smaller circles, it may well be pointed out that it does not correspond to ethnographic (empirical) reality. "It merely describe(s) a theoretical diagram, purporting to reorganize ethnographic data which, at the observational level, do not clearly exhibit those hidden properties . . ." (Lévi-Strauss, 1960a, p. 49).

The purpose of the three diagrams (represented in a general form as one in this discussion) is to show "how marriage relations, social structure, village lay-out, religious representations, etc., *are all part of a system* (italics ours), the difference being that, in each case, they are assigned different functions, or—to express it in diagrammatic terms—they are permuted in different topological positions. To put it differently, what a given society says in terms of marriage relations, is being said by another society in terms of village lay-out, in terms of religious representations by a third, etc." (Lévi-Strauss, 1960a, pp. 50–51).

The whole point being that given an ethnographic problem of some complexity (the dyadic/ternary problem, or diametric/concentric problem), which is found expressed differently in societies that are distributed widely over the world, it is possible to design a didactic-conceptual representation, in the manner of a system of elements, *the relational properties of which are identical*, despite the fact that the elements themselves are of disparate nature in each case. We can locate, at an underlying level, a common structure that was certainly unapparent at the beginning of the analysis, and would forever have remained so, had we stuck to the level of the empirical facts.[6]

This brings us to a consideration of what Lévi-Strauss means by the term *model*. If this discussion is somewhat lengthy, it is because the issue is critical, and will serve to lead the discussion to three subjects, (1) the categorical, methodological, and theoretical differences between the "Lévi-Strauss" point of view, and the "Radcliffe-Brown" point of view (the last of which we examined at length in the last chapter), (2) the logical and epistemological entailments of this conceptual posture (which will lead us to a discussion of the positivistic application of alliance theory), and (3) the semantic problems that are implicit in Lévi-Strauss' ("and others") use of the word *model*, and its place in the epistemology and methodology of social science as a whole.

In order to give the background of the more substantive issues involved in the study of what Lévi-Strauss (1949) has called *échange restreint* (hereafter *restricted exchange*) and *échange généralisé* (hereafter *generalized exchange*), let us recapitulate briefly some of the discussion of *Les Structures Élémentaires de la Parenté*. Let us also remember that this brief summary does not do justice to the amplitude of the argument, and represents but a small part of the contribution that Lévi-Strauss and his followers have made to the study of social organization.

Reverting to the introductory discussion on Durkheim, Mauss, and Lévi-Strauss, it can be recalled that the positive value of exchange itself provided the articulating concept between Durkheim's notion of "organic solidarity" and Mauss' conception of the centrality and symbolic importance of *prestations totales*. Briefly note the difference between this kind of a view of social

---

[6] Lévi-Strauss (1960a, p. 53) concludes: "Of course the final word should rest with experiment. However, the experiment suggested and guided by deductive reasoning will not be the same as the unsophisticated ones with which the whole process had started. These will remain as alien as ever to the deeper analysis. The ultimate proof of the molecular structure of matter is provided by the electronic microscope, which enables us to see the actual molecules. This achievement does not alter the fact that henceforth the molecules will not become any more visible to the naked eye. Similarly it is hopeless to expect a structural analysis to change our way of perceiving concrete social relations. It will only explain them better. If the structure can be seen, it will not be at the earlier, empirical level, but at a deeper one, previously neglected; that of those unconscious categories which we may hope to reach, by bringing together domains, which, at first sight appear disconnected to the observer: on the one hand, the social system as it actually works, and on the other, the manner in which, through their myths, their rituals and their religious representations, men try to hide or justify the discrepancies between their society and the ideal image of it which they harbour."

structure, and the "descent theory" point of view. In the context of descent theory, alliance between groups (affinal ties) is brought about by the negative application of the incest taboo. For any Ego in a patrilineage, there exist merely negative sanctions upon whom he may not marry (females in his own line, and possibly in his mother's patriline).

The focus in descent theory is on the domestic domain (in Fortes' 1959, 1962 terms) and it is as though the origin of the women who marry into the lineage was unimportant. The focus of interest is upon what "happens" to the women upon arrival, as it were; to what degree they are incorporated into the lineage, or the degree to which they maintain residual rights in their natal lineage. (See the following section on complementary filiation.) For alliance theorists the focus is upon the system as a whole. It is of great importance (in simplified language) where the women come from. Women are seen as the positive link between groups, and the incest taboo per se is not seen as of more than passing importance, but rather the important factors are the *positive marriage rules* that govern the movement of women, and the articulation of the social segments. Alliance theory, then, is holistic, sees the integration of the total social system as problematic (makes the assumption of entropy rather than equilibrium), and sees marital exchanges as the critical linking elements in the system.

Lévi-Strauss distinguishes between two "model concepts," to one of which he gives the appellation, *mechanical model,* to the other, *statistical model.* We will have more to say about the usage of the term *model* shortly, because, in our view, it is misapplied. According to Lévi-Strauss (1963a, pp. 283ff.), mechanical models do not admit of contingency; they are representations of the phenomenal world "on the same scale as" the phenomena themselves. There is much terminological confusion here, and as Nutini (1965, p. 709) points out, Lévi-Strauss does little to help us out, although his comments in the article, "The Future of Kinship Studies" (Lévi-Strauss, 1965), serve to elucidate the matter in the context of a discussion of Crow-Omaha systems. The phrase "on the same scale as" suggests, that Lévi-Strauss is attempting to represent states of social systems (marriage systems in the main) on a homomorphic plane, all the while maintaining the relational and positional properties of the idealized phenomena under discussion.

Take, for example, the very important construct "elementary structure." In an elementary structure (speaking in terms of marriage choices or possibilities) "the important fact . . . (is) . . . that the contemplated spouse, whether preferred or prescribed, is selected for the reason that he or she belongs to a particular social group or to a given category of kinship, in other words, because the relationship between the intermarrying pair is defined in terms pertaining to the social structure" (Lévi-Strauss, 1965). The universe of discourse is delimited to the conceptually "mappable" social structure, and marital exchanges take place within the universe, thus enabling the observer to construct (out of the "ethnomodel" of the natives, and his own observations) an idealized representation of marital exchange. This representation will be a simplified version of the reality, and like a small-scale mock-up of the idealized form (somewhat like the Platonic *idea*) of a class of phenomena, will be of the same scale as the phenomena it represents.

Let us take the familiar concrete example of a society practicing what has been called asymmetric exchange, or more roughly, matrilateral cross-cousin marriage. Such a system requires three elements (representing three conceptual social entities, or groups). In Figure 5–4, we can see that the women "flow" in one direction, women in $A$ go to $B$, and women in $B$ go to $C$, and for the purpose of this idealized representations, we shall posit that the system is closed and circular such that women in $C$ go to $A$.

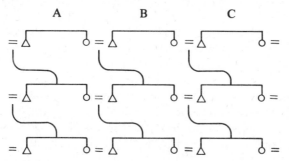

Figure 5–4.  *Idealized, Simplified Representation of a System of Asymmetric Exchange.*

At this point all we have to concern ourselves with are the relational and positional properties of the "model," which is presented topographically in this didactic form.

Conceptually then we can say there are three elements, related dyadically; that is, from the point of view of $B$, there exist two relations that connect the three entities, and insofar as we are discussing the diagram in terms of marriage alliance we can call these relations wife-giving relations and wife-receiving relations. Once again, as in the discussion of dualistic systems, we see the simultaneous emergence of triadic elements (or *terms*) within a system of dyadic relations.

It must always be remembered that this is an idealized representation. If we take this scale model (model here in the sense of representation) of an underlying (unconscious) paradigm, which serves to explain the complex marital and symbolic elements of the society, to be a representation of the ensemble of actual (concrete) social relations, we would be making a grave error. And it is precisely this error that has afflicted the discussion of asymmetric alliance since the publication of "Marriage, Authority and Final Causes" (Homans and Schneider, 1955).

The implications of this statement take us slightly further afield, but no matter. Once the underlying methodological (and perhaps philosophical) implications of this mode of thinking are clear, then the errors and misconceptions that have pervaded the literature on asymmetric exchange will be clarified.

Briefly the use of the term *model* in context of scientific theory is strictly defined. (We go into this later.) A theory is an interpretation of an uninterpreted calculus and the function of the calculus is to furnish a semantically invariant language for the discussion of relations. The "theory" is an interpretation of the calculus, consisting of law-like generalizations, and correspondence rules that connect the theory with empirical data. A model is an alternative interpretation of the calculus, used because it is simpler to understand. When, for example we speak of electrical "flow" in terms of the theory of hydraulics, we are using a "model" of fluids simply because our minds can more easily apprehend the more concrete phenomenon. The validity of the model, however, lies in the fact that the theory of hydraulics is derived from the same relational statements, from the same abstract calculus as is the theory of electricity. Thus to speak of "voltage" in terms of pressure is more than metaphorical; the relation between this variable and others in the calculus is the same both for water flow and electrical flow.

In social anthropology we cannot yet attain to such stringent requirements for the formulation of our theoretical statements (although we are approaching this ideal in some parts of kinship theory. (See Chapter Eleven.)

Therefore it is misleading to use the term *model*, which has an established usage in scientific parlance when we are discussing the representations of phenomena such as dualistic systems or asymmetric alliance.

It is preferable to speak of "ideal types" (of social structures) in this case. Asymmetric exchange we regard as an ideal type, or idealized typification of a class of social structures. The kind of theoretical formulation constituted by this sort of typology is surprisingly complex (see Rudner, 1966, pp. 54–63; see also Nagel, 1961, pp. 463–466).

First we must establish the universe of discourse. In our case the universe is established on the basis of three variables, the semantic boundaries of which delimit the universe. The three variables are (1) incest rules, (2) marital choices, (3) and the social space that it is *convenient*[7] to designate in terms of genealogical positions. By delimiting the universe of discourse we can proceed with two kinds of statements. First, we can specify the *state boundaries* of the marriage systems under consideration, or be explicit about what we are talking about, and more important, what we are not talking about. Second, we can introduce order into the typological classification by the application of an ordering relation in terms of the applicability of our three variables. Our first ideal type can be called *elementary structure*.

---

[7] This is a procedural convenience, not an epistemological commitment to the "nature" of the space we are examining. See Chapter Two for discussion of the semantic and substantive aspects of the nature of social spaces.

In this case the incest variable takes a positive value, the marital choice variable takes a positive value, and the social space variable takes a positive value. By which we mean that the incest taboo "pumps women out" (as in all systems). There is a "positive marriage rule" (indicating the marital destiny of the women), and the social system is bounded, or closed. Our second ideal type has been called *Crow-Omaha system*,[8] where the incest variable takes a positive value, the marital choice variable takes a negative value, and the social space variable takes a positive value.

In a Crow-Omaha system (see Lévi-Strauss, 1965, p. 20) the incest rule applies, but there is no positive marriage rule. Generally one may marry anyone who is neither a member of one's own line or of parent's line. This introduces contingency, but still permits a bounding of the social universe within which marriage may take place—even though this universe is of a higher order of magnitude than in elementary structures. This becomes clear when we consider Lévi-Strauss' (1965, p. 20) statement on the amplitude of marriage choice in Crow-Omaha systems,

. . . there are in a group containing only two prohibited clans, the mother's and the father's, twenty-three thousand four hundred and thirty-six (23,436) marriage types for an overall figure of seven clans, three million seven hundred and sixty-six thousand, one hundred and forty (3,766,140) for fifteen clans, and two hundred and ninety-seven million, four hundred and twenty-three thousand, eight hundred and fifty-five (297,423,855) for thirty clans. Three clanic interdictions instead of two would lower the figures but slightly.

The third type is called *complex systems*, where incest is positive, marital choice negative, social space negative. The three types can be represented in Table 5–1.

Table 5–1. Ordering of Three Types of Social Structure

| | Variables | | |
| Ideal type | Incest rule | Social space | Marital choice |
| --- | --- | --- | --- |
| **Elementary structure** | + | + | + |
| **Crow-Omaha system** | + | + | − |
| **Complex system** | + | − | − |

In the case of elementary structures, marital choice can be said to be determined or ordered within the boundaries of the system. In the case of Crow-Omaha systems the same is true, but the degree of determination is of a

[8] For those students who may be accustomed to the American and British usage of "Crow-Omaha," it should be pointed out that Lévi-Strauss uses these terms in a different manner, and the best exposition is in Lévi-Strauss (1965).

vastly diminished magnitude in comparison with the elementary structure. Second, in an elementary structure, the incest restriction and the marriage prescription are but alternate formulations of the same code. In Crow-Omaha systems, this is not the case; the incest restrictions merely pose the limiting case and the marriage choice is contingential.

Let us now examine the logical entailments of the decision to treat these constructs as ideal types. Claims made for the nature of ideal types are complicated and at times conflicting (cf. the conflicting views of Weber on this subject, Weber, 1949). The designation *elementary structure* (one of the constituent terms of which is *asymmetrical system*) is to be construed as a *term*, in the analytic sense, and *not* as a nonanalytic statement that asserts some state. This is critical. Nonanalytic assertorial statements are subject to empirical disconfirmation by *extralinguistic* reference; therefore by definition they are contingential in nature. Take a trivial example. An analytic designation is axiomatic in nature. It states that within the context of a set of statements, there is some $x$, which can be designated $y$. A class term such as *Martian* could be said to be an analytic designation within the context of a set of statements pertaining to some system under discussion. The statement, "Martians arrive daily in flying saucers," is nonanalytic, and assertorial, subject to disconfirmation by empirical, or extralinguistic reference. We can form sets of analytic statements, of the form, "There is an $x$, such that for any $x$ that has the characteristic $i$, then it has the characteristic $j$," but we would be stating that within the analytic context of the statement, there can be assumed to be a noncontingent relationship between $i$ and $j$.

*Ideal type*, in this sense, refers to such constructs (or better, *predicates*) as "perfect competition," "totalitarian state," and includes "asymmetric alliance system." One of the qualities of such predicates is that (Rudner, 1966, p. 55):

In a system of fully metricized concepts an ideal type or idealization is employed to talk about what *would* (if it did exist) exemplify extreme values of some variable ranging over the system's entire universe of discourse. For example, the concept *ideal gas* designates gases, or gaseous states, in which both the volumes and the masses of molecules assume the extreme value zero.

Again, it should be noted that these ideal types have no special methodological role, however much they may have heuristic value. As Lévi-Strauss points out (1965, p. 18),

It should be kept in mind, however, that the notions of "elementary structures" and of "complex structures" are purely heuristic—they provide a tool for investigation—and *they cannot be used alone to define a system*. (Italics ours.)

Similarly all systems have a "complex" aspect, deriving from the fact that more than one individual can usually meet the requirements of even the most prescriptive systems, thus allowing for some freedom of choice.

This statement will be recalled when we come to consider one of the problems in the study of asymmetric structures, namely the purported difference between "preferential" and "prescriptive" systems. Like designations such as *totalitarian society* or *perfect competition, system of asymmetric alliance* is a shorthand term, a convenient rubric used to refer to a complex set of statements that describe the phenomenon in question. Speaking semantically, such idealizations do not describe anything (Rudner, 1966, p. 57), ". . . there is no entity, process, or state of affairs to which the idealization stands in designatory or descriptive relation. This is, of course why they are called 'idealizations.'" And further, if it becomes known that there is no set of conditions corresponding to the postulated relational properties of the idealization, this does nothing to impair the heuristic utility of the idealization. There is, quite simply, no empirical content to an idealization.

One might inquire, then, what possible value these idealizations might have. Let us answer this question, first in the general-philosophical context, and then in the context of alliance theory as it pertains to asymmetric alliance systems. Rudner (1966, p. 62) puts it as follows,

Such idealizations comprise universal generalizations (lawlike sentences) that may be true even though they "fail to describe anything." Their methodological (as distinct from their heuristic) task is to function explanatorily, and when they succeed in doing so (e.g. as in physics) it is through their subsumption under more general, independently evidenced theories which provide them (as well as other statements) to the explanations in which they do figure. Their failure to achieve significant explanatory power in the social sciences is a result of the paucity in such disciplines of the requisite general theory.

It should be pointed out that our vocabulary throughout this explanatory section is not the same as that used by Lévi-Strauss. It should be noted that we have studiously avoided the term *model* except in the explication of Lévi-Strauss' own terminology, namely, "mechanical model" and "statistical model." We do not believe that the cause of explication is well served by the use of the term *model*, which has a specific semantic content in methodological discourse. Discussions of Lévi-Strauss' work that are oriented to the justification of the scientific validity of the term *model* represent attempts to justify the use of a term, which, for all the pleasing overtones it might have in connection with the discussion, is, in fact, misapplied.[9] Strictly speaking, a model *must* have a strict correspondence to the empirical level. A model is a more familiar representation of a *theory* (and therefore is a theory itself), and a theory can be spoken of as (Gregor, n. d.) "a set of . . . systematically related propositions, which include among them some lawlike generalizations,

[9] These astringencies do not apply to explications of the larger aspects of Lévi-Strauss' work. We omit, here, to consider the wider applications of the notion of system, and the role of these conceptions in the framework of contemporary scientific work. (But see Nutini, 1967.)

*and which can be assigned specific truth values via empirical tests*" (italics ours). The structure that the model represents is isomorphic with the structure of the theory and merely serves to enable dull readers to discern the structural form more clearly. As Hertz (1894, Introduction, quoted in Braithwaite, 1955, p. 91) puts it, ". . . we make for ourselves internal pictures or symbols of external objects and we make them of such a kind that the necessary consequences in thought of the pictures are always the pictures of the necessary consequences in nature of the objects pictured . . . . When on the basis of our accumulated previous experiences we have succeeded in constructing pictures with the desired properties, we can quickly derive by means of them, as by means of models, the consequences which in the external world would only occur in the course of a long period of time, or as a result of our own intervention."

The general principles of constructing a model can be briefly summarized. Nagel (1961, p. 91) distinguishes three components of a theory: (1) an abstract calculus that is the logical skeleton of the explanatory system, and that "implicitly defines" the basic notions of the system; (2) a set of rules that in effect assign an empirical content to the abstract calculus by relating it to the concrete materials of observation and experiment; and (3) an interpretation or model for the abstract calculus, which supplies some flesh for the skeletal structure in terms or more or less familiar conceptual or visualizable materials. And formally speaking (Braithwaite, 1955, pp. 89–90), ". . . If we have before us two deductive systems which are each interpretations of the same calculus, in the first of which the interpretation of the initial formulae containing the theoretical terms is epistemologically prior to that of the derived formulae not containing these theoretical terms, whereas in the second interpretation the reverse is the case, the derived formulae being the epistemologically prior, the first deductive system will be said to be related to the second deductive system as *model* is to *theory*" (Braithwaite's italics). In social anthropology we have not reached the point where a true theory can be stated in any domain. However, as will become evident in the later chapters, particularly Chapter Eleven (Omaha systems), in some parts of kinship theory we are approaching it.

It is less ambiguous then to speak of Lévi-Strauss' formulation of a "mechanical model" of an asymmetric exchange system as an *idealization*, and not a model in any formal-theoretical sense. Failure to do so has led to a number of errors, two of which we will examine here. We can call the two errors, for shorthand convenience, the interpretive error, and the positivistic error. That they are inextricably linked will become obvious in the exposition.

## THE INTERPRETIVE ERROR

For argumentative convenience let us examine Coult's (1962) defense of Homans and Schneider (1955), and his attack on the purported act of demolition of the "theory of sentiments" carried out by Needham in "Structure and Sentiment" (1962a).[10]

Homans and Schneider took Lévi-Strauss' diagram[11] to be a literal representation of actual social relations between people, each position in the diagram corresponding to a genealogical position, as though it were some Ego's family tree. They put the question, "Why is it that matrilateral cross-cousin marriage is better for society than the patrilateral form?" and suggested that Lévi-Strauss had spoken only in terms of *final* causes, whereas they were concerned with efficient cause explanation.[12] Both a final and an efficient cause were necessary for an explanation and their role was to play Darwin to Lévi-Strauss' Lamarck (Figure 5–5).

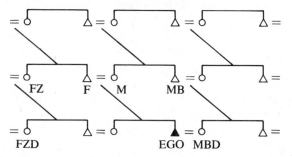

*Figure 5–5. Matrilateral Cross-Cousin Marriage (Homans and Schneider, in Homans, 1962, p. 210)*

Note the "genealogical relations" that have been marked in. Briefly the Homans and Schneider hypothesis is as follows: In a patrilineal society jural authority over the male child (Ego) lies with the father and his line (which includes father's sister), whereas the mother's brother is outside the line. Relations with the father are characterized by respect, and distance, whereas relations with the mother's brother are characterized by warmth and closeness. In a condition, then, wherein Ego had to choose a cross cousin for a marriage partner, which cross cousin is he going to choose, the child of the warm supportive mother's brother, or of the cold-fish father's sister? Clearly he would choose the mother's brother's daughter. Turnabout is the case in a matrilineal society: mother's brother becomes the locus of jural authority,

[10] We need not examine the serial shifts of position by Needham and his detractors over the years insofar as it has become clear that the argument is (except in its larger dimensions) a genuinely factitious red herring.

[11] See Figure 5–4, p. 115.

[12] ". . . a final cause theory states that an institution is what it is because it serves some purpose. But the weakness on all final cause theories was pointed out long ago by Aristotle. In his parable the house is there that men may live in, but it is also there because the builders have laid one stone upon another. Or, no final cause without an efficient cause." (Homans and Schneider, 1955.)

the cold and distant figure of respect, whereas father's sister is the warm supportive one. If one had to choose between cross cousins one would choose the father's sister's daughter. Coult (1962, 1963) has persisted in this line of thought and presented several refurbishings of the argument. In the context of cross-cousin marriages, Coult says that we have omitted to consider the role of the person who "gives away the bride." In a patrilineal society mother's brother has jural authority over his daughter, whereas father's sister's husband has control over father's sister's daughter. Therefore, under the assumption that "cognates" are closer than "affines," Ego will choose to marry MBD. In the matrilineal case, the father has the power of disposal over the patrilateral cross cousin (he is MB to Ego's FZD), whereas the locus of authority over MBD is her MB, or an affinal MBWB. On the assumption that persons who have control over a marriageable woman will arrange her marriage to the nearer relative, then clearly, in a patrilineal society Ego will marry his MBD, whereas in a matrilineal society will marry his FZD. The argument is adroit and the correlation between lineality and directionality of cross-cousin marriage and the authority-locus and the direction of cross-cousin marriage is high, well beyond the chance expectation and the hypothesis is confirmed.

However, the hypothesis is both confirmed and misconceived. It is misconceived because the diagram is an idealized representation of a set of relations, and does not refer to actual people at all. There is a rule in any debate about not attacking the analogy, which is precisely what Homans and Schneider and Coult have done. Let us be clear on this point. If one were to construct a model for the kinetic theory of gases using billiard balls as representations of the molecular activity of the gas, and someone were to attack the theory on the ground that it didn't take into account the numbers on the snooker balls —we would have an analogous situation. The triangles and circles on the diagram do not represent people, they represent points between which relationships exist in a certain "type" of social order (asymmetric exchange), and to mistake them for people is to mistake entirely the point of the representations.

Now to some extent it can be said that the vertical lines (*A*, *B*, and *C*) represent descent groups in those many cases where asymmetrical exchange is found in the context of unilineal descent. Coult (1962) has advanced the further thought that, given this alone, and given that the genealogical class represented by a given triangle or circle is a class, "one of whose members is *actual* mother's brother's daughter," then although the mother's brother's actual daughter may not be the person to whom Ego is to be married, and although actual mother's brother is no longer the father of the bride, he is a senior member of the corporate group (wife-giving lineage) from which Ego will draw his wife. Therefore in the revised hypothesis, the triangle representing the mother's brother's "position" need not represent an actual person, but can stand for the class of people of which mother's brother is but one member. The psychological (or sociopsychological) rationale holds: Ego will tend to marry a cross cousin who is under the control of the corporate group to the senior member of which Ego stands in appropriate sentimental relation. Once again the point is missed, and in order to demonstrate the actual complexity of social relations we shall look at Leach's expositions on the Kachin system of marriage (Leach, 1951, 1953, 1954) to see both why it is that a sentimental explanation cannot explain, and what that infernal diagram represents. We can then conclude with a summary statement on the role of analogy and model in social anthropology, and come full circle to Lévi-Strauss' analysis of dual systems, and give a synthetic view of the underlying methodological assumptions implicit in his approach.

We will not attempt to sum up all the objections to the sentimental position. The interested reader can refer to Schneider (1965a) for a bibliographic summary of this extended argument. We have also omitted to mention the major logical objection to the theory of sentiments, namely, that it is methodologically unsound to postulate a general condition (authority ascription and sentimental disposition of actors in a patrilineal society as against a matrilineal society), which is widely distributed (patrilineality and matrilineality being widely distributed), as the efficient cause of an institution (cross-cousin marriage), which occurs relatively rarely. In fact Lévi-Strauss' book (1949) is not about this rare phenomenon; it is an essay in structure and the mediating value of exchange and the construction of models, rather than a close examination of an ethnographic curiosity.

The difficulties of relating the idealized formulation to the empirical case can be studied using the background of Homans, Schneider, and Coult, as against the descriptive and analytic work of Leach, and then attempting to coordinate the two.

## ALLIANCE RELATIONSHIPS IN KACHIN

Conceptually there exists a stable and central relationship in Kachin society, which is called the *mayu-dama* relationship and is glossed as "affinal relationship." (Leach, 1954, p. 136 and *passim*.) "When a marriage has occurred, *mayu* denotes the relationship of the wife's lineage to that of the husband, *dama* denotes the relationship of the husband to that of the wife." (Leach, 1954, *ibid*.)

The preferred marriage "is not between mother's brother's daughter and father's sister's son, but between *classificatory* mother's brother's daughter and father's sister's son. (Kachin *nam* and Kachin *gu*.) It is only among chiefs, whose circle of kinsfolk is necessarily somewhat restricted, that an orthodox marriage with *nam* implies marriage with a real mother's brother's daughter or any near relative. A commoner male normally has a wide range of *nam* to choose from, including for example any lineage sister of the wife of any of his father's lineage brothers. In many cases the actual relationship between *gu* and *nam* is very remote, but in Kachin eyes any *gu-nam* marriage is strictly orthodox. An important corollary of this is that the class status implications of the Kachin marriage rule operate with much more marked effect among the aristocratic classes (who tried on the whole to marry near relatives) than among the commoner clans (who do not)" (Leach, 1953, p. 87; italics in original).

The implications of these statements are interesting. Under the logical restriction of *classification* it becomes clear that our gloss of *gu* and *nam* in genealogical terms is a clear misnomer. It is indeed rare that such marriage takes place in the sense of *actual* FZS marrying MBD. The definition of *gu* and *nam* is a function of (1) previous marriage of the lineages and (2) the number of local lineage-like groups that are available for a marital selection. It would seem, then, that to speak of the relationship between *gu* and *nam*, or of the *mayu-dama* relationship between wife-giving and wife-receiving groups as being genealogically conditioned is extremely misleading. And with that, the argument from sentiments, or authority—both of which have their locus in the individual (here genealogically defined)—fails irredeemably. As Leach has said in direct answer to Coult and the revised theory of sentiments (Leach, 1963, p. 77),

A Kachin for example must marry a *nam*, that is a girl junior to Ego who is a member of any *mayu* (wife-giving) lineage with respect to Ego. There will ordinarily be at least half-a-dozen such lineages and there is no statistical likelihood that the chosen bride will be of the same lineage or even of the same clan as Ego's own mother.

Leach's work is particularly apposite because he is well aware of the distinction between the simplified representation of the alliance system, and the ethnographic reality. All his work on alliance systems (Leach, 1945, 1954, 1963) reflects this awareness. He is therefore especially cognizant of the pitfalls inherent in the interpretation of the representations of asymmetric exchange in the diagrams of Homans and Schneider, Lévi-Strauss, Needham, and so on. This reply to Coult, and to the social-psychological theory of sentiment-authority well illustrates the interpretive error.

## THE POSITIVISITIC ERROR

What is here called the *positivistic error* arises from the attempt to take the idealization of asymmetric exchange systems and correlate it in detail with ethnographic cases. Needham's name is inextricably linked with this attempt, and with his prolific reanalyses of ethnographic materials he has managed to (1) becloud the discussion of symmetric alliance with the false dichotomy between "prescriptive" and "preferential" alliance systems and (2) demonstrate quite convincingly the precise opposite of his central and perduring thesis that first, matrilateral systems of alliance systems exist *in puris naturalibus* in the world (they don't); and second that patrilateral alliance systems do not and cannot exist (logically, they can; empirically, they do).

Needham's major complaint (again engendered by the misinterpretation of Lévi-Strauss' idealization of asymmetric systems perpetrated by Homans and Schneider) is that these latter do not make the fundamental distinction between "preferential systems" and "prescriptive systems." Needham states that Lévi-Strauss was concerned only with prescriptive systems. (This turned out to be a novel interpretation of Lévi-Strauss' intention, at least to Lévi-Strauss. See Lévi-Strauss, Ms., n. d.) Upon this conceptual misapprehension has foundered analysis after analysis of asymmetric alliance. For Needham (1962a, pp. 8–9) the issue is clear.

> The term "preferential" implies that there is choice, and in the context of marriage that there is choice between a number of persons (distinguished genealogically, for example, or categorically) who may all be married.
> ... The term "prescriptive," on the other hand, has quite different connotations. In this case the emphasis is on the very lack of choice: the category or type of person to be married is precisely determined, and this marriage is obligatory.

Upon the introduction of the elements of choice one passes from a discussion of "elementary structures" to that of "complex structures" and therefore out of the scope of Lévi-Strauss' general theory of alliance. In preferential systems, the set of empirical entailments, correlates of the marital alliance, simply do not exist.

What Needham is saying is that there are societies in the world that can arrange alliances in a "mechanical" fashion, admitting of no contingency, and his repeated attempts to find them have resulted in indefensible postures. Had he not insisted on ignoring the weight of the evidence of (1) ethnographers; (2) statistical analysis; (3) the mathematical adepts who constructed models of systems to show that they could not work; (4) and the computer simulations that carried out the logic of the mathematical and demographic models, his erroneous formulation would have been permitted to die quietly, and his genuine contributions on the symbolic (total structural) aspects of social system types would have been sufficient to put us permanently in his debt.

## THE ETHNOGRAPHER'S OBJECTION

As Schneider (1965a) has pointed out so clearly, Needham has tortured the ethnography repeatedly to make the facts fit his model of asymmetrical systems. For Needham all the parts must fit together, the dualistic symbolic system, the asymmetric kinship terminology (principally FZD $\neq$ MBD); the presence of lineages (in which Lévi-Strauss mistakenly concurs). When the ethnographic reports are at variance with the elements of the model, then, the errors must lie in the ethnography. As Schneider (1965a, p. 69) puts it,

Needham takes the ethnographic report and matches it against his model, his type. Every deviation of the ethnography from one or another element in the type suggests to Needham that *the ethnography* (italics his) is wrong in one way or another. Needham never alters his type to accommodate the ethnography. Needham never changes the model to fit the data.

Of course, the type (idealization) in our terms is by definition *nondisconfirmable* by reference to the empirical level. The idealization has no empirical content; its value is entirely heuristic. Therefore we need not seek for an empirical case that fits the idealization. Whether an empirical replica can fit the model or not (and it surely cannot), the idealization retains its value.

The "positivistic error" perpetrated by Needham can be exhibited by the examination of specific cases and attempting to demonstrate the physical reality of the movement of women through class memberships (i.e., through a statistical examination). In the case of the statistical examinations (see Ackerman, 1964, 1965; Goehegan and Kay, 1964; Cowgill, 1964; Muller, 1964; Wilder, 1964; Needham, 1966), given the ethnographic facts and demographic parameters, it seems clear that the Purum cannot and do not conform to Needham's model.

As for the impossibility of systems of patrilateral cross-cousin marriage, mathematical simulations (Livingstone, 1959) have shown that it is quite possible for patrilateral systems to exist, and a number (between two to six, depending on how strict your criteria are) have been found in the world (see Schneider, 1965a, p. 70, for brief comment).

As for the preferential/prescriptive dichotomy, *all* systems are preferential; it is demographically impossible to have "true" MBD marriage, in any society over time—the system breaks down as the computer simulation of Kunstadter *et al.* (1963) has shown.

It seems clear that prescriptive marriage cannot exist empirically (Lévi-Strauss, 1965, pp. 16–18). Ethnographic evidence and computer simulations are against it, and not a single ethnographic case appears to be extant. And more, consistently, the wrong question is asked or the wrong comment made. Needham, for his part (1961, p. 98), seems incensed at the "gust of amusement that blows through the pages of the *Bijdragen,*" when Berting and Philipsen (1960, p. 58) suggest that it is perhaps risible that a Purum lineage (Needham, 1962a, p. 87) which participates in 16 . . . cycles . . . supplies only three women and receives seven." He asks the question, "Why not?" We ask the question, "Who cares?" Whether in fact the lineage appeared in a derisively high or low number of cycles is clearly beside the point. The representation of an asymmetric system can exist apart from the fact that the actualization of the model exists or not. Lévi-Strauss, Needham and Leach, or anyone is perfectly at liberty to discuss social systems in terms of ideal types, providing they do not make the mistake of reifying the type, and then searching for it in the world. *Homo economicus* also represents an ideal type, but we should be hard put to discover such a person even among the most penny-pinching petit bourgeois population. The same is true of patrilateral cross-cousin marriage. The model can exist perfectly well without its enactment, in fact, does exist (Lévi-Strauss, 1965, p. 16) "not only in the mind of the anthropologist who can represent it in diagram form, but also in that of most of the natives who advocate, permit, or *reject* this formula." (Italics his.) Any system is preferential at the level of reality (Lévi-Strauss, 1965, p. 17) simply because it is impossible to realize a prescriptive system empirically. At the level of the model, however, systems are prescriptive, simply because the (mechanical) model is a noncontingent idealization of the kinds of relations that hold in the ideal case.

# Chapter Six

# Alliance Theory: Part II— Applications

The emphasis on the construction of mechanical models, and on the central importance of the (abstract) relationship as the more effective frame of reference for the construction of theory does not end with the consideration of asymmetric exchange. Certainly it has led, tendentiously and perniciously, into the construction of the defense of "total system" models (Schneider, 1965a, Conclusion) and the search for empirical cases, but alliance theory is more than that. It is a point of view. It is a way of looking at social relations in the construction of what are commonly called "Theories of the middle range" i.e., theories which restrict their scope to particular social systems. Alliance theory has proved to be a useful antidote to the British social structuralist view of society—the only structural view that had received extensive publication and documentation up until the middle 1950's.

The view of the British structuralists can be briefly and schematically compared to that of the alliance theorists before we examine some of the differences and arguments that have grown up out of the differential application of these two points of view. *Descent theory* (as we have called it in a previous chapter) represents an internal view of the society. Working from the inside out, it is a view from the actor's point of view, using the actor as point of reference, rather than the system as frame of reference. It is analytic in the sense that it dissects the role commitments of the actor and the constraints upon his conduct, and extrapolates from the individual through the groups to which he is most closely identified (conjugal dyad, family, extended family grouping, minimal lineage, minor lineage, and so on) to the whole society. At each point of reference, it sets up contrast levels (rather like the linguists' taxonomy) until the picture of the whole society is complete. It therefore emphasizes the points at which units are distinguished, rather than how they are joined, or what might be the nature of the positive link between social units of the same level of contrast.

*Alliance theory*, on the other hand (as the name implies), emphasizes the links between categories, and sees the central relationship that articulates social actors, in *marriage*. Whereas descent theory emphasizes *filiation*, or the discontinuity within continuity that exists in intergenerational relations as the central articulating distinction (thus *descent* theory), alliance theorists tend to view filiative links as continuities, as potential links, not yet actualized, *between social categories*. If our usage of the term *analytic* is supportable in connection with descent theory, then we could view alliance theory as synthetic, in that it interests itself in the system within which the links (exchanges) have positive value and take their positive value from the constitution of the system as a whole. Marriage in descent theory tends to be the negative result of the application of the incest taboos. In the alliance view, it is brought about by the positive value (resulting from the system) attached to exchange. The utility of alliance theory is generally to be found in the analysis of closed systems, i.e., systems that can be conceptually limited to an ordered universe of linked categories. (But see Beattie, 1957–1959, for his use of alliance theory in the discussion of Nyoro kinship.) However, in what Lévi-Strauss (1949, 1965, *passim*) has called "complex societies" and "Crow-Omaha" systems descent theory has been generally found to be more efficacious. It is no coincidence, then, that descent theory was developed in connection with the studies of tribal Africa, where populations of immense size had to be coped with, whereas alliance theory was developed out of an examination, not of "the ensemble of social relations" per se (Radcliffe-Brown, 1964), i.e., not out of an "etic" examination of the content of social actors, but rather out of a study of the relations between groups and categories (because the central form of exchange (marriage) takes place between categories). It is inevitable, then, that alliance theory should concern itself with the solidarity as well as the totality of the group, whereas descent theorists interest themselves more in the "complex scheme of individuation" (Fortes, 1953, p. 33) characteristic of a given social entity.

So long as we regard descent theory and alliance theory as complementary, each of which has relevance in the analysis of some "kinds" of society, then there can be no competition between them. But, this is not always the case. In the last part of this chapter we examine a number of instances where there is competition between "alliance" and "descent" theory, and review some of the more important controversies that have stemmed from these competing points of view. We will make a brief *tour d'horizon*, examining, (1) the problem of what Fortes has called "complementary filiation," (2) the problem of whether Dravidian systems are best regarded from the point of view of unilineal (or bilineal) structures, or as alliance networks, and

(3) the problem of whether Australian section systems, particularly the "Murngin anomaly" is best regarded from a descent or an alliance point of view.

## COMPLEMENTARY FILIATION VS. AFFINAL CONNECTIONS

In the discussion that arose out of the problems of interlineage relations (particularly in the matter of bride price, marital stability, and divorce) we encounter a very instructive impasse between the alliance and the descent point of view. The problem centers upon the role of marriage and filiation in the articulation and integration of social groups (lineages). From the preceding remarks in this chapter and from the chapter on descent theory, one can guess with little effort that alliance theorists see marriage as central, whereas descent theorists concentrate upon the intergenerational relation between parents and children.

Leach (1957), assessing the value of the Gluckman hypothesis, a *locus classicus* of descent theory, suggested that the alleged correlation between "Father Right" or lineage strength and bride price + divorce was ethnographically nonpredictive in the case of three societies which he examined, "Ordinary Jinghpaw," Gauri Kachin, and Lakher (see remarks in Chapter Four). It appeared (counter Gluckman) that the strongly patrilineal Lakher do not relinquish rights in personam over their sisters, but rather "hire out" their procreative powers. And although bride price is high, divorce is frequent. With the "Ordinary Jinghpaw," however, where patrilineages are equally strong, rights in personam are relinquished to the lineage into which she marries, divorce is impossible, and bride price low. The correlation among bride price, transfer of rights, and frequency of divorce is reversed. Leach proposes another explanation (Leach 1961b, p. 120):

... In the Lakher case, the sibling link between the bride and her own patrilineage is never threatened. If the affinal link ... becomes ineffective it is the marriage itself that is allowed to come to an end. This is in contrast to the "Ordinary Jinghpaw" case where the marriage is deemed unbreakable but the sibling link between the wife and her brothers can become ineffective.

In Leach's view, the sibling link is intrinsically more durable than the marital tie, and therefore to him (conceptually) the unilineal units are effectively discrete, and marriage per se cannot create both the complex individuation and solidarity-equilibrium that is a system perquisite. Such solidarity is created not by the marital tie per se, but rather by the continuing affinal relationships between these discrete groups; and marriage and bride wealth is merely an expression of the pre-existent relationship, which his informants refer to as *mayu-dama*, *ngazua-patong*, and so on. In contrast he disagrees with Fortes who has discussed the descent theory position because (Leach, 1961b, p. 122)

... for Fortes, marriage ties, as such do not form part of the structural system. They are of interest only because they serve to distinguish the individuals from one another.

For Fortes, the marriage of two individuals, the exchange of rights, and bride wealth become of structural significance upon the birth of the child. Fortes states (1959, p. 209),

Leach thinks that it is the relationship of marriage and its concomitant relationships of affinity that form the "crucial" link between corporate descent groups and the Kachin type system. I would put it the other way around and say that marriage and affinity are the media through which structurally prior politico-jural alliances and associations are expressed and affirmed, and I would contend that they are effective as such media *because they give rise to matrilateral kinship bonds.* (Italics ours.)

In the Fortesian view (*ibid.*) kinship is prior to affinity, and the web of kinship produced by the proliferating matrilateral bonds, in a patrilineal system, constitute the effective check upon the fissive and centrifugal tendencies of the descent groups. In closed systems of asymmetric alliance, marriage "is a means of implementing a relationship of amity derived from matrifiliation" (Fortes, 1959).

The problem of complementary filiation is directly and closely linked to the problem of the status of wife/mother in a patrilineal system, husband/father in a matrilineal system, and the status of MB and FZ. Do we regard the kinship status, which is residual to the descent rule (i.e., M and MB in a patrilineal system, F and FZ in a matrilineal system), as consanguineals or as affinals? Here the distinction between the alliance and descent position grows. To descent theorists the kinship statuses in the complementary position are consanguineal (Fortes, 1959, p. 194): (". . . Does he [Leach] really believe that a person 'is related to kinsmen of his two parents' . . . 'because his parents were married' and not 'because he is the descendant . . . of both parents'?").

Leach replies (1961b, p. 10) that we might indeed take this point of view, along with his general admonition to take each case as it comes.

... If the Trobrianders say—as they do say both in word and deed—that the relation between a father and his son is much the same as the relation between male cross-cousins and as the relation between brothers-in-law, but absolutely different from the relations between a mother and her child, then we must accept the fact that this is so. And in that case we only delude ourselves and everyone else if we call such a relation *filiation.* (Italics his.)

Fortes, is not particularly concerned about marriage in his theory of kinship (Fortes, 1959, p. 194), "The *marriage* of the parents is sometimes not even essential for the recognition of paternity by the genitor and the consequent acknowledgement of kinship between the 'illegitimate' offspring and the kin of the genitor."

Leach's accusation (1961b, *passim*), that Fortes has evolved the concept of "complementary filiation" simply because it worked in two societies (the patrilineal Tallensi, and the matrilineal Ashanti) where other observers might have postulated a form of double descent, is not quite fair, but it does raise the problem of what *can* unilineal descent refer to, if, wherever it is encountered, we find that it is offset by a complementary activation of rights and duties in the residual line.

The resolution of this problem has led Fortes, Goody (1959), Gough (1959a), and Freeman (1961) into a terminological morass, which has laid the whole scheme of complementarity open to comment and suspicion. Citing Laura Bohannon (1952 and see Chapter Four, this book), Fortes sees matrilineal filiation (in a patrilineal society) as a vehicle whereby the "complex scheme of individuation" takes place in a society having unilineal descent groups. By virtue of the bonds of consanguinity between Ego and the mother's descent line (i.e., the MB/ZS relationship), the individual becomes differentiated (along with his own full siblings who share the same body of agnatic and matrilateral kinsmen) from the other members of his lineage. *Descent* is seen as an construct formulated in terms of the system-as-a-whole, or in Fortes' terms, as emanating from the jural-political domain. It is the principle of descent (shades of Radcliffe-Brown) that aligns kinsmen into discrete corporate groups. In contrast, bonds of matrilateral filiation are seen as emanating from the *domestic* field, or domain of kinship, and it is the interaction of the integrative and centripetal bonds of matrilateral kinship, together with the centrifugal (and potentially fissive) ideology of discrete descent groups, which both orients the individual and organizes the diverse groups of the social system.

But what is the substantive and conceptual nature of the matrilateral (or complementary) bonds of kinship? It is at this point that technical terms begin to proliferate, the conceptual scheme complicates, and what has heretofore appeared to be a clear statement of relations deteriorates into fuzzy categories, ill-defined distinctions and parlous reifications. Under a system of unilineal descent (we take the patrilineal case as our example) the role of the sexes in the transmission of rights, duties, obligations, and so on is very different. Offices, property, rights over women, and so forth pass through males. Females also retain rights in their lineage, but these are *residual* rights. In fact, in Goody's (1959) parlance, these residual rights pertain to *shadowy claims* upon her natal corporation's property. Among the Ashanti, for example (matrilineal group) the child cannot exercise rights over land in his father's lineage, but retains rights to hospitality and certain ritual rights. These ". . . residual rights with their concomitant moral and ritual claims and associated affective bonds . . . belong primarily to the domestic domain, or what is sometimes spoken of as the sphere of interpersonal or cognatic kinship" (Fortes, 1959, p. 195).

The problem of how shadowy a shadowy right can be, or how residual a sibling can be, or how strong a lineage can be is nettlesome. There appear to be a number of unoperationalized interdependent variables, or at least, a remarkable elasticity of construct, which suggests that the degree of semantic invariance in the technical vocabulary is less than what might be desired.

What is at issue here, as Schneider (1965a, pp. 55ff.) points out, is the type of society, or rather what is meant by each commentator by "a certain type of society," or a "kind of social order." Briefly, for Leach, and Lévi-Strauss the shadowy residual claim does not arise out of itself (i.e., residual rights), but rather from the continuing expression of alliance between groups when a marriage either created these bonds, or maintained bonds that had been in effect for some generations. Mother (in a patrilineal system) and father (in a matrilineal system) can be usefully viewed as affinals, and a fortiori, so can MB, and FZ (in patrilineal and matrilineal systems respectively).[1] If asymmetric alliance is being discussed, as in the case of the Kachin, the relative efficacy of the alliance point of view is fairly clear. *Conceptually* enduring affinal relationships between unilineal descent groups, or local groups, do persist transgenerationally, corresponding to the Kachin conception of *mayu/dama*, or Lakher *patong/ngazua*. But in the case of a social system characterized by unilineal descent groups with no positive marriage rule, by no enduring relation between conceptual entities (*mayu/dama*), but merely an exogamous prescription, the situation changes, and it becomes less productive to postulate the conceptual perquisites of an alliance system in the absence of such stable relationships.

The point is that each "school" has in mind a "type of society" to which it is intellectually committed. The advantage, or the relative clarity, of the Leach–Lévi-Strauss point of view lies in the fact that they are in no doubt as to the nature of their model, or representation. It is an ideal type, and although they too fall from grace from time to time, and seek verification (in substantive detail) of their type, they are not as addicted to it as are the Fortes-Goody-Freeman-Gough "school." For Fortes, alliance does not represent an important structural principle. For Leach it most surely does. And the fact of the matter is, that to insist that one model has *eo ipso* greater efficacy and productivity in the analysis of all ethnographic cases is imperialistic and futile. Leach seems to agree when he states (Leach, 1961b, p. 123),

I suspect that, in the end, we may have to distinguish two entirely different categories of unilineal descent systems. There is the category into which most of the African lineage systems seem to fall and which would include the non-exogamous lineages of Islamic Western Asia. In this case the ongoing structure is defined by descent alone, and marriage serves merely to create a "complex scheme of individu-

---

[1] Leach equivocates, or "picks away from a sheltered position" in Schneider's (1965a, p. 51) phrase, and needs the warrant of ethnographic data to bring him out into the open to comment on the "kind of system" he is discussing.

ation" within that structure. In contrast, there is the category of those societies in which unilineal descent is linked with a strongly defined rule of "preferred marriage." In this latter case "complementary filiation" may come to form part of the permanent ongoing structure, but to understand how this comes about we need to consider economic and political factors as well as the kinship structure in isolation.

## THE DRAVIDIAN CASE

But not all the cases are so (relatively) clear cut as the problematic efficacy of complementary filiation in the analysis of "African systems" or in "Asian systems." We now turn to an analysis of cases where there is competition between these points of view—the first case in point being the Dravidian controversy. Dumont's work is applicable here as well as that of Radcliffe-Brown (Dumont, 1950, 1953a, 1953b, 1957, 1966; Radcliffe-Brown, 1953).

An exposition of the various analyses of Dravidian kinship will enable us to view in a more restricted (ethnographic) domain precisely how the dialectical relationship between descent and alliance is developed and applied. It will also lead us into a brief discussion of Australian section systems and to the analysis and examination of Murngin social organization. (It should be noted that this section is not a contribution to the discussion of Dravidian systems; the Dravidian example is used here to illustrate the difference between descent and alliance points of view.)

Dravidian systems on the surface appear to be simplicity itself. They are patrilineal systems associated with matrilateral cross-cousin marriage. But early analysis (perhaps under the influence of Radcliffe-Brown) visualized them in a different manner. Emmeneau (1941, p. 174–5) states, for example, ". . . the generalized South-Indian culture background includes exogamous patrilineal sibs with marriage forbidden also within the matrilineal line to degrees that vary from community to community."

From this we conclude that the characteristic form of Dravidian social organization was a system of matrilineal and patrilineal exogamy, of an underlying system of double descent. Such at least is the "descent view" of the matter. As we shall see shortly, this penchant for finding underlying double descent in closed marriage systems was widely followed not only in South India but also (see Radcliffe-Brown, 1930, 1951) in Australian systems such as the Kariera and Aranda.

To Radcliffe-Brown (reminiscent of the latter position adopted by Fortes in the discussion of complementary filiation), Dravidian and Kariera systems were systems in which actors were related consanguineally, and in fact there were no kinship terms nor social positions that were affinal. The system was closed—any Ego married a consanguineal. From his knowledge of Australian systems, Radcliffe-Brown (1953, p. 112) was able to assure us that "amongst the Australian natives the maternal uncle is thought of as the brother of Ego's mother, and not as the brother-in-law of the father." Essentially, for Radcliffe-Brown, Kariera and Dravidian systems are closed systems; the kinship positions are marked and mapped by kinship terms that refer to consanguineals, and the internal dynamics of the system (the relational properties) are solely mappable in terms of these. How else can this be, for example, if we take the extreme Nayar case (see Chapter Two and references) where the mother's brother is the head of the *taravad* (matrilineage), whereas the father, who may have been or might be at present no more than a *sambandham* lover or one of the lovers of the mother, is such an unstable element in the system? Is it logical, asks Radcliffe-Brown, that the kinship universe should be based upon the affinal tie (between brothers-in-law), a tie that is activated sporadically, or serially by a variable number of individuals (the lovers), rather than the solid enduring *consanguineal* connection between a mother and her brother?

In the Nayar case the question of whether the tie between Husband/ Father is consanguineal or affinal, (*pace* Radcliffe-Brown) is all the clearer. The link between *taravad* is clearly not one of consanguinity, despite the fact that the MB link can be best seen as a consanguineal link. The very instability of enactment of the H/F role, the very fact that any number of actors from H/F's descent group can take over the sexual role indicates that rights in personam among the Nayar are derived from the link between groups, and it is this kind of continuing link between groups brought about through the medium of marriage that we refer to as the *alliance link*.[2]

It we are to reconceptualize Dravidian, and by extension Kariera (Aranda, and so on), systems as systems of alliance rather than as artifacts of underlying double descent we must address ourselves to two topics: (1) the meaning of kinship terms (Radcliffe-Brown: "I can assure Mr. Dumont that amongst the Australian natives the maternal uncle is thought of as the brother of Ego's mother and not as the brother-in-law of the father.") and (2) the sociological correlates of role separation (where it exists) as between MB and WF, and hope to show that MB acts in an "affinal" rather than a "consanguineal" fashion.

## DRAVIDIAN KINSHIP TERMINOLOGY

Dumont's (1950, 1953a, 1953b, 1957) argument is essentially that the dichotomization of kin terms that occurs in Dravidian (and Kariera) systems is a direct reflection of the natives' own model of their systems as consisting in two kinds of people, kinsmen (consanguineals) and allies (affines). This is counter to Rivers, Emmeneau, and Radcliffe-Brown who see the cross-parallel distinction as the criterion by virtue of which the dichotomization takes place, and counter to Romney and Epling (1958) who dichotomize on the basis of sociogeography ("own group" vs. "other group"). A componential analysis of the kinship terminology does not enable us to choose between these variant interpretations—we can represent the componential spaces in such a way as any of the interpretations will be served by any point of view. (See Burling, 1964, and Romney and D'Andrade, 1964a, on

[2] For an alternative view, see Mencher and Goldberg (1967).

this very point.) Briefly described, Dravidian terminology makes distinctions of generation: the variable having five values, $+2$, $+1$, $0$, $-1$, $-2$ corresponding to the generations of grandfather, father, own, son's and grandson's. Sex of relative is a second distinction, whereas the third opposition is the problematic one, being either (1) lineals vs. collaterals, (2) cross vs. parallels, or (3) kinsmen vs. allies.

Table 6–1. Diagram of Terminological Spaces in Dravidian Kinship

| Generation | | Male | Female | Male | Female |
|---|---|---|---|---|---|
| $+2$ | | A (with female variant A′) | | | |
| $+1$ | | B | C | D | E |
| $0$ | > Ego | F | G | H | I |
| | < Ego | J | K | L | M |
| $-1$ | | N (+ fem. variant) | | O (+ fem. variant) | |
| $-2$ | | P (+ fem. variant) | | | |

NOTE. In 0 generation there exists the distinction of relative age.

(After Dumont, 1953, p. 36.)

The issues then revolve around the semantic content of the dichotomizing component, represented by the double line in generations $+1$, and $0$. Dumont's theoretical stance is unabashed—an alliance theorist, he sees marriage as central in creating a relationship between two persons of different sexes, also serving to connect their groups (see Dumont, 1953a, p. 35). But more than that he is convinced that the Dravidians see things his way as well. Although the natives "do, when tracing relationships pass from one line to another these are not among their basic characteristics and are not in the least expressed in theory" (Dumont, 1953a, p. 35). What we see here is not a categorical discontinuity by the distinction of generation applied to a continuing relationship of perpetual affinity. Our mode of expressing the content of a "positive marriage rule" by stating that in a Dravidian system Ego marries mother's brother's daughter is a misnomer, and an ethnocentric misnomer at that. A Dravidian does not establish a marital relationship with a relative standing in a specified consanguineal relationship to him; rather he marries an *affine*. The stable perduring characteristic between the two groups is one of affinity, and not one of lineality vs. collaterality.

But the argument from terminology (or structural semantics—see Chapter Nine) is illusory. Each interpretation of the diagram is equally valid. To demonstrate what to this point can only be the intuition of an ethnographer who is extremely well versed in the culture of South India, Dumont (1957) comes to cases, and sociological cases at that, to display his point. As with the discussion of complementary filiation, the position of "mother's brother" is taken as the hinge of the argument. Dumont states that if he can demonstrate that MB is clearly an affine (better labelled as an affine rather than as a consanguineal), then a fortiori the more distant collaterals can be assumed to be affinals, and the case can be demonstrated. In Dumont (1957) two such cases are adduced. In the first case the cycle of prestations that center upon marriage is examined. In the case that Ego marries a woman who is not his MBD (MBD marriage with the Pramalai Kallar,[3] being highly preferential for eldest son only), it is clear that the actor equation MBD-WF will not hold, and separate actors will occupy separate roles. From his father-in-law Ego receives a series of gifts that culminate in the giving of household items at the time of his departure from his father's household, and the birth of his first child. The cycle of prestations between Ego and father-in-law thereupon ceases, but the bond is activated between father-in-law and Ego's son. The next step in the development of the cycle of prestations is for father-in-law to pass the giving obligation to his son, i.e., a secondary cycle is initiated between Ego's child and his or her maternal uncle. When Ego's child enters upon puberty ceremonies (if a girl) or initiation (if boy), the mother's brother (child's maternal uncle) is of exceeding great importance, but upon the marriage of this child the cycle of prestations ceases, being replaced by a new cycle, between Ego's married child and his father-in-law. In the case that Ego's child marries a woman not-MBD then new actors are assigned to the roles according to the affinal tie. Ego's child enters into prestatory relations with his father-in-law and subsequently his brother-in-law just as Ego did before him. Accordingly, it is in those nonregulated marriages, in those marriages where the positive marriage rule is not followed, that we can separate out the status of the actors who are involved in the prestation cycle. Where the positive marriage rule is followed, where father-in-law and mother's brother are the same individual, it is impossible to distinguish between them. It is clear then that if we were examining a "prescriptive system" in which every Ego married his MBD, there could be no argument. But inasmuch as the Dravidian system is highly preferential, we are able to separate out the actors, by virtue of the functional significance of their activity in the prestation cycles associated with marriage, and continuing through the life cycle. And it becomes clear that these important functions (ascribed to the *consanguineal* MBD by descent theorists) are only carried out by the MBD if he is *also an affinal*. If he is not an affinal, the continuing exchange relations are carried out by the actor who is the affinal. Therefore we can fairly designate the central relationship of Ego/MBD as an affinal

[3] The Pramalai Kallar are a "politically unitary subdivision of the large Tamil caste of Kallar . . . (and) form the dominant caste of an area west of Madura city" (Gough, 1959b, p. 202).

relationship, because MB carries out affinal-like activities with respect to his sister's son.

A second ethnographic example can be drawn from the behavior of actors during the wedding ceremony. There are two important roles to be enacted during the marriage ceremony—one that can be called the "father-in-law role" (that of remaining with the bride in her house), and second the "mother's brother role" (consisting in introducing the bride or groom [one's own nephew or niece]). Obviously role conflict will obtain if the roles are mutually exclusive and the marriage is a regulated one according to the positive marriage rule of matrilateral cross-cousin marriage. In such a case WF = MBD, and conflict exists in that two men cannot be in two places at once. In this case we will be interested to see which role will be enacted by the actual MBD/WF. Again it is the affinal role; actual MBD/WF stays in the house of his daughter, while sending his younger brother to enact the "mother's brother" role as his replacement.

Dumont chooses the mother's brother role for examination, not only in view of the stricture of Radcliffe-Brown that Australians *do* have mother's brothers, but because in South India it is the role of greatest importance. He feels that, once it is demonstrated that the mother's brother role is "affinal" in essence, then a fortiori it can be inferred that other matrilateral roles are such. In view of the evidence that he adduces to demonstrate that Dravidian kinship is terminologically bifurcate, and that sociologically the bifurcation can be best described in terms of kinsmen, and allies (affines), Dumont concludes (1957, p. 37),

... the maternal uncle's role is a part of an alliance pattern, and ... there is a fundamental difference between such links and those which constitute descent groups. This is so true that, far from being a remnant of matrilineality, the role would be found to be much weaker in matrilineal groups, where the father's sister would be more in evidence in the affinal role. What is true in the old idea is that there is a principle which balances patrilineality, which has at the same time a projective or filiation aspect and at first sight a maternal one, and which for these reasons was confused, naturally enough, with descent. But, if the complementary principle is bound to make use of relatives who are not integrated in the descent group, it does not integrate them in turn in another descent group. There is a balance of forces, but the forces are not of the same nature. The descent group ties are counterbalanced by a system of ties which do not link mechanically whole descent groups, but regulate and at the same time generalize individual ties.

Let us here recapitulate the issues involved in the discussion of the Murngin system of section, kinship, and alliance, and then evaluate the contribution of Dumont (1966) and "alliance theory." If the section appears lengthy, let indulgence be given; the issues are complex, and the case has been widely discussed.[4]

[4] Barnes' projected "Inquest on the Murngin" is not as yet available at the time of writing.

We can begin with a discussion of the "fit" of the kinship terminology of Murngin, with the section systems. There are 71 relatives recognized in Murngin: seven sets of sibling groups, or seven lines, as Radcliffe-Brown (1951) calls them.[5] The odd relative is made up of the distinction of elder and younger brother. This is Warner's statement on the matter, and with Warner we shall stick, despite the attempts of Josselin de Jong (1952), or more blatantly Lawrence and Murdock (1949) to "explain" the system by the addition of another "line" of kinsmen.

In addition the Murngin have a system of eight subsections (themselves divided by sex), which regroup the kinship terms. This regrouping process is governed by the following rules. (See Chapter Twelve.)

i. The rule of alternation of generation, which assigns a man, his paternal grandfather, and his son's children to the same subsection.
ii. This rule assigns all members of ego's own moiety to the same set of subsections as his own line; conversely, members of the opposite moiety are assigned to opposing sections.
iii. A final rule divides each kinship personality "into two" (Warner, 1958, p. 117).

Each subsection has a male and female term. The eight subsections—four in each moiety—are (Warner, 1958, p. 118)

Moieties

| Dua | | Yiritija | |
|---|---|---|---|
| | Subsections | | |
| $A^1$ | m. Buralung<br>f. Kalint | $B^1$ | m. Narit<br>f. Naritjin |
| $A^2$ | m. Ballung (Belin)<br>f. Billindjint | $B^2$ | m. Burlain<br>f. Burlaindjint |
| $D^1$ | m. Wamut<br>f. Wamutjin | $C^1$ | m. Kaidjawk<br>f. Koitjin |
| $D^2$ | m. Kamerdung<br>f. Kamindjint | $C^2$ | m. Bangardi<br>f. Bangarditjin |

We can ignore, for the moment, because of its structural unimportance, the division of each subsection by sex, and will substitute letter-designations $A^1$, $A^2$, $B^1$, $B^2$, $C^1$, $C^2$, $D^1$, and $D^2$ for the eight subsections. Let us partially apportion kinship terms to the sections. Taking Ego as a member of $A^1$, then his paternal grandfather and his son's son will also be in $A^1$. This is precisely the same as the Aranda eight-section system, and gives us no

---

[5] Five generations of siblings (male and female) in seven lines = $5 \times 2 \times 7 = 70$, plus the odd one created by the older/younger distinction = 71.

difficulty; the patrilineal "cycle" has twice the duration that it has in a four-section system, as we would expect. Marriage is complex, and the nub of the problem. We are told that mother's brother's daughter marriage is the preferred form of alliance in Murngin. Or as Radcliffe-Brown puts it (1951, p. 42),

(Marriage) ... type is asymmetrical; a man may not marry the sister of sister's husband. The marriage of a man is with the daughter of a "mother's brother" and in some instances he has a claim to the daughter of his own mother's brother. But no one may marry the daughter of his father's sister or of any woman who is by the kinship system a "sister" of the father. Thus a man may marry a woman of his own mother's patrilineal clan, but may not marry the daughter of a woman of his own clan. The relation between cross cousins is asymmetrical.

This type is called by Radcliffe-Brown, the Karadjeri type of marriage, and is found with "four class" systems in the Karadjeri tribe, with eight "classes" in the Murngin, with patrilineal moieties in the Yir Yiront of North Queensland, and apparently in the almost extinct Larakia which had no "classes" (Radcliffe-Brown, *ibid.*).

Thus we have an anomaly, a symmetrical class-system, with asymmetrical marriage with the maternal cross cousin. On the face of it, it is impossible, as a moment's calculation will show. Let us suppose, as we do generally in the examination of Australian section systems, that there are two exogamous restraints. First one must marry outside one's own moiety. A Dua ($A$ or $D$) must marry a Yiritija ($B$ or $C$). Second, one must not marry a person who carries the same numeral designation as one's self (i.e., a 1 must not marry a 2). Further, let us take Elkin's word (and phrasing) that the Murngin in reckoning section designation of the child ... "throw away the father" (i.e., the section designation of the child is not determined by his father's designation). Given these three conditions let us plot marital destinies starting with an $A^1$ male. Ego is $A^1$ and therefore marries a $B^2$ and their child is $C^2$. ($A \neq B$, [rule one], $1 \neq 2$ [rule 2], child's section designation is not determined by father's [rule three].) The mother's brother of the child is a $B^2$ (same as the mother—siblings share section designation), who marries an $A^1$, and their child has designation $C^1$. But these are precisely the children who marry by virtue of the positive marriage prescription of MBD marriage. The first child (a $C^2$ has to marry his MBD, who is a $C^1$; but this is in violation of the rule that people of the same moiety cannot marry. ($C^1 \neq C^2$.) We are at an impasse.

It was this dilemma, in the main, that led Murdock and Lawrence to postulate the existence of an eighth descent line and to reify Warner's diagram of the kinship terminology into putative (but nonexistent) lines of patrilineal descent, which, combined with moiety division and alternating generation, produced the 32-class system that Radcliffe-Brown subsequently ridiculed. It was this dilemma, as well, that led Radcliffe-Brown to ignore the section system as a possible determinant of marriage and to point to "alternate marriages" as means of keeping the sections and the kinship terminology (his primary determinant, or regulator) in step.

The resolution of the problem, however, appears to lie elsewhere. As Dumont (1966) has pointed out, it has been the "spell of underlying descent groups" that has created the dilemma, and until we dispose of the notion of Australian marriage as being merely the negative residue of exogamous prohibitions brought about by cross-cutting descent groups we cannot simultaneously account for (1) asymmetrical cross-cousin marriage and (2) a symmetrical eight-section system in conjunction with each other, and each with its own place in the social organization.

Lévi-Strauss gets us part of the way, although he too succumbed to the "spell of underlying descent groups." Let us begin with a brief recapitulation of the ethnographic background of Australian section systems.

The basis of Australian social groups is the local horde. In a four-section system (Kariera is the type case) there are two "kinds" of local groups (called by many, "our side," and "the other side"). Each local group is divided in two (and depending on one's theoretical orientation, one can call the divisions matrimoieties, or divisions into alternating generations). Thus a 2 × 2 division yields four "classes" or sections. In the eight-subsection systems (Aranda the type case), there are four kinds of *local groups*, once again bifurcated, the nature of the bifurcation depending, in this case as before, upon one's theoretical predisposition. Marriage in the Aranda case is such that (in Radcliffe-Brown's terms, 1951, p. 42) "a man's mother-in-law . . . should be the female cross-cousin of his mother, the daughter of a mother's mother's brother, or of a mother's father's sister. The system is symmetrical; and man's mother is mother-in-law to the son of his assigned mother-in-law. The relationship between cross-cousins is symmetrical."

Assigning, then, letters to the four local groups (*A, B, C, D*), and numbers to the secondary bifurcation (1, 2), we can follow Lévi-Strauss in summarizing marriage and section assignment in Table 6–2.

Table 6–2. Marriage and Section Assignment (Aranda)

| Man's section | His wife's section | Children's section |
|:---:|:---:|:---:|
| $A^1$ | $B^1$ | $D^2$ |
| $A^2$ | $B^2$ | $D^1$ |
| $B^1$ | $A^1$ | $C^1$ |
| $B^2$ | $A^2$ | $C^2$ |
| $C^1$ | $D^1$ | $B^1$ |
| $C^2$ | $D^2$ | $B^2$ |
| $D^1$ | $C^1$ | $A^2$ |
| $D^2$ | $C^2$ | $A^1$ |

(Adapted from Lévi-Strauss, 1949, p. 211).

Or diagrammatically, as follows, displaying the *couples* (or sections that are assigned to alternate generations). (Lévi-Strauss, 1949, p. 211.)

$$
\begin{pmatrix}
A^1 & = & B^1 \\
A^2 & = & B^2 \\
C^1 & = & D^1 \\
C^2 & = & D^2
\end{pmatrix}
$$

The diagram can be read off as follows: A man of $A^1$ marries a woman of $B^1$ and their children are $D^2$. Subsequently a $D^2$ male will marry a $C^2$ female and their children (as indicated by the arrow) will be $A^1$; thus within two generations the cycle is closed: the *couple*[6] is $A^1$ and $D^2$, and if Ego belongs to $D^2$ then father and son will belong to $A^1$. The "matrilineal cycles" (the section of the mother, and the section of the child constitute a *cycle*) are longer: $A^1 \rightarrow C^1 \rightarrow A^2 \rightarrow C^2$ and finally return to $A^1$, and in the second matrimoiety, $B^1 \rightarrow D^2 \rightarrow B^2 \rightarrow D^1$, and finally return to $B^1$. The structure of the cycle (in an eight-subsection system) is transformed, compared to the four-section system, while the marriage *pairs* and the structure of the *couples* remain the same. That is, if we begin with an $A^1$ mother, then her child will be a $C^1$, and her child's child an $A^2$, her child's child's child a $C^2$, and finally in the fifth generation the *cycle* will be closed with a return to $A^1$.

The section system and the kinship system are in harmony. The prescribed section from which one draws one's wife contains only permitted women.

The appropriate section can be described (following Maybury-Lewis' [1965] comments) as a class of women, one of whose members is actual mother's mother's brother's daughter's daughter.

The Murngin system, according to Lévi-Strauss' analysis, conforms to this type, but in a complex manner. It is characterized by eight sections and first cousin matrilateral cross-cousin marriage. In the first characteristic it resembles the Aranda system, but in the second (loosely) resembles Kariera.[7]

Elkin (1953) and Radcliffe-Brown (1953) have suggested that the Kariera state that they themselves prefer to marry MBD, although FZD marriage is relatively common. Figure 6–1 displays the conceptual relations that obtain given a cultural rule that permits marriage with both cross cousins. It also maps both the kinship terminology and the sections in the most economical fashion, but does not allow for the declared matrilateral preference on the

[6] Note the three terms, which are Radcliffe-Brown's, (1) a *pair* refers to the sections of (a) husband and (b) wife; (2) a *couple* refers to the sections of (a) father and (b) son respectively; and (3) a *cycle* refers to the sections of (a) mother and (b) child respectively (Lévi-Strauss, 1949, p. 203).

[7] Most analysts' constructions assume that marriage in Kariera takes place with a woman from a class of which MBD/FZD is a member. Or, marriage is said to take place with a bilateral cross cousin. We can display the system simply in a diagram.

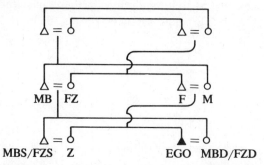

*Figure 6–1. Simplified Representation of Bilateral Cross-Cousin Marriage in Kariera.*

part of the Kariera. It is in the resolution of this anomaly that we return, after this long example, to the "alliance point of view."

Lévi-Strauss has a simple way of conciliating the rule of matrilateral cross-cousin marriage, and the eight-section system. In the "normal" form of marriage we find the cycles and couples in pure Aranda form, as we would expect.

$$\left( \begin{array}{ccc} A^1 & = & B^1 \\ A^2 & = & B^2 \\ C^1 & = & D^1 \\ C^2 & = & D^2 \end{array} \right)$$

But in the optional system of marriage, we find alternative marriage choices, which can be diagrammed as follows:

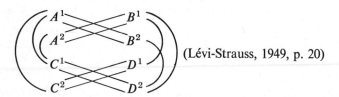 (Lévi-Strauss, 1949, p. 20)

Given the moieties and the subsection names,[8] we can see that (Lévi-Strauss, 1949, p. 217)

[8] Yiritcha Moiety      Dua Moiety

Subsections:

| Ngarit | Buralang |
| Bulain | Balang |
| Kaijark | Karmarung |
| Bangardi | Warmut. |

(Lévi-Strauss, 1949, p. 217.)

. . . a man of Ngarit section can marry either a woman of Balang, or a woman of Buralang section. A man of Bulain section can choose between a woman in Buralang and a woman in Balang. A man in Kaijark marries either into the Warmut subsection, or in the subsection Karmarung, etc. Whatever the type of marriage practiced the children belong to the same section (opposite to father's but same moiety). (Translations ours.)

Lévi-Strauss by combining "regular" and alternative marriages was able to bring into line the marriage rule and the section designations, neither of which Radcliffe-Brown (who ignores the sections), Josselin de Jong (who created an eighth patriline), nor Murdock and Lawrence (who reified Warner's diagram lines and created a 32-section system) were able to do.

Still, Lévi-Strauss did not clear up the ambiguity over whether, in fact, the lines in Warner's diagrams were agnatic descent lines, and whether, in fact, we have in Murngin a complex system of descent, or a system of alliance.

Take Kariera for example. Classic analysis (Radcliffe-Brown, 1930) indicates that the Kariera four-section system is the result of the intersection of patrimoieties and matrimoieties. The marriage rule (bilateral cross-cousin marriage, or marriage with a female from a class that is designated minimally by the genealogical reference MBD/FZD) is the result of exogamy with respect to one's own patriline and one's own matriline, leaving a single eligible class. But (see on this point, Romney and Epling's [1958] analysis), there *are no* reported matrimoieties.

The Kariera do not recognize matrimoieties. They do, however, recognize the positive value of a marriage rule that brings about the interrelation of the local groups of the Kariera linguistic group. The integrative principle is not the negative residue of rigorous matri- and patri-exogamy, as Radcliffe-Brown would claim, and as Lawrence claims, but rather in the positive exercise of the exchange function. As Dumont points out (1966, p. 236), *Given the rule of patrilineal filiation and the rules of intermarriage, the rule of matrifiliation is entailed.* (Italics his.) True, if one is interested in examining the internal relations of a local group, one will perforce be interested in the patrilineal kin ties that permeate the local horde, and the genealogical status of inmarrying women. But this is a bits-and-pieces approach to the system. If one is interested in the system-at-large it is more accurate ethnographically, and more parsimonious theoretically, to begin from the point of view of alliance and exchange.

If one does not, then, one is forced to one or the other of the horns of a dilemma. Either (1) it is impossible to regard the Australian marriage systems as being of a single type, and therefore one must introduce "anomalous" cases such as the Murngin, or (2) one must introduce elements into the analysis ("Murdock marriages" in Radcliffe-Brown's [1951, p. 52] parlance), which are so far from the ethnographic accounts as to give the feeling that they are derived wholly from the imagination of the ethnographer (32 marriage classes plus rigorous exogamy in a group characterized by alternate marriage (see Webb, 1933, *passim*).

Given Lévi-Strauss' insight that the "regular" and "alternative" forms of marriage are of structural importance, the interpretation of the Murngin system is really quite simple. The anomaly of a symmetrical section system (eight subsections like Aranda), and an asymmetric marriage rule (mother's brother's daughter marriage) can be ingeniously fitted together. We can summarize briefly.

Beginning with a Kariera, four-section system, and a marriage rule that prescribes regular and alternate forms, we see readily that for Ego there are two divisions that are relevant to him.

In the four-section system it will be remembered that section $A^1$ took wives from section $B^2$, $A^2$ took from $B^1$, and so on. With alternative marriage in an eight-section system, we divide the sections into two subsections, and following Dumont refer to the subsections by the designatory letters $a$ and $b$. Thus $A^1$ section comes to be divided into $A^1a$, and $A^1b$; whereas section $B^1$, in turn, becomes designated by the formulae $B^1a$, and $B^1b$. In order to display and demonstrate the Murngin marriage cycles in the context of matrilateral cross-cousin marriage, all we need to do is to see that "regular" marriages alternate with "alternate" marriages, such that if my father made a "regular" marriage, I shall make an "alternate" marriage, my son will make a "regular" marriage, and so on.

Dumont (1966, p. 248) illustrates with a diagram.

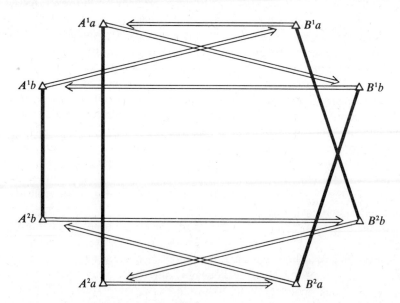

*Figure 6–2. Asymmetrical Intermarriage in an Eight-section System (one half of the hypothetical Murngin system: adapted from Dumont, 1966, p. 247).*

Figure 6–2 is to be read as follows. The arrows indicate the direction from which women *come*. Reading from the top $B_1a$ gives women to $A_1a$, whereas $A_1a$ gives women to $B_1b$. The solid lines indicate the line of filiation. But, let it be recalled that the Murngin "throw away the father" and therefore the section designation of the child will be indicated by the solid vertical line which connects the wife-giving section to the section of the child.

Let us follow the chain of marriages over five generations to see how the circle is completed.

$$
\begin{array}{c}
B_1a \doteq A_1b \\
\;\;| \\
A_2b \doteq B_2a \\
\;\;\;\;\;| \\
B_1b \doteq A_1a \\
\;\;\;\;\;\;\;| \\
A_2a \doteq B_2b \\
\;\;\;\;\;\;\;\;| \\
B_1a
\end{array}
$$

(cf. Dumont, 1966, p. 241.)

And the marriage system can perhaps be seen best in a more traditional diagram which we can adopt from Josselin de Jong (1952, p. 60). Perhaps the easiest way of reading this diagram (Figure 6–3) is to go across sibling lines rather than down generations. The diagram displays how alternation of marriage, symmetrical sections, and matrilateral cross-cousin marriage can be harmonized. Figure 6–3 accords with Dumont (1966, p. 247), but dis-

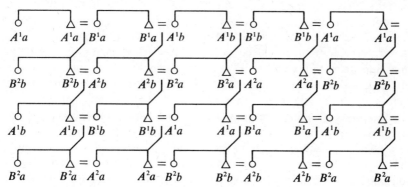

Figure 6–3. *Alternating Marriage and Murngin Section System (after Josselin de Jong, 1952).*

plays the consanguineal alignments more clearly. Note alternation of generation between generations, marked by sucessively 1, 2, 1, 2. Note also that the number of lines has been reduced for the purposes of simplicity. The pattern of alternate marriage can be better seen in Dumont's diagram (see Figure 6–2).

The point of this demonstration is simply as follows. If we focus on the possibilities of marriage alternation, the logical (subsection) entailments of such marriage practices, then the "riddle of the Murngin" can be solved. If we insist (as Romney and Epling do *not*), that section systems, and by extension Dravidian systems, can exist only in the presence of cross-cutting descent groups, we not only display a predisposition to view the data in a prejudicial manner, but more, we are led to impasses from which we cannot extricate ourselves. Lineality does, ordinarily, apply in Dravidian and Australian section systems.[9] The unique configuration, however, of these systems arises out of the dialectic between lineage and marriage rule. To deny the importance of the second in favor of the first in order to impose classificatory order may be psychologically fulfilling, but it is neither ethnographically accurate nor explanatory. The point of bringing out the Murngin case was not to indulge in the provoking and stimulating intricacies of the complex social organizations of Australia, but rather to show that two "kinds of social order" or "two ways of viewing social organization"— descent *and* alliance—can be seen to be complementary. To stress one as against the other is to lead to confusion. To set both points of view in dialectical relation is, at least in this case, to bring order and understanding.

## CONCLUSION

In Chapters Five and Six we have tried to indicate a number of things. Alliance theory in the most basic sense represents an attempt to formulate structures in terms of relations rather than in terms of concrete elements. It seeks to reconceptualize the concrete facts of ethnographic phenomena in such a way that generalized structural forms can be seen in disparate cases, and these forms are seen to underly the cultural phenotypes which they represent. It may well be said that (see Maybury-Lewis, 1960) these first approximations to "true" structural analysis are misapplied, misdirected, and misleading. The methodological value of these demonstrations cannot be underestimated, however. If we may make an analogy to what might appear a similar development in the history of another science— astronomy—we can find the example of Copernicus instructive. What is now referred to as the "Copernican revolution" was seen as a "revolution" only in the selective eye of posterity. Copernicus indeed revived Aristarchus' conception of the heliocentric solar system, but his model of the universe included, as central postulates, erroneous, and nonpredictive elements that had been derived from Ptolemy, and he merely simplified by half the number of cycles that the scholastics had elaborated to "explain" the movement of celestial bodies. His models of the universe are crude and misleading—but

---

[9] Yalman (1962) has shown in the case of the Sinhalese kindred that a Dravidian terminology is perfectly consistent with a social organization that lacks unilineal descent groups altogether.

nevertheless revolutionary in their impact upon the growth of astronomy. It is perhaps the same with Lévi-Strauss' structural reconceptualization of dual systems.

In the smaller view (from the point of view of "theories of the middle range"), alliance theory has given us a fresh perspective on social structures, which has, at a minimum, given us the choice of an alternative view of social systems. The comparative-classificatory scheme of Radcliffe-Brown was a step forward, but it led inevitably to Procrustean interpretations of systems that did not fit. Thus the Murngin, for example, became a structural anomaly because they did not fit readily into the theoretical scheme then current.

There is room for more than one (or two, or more) ways of looking at social structure. Our knowledge of the logic of discovery is not so developed that we can afford to abandon any approach, if the approach yields results that can be verified, by acceptable canons of logic and/or probabilistic method. Descent theory (as of today) seems more clearly applicable to the examination of some systems rather than others. Many of the debates that have raged over the demonstration that such and such a system is an alliance system or a descent system have developed out of a psychological need to defend one's own position, and one's own view of the "type of society." The fact is that both points of view yield insights into social organization, and to reject one or the other is precipitate.

# Chapter Seven

# Mathematical Models of Marriage Systems

Mathematical models of symmetric and asymmetric alliance systems are derived from several related branches of modern mathematics; for example, graph theory, matrix algebra, the theory of games, and the theory of groups of permutations (Weil, 1949; Goldberg, 1958; White, 1963; Bush, 1963; Livingstone, 1965, 1966; and Kemeny, Snell, and Thompson, 1962a, 1965). Potentially, these models allow us to derive consequences, which are not always immediately obvious, from theoretical summaries or abstractions of "observed facts." The passage from induction to deduction need not, of course, employ the tools of logic and mathematics; but the methods of modern mathematics are particularly useful in allowing us to discern relationships between seemingly unrelated structures (Lévi-Strauss, 1955), in predicting previously unknown relations and properties, and in clarifying theoretical problems that have often been handled in an arbitrary manner. The models that are reviewed in this chapter should be carefully distinguished from the probability models of "cross-cultural research," which are closely related to the nondeterministic methods of statistical mechanics. Let us first consider some rather elementary game- and graph-theoretic models of symmetric and asymmetric alliance systems.

Mathematical models of parasitism and symbiosis suggest that various forms of "direct exchange" (symmetric alliance, trade relationships, and so on) may be considered a two-person, nonzero-sum game (Rapaport, 1963, pp. 546–549). We begin this section with a general note on symbiosis. Ecologists refer to organisms who live together in close physiological union as symbionts, and distinguish the condition of symbiosis from commensalism (in which the partners are not irrevocably committed to exist together) in terms of the following characteristics: (1) the intimacy of the relationship;

(2) the obligatory nature of the association; and (3) the mutuality of the resultant advantages. In a mathematical model of "symbiotic exchange," we consider the exchange between two societies, or groups ($X$ and $Y$) of commodities (e.g., women, labor) in the respective amounts $x$ and $y$. A porportion $p$ of the output of a given commodity is exchanged for a proportion $q$ of the output of the commodity produced by group $Y$. Each group, therefore, retains a proportion $p = 1 - q$ of its own output. The following assumptions are made

1. The commodities received by each group represent a positive, logarithmic contribution to that group's utility, and
2. Because of the labor involved, there is a negative, logarithmic contribution to a group's utility that is proportional to the output.

If we designate the utilities $S_x$ and $S_y$ (Rapaport, 1963, p. 547), then

$$S_x = \log (1 + px + qy) - \beta x, \quad \text{and} \tag{1}$$

$$S_y = \log (1 + qx + py) - \beta y. \tag{2}$$

Given any set of strategies (each descent group, village, or player has a continuum of strategies in the $x$- and $y$-space), the numerical values of the utilities may be computed by determining the values of $x$ and $y$ (the amounts of the respective commodities in locally defined units of measurement), $q$ (the proportion of group $X$'s output of the designated commodity that is received by group $Y$), and $p$ (the proportion of the retained output of the designated commodity), and solving for $S_x$ and $S_y$.

In choosing his strategy each player (group) naturally wishes to maximize his utility. But since he controls only one of the variables, all he can do is make the "best response" to each strategy chosen by his opponent, that is, choose that value of his variable which maximizes his own utility, *given* the choice of output by the other (Rapaport, 1963, p. 547).

In order to maximize its utility a group will attempt to regulate its output to bring the points $(x, y)$ on its own optimal line (Cournot lines). These optimal lines are defined by the following equations (Rapaport, 1963, p. 547):

$$L_x: px + qy = \frac{p}{\beta} - 1, \quad \text{and} \tag{3}$$

$$L_y: qx + py = \frac{p}{\beta} - 1, \tag{4}$$

and are obtained by setting $\partial Sx/\partial x$ and $\partial Sy/\partial y$ equal to zero (Rapaport, 1963, p. 547).

Intertribal relations in which commodities of one sort or another are exchanged, and various forms of intratribal exchange, or "retention" (symmetric alliance), have traditionally been characterized in communication concepts or in terms of such vague functionalist notions as "social" or "ecological" equilibrium. By assigning numerical values to utilities, and by considering a continuum of strategies (in the product space $x$, $y$), it is possible to define precisely such notions as "stable equilibrium" ($p > q$). The ethnographic or ethnological problem is to identify categories of behavior that obey the differential equations; for then interpretations are automatically supplied for all results that are deduced from the equations (cf. Kemeny and Snell, 1962b, pp. 4, 24–34). It is of some interest

to note that at the stable equilibrium neither of the two individuals (or groups) does as well as he could at the "Pareto point," at which the joint payoff is maximized. But the Pareto point cannot be reached if each individual "tries" to maximize his own utility. It can be reached only if the two coordinate their outputs . . . or if each attempts to maximize the joint payoff instead of his own (Rapaport, 1963, p. 548).

A consideration of a possible strategy continuum underlying restricted exchange underscores the model properties of the construct "symmetric" and allows us to account for the occasional and statistical asymmetry of ideologically symmetric systems. In the context of the political ideology and composition of descent groups (cf. Chapter Four), we have considered other methodological approaches to the strategic options and probability continua underlying jural formulations. If a statistical run of actual patterns of exchange could be shown to define a utility that approximates minimaximization, then the naive assumptions of complete conformity which certain structural-functionalists make "would have to be taken under further advisement" (Davenport, 1960, p. 10; Buchler and Nutini, 1968a).

We are now in a position to consider the Rapaport (1960, 1963) model of cooperation and exploitation in the general context of institutionalized reciprocity. Leach (1961b, p. 79) distinguishes three types of exchange relationship:

i. Relationship between social groups is expressed by the simultaneous or nearly simultaneous exchange of goods—the Trobriand Kula might be taken as an example (Leach, 1961b, p. 79).
ii. Relationship between social groups is expressed by the simultaneous or nearly simultaneous exchange of women—the Australian Kariera and Aranda marriage systems might be taken as examples (*échange restreint* in Lévi-Strauss' terminology) (Leach, 1961, p. 79).
iii. Relationship between social groups is expressed by the exchange of women for goods—formalized systems of asymmetrical cross-cousin marriage (*échange généralisé* in Lévi-Strauss' terminology) provide examples of this pattern (Leach, 1961b, p. 79).

In diagrammatically representing these exchange relationships, recall that each group controls a separate coordinate: $Y$ can move only vertically; $X$ only horizontally (cf. Rapaport, 1960, pp. 65–67). If we identify symmetric, direct, or simultaneous exchange (i. and ii.) with "stability," then the optimal lines in such a case are shown in Figure 7–1,

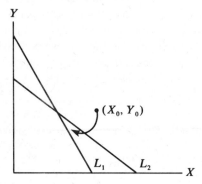

*Figure 7–1.   The Optimal Lines for Symmetric Exchange (adapted from Rapaport, 1960).*

and we may examine some formal properties of symmetric exchange.

Exchange is stable or symmetric if $X$'s optimal line is steeper than $Y$'s. If the labelling of the axes were interchanged, then stability would be indicated by the slope of $Y$'s optimal line. We have previously indicated that this will be the case if $p > q$.

The unstable situation is, however, of more general interest. Leach (1961b, p. 84) suggests that the two most general principles that govern the Kachin marriage system and, by implication, many other asymmetric systems, are "that a man will do everything possible to avoid marrying into a class beneath him, and that a man will seek to make the maximum profit—either in terms of brideprice or political advantage—out of the marriage of his daughters" (Leach, 1961b, p. 84).

In terms of Leach's (1961b, pp. 85–86) analysis, the general structure of the system may be described as "hypergamy reversed": "Women may marry into their own class or the class below, but never into the class above" (Leach, 1961b, p. 85). In this model situation, a man of a chiefly or aristocratic class seeks to maximize his profit—measured by bride price or political advantage—and consequently introduces an element of instability into the system. In Rapaport's (1960, p. 68) terminology, men of high ranking lineages rely on the efforts of others more than on their own. This statement should not be given too literal an interpretation. We simply mean that high ranking lineages derive their status, prestige, and political advantage from low ranking lineages: these are derived rather than endo-produced commodities. The instability ($q > p$) of the asymmetric case may be represented by letting the slope of $Y$'s optimal line exceed the slope of $X$'s (Rapaport, 1960, p. 66):

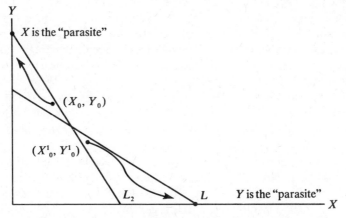

Figure 7–2.   The Instability $(q > p)$ of the Asymmetric Case
(adapted from Rapaport, 1960).

There is a sense in which our use of the term *parasite*, and the mathematical definition—from analytic geometry—of a parasitic relationship is theoretically interesting. There is a fundamental difference between the types of commodities exchanged in unstable systems. Women are natural products procreated by other biological individuals: they are alike so far as nature is concerned and can be considered as different only from the "cultural angle" (Lévi-Strauss, 1966, pp. 123–124). A homogeneous natural product is declared culturally heterogeneous; consequently they have to be exchanged (Lévi-Strauss, 1966, p. 125). Conversely, status and political advantage are culturally manufactured social products that are, in most societies, scarce commodities. To exchange natural products that are produced by all classes and are different or of a higher value only from a cultural angle, for intrinsically scarce commodities is, in a sense, to "produce nothing." This position defines a family of transformations that maps asymmetric exchange systems onto the mathematical theory of parasitism. If $X$ is a chiefly lineage and $Y$ is a low ranking or commoner lineage, then the situation may be mathematically represented by (Rapaport, 1960, p. 70):

$$qx + py = p/\beta - 1 \text{ is } Y\text{'s optimal line, where } X = 0^0. \qquad (5)$$

Consequently, $Y$ must "produce prestige" to satisfy the equation $Y = 1/\beta - 1/p$, where $\beta < p$ is assumed throughout (Rapaport, 1960, p. 70). The resultant utilities are

$$Sx = \log (1 + q/\beta - q/p), \qquad (6)$$

$$Sy = \log (p/\beta) - 1 + \beta/p. \qquad (7)$$

It is instructive to compare the Kachin alliance system with the Natchez class system (Swanton, 1911; Goldberg, 1958; Fischer, 1964). We have characterized the Kachin system, on a mathematical plane, as unstable or "self-destructive," for large bride price payments always move from commoners towards aristocrats and from aristocrats towards chiefs. From this property, Lévi-Strauss (1949, p. 325) infers that Kachin marriage classes will transform themselves into privileged classes of the Natchez type, and it is suggested that this is *"en contradiction avec le système, et doit donc entraîner sa ruine."* Leach (1961b, p. 89) has pointed out, however, that the main item in a bride price is a gift of cattle, "and cattle, among the Kachin, are a consumable commodity" (Leach, 1961b, p. 89). Through a process of redistribution in religious feasts, perishable wealth is converted into imperishable prestige "through the medium of spectacular feasting. The ultimate consumers of the goods are in this way the original producers, namely, the commoners who attend the feast" (Leach, *ibid.*). Despite the instability or asymmetry of the kinship system, the organization is in economic and political balance.

In a similar manner, the Natchez paradox derives from the following unstable or asymmetrical properties of Swanton's "collated model" of the Natchez class system:

1. There were four Natchez classes: Suns, Nobles, Honored, and Stinkards. The three upper classes had obligatory class exogamy and were obliged to marry members of the lowest (Stinkard) class.
2. Although social class membership was "generally matrilineal," the children of Sun men and Stinkard women became members of the Noble class, and the children of Noble men became members of the Honored class. The Nobles and Honored would therefore reproduce themselves through the progeny of their own women, as well as "receiving an additional increment in each generation by incorporating the descendants of Stinkard women married to Sun and Noble men" (Fischer, 1964, p. 53).
3. Depending on the initial size of the Sun class, the total size of the population, and the rate of polygyny in the Noble and Sun classes, a demographic crisis would ensue, given the jural framework of the system, in a computable number of generations (Fischer, 1964, p. 54; cf. Hart, 1943; Quimby, 1946). In the Kachin case, the instability of the system derives from the movement of prestige commodities; in the Natchez case, the instability derives from the movement of the offspring of "mixed marriages."

If we let a positive sign (+) stand for the "upward" movement of women, children, or prestige commodities, and a negative sign (−) stand for "downward" movement, then the situation may be roughly represented by

|  | Kachin | Natchez: Suns, Nobles, Honored | Natchez: Stinkards |
|---|---|---|---|
| Hypergamy | − | − | + |
| Return goods | + | − | + |

Goldberg (1958, p. 239) conveniently summarizes the reported Natchez descent and marriage rules in tabular form, in which each cell entry gives the class of a child in the corresponding margin and an $X$ indicates that the corresponding marriage is not allowed.

**Table 7–1. Natchez Marriage and Descent Rules**

|  |  | Father | | | |
|---|---|---|---|---|---|
|  |  | Sun | Noble | Honored | Stinkard |
|  | **Sun** | × | × | × | **Sun** |
|  | **Noble** | × | × | × | **Noble** |
| **Mother** |  |  |  |  |  |
|  | **Honored** | × | × | × | **Honored** |
|  | **Stinkard** | **Noble** | **Honored** | **Stinkard** | **Stinkard** |

(Adapted from Goldberg, 1958, p. 239, Table 4.3).

Goldberg's mathematical analysis of the Natchez system is based upon three assumptions: (1) each social class has an equal number of men and women in each generation; (2) each individual in the system marries once and only once; and (3) each married couple has exactly one daughter and one son. Goldberg (1958, pp. 240–241) develops a system of equations for the system, puts these equations into matrix form, performs a number of operations on this matrix and arrives at a column vector, which gives the number of either women or men in each of the four classes in any generation $n$. It is clear from this solution that there will be a limiting stable distribution *only if* Suns and Nobles are initially absent from the population. But with Suns and Nobles present, "The number of Stinkards decreases with $n$ until there are an insufficient number of Stinkard men to marry all the Sun, Noble, and Honored women as required by the marriage rules. Thus the social system as described cannot persist" (Goldberg, 1958, p. 241).

Fischer (1964, pp. 55–61), in his discussion of Goldberg's analysis, poses several possibilities: the model is inadequate or the ethnographic reports are mistaken. He (Fischer, 1964, p. 61) suggests that Natchez society may have been approaching an internal class-demographic crisis, but suggests a differential fertility solution to account for demographic viability. For it is clear that "once we introduce the assumptions of differential fertility of upper-class males and females in class-exogamic marriages and of a certain number of unmarried or late marrying individuals in times of class imbalance we see that increases in the Noble and Honored classes are not necessarily irreversible" (Fischer, 1964, p. 59).

These analyses point to a more general problem in the mathematical analysis of marriage systems: the resultant models fail to reckon with criterial anthropological problems. They have a relatively low information value for the social anthropologist. In the Natchez case, we might pose the following query: What significant issues are raised for ethnological theory? As we see it, these issues involve the relations of rules to behavior, the status of jural formulations in anthropological studies, and the types of rules that may be used for describing cultural systems. These issues are closely related. Rather than assuming that jural rules operate as absolute constraints on behavior, or, in the case of marriage systems, have prescriptive entailments, we assume that jural formulations are essentially probability statements, that they do not operate as absolute constraints on behavior. Further, as we have noted in previous chapters, it is of considerable importance to distinguish between ground rules that structure the basic cultural framework within which decision making occurs and strategy rules that allow individuals to operate within the options provided by the ground rules. Swanton's (1911) rules for the Natchez class system, which derive from early French reports, may quite reasonably be regarded as an idealized account of Natchez ground rules relevant to descent and marriage. Although these rules certainly have mathematical implications, it may be more productive from the viewpoint of ethnological theory to simulate the type of strategy rules that might have operated in a society with Natchez-type ground rules. Such an approach may be equally applicable to ground rule descriptions of this sort in other areas of the world. Our most basic assumption would not be a demographic one: it is simply that the Natchez knew what they were doing.

It is instructive, however, in many instances, to simulate the demographic processes of actual communities, taking into account such variables as child mortality, differential fertility, and so on. Simulations of this sort have yielded important preliminary results for both asymmetric and endogamic systems (Kunstadter et al., 1963; Gilbert and Hammel, 1966). For example, it seems that there is a close fit between (1) the probability of FBD marriage given by some relatively simple mathematical models and the results of a computer simulation, and (2) probabilities for FBD marriage derived from a mathematical model and the Gilbert-Hammel simulation (even though substantial differences exist between the demographic characteristics of the particular village in question and those characteristics assumed by the simulation).

Computer simulations are clearly complementary to formal axiomatic approaches. In a sense, simulated parameters are the axioms of computer programs that are designed to perform operations other than data processing and analysis. And both approaches suggest that any substantial progress in the analysis of marriage systems must ultimately be concerned with stochastic as well as deterministic processes. In speaking about jural rules as absolute constraints on behavior, social anthropology has managed, in a most consistent manner, to divorce itself from major methodological advances in the other behavioral sciences, which regard decision processes as the core problem in the study of behavioral systems.

## ASYMMETRIC ALLIANCE: GRAPH–THEORETIC MODELS

Informal as well as formal axiomatizations of asymmetric alliance systems often are based upon a tripartite division: wife-givers, wife-takers, and lineal kin. A cardinal rule of such systems on the plane of model construction is wife-givers and wife-takers are mutually exclusive categories. In terms of graph theory, generalized alliance systems are a type of directed graph or digraph known as tournaments. These graphs are mathematically isomorphic with (1) peck right relations in chickens (Rapaport, 1949); Lévi-Strauss' (1963a, pp. 227–228 orig. 1955) ordering of the variants of the Hopi myth of the origin of Shalako; and (3) the outcomes of a round robin tournament (Moon, 1963; Fulkerson, 1965; Livingstone, 1968).

For Livingstone's (1968) graph-theoretic model of the alliance relations between clans, we consider a matrix of 0's and 1's, where: (1) when clan $i$ gives women to clan $j$, the matrix entry $a_{ij} = 1$; when clan $i$ does not give women to clan $j$, the matrix entry $a_{ij} = 0$; consequently, all $a_{ii} = 0$, and if $a_{ij} = 1$, then $a_{ji} = 0$, so that for all $i$'s and $j$'s, $a_{ij} \cdot a_{ji} = 0$.

The result is an $n \times n$ skew symmetric matrix, when $n$ is the number of clans in the society. Since the row totals for the matrix are the number of clans each clan gives women to and the column totals are the number each clan receives women from, and all clans have one or the other relation with all the others, $a_i + a_j = (n - 1)$ and $\sum_{ij} a_{ij} = n(n - 1)/2$. For any such matrix the rows can be rearranged so that $0 \le a_1 \le a_2 \cdots \le a_n$ (Livingstone, 1966, p. 8; cf. Rapaport, 1963, p. 543).

Using this form of representation, a skew symmetric matrix and digraph for the "ideal marriage relations among Purum clans" is formulated by Livingstone (1968):

Clans

| | ♂ | M | MK | K | T | P | Total |
|---|---|---|---|---|---|---|---|
| | ♀ | | | | | | |
| Marrim | M | 0 | 1 | 1 | 0 | 1 | 3 |
| Makan | MK | 0 | 0 | 0 | 1 | 0 | 1 |
| Kheyang | K | 0 | 1 | 0 | 0 | 0 | 1 |
| Thao | T | 1 | 0 | 1 | 0 | 0 | 2 |
| Parpa | P | 0 | 1 | 1 | 1 | 0 | 3 |
| | Total | 1 | 3 | 3 | 2 | 1 | 10 |

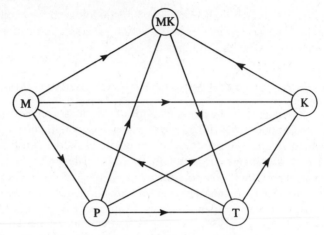

Figure 7–3.   The Ideal Marriage Relations Among the Clans of the Purum.

The matrix and digraph for Lévi-Strauss' (1949, p. 303; cf. Leach, 1951) Kachin model is (Livingstone, 1968)

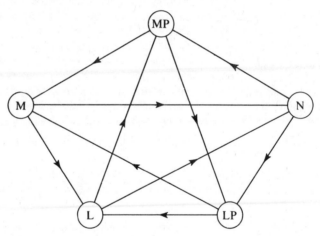

Clans

| | ♂ | M | MP | N | L | LP | Total |
|---|---|---|---|---|---|---|---|
| | ♀ | | | | | | |
| Maran | M | 0 | 0 | 1 | 1 | 0 | 2 |
| Marip | MP | 1 | 0 | 0 | 0 | 1 | 2 |
| Nkhum | N | 0 | 1 | 0 | 0 | 1 | 2 |
| Lathong | L | 0 | 1 | 1 | 0 | 0 | 2 |
| Laphai | LP | 1 | 0 | 0 | 1 | 0 | 2 |
| Totals | | 2 | 2 | 2 | 2 | 2 | 10 |

Figure 7–4.   The Ideal Marriage Relations Among the Kachin (after Lévi-Strauss, 1949, p. 303).

Table 7–2. The Ideal Marriage Relations and the Actual Marriages Among the Purum

(♂ = columns, ♀ = rows)

| | | $M_1$ | $M_2$ | $M_3$ | $M_4$ | $MK_1$ | $MK_2$ | $K_1$ | $K_2$ | $T_1$ | $T_2$ | $T_4$ | $P$ | Total |
|---|---|---|---|---|---|---|---|---|---|---|---|---|---|---|
| **Ideal** | $M_1$ | | | | | 0 | 1 | 0 | 0 | | | | 1 | 2 |
| | $M_2$ | | | | | 1 | 1 | 0 | 0 | 0 | 0 | 1 | 1 | 4 |
| | $M_3$ | | | | | 0 | 1 | 0 | 0 | 0 | 0 | | 1 | 2 |
| | $M_4$ | | | | | 0 | 1 | 1 | | 0 | 0 | | 1 | 3 |
| | $MK_1$ | 1 | 0 | 1 | 1 | | | 0 | | 1 | 1 | 1 | 0 | 6 |
| | $MK_2$ | 0 | 0 | 0 | 0 | | | 0 | | 1 | 1 | 1 | 0 | 3 |
| | $K_1$ | 1 | 1 | 1 | 0 | 1 | 1 | | | 0 | 0 | 0 | 0 | 5 |
| | $K_2$ | 1 | | 1 | | | | | | | | | | 2 |
| | $T_1$ | | 1 | 1 | 1 | 0 | 0 | 1 | | | | | 0 | 4 |
| | $T_2$ | | 1 | 1 | 1 | 0 | 0 | 1 | | | | | 0 | 4 |
| | $T_4$ | | 0 | 1 | | 0 | 0 | 1 | | | | | | 2 |
| | $P$ | 0 | 0 | 0 | 0 | 1 | 1 | 1 | | 1 | 1 | | | 5 |
| | **Total** | 3 | 3 | 6 | 3 | 3 | 6 | 5 | 0 | 3 | 3 | 3 | 4 | 39 |
| **Actual** | $M_1$ | | | | | | | | | | | | 4 | 4 |
| | $M_2$ | | | | | 5 | | (2) | (2) | | | | 4 | 13 |
| | $M_3$ | | | | | | | | | | | | | 0 |
| | $M_4$ | | | | | | | 2 | | | | | 10 | 12 |
| | $MK_1$ | 4 | | | 1 | | | | 2 | 2 | 10 | 2 | | 21 |
| | $MK_2$ | | | | | | | (1) | 2 | | 2 | | | 5 |
| | $K_1$ | 3 | | | (2) | 18 | 2 | | | | | (1) | (3) | 29 |
| | $K_2$ | 1 | | | 1 | 3 | | (3) | | | | | 3 | 11 |
| | $T_1$ | | 2 | 4 | | | | 3 | 4 | | | | | 13 |
| | $T_2$ | | 4 | | | | | 1 | | | | | | 5 |
| | $T_4$ | | | | | | | 4 | 1 | | | | | 5 |
| | $P$ | | | | | 2 | | 10 | 1 | 6 | 4 | | | 23 |
| | **Total** | 8 | 6 | 4 | 4 | 28 | 2 | 26 | 12 | 8 | 16 | 3 | 24 | 141 |

In both instances, the recorded wife-giving/wife-taking relations

$$\left[\sum_{i,j} a_{ij}\right] = 10, \quad \text{or} \quad n(n - 1)/2.$$

The score structure or row totals for the Purum model is (1, 1, 2, 3, 3); for the Kachin, (2, 2, 2, 2, 2). A complete hierarchy would have a score structure of (1, 2, 3, 4, 5), whereas the score structure of the "Kachin model" describes a system at equilibrium; Purum and Chawte (Livingstone, 1968) are, so to speak, intermediate cases. The Landau (1951; Rapaport, 1963, p. 543) hierarchy index may then be used to measure the departure of a given score structure from that of a complete hierarchy.

$$h = \frac{12}{N^3 - N} \sum_j \left( r_j - \frac{N-1}{2} \right)^2, \qquad \text{where}$$

$h$ is maximal ($=1$) for a complete hierarchy, $r_j = (N-1)/2$, ($j = 1, 2, \ldots, N$), $h = 0$, for an "egalitarian" order.

One step away from equilibrium would have one clan giving wives to $(n + 1)/2$ and one clan giving wives to $(n - 3)/2$ clans. There are $n!/(2!(n - 2)!)$ combinations of the clans which would result in this pattern and the variance is $2/n$. Two steps away with two clans giving to $(n - 3)/2$ and two clans to $(n + 1)/2$, the number of combinations is $6n!/(4!(n - 4)!)$ and the variance is $4/n$. Three steps away the variance is $6/n$ and at further steps it is $2x/n$ where $x$ is the number of steps away from the equilibrium order. Evolution of the social structure toward equilibrium would tend to reduce the variance in the number of clans each clan gives wives to. This seems quite similar to R. A. Fischer's Fundamental Theorem of Natural Selection which states that the amount of genetic change is proportional to the variance in fitness (Livingstone, 1965, p. 151).

The Landau hierarchy index provides a measure of the "evolution toward equilibrium" of generalized exchange systems, or of the relationship between an ideal ("egalitarian") order of exchange, on the one hand, and the actual scheme of alliances, in any particular case, on the other. Further, this measure suggests a method for (a) comparing status hierarchies from different domains, and (b) scaling various types of structures in terms of the degree to which they approximate a "complete hierarchy."

Mathematically, then, a generalized exchange system is described by the same graph as a round robin tournament: both are asymmetric digraphs, are unilateral, and have at least three points (Harary, Norman, and Cartwright, 1965, pp. 289–290). Translating wins and losses in tournaments into the language of marriage systems, we may say that to take a woman is to lose, to give a woman is to win. Consequently, we can speak of the outdegree of a point $v_i$ (any group that gives women) as the number of victories won by player $v_i$ (women given), in terms of Livingstone's analysis. The outdegree of a point $v_i$ is the points' score ($s_i$). What, then, is the score sequence of a generalized exchange system, or tournament ($T$). It is defined by the following theorem.

*Theorem.* A sequence of nonnegative integers $s_1 \leq s_2 \leq \cdots \leq s_p$ is a score sequence if and only if their sum satisfies the equation (Harary *et al.*, 1965, p. 291)

$$\sum_{i=1}^{p} s_i = \frac{p(p - 1)}{2} \text{ and,} \tag{1}$$

if the following inequalities hold for every positive integer $k < p$:

$$\sum_{i=1}^{k} s_i \geq \frac{k(k-1)}{2}. \qquad (2)$$

The score sequence for Livingstone's representation of the Purum alliance system is (1, 1, 2, 3, 3), which satisfies Equation 1, as the sum of the scores is 10, and the inequalities of Equation 2 are satisfied by

$$
\begin{aligned}
k &= 1, & 1 &\geq 0 \\
k &= 2, & 1 + 1 &\geq 1 \\
k &= 3, & 1 + 1 + 2 &\geq 3 \\
k &= 4, & 1 + 1 + 2 + 3 &\geq 6.
\end{aligned}
$$

Consider some of the theoretical and methodological implications of graph theory as a "descriptive model" (cf. Kemeny and Snell, 1962b, p. 6) in social anthropology.

In his critique of the Homans-Schneider (1955) theory, Needham (1962a, p. 79) considers marriages outside the mother's clan in the Purum system of descent and alliance. From an analysis of marriages from three villages, Needham (1962a, p. 79) illustrates "that no fewer than 26 (48.1 per cent) are with women of clans other than that of the mother." This distribution is described by Livingstone's score sequence, which satisfies Equations 1–2. Needham (1962a, p. 79) contends that this distribution has grave consequences for the Homans-Schneider theory, for

Their argument applies specifically and exclusively to marriage with the first cousin. It is conceivable that a theory of sentiments might help to elucidate marriage with such a close relative; but it is not readily conceivable how it could possibly apply to a situation in which nearly half the women married come from clans other than that of the mother. How could it ever be thought likely that marriages with all such women should be "sentimentally appropriate" in the way proposed by Homans and Schneider (Needham, 1962a, p. 79).

Is there any way of "testing" the Homans-Schneider theory, other than by correlational analysis or by an empirical analysis of marriage distributions in individual systems? We will attempt to demonstrate one of a family of interesting approaches to this problem.

That a certain class of marriage systems is defined by asymmetric properties and that this class is minimally defined by three points, clans or local groups, are important theoretical abstractions from factual observations. Recognizing that the formal properties of these systems are similar to that class of directed graphs known as tournaments, allow us to deduce consequences, which may not be immediately obvious, from our theoretical statements. The theorems of digraph theory are valid assertions about any empirical structures, such as asymmetric alliance systems, which satisfy the axioms of digraph theory. "The theorems thereby give additional information about empirical structures" (Harary *et al.*, 1965, p. 3). Consider the Purum case. For an asymmetric alliance system with five clans, or points, it is immediately obvious that, at the very least, several clans must exchange women with clans other than the mother's clan, if Equation (1) is satisfied; or $\sum_{i=1}^{p} s_i = 10$. Furthermore, by mathematical deduction, we have arrived at a general property of asymmetric systems which should be carefully distinguished from features of individual systems which are the product of empirical analysis. Virtually all of the theorems developed for tournaments allow us to derive general conclusions about asymmetric systems.

We would like to summarize this brief discussion of mathematical models of marriage systems in the following terms. At this stage in the development of anthropology, mathematical models may serve a dual purpose: (1) allowing us to see formal relationships between the properties of structures that are neither obvious nor trivial, and (2) providing us with interpretations for results that are deduced from our equations, allowing us to go beyond the information given. What is perhaps of most importance, at this point, is the development of constructions that entail logical and epistemological considerations, "which are most commonly known as coordinative definitions, designed to solve the problem of applying formal or analytical systems to empirical reality" (Nutini, n.d., p. 27).

# Chapter Eight
# Methods for the Analysis of Kinship Terminology

Whereas European anthropologists have been concerned with the meaning of kinship, meaning in the sense of the relationship of the kin system to the total society in which it occurs, recent American work has been concerned with definitions and classifications of kin terms and kin systems. *Meaning* has been restricted to attempts to map precisely the semantic components necessary to define kin-class assignment, attempts that owe much of their inspiration to modern linguistics, both structural and generative. The object has been, first, to discover the least number of criteria that would serve to distinguish one kin term from another. For instance, we could say that *son* differs from *father* in one component only, that of generation. Next, an analysis of the system is made, in which various formal orderings of the data are used to describe the relationships between classes of kin. The hope is that such structuring of the data will make it easier to understand and to compare, and also that the anthropologist's arrangements correspond to and are predictive of natural ordering, that is, the ordering that "makes sense" to the native informant.

In this section we present three methodological approaches that are of particular importance in the following chapters and we discuss the question of psychological reality of some of the classificatory schemata.

The first approach consists of a general introduction to transformational analysis, with particular reference to the domain "kinship terminology." The generality of our discussion allows us to suggest, on a provisional basis, that such a method of analysis may be interpreted substantively, as well as formally. This we hope to illustrate when, following Aoki (1966), distinctive features are mapped on transformations. If such an interpretation is accepted,

[165]

then we are led to the conclusion that transformational analysis may tell us something of interest about the structure of culture itself, as well as about our own view of this structure (but cf. Berlin, Breedlove, and Raven 1966, p. 275).

The second approach we discuss, in somewhat general terms, is scalogram analysis. And, finally, we review the basic concepts and operations of componential analysis.

## TRANSFORMATIONAL ANALYSIS

In formulating transformation rules, we begin with a set of theoretical constructs (rules and corollaries), which are intuitively derived from the data, and we demonstrate that these constructs will predict end products (kin-class assignments) that replicate the data. The adequacy of these theoretical constructs may be determined by observing whether their end products are, in fact, an accurate description of the data, and whether the operations producing these data are more economical than the operations of any alternative account that might be formulated.

A formalized theory of this sort will assign denotative types (biological kin types) to conceptual classes in very much the same way that a deductive theory provides an enumeration of a set of theorems. In this respect, a formalized theory will provide an enumeration of kin-class assignments in a manner similar to the way that a linguistic theory generates the grammatical sequences that are the sentences of a language. However, transformational analysis is based on semantic elements and such a semantic theory produces *meaningful* strings of concatenated primary kin types, whereas a grammar generates sentences that are grammatical, but not necessarily meaningful (Chomsky, 1957, p. 15).

A formal account of a body of empirical data may be distinguished from functional or historical accounts by its sufficiency and its economy. The sufficiency of a formal account consists in its ability to predict accurately and completely the elements of the body of data which is to be accounted for. The economy of a formal theory consists in its ability to minimize the number of causes necessary to account accurately for the empirical data. A formal theory consists of (1) a set of primitives or symbol tokens and (2) set of rules, sentences, or axioms. When the latter are applied to the former, the theory will predict back the data in question. That is to say, in formal terms, the assignment of any kin type to a labeled kin class is deducible, as a theorem, from the axiom set (i.e., the rules and corollaries) or calculus. A formal theory of this type satisfied the criterion of descriptive adequacy but not the higher-order criterion of explanatory adequacy.

The theoretical constructs from which we derive kin-class assignments take the form of rewrite rules. A rewrite rule is a formulation that changes one set of symbols (in our case, kin types) into another set of symbols. Two types of rules must be formulated to account for kin-class assignments: expansion and reduction rules, on the one hand, and transformation rules, on the other.

Expansion and reduction rules belong to the same logical type; one is obtained from the other by interchanging the terms of a proposition. An expansion rule may be represented abstractedly as $X \rightarrow XY$, where this is to be read as an instruction to rewrite $X$ as $XY$ in whatever context $X$ occurs. All the following derivations are correct applications of the foregoing instructions:

$$
\begin{aligned}
X &\rightarrow XY \\
&\rightarrow XYY \\
&\rightarrow XYYY \\
&\rightarrow XYYYY
\end{aligned}
\tag{1}
$$

$$
\begin{aligned}
ZX &\rightarrow ZXY \\
&\rightarrow ZXYY \\
&\rightarrow ZXYYY
\end{aligned}
\tag{2}
$$

$$
\begin{aligned}
XZ &\rightarrow XYZ \\
&\rightarrow XYYZ \\
&\rightarrow XYYYZ
\end{aligned}
\tag{3}
$$

$$
\begin{aligned}
ZXW &\rightarrow ZXYW \\
&\rightarrow ZXYYW \\
&\rightarrow ZXYYYW
\end{aligned}
\tag{4}
$$

The instruction to rewrite $X$ as $XY$ may be restricted to certain contexts by preposing or postposing three dots to the symbols in a formulation. Thus, $\ldots X \rightarrow \ldots XY$ is to be read as an instruction to rewrite $X$ as $XY$ only when $X$ is preceded by one or more symbols. Of the four derivations shown, only the second and fourth would now be acceptable interpretations of the instruction to rewrite $\ldots X$ as $\ldots XY$. The first and third are unacceptable interpretations because $X$ is not preceded by a symbol at any step in the derivation.

The instruction to rewrite $X$ as $XY$ may also be restricted to certain contexts by postposing three dots to these symbols. Thus, $X \ldots \rightarrow XY \ldots$ is to be read as an instruction to rewrite $X$ as $XY$ only when $X$ is followed by one or more symbols. Of the foregoing derivations, only the third and fourth would be acceptable interpretations of the instruction to rewrite $X \ldots$ as $XY \ldots$. The first and second are unacceptable interpretations of the instruction because $X$ is not followed by a symbol in the initial step of the derivation.

A reduction rule may be formulated by a process of logical conversion from an expansion rule, that is, by interchanging the terms in an expansion statement. An expansion rule of the form $X \rightarrow XY$ may be converted into a reduction rule of the form $XY \rightarrow X$. A set of reduction rules may therefore be represented abstractly as (a) $XY \rightarrow X$, (b) $\dots ZW \rightarrow \dots Y$, and (c) $XW \dots \rightarrow Z \dots$. The operation of these rules (a, b, c) may be clarified by using them to reduce a string of symbols ($XXWW$), as follows:

$$
\begin{aligned}
XXWW &\rightarrow XZW & \text{(by rule c)} \\
&\rightarrow XY & \text{(by rule b)} \\
&\rightarrow X & \text{(by rule a).}
\end{aligned} \tag{5}
$$

At each step in the foregoing derivation, it should be noted, one and only one rule (a, b, or c) will operate upon a string of symbols. This is a desideratum. If two or more rules will operate upon a kin type string then an ordering rule must be formulated that specifies the order in which the rules may be applied. It is preferable that rules do not conflict with one another.

A reduction series is terminated when there remain no symbols in a derivation that are to be found in the appropriate context and combination on the left side of a reduction rule. Although $X$, in the terminal step of the foregoing derivation, is represented on the left side of rules (a) and (c), its context is restricted to the forms $XY$ and $XW \dots$, respectively. The functional difference between expansion and reduction rules may be summarized as follows: An expansion rule will "project" from a genealogical kernel to an infinite set of kin-class assignments; a reduction rule will reduce an infinite set of kin types to the genealogical kernels to which they are structurally equivalent. A genealogical kernel is, in formal terms, a terminal derivation.

Transformation rules differ from both reduction and expansion rules. A transformation rule specifies that one symbol is to be substituted for another symbol in a string of symbols, without expanding or reducing the number of symbols in any given derivation. A set of transformation rules may therefore be represented abstractedly as (1) $WW \rightarrow ZW$, (2) $\dots ZX \rightarrow \dots WY$, and (3) $ZY \dots \rightarrow XW \dots$. These transformation rules and the reduction rules already cited are applied together in the following derivation:

$$
\begin{aligned}
ZWWZX &\rightarrow ZZWZX & \text{(by rule 1)} \\
&\rightarrow ZYZX & \text{(by rule b)} \\
&\rightarrow XWZX & \text{(by rule 3)} \\
&\rightarrow ZZX & \text{(by rule c)} \\
&\rightarrow ZWY & \text{(by rule 2).}
\end{aligned} \tag{6}
$$

We begin this derivation with a string of symbols ($ZWWZX$) and a set of rules. At each step, we scan the rules in order to determine the transformations or reductions that we are instructed to perform upon the string. When we have produced a string for which there are no additional reduction or transformation instructions, a derivation is terminated.

In an analysis of Nez Perce and Proto-Sahaptian kinship terms, Aoki (1966, pp. 361–362) has formulated transformation rules in terms of distinctive features. Before reformulating the foregoing rules, consider briefly the notion of distinctive features in a somewhat more inclusive linguistic and ethnological context. First consider the Jakobson-Halle (1956; Jakobson, Fant, and Halle, 1961) theory of "the feature level of language," and then Lévi-Strauss' (1966) "ethnological mapping" of distinctive features in the form of transformation rules.

"Linguistic analysis gradually breaks down complex speech units into morphemes as the ultimate constituents endowed with proper meaning and dissolves these minute semantic vehicles into their ultimate constituents, capable of differentiating morphemes from each other" (Jakobson and Halle, 1956, pp. 3–4). In the Jakobson-Halle theory of "the feature level of language," distinctive features are formulated in terms of binary choices; a linguistic message confronts a listener with a series of yes-no decisions. On the phonological level as well, the bundles of features called *phonemes* are characterized by similar oppositions albeit of a physical and motor kind; thus, the grave/acute opposition is "correspondingly opposed by the distribution of energy at the ends of the spectrum and on the motor level by the size and shape of the resonating cavity" (Jakobson and Halle, 1956, p. 4; cf. Jakobson, Fant, and Halle, 1961; Jakobson, 1962). For example, the minimal distinctions (grave vs. acute and diffuse vs. compact) in the pair *bitter/detter* are acoustically characterized by a concentration of energy in the lower (vs. upper) frequencies of the spectrum, and by a higher (vs. lower) concentration of energy in a relatively narrow, central region of the spectrum, accompanied by an increase (vs. decrease) of the total amount of energy, respectively (Jakobson and Halle, 1956, pp. 29, 31).

Codes of this type are usually referred to as digital devices; they are of a plus/minus, yes/no type. Conversely, devices of a more-or-less type, those which deal with measured quantities, and the connections between these quantities, are known as *analog-mechanisms*. Structural semantics, as practiced by Lévi-Strauss (e.g., 1945, 1955, 1963a, 1964, 1965, 1967), involves, for the most part, the (a) study of binary processes in the operation of cultural systems, and (b) assumption that binary oppositions ("distinctive features") may be established on an a priori basis (cf. Buchler, 1966c). More precisely, it is assumed that a finite number of oppositions are permuted in a limited series of combinations that underlie folk classifications. "Lévi-Strauss would like to believe that cultural systems can be shown to incorporate a very limited number of universal cultural distinctive features" (Leach, 1965, p. 775).

For example, in his discussion of Needham's (1954, 1959b) study of Penan mourning terms, Lévi-Strauss (1966, pp. 194–198) accounts for (a) necronyms (mourning terms), (b) teknonyms, and (c) autonyms, as well as three types of periodicity in the passage from one form to another, in terms of two dimensions, formulated in binary terms.[1] Let us first attempt to clarify the distinction between necronyms, teknonyms, and autonyms. When one's elder brother (or sister) dies, his (or her) siblings and parents relinquish their autonyms (e.g., John, Mary) or teknonyms (Bob's father *or* mother) and are addressed as "elder sibling dead" *or* "elder child dead" (by necronym). At the birth of a new child, siblings go from necronym to autonym and parents from necronym to teknonym. Teknonyms and necronyms are relational categories, as they state a relationship between Ego and another person. There are, however, two relevant distinctions: (1) necronyms define a relation only to declare it extinct; (2) teknonyms define a relation, as well as designate a unique individual.[2] An autonym defines an opposition between "self" and "others," rather than declaring a relation. There are, then, two features: (1) Relation, stated (+) or absent (−); (2) Opposition between self and others stated (+) or absent (−). Thus, the relation between necronyms and autonyms is one of inverted symmetry.

| Features | Necronym | Autonym | Teknonym |
|---|---|---|---|
| **Relation, present (+) or absent (−)** | + | − | + |
| **Oppsoition, present (+) or absent (−)** | − | + | + |

Or

$$\text{Necronym} \rightarrow \begin{bmatrix} + R \\ - 0 \end{bmatrix}$$ I exist by virtue of the relationship with my dead son. I am *not* an individual as *opposed* to all the world but a class member of those "eldest sons dead." I am not a unique event, but rather a member of a set.

$$\text{Autonym} \rightarrow \begin{bmatrix} - R \\ + 0 \end{bmatrix}$$ I am myself as against all the world. I am a unique event.

$$\text{Teknonym} \rightarrow \begin{bmatrix} + R \\ + 0 \end{bmatrix}$$ I am a unique event, set off as opposed to all the world by virtue of my relation to my child.

These distinctive features constitute the ultimate constituents capable of differentiating sememes from one another (cf. Jakobson and Halle, 1956, pp. 3–4). What we have done here is an exercise in analysis, demonstrating

[1] A *necronym* is a designation that is applied to a person by virtue of his relation with a deceased relative. An approximate example would be "eldest son dead"—a name applied to a person whose eldest child had died. A *teknonym* is a designation applied to a person by virtue of his relation to his child. An example might be "Bob's father." An *autonym* is applied to a person independent of his relation to other relatives, living or dead. Christian names for us are autonyms.

[2] In our view *John* as in *John* Bull and *John* Bright are homonyms. Their referential meaning is different in each case.

that if we use formal criteria of a binary kind, we can differentiate between name-types in an economical and clear manner.

But the point of the exercise is not to introduce the reader to "mourning terms" in Penan, but rather suggest that the same kind of method of explanation is useful in the formulation of transformation rules. If we can reduce primary kin types to bundles of distinctive features, and if we can display the transformation rules in a matrix of distinctive features, we may well be able to economize on our presentation of transformation rules, and thereby achieve a greater parsimony for our presentation as a whole.

First (following Aoki, 1966) we have to define our eight primary types in terms of binary principles (present/absent), and then reformulate the transformation rules in matrix form, utilizing these binary features. Next we will see that by so doing we can reduce each type of transformation rule (half-sibling, strong merging, weak merging) with its corollaries to one statement in the form of a distinctive feature matrix.

The features used by Aoki (1966, p. 361) to define eight primary kin types depend upon three of the eight "principles of relationship" enumerated by Kroeber in 1909

| *Kroeber* | *Aoki* |
|---|---|
| 1. The difference between persons of the same and of separate generations. | 1. Generational removal. |
| 2. The sex of the relative. | 2. Masculinity. |
| 3. The distinction of blood relatives from connections by marriage. | 3. Consanguinity. |

As the opposition for feature **1** (generational removal) does not indicate either direction or degree of removal, a seniority feature (4) is introduced. With these four features, either present (+) or absent (−), we can define the eight primary kin types.

The matrix follows

| Features | F | M | B | Z | S | D | H | W |
|---|---|---|---|---|---|---|---|---|
| **Masculinity** | + | − | + | − | + | − | + | − |
| **Generational removal** | + | + | − | − | + | + | − | − |
| **Seniority** | + | + | − | − | − | − | − | − |
| **Consanguinity** | + | + | + | + | + | + | − | − |

Thus, the kin type F would be written:

$$\begin{bmatrix} + \text{ mas.} \\ + \text{ g.r.} \\ + \text{ sen.} \\ + \text{ con.} \end{bmatrix} .$$

Juxtaposition of primary kin types is indicated by juxtaposing "bundles" of features:

$$MB \rightarrow \begin{bmatrix} -\text{ mas.} \\ +\text{ g.r.} \\ +\text{ sen.} \\ +\text{ con.} \end{bmatrix} \begin{bmatrix} +\text{ mas.} \\ -\text{ g.r.} \\ -\text{ sen.} \\ +\text{ con.} \end{bmatrix} .$$

Constraints on the application of rules are rewritten as follows:

1. Preposed dots: $\ldots ZY \rightarrow \ldots X$, as

$$\begin{bmatrix} \quad \end{bmatrix}\begin{bmatrix} \quad \end{bmatrix} \rightarrow \begin{bmatrix} \quad \end{bmatrix} \text{ in env. } X \underline{\quad},$$

where $X$ = the constraints imposed on rewrite rules by $\ldots$ preposing *or* postposing kin types.

2. Postposed dots: $ZY \ldots \rightarrow X \ldots$, as

$$\begin{bmatrix} \quad \end{bmatrix}\begin{bmatrix} \quad \end{bmatrix} \rightarrow \begin{bmatrix} \quad \end{bmatrix} \text{ in env. } \underline{\quad} X.$$

3. Either preposed or postposed dots and Mars or Venus symbols: $\male X \ldots \rightarrow \male Y \ldots$, as

$$\begin{bmatrix} \quad \end{bmatrix} \rightarrow \begin{bmatrix} \quad \end{bmatrix} \text{ in env. } [+\text{ mas.}] \underline{\quad} X.$$

Thus, the four half-sibling rules may be written:

$$1: \quad FS \rightarrow B \overbrace{\begin{bmatrix} +\text{ mas.} \\ +\text{ g.r.} \\ +\text{ sen.} \\ +\text{ con.} \end{bmatrix}}^{A} \overbrace{\begin{bmatrix} +\text{ mas.} \\ +\text{ g.r.} \\ -\text{ sen.} \\ +\text{ con.} \end{bmatrix}}^{B} \rightarrow \overbrace{\begin{bmatrix} +\text{ mas.} \\ -\text{ g.r.} \\ -\text{ sen.} \\ +\text{ con.} \end{bmatrix}}^{C}$$

$$2:\ MS \to B\ \begin{bmatrix} -\ \text{mas.} \\ +\ \text{g.r.} \\ +\ \text{sen.} \\ +\ \text{con.} \end{bmatrix} \begin{bmatrix} +\ \text{mas.} \\ +\ \text{g.r.} \\ -\ \text{sen.} \\ +\ \text{con.} \end{bmatrix} \to \begin{bmatrix} +\ \text{mas.} \\ -\ \text{g.r.} \\ -\ \text{sen.} \\ +\ \text{con.} \end{bmatrix}$$

$$3:\ FD \to Z\ \begin{bmatrix} +\ \text{mas.} \\ +\ \text{g.r.} \\ +\ \text{sen.} \\ +\ \text{con.} \end{bmatrix} \begin{bmatrix} -\ \text{mas.} \\ +\ \text{g.r.} \\ -\ \text{sen.} \\ +\ \text{con.} \end{bmatrix} \to \begin{bmatrix} -\ \text{mas.} \\ -\ \text{g.r.} \\ -\ \text{sen.} \\ +\ \text{con.} \end{bmatrix} .$$

Consider (1). First, in column A we score F on the features mas.(+), g.r.(+), sen.(+), and con.(+) and juxtapose this bundle of features to the scored features underlying the kin type S (in column B). As there are no contextual constraints $[X, \mp \text{mas.}]$ on these juxtaposed bundles of features, we reduce (A) and (B) to (C: + mas., − g.r., − sen., + con.) in whatever context they (A, B) occur.

$$4:\ MD \to Z\ \begin{bmatrix} -\ \text{mas.} \\ +\ \text{g.r.} \\ +\ \text{sen.} \\ +\ \text{con.} \end{bmatrix} \begin{bmatrix} -\ \text{mas.} \\ +\ \text{g.r.} \\ -\ \text{sen.} \\ +\ \text{con.} \end{bmatrix} \to \begin{bmatrix} -\ \text{mas.} \\ -\ \text{g.r.} \\ -\ \text{sen.} \\ +\ \text{con.} \end{bmatrix} .$$

One of the advantages of formulating transformation rules in terms of distinctive features is that we are able to combine rules. For example, the four half-sibling rules may be combined in a single *"alpha-rule"* (Aoki, 1966, p. 361):

$$\begin{bmatrix} \\ +\ \text{g.r.} \\ +\ \text{sen.} \\ +\ \text{con.} \end{bmatrix} \begin{bmatrix} \alpha\ \text{mas.} \\ +\ \text{g.r.} \\ -\ \text{sen.} \\ +\ \text{con.} \end{bmatrix} \to \begin{bmatrix} \alpha\ \text{mas.} \\ -\ \text{g.r.} \\ -\ \text{sen.} \\ +\ \text{con.} \end{bmatrix}, \text{ where } \alpha = \pm.$$

An "alpha-rule" is merely a written convention allowing us to combine both plus and minus features in the same expression. Where NO feature marker appears, the feature is immaterial; it can take any value, and it does not depend on any other expression as to which value is assigned. For example, the matrix

$$\begin{bmatrix} +\ \text{g.r.} \\ +\ \text{sen.} \\ +\ \text{con.} \end{bmatrix}$$

carries the meaning "parent of either sex." An alpha ($\alpha$) is introduced in expressions to indicate that whatever value is assigned to the expression where it first appears will be subsequently assigned wherever the alpha appears. For example, given two matrices

$$
\begin{bmatrix} \alpha \text{ mas.} \\ + \text{ g.r.} \\ + \text{ sen.} \\ + \text{ con.} \end{bmatrix} \rightarrow \begin{bmatrix} \alpha \text{ mas.} \\ - \text{ g.r.} \\ - \text{ sen.} \\ + \text{ con.} \end{bmatrix}
$$

would mean (1) F → B and (2) M → Z. If alpha has a plus value in the first expression, then it will in the second. When we assign a minus value in the first expression (M), then so also we will assign a minus value in the second. When an alpha is followed in a subsequent matrix by a minus alpha, then we must change the value assignment. Thus the following matrix would read, (1) FZ → M (2) MB → F:

$$
\begin{bmatrix} \alpha \text{ mas.} \\ + \text{ g.r.} \\ + \text{ sen.} \\ + \text{ con.} \end{bmatrix} \begin{bmatrix} -\alpha \text{ mas.} \\ - \text{ g.r.} \\ - \text{ sen.} \\ + \text{ con.} \end{bmatrix} \rightarrow \begin{bmatrix} -\alpha \text{ mas.} \\ + \text{ g.r.} \\ + \text{ sen.} \\ + \text{ con.} \end{bmatrix} .
$$

A summary can be given as follows. The framework of distinctive features has two parts: the substantive and the formal. The substantive is made up of a small number of features that are, we may assume, *minimally necessary* for describing all the kinship terminologies of the world. The formal properties of distinctive features may be defined by the following concepts: (1) they are relational; (2) they are binary; and (3) they make up segments such as primary kin types in the form of complexes of features rather than in the form of indivisible units. A plus mark indicates a feature which the segment or kin type in question does possess; a minus mark, a feature which the segment does not possess. The logic, however, can be thought of as three-valued because a zero can be used and zero in a "code book" means either plus or minus. Further, the questions which the analyst asks of each kin type are disjunctive either/or questions rather than yes/no question, for the absence of an attribute $X$ usually means the presence of another attribute $Y$, and the presence of $X$ conversely means the absence of $Y$. This implies implicational rules of the form Is it *male*? If no (−), then it is *female*. Thus it is difficult to state that the logic underlying the distinctive feature framework is truly binary.

## SCALOGRAM ANALYSIS

Scaling may be defined as a process for ordering qualitative data within hierarchies. Although scalogram analysis was initially developed for attitude measurement, Guttman (1944, p. 142) has emphasized that "Scaling analysis is a formal analysis, and hence applies to any universe of qualitative data of any science, obtained by any manner of observation." The most basic concept of scale theory is the universe of attributes. The universe consists of all the attributes that define the concept being measured. If we are interested in Iroquois-type kin systems, the term *attribute* may be used interchangeably with qualitative variable and our qualitative variables will be terminological equations (e.g., FZS = MBS). The determination of the presence or absence of any given variable must be determined for each unit (system) that is to be scaled. Any system must receive either a positive (+) or a negative (−) score for the terminological equations that define the concept of an Iroquois system. If a system receives a positive score for variable $X$ (e.g., FZS = MBS), then it cannot receive a negative score (FZS ≠ MBS) for the same variable; in Guttman's (1950c, p. 335) terms, a system cannot score in the opposite categories (FZS = MBS and FZS ≠ MBS) for any item (variable).

There are several limiting conditions on the "transformation" of terminological equations into scale variables. (1) A given equation must be reported for all systems or for a sizeable proportion of the terminological systems under consideration. (2) Given condition (1), a terminological equation must "maximize" the coefficient of reproducibility; that is, an equation that greatly increases scale errors is rejected. Other than this methodological criterion, we impose no other constraints on the introduction of equations. The base variable, however, must, by definition, be reported for all systems and must be justified by some theoretical rationale (e.g., the Spier or Murdock definitional criteria). To be somewhat more specific,

1. We will see that Iroquois or Omaha systems as traditionally defined vary enormously with respect to their formal properties.
2. They vary so widely that we might be led to assume that the label *Iroquois or Omaha system* is meaningless. It subsumes systems that are so different from one another that it might be better to discard this holistic notion and break down so-called Iroquois systems into their constituent types.
3. If we are *not* to do this we must show that the concept of "Iroquois or Omaha system" is unitary, by demonstrating that a scale of Iroquois or Omaha systems is a unidimensional scale—which means, in turn, that we are measuring one thing, and not a heterogeneous mixture of things.
4. We will assume that if our coefficient of reproducibility is high (over .90), then the traditional concept is unitary. Empirically we will have shown it is unidimensional, and that Spier, Murdock, and Lowie were able (despite the wide variation in empirical systems) to discriminate criteria that differentiated a system type from other system types. In this sense our capacity to scale systems will validate the type classification.
5. The Lounsbury classification of kinship terminologies (cf. Chapters Ten, Eleven) differs from the Murdock-Spier-Kirchoff typology only in the assignment of criteriality to a wider segment of the genealogical space.

It is a more ethnologically meaningful typology; it is not a measure. Mapping kinship terminologies onto the machinery of scalogram analysis provides a weak (ordinal) measure of ethnological constructs. Scalogram analysis therefore provides a primitive measure rather than merely another primitive typology. (But cf. Scheffler, 1967.)

We begin our analysis with a finite set of variables (derived from the data), which define the concept being measured. The rank order of these variables divides the initial group of systems into subsets; these subsets are what Guttman calls *scale types*. A scale type refers to all the kinship systems that display the number of terminological equations defining the type. The systems are ordered from 1, 2 . . . *n*, according to the number of equations—the greater the number, the higher the scale type. Individual scores for systems are determined by assigning integers in order (e.g., 1, 2, 3, 4, 5) to the scale types. Additional variables may increase the number of scale types; they will not interchange the ordering of systems that have previously been scaled. We arrive at an important methodological point for the scales that has been constructed in this study; they by necessity deal with a "sample" of variables, but scalogram theory shows that if the universe of attributes measures a single variable (e.g., the concept of an Iroquois system), then the same rank order of systems will be obtained regardless of which sample of attributes (terminological equations) is drawn from the universe (Guttman, 1950a, p. 81). The notion that a universe of attributes measures a single concept is referred to as unidimensionality.

The unidimensionality of a scalogram account assures us that the scalable attributes are the predictable consequences of an underlying principle. The scale measures the logical unfolding of the principle in question; the logically possible forms through which Iroquois systems may transform are reduced to a single variable (terminological equation) at each scale step, thus allowing us to demonstrate that logical priority can be assigned to certain terminological equations.

The basic methodological problem in scaling is determining the arrangement of the variables that will yield the maximum coefficient of reproducibility. The computation of the coefficient of reproducibility (Guttman, 1950a, p. 77) is

$$1 - \frac{\text{no. of errors}}{\text{no. of equations}} \times \text{no. of societies.}$$

The coefficient expresses the relationship between the multivariate distribution of a scale without errors and the obtained multivariate distribution in any particular case (Guttman, 1950a, p. 77). The reliability of any scale is indexed by the extent to which repeated measurements may be expected to result in similar results (cf. Green, 1954, p. 339). The aspect of reliability we are concerned with has been variously called *test-retest reliability* (Guttman, 1945, 1946) and *stability*. If the body of data being scaled is not subject to conscious modification, then the reliability of a scale is assured.

Before we state the predictive properties of a scalogram matrix, let us take a simple example for those unfamiliar with the Guttman technique. Those familiar with scaling should skip this section. Some years ago one of the authors was attempting to construct a Guttman scale of acculturation in a Mexican village. He gave a questionnaire to a sample of subjects and asked them among other things to report on the following items:

1. whether they spoke any Spanish;
2. whether they (if respondent was female) or their wives wore shoes;
3. whether they had listened to the radio in the past week;
4. whether they had bought a newsmagazine over the past six months.

After the answers to these questions were collated it was found that a large percentage of the population spoke some Spanish; a smaller proportion (women or wives) wore shoes; a still smaller proportion listened to a radio (once a week or more); and a still smaller proportion had bought a newspaper or magazine in the past six months. These were not the only items that were asked, but will do for illustration. The question was then put to the data to see if any of those whose wives wore shoes did not speak any Spanish. The number was almost nil. Next whether any of those who listened to the radio more than once a week did not wear shoes or speak any Spanish. The number was small. Lastly, whether any of those who had at some point in the past year bought a newsmagazine had not listened to the radio over the past week, had women who did not wear shoes, or did not speak Spanish. Again, the number of respondents was very small. Thus, out of this data we could construct a Guttman scale, knowing that if a person bought a newsmagazine, the chances were extremely high that they would (1) listen to the radio, (2) have women who wore shoes, and (3) speak at least a little Spanish. We could diagram the scale as follows:

| | Response Type | | | |
|---|---|---|---|---|
| Item | I | II | III | IV |
| 1. Speak Spanish | YES | YES | YES | YES |
| 2. Wore shoes | No | YES | YES | YES |
| 3. Listened radio | No | No | YES | YES |
| 4. Newsmagazine | No | No | No | YES |

Assuming that all the answers given by the respondents were of this type, the coefficient of reproducibility would be 1.000. With any Guttman scale of kinship systems the problem is the same. Take the example of Iroquois kinship terminologies. Instead of respondents we have reported Iroquois systems (and as we shall see there are 41 systems under examination). Instead of substantive behavioral questions we have terminological equations. And the type number corresponds to the number of terminological equations that are reported in the data. In two systems, for example (Ittik and Kapauku), there are four terminological equations; in these systems (1) FZS = MBS, (2) FZD = MBD, (3) FBS = B, and (4) FBD = Z. Therefore, for convenient shorthand we say that this is a type four Iroquois system. The full roster of terminological equations is found in type ten systems; there are ten terminological equations by which we index these systems. Equation number 10 is M = MZ. If we know that an Iroquois system displays this equivalence, then the chances are extremely high that it will display the other nine, just as we knew (in the example) that if a person had bought a newsmagazine in the past year, the chances were extremely high that they would have responded affirmatively to the other three questions.[3] With this example in mind, let us state in more formal terms what the scale predicts in the case of Iroquois kinship systems. The following rule will clarify the predictive properties of the scale.

In the case that an equation is not reported in the data we can predict the probable presence of the equation by knowing the predictability of the whole scale. If we find, for example, that an ethnographer reports that in a system, for example, Guahibo (see page 222), displays the terminological equation F = FB, which is scale type nine (see page 223), but the ethnographer does not report whether equations eight and seven are present (merging of all −2 generation consanguineals; merging of all +2 generation consanguineals), we can predict with 95.5 per cent accuracy that these equations are present from our knowledge of the coefficient of reproducibility. It is 95.5 per cent certain then that the Guahibo do, in fact, merge all −2 generation relatives into one term (variable eight) and that they do merge all +2 generation relatives into one term (variable 7).

The following graphic rule will clarify the predictive properties of the scale:

When a ± is preceded by a 0 or a ±, predict downward, filling in the terminological equation that is located on the axis which is denoted by the 0 or ± in question. The methodological notion predict downward indicates that ethnographically unreported terminological equations may be predicted on a probabilistic basis, if they are superseded on the scale (for the system in question) by a positive score (+) for any terminological equation. On a statistical level, the probability that predictions of this sort are accurate is indicated by the coefficient of reproducibility of the Iroquois scale. A scale with a coefficient of reproducibility of 0.955

---

[3] It should be noted that many of these equations are characteristic of other "types" of terminological systems (Scheffler, 1967); however, the most basic discussions of ordinal measures invariably indicate the distinct importance of considering the interrelationship of scale variables in a matrix, rather than isolated items.

indicates that the probability of accurate downward prediction for any unreported equation is 0.955.

From this rule several limitations on predicting equations follow:

a. When there are no ±'s which supersede a 0 in the hierarchy the rule does not apply, to that 0.
b. The generating rule applies only to 0's or ±'s. A dash (—) indicates that a unit has scored in the nonscalable category of an item (Guttman, 1950c, p. 335).

In the following diagram, all of the items (regardless of their content), i.e., 1–4, may be generated, for individual three, as all of the items score in the scalable category, viz., all axes receive a positive score for individual three. Items four, three, and one may be generated for individual two, as there is no information (0) for item three, and item two has scored in the nonscalable category (—). Items one and two may be generated for individual one, as there is no information for variable three, and it is not superseded in the scale by a positive score. Item four has scored in the nonscalable category, and consequently cannot be generated.

|  |  | 1 | 2 | 3 |
|---|---|---|---|---|
| Variables | 4 | — | + | + |
|  | 3 | 0 | 0 | + |
|  | 2 | + | — | + |
|  | 1 | + | + | + |
|  |  | 1 | 2 | 3 |

Systems

An increase in the number of scale types or "cutting points" results in the expansion of the predictive range of the scale. Terminological equations that differentiate the existing number of scale types are of greater intrinsic methodological significance than items that do not increase the predictive range of the scale.

What, then, is the general theoretical rationale of scalogram analysis in comparative social anthropology, and the significance of the scale types, in relationship to the typology of kinship terminologies that is derived from the transformational approach? In order to clarify the discussion, let us consider a "class" of important ethnological concepts: residence rules (Buchler, 1967a).

Residence concepts, which are used for comparative purposes, are based on criteria, "which are independent of any particular culture. That is why we define types of residence in terms of physical alignments of persons differentiated by genealogical (biological) considerations. The criteria are of necessity extra-cultural" (Goodenough, 1956b, p. 29; and see Chapter Three). On a comparative plane, the "structures which the anthropologist describes are models which exist only as logical constructions in his own mind" (Leach, 1954, p. 5). Although theoretical concepts in anthropology do not derive their meaning from their use as symbols in a calculus, which in physics is interpreted as an applied deductive system (Braithwaite, 1955, p. 51), the problem of translation from logical constructions to directly observable entities is essentially similar. For example, electrons

are logical constructions out of the observed events and objects by which their presence can be detected; this is equivalent to saying that the word "electron" can be explicitly defined in terms of such observations. Every sentence containing the word "electron" can, on this view, be translated without loss of meaning into a sentence in which there occur only words which denote entities (events, objects, properties) which are directly observable (Braithwaite, 1955, pp. 52–53).

What we have referred to as "the translation problem" brings us back to the ordinal definition of theoretical concepts. We have previously noted that an ordinal scale measures the range of empirical variance that is accounted for by specific theoretical concepts. But the variables used to measure this variance do *not* denote entities that are directly observable. These variables are mediating theoretical concepts: they are criteria (for classifying individual systems) that are essentially ethnological and are related to observable entities in a more direct fashion than general theoretical concepts. In terms of the comparative-statistical method (as distinguished from other forms of comparison) it is only necessary that theoretical concepts have sociological significance for the analyst, in the sense that they can be indirectly related to observable entities through criteria (or mediating concepts) that are ethnologically meaningful. We define ethnologically "meaningful criteria" as *criteria that minimally provide an ordinal measure of the variance that is accounted for by the "boundaries" of theoretical concepts.*

Scalogram analysis has a wider application in social anthropology than kinship systems. Some recent applications of scalogram analysis in anthropological studies can be mentioned and some of the methodological and theoretical problems that are raised by this form of analysis.

Goodenough (1965b, p. 8; cf. Goodenough, 1951) has suggested that the distribution of duties in the identity relationships in which people participate is a function of several independent considerations: for example, deference, cordiality, and display of affection, sexual distance, and so on. "The several duties that in different combinations indicate socially significant differences along one such dimension will be mutually distributed in identity relationships according to the patterns of a 'Guttman scale'" (Goodenough, 1965b,

p. 9). In this context, the analysis of scales will allow us to determine the minimum number of dimensions that will account for the distribution of "all culturally defined duties in a system of social relationships" (Goodenough, 1965b, p. 9), and (2) to determine duties that are functions of the same dimension. Scalogram analysis may allow us to develop objective measures of anger, insult, and flattery in alien cultural contexts.

A Guttman scale that is developed for comparative materials, such as the Iroquois and Omaha scales in the following chapters, raises two types of problems. (1) the rank order of systems must be accounted for, explained, or interpreted in a theoretically adequate manner; (2) The coefficient of reproducibility may be inflated if independent cases of co-occurrence, falling within the same scale type, are not carefully distinguished from cases that are the product of historical diffusion (Galton, 1889a; Naroll, 1961, 1964; Naroll and D'Andrade, 1963). Only (1) is relevant to both comparative and ethnographic scales. Consider, for example, the partial interpretation that Kay (1964, p. 164) develops to account for a scalogram of durable consumer goods ownership that "expresses popularity of an item as a function of two variables":

$$\text{net utility} = \text{utility} - \text{money cost.}$$

This function accounts for the empirical observations that scale items such as (1) radio, (2) primus stove, and (3) bicycle, scale on a single dimension and that they do not scale according to cost (Kay, 1964, p. 164). In a comparative context, theories must be generated that will account for the range of empirical variance that is measured by a Guttman, or any other scale model.

## COMPONENTIAL ANALYSIS AND AMERICAN KINSHIP TERMINOLOGY

In the final section of this chapter we present an introduction to componential analysis with particular reference to American kinship terminology. (In the next chapter componential analysis will be considered in a more formal context and in relation to other linguistically derived methods in social anthropology.) Three views of the American kinship system that have arisen from the use of this technique are examined and the theoretical implications of these alternative formulations are considered in our concluding section. At the outset, let us consider the substantive results reported by three analysts (Wallace and Atkins, 1960; Romney and D'Andrade, 1964a; and Goodenough, 1965a).

Quite simply a componential analysis "defines all of some set of words in terms of the same semantic dimensions or components. The meaning of each word in the set appears as a unique bundle of values on the common dimensions. The meaning of *father*, for instance, is: a *male* relative in the *direct* line belonging to the *ascending* (or higher) generation. Or, more briefly, father is: male, direct, ascending. *Niece* has the meaning: female, collateral, descending" (Brown, 1965, p. 307).

One method of doing a componential analysis is as follows (following Goodenough, 1956a). First one must establish the morphemes that belong to the domain of analysis. One must take all the expressions "whose denotata make it appear upon inspection that there may be some common element to their significata" (*ibid.*, p. 198).

Goodenough (1956a, p. 198) discusses the discovery procedure whereby the universe is determined,

> There are two procedures we can follow. One approach is to start with an expression such that a sample of its denotata seems most clearly to put it in the realm of kinship. Any other expression whose denotata suggest that it complements the first in some way, must, by virtue of complementation, relate to another partition of the same universe of which the first is also a partition. An expression, moreover, whose denotata are entirely included within the denotata of another expression, or within the denotata of a complementary set of expressions, must also signify a partition of the same universe to which the latter expressions belong. Another approach is to start with an expression whose denotata appear to cover the entire universe in question and which appears, therefore, to signify something that we would translate, in this case, as "kinsman." All expressions whose denotata are entirely included within the denotata of this expression will belong to the universe of kinship.

We now wish to discover the "meaning" of these kin terms (the *significatum* of each term in Morris' [1946] sense). The first step in determining the meaning is to write out all the designata of each term, i.e., map the term onto all its biological kin types. If the term under analysis were *uncle*, we would write out the list of biological kin types which the term mapped onto, i.e., MB, MZH, FB, FZH. We will do this for all the terms in the domain.

The next step is to find the core term (or kernel) of each range of biological kin types (in our example, the "range" of *uncle* is MB, MZH, FB, FZH). A notational system such as that of Romney (in Romney and D'Andrade 1964, and Romney 1965) is of great utility here, but we can proceed in this oversimplified example without it. Here we can intuit (utilizing Kroeber, 1909) that the kernel for the range of *uncle* is "male of first ascending generation, collateral."[4] In the same way the kernel is discovered for the range of *aunt* (female of first ascending generation, collateral), *grandfather* (male of second ascending generation, lineal), *cousin* (any sex relative of own generation collateral), until we have kernels for all the ranges, i.e., until we have established the "core term" for each and every kin term. We then define the terms by the least number of criteria by which they are distinguished. These

---

[4] We intuit the result here. There are well-developed procedures for establishing the kernel which we will discuss in Chapter Ten.

criteria are components, and we hope that the components will distinguish each kin term from every other, and each kin term will be identified by the bundle of components that define its space in the domain.

"A componential analysis is economical since it uses fewer semantic components than there are terms to be defined . . . . A componential analysis, furthermore, shows how the meaning of each term is like and unlike the meaning of each other term in the set. A componential analysis also describes the degree of similarity in meaning for any two terms in a set" (Brown, 1965, pp. 307–308).

## COMPONENTIAL ANALYSIS OF ENGLISH–AMERICAN KINSHIP

As we mentioned earlier, the three major published attempts to describe English-American kinship terminology via componential analysis are, in order of appearance, Wallace and Atkins (1960), Romney and D'Andrade (1964a), and Goodenough (1965a). Although they might appear at first glance to be similar, in fact they differ in several crucial ways. Consider Wallace and Atkins' analysis first. As we go on the componential models become more and more complex.

Wallace and Atkins attempt to place the following kin terms within a genealogical space: *grandmother*, *grandfather*, *father*, *mother*, *son*, *daughter*, *grandson*, *granddaughter*, *uncle*, *aunt*, *brother*, *sister*, *nephew*, *niece*, and *cousin*. They explicate the ranges of these terms in the way we have already briefly indicated, omitting, however, to consider affinals in any of the ranges.[5] They hypothesize that "three dimensions will be sufficient to define all the terms, sex of relative . . . , generation, . . . and lineality" (Wallace and Atkins, 1960, p. 61). Sex of relative has two values, male and female. Generation has five values, (1) two generations above Ego, (2) one generation above Ego, (3) same generation as Ego, (4) one generation below Ego, and (5) two generations below Ego. Lineality has three values, (1) lineal, (2) colineal, and (3) ablineals. "Lineals are persons who are ancestors or descendants of Ego; co-lineals are non-lineals, all of whose ancestors include, or are included in all the ancestors of Ego; ablineals are consanguineal relatives who are neither lineals nor co-lineals" (Goodenough, private communication in Wallace and Atkins, 1960, p. 61). In this way they can partition the set of consanguineal relatives so that each term falls into its separate subset. The components of sex of relative, generation, and lineality partition the set such that each kin term occupies a position, and each term has its position. The partitioning is mutually exclusive and jointly exhaustive. In their view a graphic representation of English-American kin terms (or their selected subset of such terms) would look like Figure 8–1.

---

[5] For *uncle* they do not include MZH, nor for *aunt* FBW.

|  | $C_1$ | | $C_2$ | | $C_3$ |
|---|---|---|---|---|---|
|  | $a_1$ | $a_2$ | $a_1$ | $a_2$ | $a_1 a_2$ |
| $b_1$ | grandfather | grandmother | uncle | aunt | cousin |
| $b_2$ | father | mother | | | |
| $b_3$ | (Ego) | | brother | sister | |
| $b_4$ | son | daughter | nephew | niece | |
| $b_5$ | grandson | granddaughter | | | |

Figure 8–1.  *A Componential Representation of American-English Consanguineal Core Terms (Wallace and Atkins, 1960, p. 62).*

The paradigm presented in Figure 8–1 conveys a great deal of information in a much more economical fashion than "traditional" forms of kinship analysis with their lengthy lists of terms, and explication of range sets in biological kin type lists. From the definition given by the location of each term we can generate all, and only, the appropriate kin types that designate the kin term in question. Any "same generation, ablineal" relative is a cousin, and we can spin out lists of kin types that fit the designated criteria, knowing that any English speaker (once he understood our nomenclature) would generate the term *cousin*.

The problem then lies not in the accuracy of the paradigmatic description, but rather in another consideration. Is this the only account that can be given of English-American kinship? If there are others, then, on what grounds do we choose among them. A second question (both are posed by Wallace and Atkins) has to do with the validity of such a description. Does the informant agree that "that's the way it really is?" Can we say that in some sense the distances from Ego in the paradigm roughly represent psychological distance? Does the paradigm represent his cognitive map of the situation?

Romney and D'Andrade and Goodenough would say that this diagram is not psychologically accurate, that it "doesn't feel right" or it doesn't represent the cognitive mapping of the informant. Goodenough rejects this mapping on intuitive grounds, boggling at the emplacement of sibling terms apart from the set of "lineal terms," *father, mother, son,* and *daughter.* "It didn't seem right to me to have the major taxonomic level in the system (as represented by degree of collaterality) separating the terms *brother* and *sister* from *father, mother, son* and *daughter,* with which I somehow felt they belonged . . . . Grouping them with *aunt, uncle, nephew* and *niece* just didn't sit right" (Goodenough, 1965a, p. 260). Goodenough divides his kin terms in terms of the transforming operations they can be subjected to by the use of such morphemes as *step*, *-in-law*, *foster*, *first* (as in *first* cousin), *great* (as in *great-grandfather*), and so on. Thus, to Goodenough one set of terms belong together in the sense that they are closer to each other than to those terms not in the set, and they are those kin terms that admit the transform operation with *step-*, *-in-law*, and *foster*. These are, of course, the terms *my father*, *my mother*, *my son*, *my daughter*, *my brother*, *my sister*. Another set wôuld be made of the terms that "enter into constructions with the adjective *great(grand)* to form the open ended set of derivative terms of which *my grandfather*, *my great-uncle*, *my great-great-grandniece* are examples" (Goodenough, 1965a, p. 270). A third set is made up of the one term (*cousin*) that enters into constructions with the adjectives first, second, third, and does not enter into constructions with *step*, *-in-law*, *foster*, or *great(grand)*.

For the purposes of comparison with Wallace and Atkins and Romney and D'Andrade we need go no further, but will merely mention that Goodenough has done the only complete analysis of the 47 kin terms in his dialect, partitioning the complete set with ten "discriminant variables."

If we examine the fifteen kin terms that Wallace and Atkins used for their example of a componential analysis of English-American, we find that Goodenough requires five variables to partition his set. On the face of it we should reject his analysis on the grounds that Wallace and Atkins required only three, but, clearly Goodenough is aware of their solution, and prefers his own for the very good reason that with five dimensions he can partition the set in a way that he "feels" is correct as a speaker of Yankee.[6]

The five variables areas follow 1. Degree of collateral distance between Ego and alter "which is coded for two values" 1.1 "less than two degrees of distance" and 1.2 "two or more degrees of distance" (Goodenough, 1965a, p. 273).[7]

---

[6] Actually, the discrepancy is not so great as it might appear. If we omit to consider Ego (as do Wallace and Atkins, wrongly, in our opinion) for the purposes of considering the number of possible discriminations that the cross products of the variable values will yield, we find there is little discrepancy at all. Wallace and Atkins, as will be remembered, give lineality 3 values, generation 5 values, and sex 2. The total possible two-dimensional spaces amount to 30 in their paradigm. Goodenough utilizes two values for variable 1 (degree of collateral distance), two for variable 2 (degree of genealogical distance between Ego and alter), two for variable 4 (lineality), two for variable 5 (generation seniority), and two for variable 6 (sex of alter). In a two-dimensional space this cross product yields the total of 32 possible partitions to form the paradigm.

[7] Collateral distance can operationally be said to be the number of genealogical links necessary to get from Ego's lineal through whom the relationship is traced. Thus, (first) cousin would be two degrees of collateral distance away from Ego, because one would count through Ego's parent to parent's sibling (one link) to parent's sibling's child (one link more for a total of two), and FFFBSSS would be four degrees of collateral distance away. One would count the number of links through Ego's lineal through whom the relationship was traced (FFF), and would count BSSS as four links from this lineal (thus Lounsbury, 1956).

A second variable which Goodenough utilizes is "genealogical distance" which can be said to take four values (of which only two are necessary if we exclude Ego from the analysis of the restricted number of kin terms in the Wallace and Atkins analysis). He defines a unit of genealogical distance "vertically as the space between a genitor or genetrix and his or her progeny, and horizontally as the distance between two individuals with a genitor in common" (Goodenough, 1965a, p. 273) and if we omit to consider = or affinal as marking spatial removal, then we can locate Ego as zero degrees distant, F, M, B, Z, S, D as one degree distant, FB, MB, and so on as two degrees distant, and so on. Variable two takes four values.[8]

2.1   zero distance (Ego)
2.2   one unit of distance
2.3   two units of distance
2.4   three units of distance

The third variable necessary for the analysis is lineality of relationship with two values.

3.1   alter and Ego in lineal relationship
3.2   alter and Ego not in a lineal relationship

The fourth variable refers to "generation seniority" and has two values.

4.1   alter in senior generation
4.2   alter in junior generation

The fifth and final variable is sex of relative with two values.

5.1   alter male
5.2   alter female

With four binary oppositions, and one open-ended variable (for comparative purposes taking only two values), Goodenough can partition the set of kin terms which Wallace and Atkins analyzed. His paradigm is reproduced in (Table 8–1).

Two immediate advantages can be seen in Goodenough's paradigm, which give it preference over Wallace and Atkins'. First, the terms for *brother* and *sister* are placed closer genealogically to Ego than *uncle* and *aunt*. As we can see by inspecting the table, *brother* and *sister* (along with *father* and *mother*) are placed at one unit of genealogical distance (2.2), whereas uncle and aunt are placed at two units (2.3). This concords not only with our "feelings" about own siblings, but also with the relative psychological distance between terms as demonstrated by Romney and D'Andrade.

---

[8] Noting the *caveat* about Ego, we can then operationally simplify the notion of genealogical distance by equating it with the number of primitive terms necessary to define a kin type.

## Table 8–1. Discriminant Variables

| Discriminant variables | | | | | Kinship terms |
|---|---|---|---|---|---|
| 1 | 2 | 3 | 4 | 5 | |
| 1.1 | 2.1 | ... | ... | ... | Ego |
| 1.1 | 2.2 | 3.1 | 4.1 | 5.1 | my father |
| 1.1 | 2.2 | 3.1 | 4.1 | 5.2 | my mother |
| 1.1 | 2.2 | 3.1 | 4.2 | 5.1 | my son |
| 1.1 | 2.2 | 3.1 | 4.2 | 5.2 | my daughter |
| 1.1 | 2.2 | 3.2 | ... | 5.1 | my brother |
| 1.1 | 2.2 | 3.2 | ... | 5.2 | my sister |
| 1.1 | 2.3 | 3.1 | 4.1 | 5.1 | my grandfather |
| 1.1 | 2.3 | 3.1 | 4.1 | 5.2 | my grandmother |
| 1.1 | 2.3 | 3.1 | 4.2 | 5.1 | my grandson |
| 1.1 | 2.3 | 3.1 | 4.2 | 5.2 | my granddaughter |
| 1.1 | 2.3 | 3.2 | 4.1 | 5.1 | my uncle |
| 1.1 | 2.3 | 3.2 | 4.1 | 5.2 | my aunt |
| 1.1 | 2.3 | 3.2 | 4.2 | 5.1 | my nephew |
| 1.1 | 2.3 | 3.2 | 4.2 | 5.2 | my niece |
| 1.? | ,,, | ... | ... | ... | my cousin |

(Adapted from Goodenough, 1965a, p. 275.)

Secondly, Goodenough's analysis explicitly puts Ego back into the gene-alogy. Wallace and Atkins had placed him in their diagram (see Figure 8–1), but had not shown any grounds for his being there. In Goodenough's scheme he has a place. Romney (oral communication) has speculated that perhaps it should go in a three-dimensional space "above" *brother* and *sister*. In Goodenough's analysis Ego is merely a "relative" of zero degree collateral distance and zero degree genealogical distance, and is the only "relative" that can occupy that space.

Romney and D'Andrade, using Wallace and Atkins' list of kin terms, propose two more structural analyses of these kin terms. One analysis groups the following as primary types; parents, siblings, and children together (separated only by sex and generation); as secondary types grandparents and uncles, aunts, nieces, and nephews; and as tertiary types, cousins. The assumption is that each group contains members that are "closer" to each other than they are to members (kin terms) outside the group. Thus, niece is closer to aunt than it is to mother. Son is closer to sister than it is to uncle, and so on. They note that this grouping is more in line with Parsons' notion of the immediacy of the nuclear family who constitute the "inner" circle of relatives (Romney and D'Andrade, 1964a, p. 153; Parsons, 1943, p. 36).

Their notational system[9] allows them, however, to prefer a third grouping, which they diagram as follows:

|      |  Direct |         | Collateral |        |      |
|------|---------|---------|------------|--------|------|
|      | male    | female  | male       | female |      |
| +2   | GrFa    | GrMo    | Un         | Au     | +    |
| −2   | GrSo    | GrDa    |            |        |      |
| +1   | Fa      | Mo      | Ne         | Ni     | −    |
| −1   | So      | Da      |            |        |      |
| 0    | Br      | Si      | Co         |        | 0    |

*Figure 8–2. Analysis of American Kinship System (Romney and D'Andrade, 1964, p. 153).*

Note the difference between this diagram (Figure 8–2), and Wallace and Atkins' diagram (Figure 8–1), and Goodenough's table (Table 8–1). Like Goodenough, Romney and D'Andrade place *brother* and *sister* in the "line" of lineal relatives, along with the ascendants and descendants of Ego. (Unlike Goodenough, Ego is not placed in the diagram.) We will remember that Wallace and Atkins put sibling terms into a separate category (with *uncles* and *aunts*, *nephews*, and *nieces* which they denoted "co-lineal"). Second Romney and D'Andrade reduce "lineality" to two values (direct and collateral in the diagram), unlike the three values in Wallace and Atkins' diagram. This accords with Goodenough, and we may remember that Goodenough was bothered by Wallace and Atkins' three-fold division as well. Most distinctive of all is Romney and D'Andrade's emplacement of *grandson* and *granddaughter*, "close" to *grandfather* and *grandmother*. Unlike Goodenough and Wallace and Atkins, Romney and D'Andrade are forced, by the logic of their notational system, to place terms close when there exist

---

[9] The notational elements are based on biological reckoning of kin relationships. The string is read from left to right, the first symbol refering to sex of speaker and the last to sex of referent.

| a | person of either sex |
|---|---|
| m | male |
| f | female |
| + | up one generation |
| − | down one generation |
| 0 | sibling link |
| = | marriage link |

Thus a+f0m would be mother's brother, a+a+a would be grandparent, m0f−m would be a man's sister's son, and so on.

only minimum differences (i.e., differences of one component) between them. If we briefly examine their components we will see why this arrangement of kin terms proceeds directly and explicitly from their assumptions. Sex of relative is one component, with two values, *male* and *female*. Lineality is another component with two values *lineal* and *nonlineal* (*collateral*). A third component of relevance to the study of this restricted set of kin terms is *reciprocity*. As Romney and D'Andrade (1964a, p. 152) state, "If two expressions" (we can think of them as kin type strings for the sake of continuity with the rest of the exposition) "are identical except for being reciprocals, then *polarity* is a distinctive variable . . . (It) takes two values, (1) senior or ascending generation (2) . . . junior or descending generation." If, for example, we write out kin type strings for grandparent we get a set of expressions which we can reduce to *parent's parent*. The reciprocal of *parent's parent* is *child's child*. These two expressions are equivalent except in the one variable of polarity, *parent's parent* taking the polarity value "ascending generation," and *child's child* taking the polarity value "descending generation" ($a + a + a$ and $a - a - a$). Romney and D'Andrade choose to align their range-sets (reduced kin types that correspond to kin terms) by this variable of polarity. Intuition enters here: there is no clearly deducible reason why they should do this, except in terms of "feel" as Goodenough says. As they put it, "We know of no way to specify a single best solution for the classification or arrangement of the five range-sets " (A *range-set* is all those terms in the diagram within solid lines, separated only by dotted lines.) "Taste, previous knowledge of the system, emphasis on core kin types, and other factors affect the outcome" (Romney and D'Andrade, 1964a, p. 152).

Given this alignment of range-sets, then, how can we validate it? What are the ways of discriminating between one analysis and another? No definitive method has yet been described but Romney and D'Andrade have developed a version of a sorting task (the Kelly Triad Test, Kelly, 1955), in which subjects are asked to decide which of three word stimuli is most "different." Controlling for sex of relative (which was demonstrated to be a consistent constant in sorting behavior) they made up triads comparing eight kin terms, by threes, each one against each other one.[10] There were 56 sortings required to complete the task. By this sorting task they could sort out those relatives which were seen to be closest (least different) and compare these perceived similarities with the hypothesized arrangement arrived at by structural analysis. Their arrangement was a great deal more predictive of similarity than Wallace and Atkins'. Subjects did put *grandfather* closer to *grandson* than to *father*. They did put *brother* closer to *father* and *son* than they did to *uncle*. Yet from Wallace and Atkins' analysis one would have expected that insofar as *brother* differed from *father* by two components that subjects would have discriminated more markedly between

---

[10] The kin terms were *grandfather, father, brother, son, grandson, uncle, cousin, nephew*.

*father* and *brother* than they did in Romney's sorting task.  So, in the two ways, or alignments, in which there was a difference between Romney-D'Andrade and Wallace-Atkins, the former seemed more accurate where the sortings were concerned.  So far as we know the Romney-D'Andrade attempt to validate a componential analysis through the use of independent measures is unique, and represents a step forward in the analysis of kinship terminology.

# Chapter Nine

# Linguistic Models for Kinship Semantics

## FOLK CLASSIFICATION: UNITS AND CONTEXTS

The previous chapter discussed three methods of analysis that have been used for kinship data; this chapter will also be concerned with systems of classification, but from a more general theoretical point of view.

Our intent in this chapter is neither to present a review of the historical antecedents of linguistic models in social anthropology nor to review all current applications and the theoretical and methodological issues that derive from these applications. Rather, we consider two categories of studies, which appear to be of particular relevance to various issues considered in this text: (1) studies that develop significant areas of methodological concern; and (2) studies that present important formal or theoretical formulations. Other models derived from linguistics, as well as other communication sciences, are considered in separate chapters.

In the analysis of systems for classifying segments of the social and natural environment, the anthropologist is essentially concerned with (Conklin, 1962, p. 120): (1) the identification of relevant syntactic segments; (2) the identification of fundamental semantic units in specified contexts; (3) the isolation of culturally significant sets of semantic units in particular domains; and (4) a translation, and marking of these units that displays all relevant semantic relationships.

The term *lexeme* has been suggested (Swadesh, 1946; Goodenough, 1956a) for fundamental or elementary units whose signification cannot be inferred from a knowledge of anything else in language; specifically, from its grammatical structure (Conklin, 1962, p. 121). *Segregate* refers to any conventionally named grouping of objects (Conklin, 1962, p. 121). The terms *lexeme* and *segregate* should be clearly distinguished from the somewhat more neutral term *category*, which may be either monolexemically labelled or covert (Keesing, 1966, p. 23; Berlin, Breedlove, and Raven, 1967). As we will see in a later section, this distinction is crucial to an understanding of such "methods of classification" as keys, paradigms, and taxonomies.

In the study of segregates or "labelled categories," explicit semantic distinctions between types of lexemic units are exceedingly useful. Although the criterial features of these types depend, in a sense, on some understanding of taxonomic structures (cf. following sections), they may, nevertheless, be profitably reviewed at this point (Conklin, 1962, p. 122).

| *Types of Lexemic Units* | *Semantic Criteria* |
|---|---|
| **1.** Unitary Lexemes | No segments may designate categories which are identical with, or superordinate to those designated by the forms in question (Conklin, 1962, p. 122). |
| **i.** Simple (unitary lexemes) | Unsegmentable. |
| **ii.** Complex (unitary lexemes) | Segmentable. |
| **2.** Composite Lexemes | One or more segments, under specified conditions, may (a) designate the same categories as those designated by the forms in question (abbreviation), or (b) designate categories superordinate to those designated by the forms in question (generalization) (Conklin, 1962, p. 122). |

Examples from American-English kinship terminology include

### Lexemes

| *Unitary simple* | *Unitary complex* | *Composite* |
|---|---|---|
| son | grandson | son-in-law |
| daughter | granddaughter | daughter-in-law |
| father | grandfather | father-in-law |
| mother | grandmother | mother-in-law |

Conklin (1964, pp. 39–41) distinguishes five methods of arrangement or "methods of classification": (1) index; (2) key; (3) paradigm; (4) typology; and (5) taxonomy.

*Index.* Of the five types of orderings, an index is the only unidimensional form of arrangement: a sequential enumeration of "lexemes" in terms of an "arbitrary dimension." A sequential cataloguing of lexical entries provides no information concerning the relevant paradigmatic or hierarchic relationships that obtain among these categories. The arbitrary dimension of alphabetic order is most frequently encountered in the sequential enumeration of entries in dictionaries and telephone directories.

*Key.* In contrast to an index form of arrangement, a key is multidimensional. The arrangement of attribute oppositions—or dichotomous exclusions—is permutable, thus producing an illusory geometrical relationship to a taxonomy. Whereas "the selection of the attributes and of a particular sequence of oppositions may be arbitrary" (Conklin, 1964, p. 40) for a key, this is never the case for a taxonomy.

A semantic key represents a branching structure or tree measure characteristic of stochastic processes (Kay, 1966, p. 22), where the initial node is the root feature, domain feature (Lounsbury, 1964b; Kay, 1966, p. 22), unique beginner (Berlin, Breedlove, and Raven, 1967), single beginner (Gregg, 1954, p. 37), or head term (Kay, 1966, p. 23), "and each succeeding node represents a selection of a single feature from some particular dimension" (Kay, 1966, p. 22).

Domain: $L_1, L_2, \ldots, L_8$

Dimensions: $D, A, B, C, D, E, F$ where features are given by

$$D \quad [d]$$
$$A \quad [a_1, a_2]$$
$$\vdots$$
$$F \quad [f_1, f_2].$$

Componential definitions are shown in Figure 9–1.

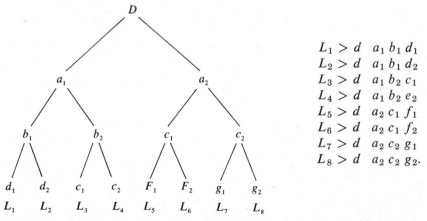

$$L_1 > d \quad a_1 \, b_1 \, d_1$$
$$L_2 > d \quad a_1 \, b_1 \, d_2$$
$$L_3 > d \quad a_1 \, b_2 \, c_1$$
$$L_4 > d \quad a_1 \, b_2 \, e_2$$
$$L_5 > d \quad a_2 \, c_1 \, f_1$$
$$L_6 > d \quad a_2 \, c_1 \, f_2$$
$$L_7 > d \quad a_2 \, c_2 \, g_1$$
$$L_8 > d \quad a_2 \, c_2 \, g_2.$$

*Figure 9–1. Key Diagram of a Perfect Tree (without taxonomy: after Kay, 1966, p. 22).*

Note:

1. Each dimension occurs at 1 and only 1 node; e.g., dimension $B$ occurs at (descends from) the unique node labelled $a_1$.
2. Except for the trivial alteration of interchanging features on the same dimensions, this is the only possible key for this structure.
3. A box diagram is impossible for this structure.
4. Only the bottom row of nodes is labelled; hence no taxonomy.

A distinction has recently been suggested between "true" tree rules, on the one hand, and "imperfect" tree rules on the other (Durbin, 1966, pp. 33–35). A true tree is characterized by hierarchical ordering, as the nodes on any given level must be "expanded differently." Consequently, a true tree is less economical than a "true paradigm" (Figures 9–2 and 9–3):

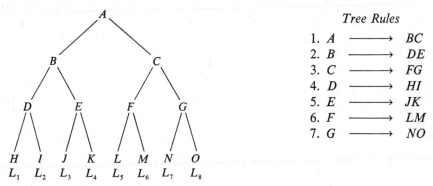

Figure 9–2.   A "True" Tree (cf. Durbin, 1966, p. 34).

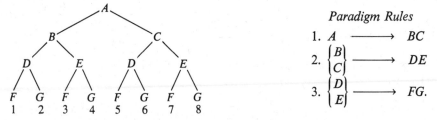

Figure 9–3.   A "True" Paradigm (cf. Durbin, 1966, p. 33).

Durbin's (1966) rule measure of economy is comparable, on one plane, to Kay's (1966, p. 22) distinction between perfect or true paradigms and trees: zero redundancy, on the one hand, and "maximal" redundancy on the other. From the componential definitions given in Figure 9–1, it is perfectly clear that no two definitions contrast on more than a single dimension. A change in the componential definition of a single feature (e.g., $a_1, a_2, b_1, b_2$) will not change it into the componential definition of another lexeme in the domain. This formulation is the meaning we attach to Kay's (1966, p. 22) notion of a true tree as a maximally redundant structure.

*Paradigm.* In a paradigmatic ordering, entities are arranged which (1) share a common feature, and (2) constitute a contrast set (Conklin, 1964, p. 40; cf. Conklin, 1962, Lounsbury, 1956). (1) is a "criterial property" of keys and taxonomies (root feature, domain feature, and so on): it (1) is, in a sense, a derivative property of paradigmatic classifications, resulting from their embedding in taxonomic structures. "In other words, any taxonomy may contain one or more paradigmatic structures, but no paradigm can include or be equivalent to a taxonomy" (Conklin, 1964, p. 41).

An abstract representation of this form of embedding is provided by Kay (1966, p. 23) in Figure 9–4.

Domain: $[L_1, L_2, \ldots, L_{15}]$

Dimensions: as in Figure 9–1.

Componential definitions:

   (1) $L_1, L_2, \ldots, L_8$ as in Figure 9–1.
   (2) $L_9 \ > d\ a\ b\ \ c$
     $L_{10} > d\ a_1 b\ \ c$
     $L_{11} > d\ a_2 b\ \ c$
     $L_{12} > d\ a_1 b_1\ c$
     $L_{13} > d\ a_1 b_2\ c$
     $L_{14} > d\ a_2 b_1\ c$
     $L_{15} > d\ a_2 b_2\ c,$

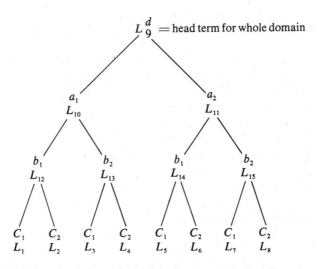

*Figure 9–4.   Key Diagram of a Perfect Paradigm, with Perfect Taxonomy.*

Note: all nodes are labelled; hence perfect taxonomy.

A coordinate set of entities such as $L_1, L_2, \ldots, L_8$, or $L_{12}, L_{13}, \ldots, L_{15}$ may be internally arranged as in a paradigm.

Consider a simple query-response "model" for the ordering of folk taxa (Berlin, Breedlove, and Raven 1967), segregates (Frake, 1962, p. 76), or "minimal classification events" (Kay, 1966, p. 21) within contrast sets (cf. Frake, 1962, p. 78; cf. Conklin, 1964, p. 34).

i. When a person reaches a decision concerning the category membership (designative reference rather than nominal usage; Conklin, 1964, p. 34) of a given object, it is assumed that a selection has been made from a set of alternative terms (Frake, 1962, p. 78).
ii. "When he asserts, 'This is an $X$,' he is also stating that it is *not* specific other things, these other things being not everything else conceivable, but only the alternatives among which a decision was made" (Frake, 1962, p. 78).
iii. Culturally appropriate responses, which are alternatives in the same environment contrast; and a series of terminologically contrasting terms or segregates form a contrast set (Frake, 1962, pp. 78–79).

Paradigmatically ordered contrasting units can be described componentially (Lounsbury, 1956, pp. 162, 192; cf. Conklin, 1964). "Componential analysis is best conceived as an analytic *process* in which the investigator searches for (a) the *dimensions* of meaning underlying the domain and (b) the mapping of the values on these dimensions (the *features* of *meaning*) onto *the set of lexemes*" (Kay, 1966, p. 20). The criteria for each category or taxon within a domain constitute that category's significatum: the significatum of any category consists of a combination or "bundle" of values on several semantic dimensions (cf. Goodenough, 1956a, p. 205). Put somewhat differently, if any feature is selected from each dimension, and the conjunction or intersection of all selected features is taken, the result is a "minimal classification event" (Kay, 1966, p. 21). A set of values on any dimension are, by definition, mutual contraries; they stand in a relation of complementarity. Where a term (or category), "which signifies a particular value on a dimension has no complementary term signifying another logically necessary value on that dimension, the existing term is said to be complemented by 'no lexeme'" (Wallace and Atkins, 1960, p. 69).

In reference to the representation of the "cognitive structure" of a domain, a paradigmatic ordering of contrasting units has been characterized as "The simplest and most elegant formal structure consonant with a psychological theory of simultaneous application of dimensions" (Kay, 1966, p. 21).

If each componential definition corresponds to a unique entity, then a domain is characterized by a "perfect paradigm" (Kay, 1966, p. 21). In a "perfect paradigm," a change in any feature, on any dimension, will change a componential definition into another componential definition. For example:

*Pair of features* [♂, ♀]:

| Componential definitions | Lexemes |
|---|---|
| (Kinsman, $G^0$ colineal, ♂) < | "brother" |
| (Kinsman, $G^0$ colineal, ♀) < | "sister" |

But, taking two lexemes from the "partial domain" considered by Kay (1966, pp. 21–22):

*Triad of features* [$G^0$, $G^1$, $G^2$]:

| Componential definitions | Lexemes |
|---|---|
| (Kinsman, $G^0$ colineal, ♂) < | "brother" |
| $\left\{\begin{array}{l}\text{Kinsman, } G^1 \text{ colineal, ♂}\\\text{Kinsman, } G^2 \text{ colineal, ♂}\end{array}\right\}$ < | "uncle" |

$G^0$: Ego's own generation
$G^1$: one generation above Ego
$G^2$: two generations above Ego

colineal: nonlineals all of whose ancestors include, or are included in, all the ancestors of Ego (Wallace and Atkins, 1960, pp. 61–62; cf. Romney and D'Andrade, 1964a, p. 147)

♂: male
♀: female

On an analytic plane, domains in which componential definitions are exclusively assigned to unique categories are probably, to some degree, the product of exclusively dichotomous, rather than continuous, dimensions. This is illustrated, in a general sense, in Kay's (1966, p. 22) abstract representation of a perfect paradigm:

Domain: [$L_1, L_2, \ldots, L_8$] (i.e., the domain contains 8 lexemes)
Dimensions: [$D, A, B, C$], where the features are given by $D = [d]$
$$A = [a_1, a_2]$$
$$B = [b_1, b_2]$$
$$C = [c_1, c_2].$$

Componential definitions:

$$L_1 > d \quad a_1 \, b_1 \, c_1$$
$$L_2 > d \quad a_1 \, b_1 \, c_2$$
$$L_3 > d \quad a_1 \, b_2 \, c_1$$
$$L_4 > d \quad a_1 \, b_2 \, c_2$$
$$L_5 > d \quad a_2 \, b_1 \, c_1$$
$$L_6 > d \quad a_2 \, b_1 \, c_2$$
$$L_7 > d \quad a_2 \, b_2 \, c_1$$
$$L_8 > d \quad a_2 \, b_2 \, c_2.$$

Box diagram (Figure 9–5):

|  | $a_1$ | $a_2$ |  |
|---|---|---|---|
| $c_1$ | $L_1$ | $L_5$ | $b_1$ |
| $c_2$ | $L_2$ | $L_6$ | |
| $c_1$ | $L_3$ | $L_7$ | $b_2$ |
| $c_2$ | $L_4$ | $L_8$ | |

Figure 9–5. A Perfect Paradigm (Kay, 1966, p. 22).

Empirically, a paradigmatic ordering of lexemes within a componential matrix is well illustrated by Wallace and Atkins (1960, pp. 60–62; cf. Romney and D'Andrade, 1964a, pp. 146–147, 152–153) representation of consanguineal core terms for American-English (Figure 9–6):

|  | $C_1$ | | $C_2$ | | $C_3$ |
|---|---|---|---|---|---|
|  | $a_1$ | $a_2$ | $a_1$ | $a_2$ | $a_1a_2$ |
| $b_1$ | grandfather | grandmother | uncle | aunt | |
| $b_2$ | father | mother | | | |
| $b_3$ | (Ego) | | brother | sister | cousin |
| $b_4$ | son | daughter | nephew | niece | |
| $b_5$ | grandson | granddaughter | | | |

Figure 9–6. A Componential Representation of American-English Consanguineal Core Terms (Wallace and Atkins, 1960).

Where:

A: *Sex*
A.1: Male
A.2: Female

B: *Generation*
B.1: two generations above Ego
B.2: one generation above Ego
B.3: Ego's own generation
B.4: one generation below Ego
B.5: two generations below Ego

C: *Lineality*
C.1: lineal
C.2: colineal
C.3: ablineal

*Lineals*: persons who are ancestors or descendants of Ego;

*Colineals*: nonlineals all of whose ancestors include, or are included in, all the ancestors of Ego;

*Ablineals*: consanguineal relatives who are neither lineals nor colineals.

Wallace and Atkins (1960, pp. 63–79) outline five methodological problem areas in the componential analysis of kinship terms and other domains.

First is *the problem of homonyms and metaphors*. Homonyms and metaphors are graphically or phonemically identical words or phrases that have different meanings. "The issue is important because it concerns both the principles of finding the boundary of the system being described and also the logical structure of semantic domains" (Wallace and Atkins, 1960, p. 63).

Pragmatically, the significance of homonyms and metaphors as an analytic problem in the study of kinship semantics derives from two considerations (Wallace and Atkins, 1960, p. 64). First, some terms that signify kin relationships may also signify nonkin relationships in "nonkin contexts"; second, the same kinship terms may either have or seem to have two or more kinship usages. However, this problem, although certainly important in ethnoscientific and linguistic research and although methodologically interesting, is from our point of view essentially a field issue. The puzzle of homonyms and metaphors may be partially settled while the anthropologist is gathering his data, by the use of elicitation frames and by proper use of control questions (Schneider, 1965b). In other words, one must be able to assume that the range of kin terms is reasonably accurate and complete before formal analysis of kin systems can begin.

As Wallace and Atkins (1960, p. 67) suggest, a resolution of the problem of polysemy and homonymy are intricately related to the analytic task of defining major boundary setting parameters (e.g., relative) for the semantic space. Examples of boundary-setting criteria include (1) constant syntactic context, (2) a type of pragmatic situation, (3) inclusion within the extension of a cover label for "kinsman" or "relatives" (Wallace and Atkins, 1960, p. 60).

*The problem of definition vs. connotation.* In the componential analysis of kinship terms, (1) the individual kin types to which a term refers are its denotata; (2) the class of these denotative types are its designatum; and (3) the distinctive semantic features of this class are its significatum (Lounsbury, 1956, p. 67). The significatum of a kinship term is a set of "contextual elements ... without which it cannot properly occur. Significata are prerequisites while connotata are probabilities and possibilities. Only the former have definitive value" (Goodenough, 1956a, p. 195). As the notion of necessary and sufficient conditions is related to a definition of the universe of denotata, the problem of synonymy must be considered. Generally, synonymy refers to a closeness of overlap among the manifestations of semological units (Chafe, 1965, p. 25). If semological units are construed as types "whose tokens are the points in experiential space that cluster in a particular target area" (Chafe, 1965, p. 25), then the manifestations of these units can be represented as circles that can be manipulated like the "circles" of Venn diagrams (cf. Chafe, 1965, pp. 25–26). Any pair of the set of referential kinship terms, *father, dad, daddy, pop, old man,* may be represented and the entire set may be regarded as a class of manifestations of a single semological unit (Chafe, 1965, p. 25). All members of this class, with the possible exception of *dad,* have nonkin homonyms or metaphoric extensions (Wallace and Atkins, 1960, p. 67)(Figure 9–7).

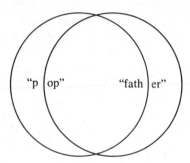

Figure 9–7.   *A Venn Diagram for a Pair of Referential Kin Terms.*

As homonymy, synonymy, and metaphoric extensions must be frequently reckoned with in structural semantics, it is of some importance to carefully distinguish these processes. A *metaphor* is

a semological unit which occurs in one or a very small number of environments, and always has a corresponding or alternative unit that can be called its *literal* correlate. A metaphor is overwhelmingly the most frequent unit in the environments where it occurs. Its literal correlate, however, can occur in all of those environments plus a large number of others from which the metaphor is excluded (Chafe, 1965, p. 34).

The Pawnee reference to corn as "Our Mother" (Lounsbury, 1956) and the referential kinship term, which includes among its denotata the English kin-type primitive *M* (= mother), have an apparent experiential similarity. But "the two units are discretely different, with different foci, different peripheries, and contrastive distributions" (Chafe, 1965, p. 34). Weinreich's (1963, p. 143) contextual resolution of a type of polysemy is essentially similar: "*blue* and *purple* have color components in the context of signs for visible objects, but these are replaced by 'affective' values in such contexts as . . . *music, . . . prose.*"

Both homonyms and metaphors are discretely different units with the same phonological representation. But whereas a metaphor occurs in one or a small number of environments, this is not the case for either unit of a homonymous pair (Chafe, 1965, p. 34): "Rather, it would seem that both units are interchangeable in all environments if they are interchangeable at all." Generally, the so-called problem of homonymy is a crucial one in kinship semantics, and "a policy of avoiding 'homonyms' in English semantic translations is something of a red herring in analysis, interfering with the development of a consistent and logical notation, influencing the choice of either dimensions and values or the size of lexicon, and interposing an arbitrary preference for one kind of logical operator (the class product) in a situation where, in general, both class sums and class products must be used anyway" (Wallace and Atkins, 1960, p. 66).

Succinctly stated, synonymy is simply an experiental similarity in the manifestation of semological units; the converse of this process is phonetic similarity, whereas the converse of homonymy is "the multiple phonological symbolization of a single semological unit" (Chafe, 1965, p. 34). The non-inclusion of various members of a semological class, in a componential analysis, which have connotations that are somewhat different from the "core terms" but which, nevertheless, have the force of significata (e.g., *pop, dad, ma, mom*) suggests that the meaning of a kinship term given by a componential account is likely to be minimal, "probably not complete in specification of culturally or linguistically relevant dimensions, and certainly devoid of most of the connotations which it will have for individuals and even subgroups in the society" (Wallace and Atkins, 1960, p. 68). All of this merely serves to remind us that componential analysis of kinship semantics generally accounts for a closed system within an essentially deductive framework, handling circumscribed problems on specific levels of analysis (Nutini, 1967, p. 50), and must be complemented by, at the very least, a more inclusive functional and contextually sensitive analysis of usage and associated attitudinal structure. If componential accounts are not related, on some level, to an opened-ended system, then the results can only be a sterile formalism.

## COMPLEMENTARITY, PARADIGMS AND SPACES

The notion of complementarity is related, on one level, to the concept of a perfect or true paradigm (Kay, 1966, p. 21; Durbin, 1966, p. 33). Each componential definition within a perfect paradigm corresponds to a unique entity or labelled minimal classification event (Kay, 1966, p. 21). Consequently, a change in any feature on any dimension will change the componential definition of any term into the componential definition of another term within the set. Values that stand in a relation of complementarity "constitute a single dimension whose two or more values are mutual contraries" (Wallace and Atkins, 1960, p. 69). Wallace and Atkins (1960, p. 69) distinguish between and suggest various implications of regular and irregular reductions of a terminological set. In the process of partitioning a universe of kinship terms and their denotata into groups and subgroups, the analyst is faced with a significant choice: at each stage of the reduction of the set, beyond the first stage, he may use "the same dimensions for the reduction of all the terms on that level, or he can use different dimensions for different groups" (Wallace and Atkins, 1960, p. 69). If the reduction of the set is regular on at least one analytic level beyond the first stage, then the universe of terms can be displayed in the same paradigm; if the reduction is irregular on any level, "then the terms cannot be displayed in the same paradigm, for their significata are not logically complementary on any dimension" (Wallace and Atkins, 1960, p. 70).

The distinction between regular and irregular reduction of terms and the mapping of a universe of terms on one or more paradigms or semantic spaces is analogous to Durbin's (1966, pp. 33–35) distinction between true and imperfect paradigmatic rules as shown in Figure 9–8.

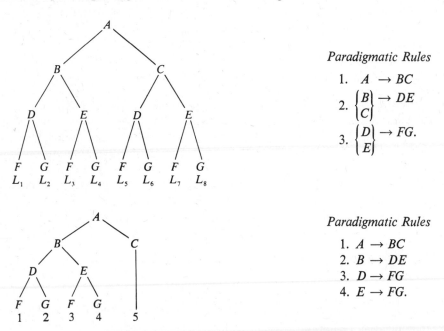

*Paradigmatic Rules*

1. $A \rightarrow BC$
2. $\begin{Bmatrix} B \\ C \end{Bmatrix} \rightarrow DE$
3. $\begin{Bmatrix} D \\ E \end{Bmatrix} \rightarrow FG.$

*Paradigmatic Rules*

1. $A \rightarrow BC$
2. $B \rightarrow DE$
3. $D \rightarrow FG$
4. $E \rightarrow FG.$

*Figure 9–8.   An Imperfect Tree and True Paradigm.*

Three types of class-product spaces may be distinguished (Wallace and Atkins, 1960, pp. 70–71). (1) *Orthogonal spaces:* An orthogonal space is a set of class products formed by all unique combinations of values from *n* independent dimensions. A perfect paradigm, a regular reduction of terms on every level of analysis, is a mapping of a universe of terms on an orthogonal space as shown in Figure 9–9.

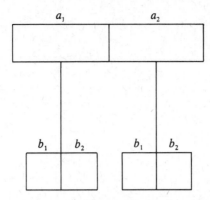

*Figure 9–9.    Ortho-space (Wallace and Atkins, 1960, p. 71).*

(2) *Nonorthogonal class-product spaces:* At least one pair of the group of dimensions from which a nonortho-space is constructed is nonindependent. "Whenever there is a negative logical entailment of at least one value on any dimension by any other value on any other dimension, the space is nonorthogonal" (Wallace and Atkins, 1960, p. 71). There are two types of nonorthogonal spaces. Type I is shown in Figure 9–10.

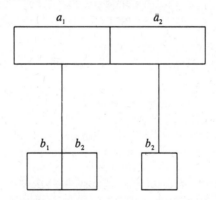

*Figure 9–10.    Nonortho-space Type I (Wallace and Atkins, 1960, p. 71).*

In Type I, all the dimensions span the same set of referents, "but at least two values from different dimensions are mutually contrary ($[a_i \rightarrow \sim b_j] \wedge [b_j \rightarrow \sim a_i]$)" (Wallace and Atkins, 1960, p. 71).

In Type II, every dimension overlaps at least one other dimension, but at least one value on one dimension is mutually contrary with each of the values on another dimension. It is rarely possible to represent all of the terms of a given kinship lexicon on a single orthogonal space, or to trans-

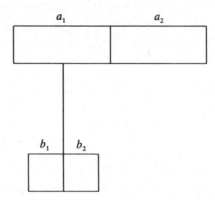

*Figure 9–11. Nonortho-space Type II (Wallace and Atkins, 1960, p. 71).*

form paradigms on nonorthogonal spaces into paradigms on orthogonal spaces (Wallace and Atkins, 1960, p. 73). (See Figure 9–11 above.)

*The problem of noncommutative relational concepts.* Wallace and Atkins (1960, p. 74) pose a question of central analytic and psychological significance: "May not the users of many kinship lexicons cognitively define at least some of their terms relationally, even though it may be possible for the ethnographer to analyze them as class products? For example, *mother* may be defined as a 'female parent,' which may be analyzed as the class product female lineal one generation above ego, whereas *uncle* may be relationally defined as the 'brother of a parent,' or, combining class and relational calculi and with more general formal implications, as the 'brother of any ascending generation lineal.'"

## PSYCHOLOGICAL REALITY

Various analysts have justified the selection of components by describing them as criteria or rational decision rules that are psychologically salient within a specific social matrix. Consequently, componential analysis of kinship terms have been said to provide psychologically real definitions; to provide a method for learning about human cognitive processes (Goodenough, 1956a). Wallace and Atkins (1960, pp. 76–79) outline two basic problems that must be reckoned with if a "psychologically real" description of a culture is to be something more than a trivial and arbitrary claim, and suggest analogous analytic contexts in mathematical physics.

*The problem of linguistic complementarity.* Various class and/or relative product definitions of a given term may allow an analyst to predict accurately the usage of the term. And the analytic prediction of usage based upon an apparent and trivial psychological definition is extensionally equivalent to a multiplicity of psychologically real definitions, or, conversely, many analytic solutions. "Just as the physicist cannot measure both the position and momentum of a particle under the same conditions, so the semantic analyst cannot state simultaneously the meaning of an event in his own language and in that of another persons' because the two languages impose different conditions of analysis" (Wallace and Atkins, 1960, p. 76).

*The problem of indeterminacy.* Wallace and Atkins (1960, p. 76) suggest an equation between multiple mappings (paradigms) for the same set of terms, or a multiplicity of solutions, on the one hand, and the physicist's relativity on the other. They proceed to enumerate some sources of indeterminacy: (a) the set of all kin-type denotata has no finite boundaries; (b) variation in the universe of denotata chosen; (c) variation in the number and identity of terms selected from a lexicon for analysis; (d) variation in the identity of the selected dimensions; (e) variation as to the use of logical operators; (f) variation in the type of class-product space; (g) variation as to inclusion or exclusion of connotative dimensions. They (Wallace and Atkins, 1960, p. 77) suggest that the essential difference between psychologically and structurally valid descriptions lies in the choice of dimensions and logical operators.

Some recent publications are directly relevant to some of these problems. In the following section some of these studies are reviewed.

Burling (1964) considers (a) the total number of logically possible solutions, (b) the implication of that number for indeterminacy, and (c) the implications of indeterminacy for semantic analysis. Logically, three items (terms) in a set may be partitioned in six ways (see Figure 9–12):

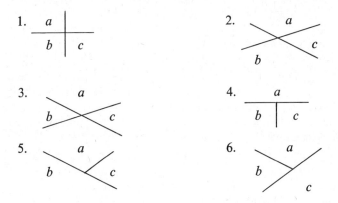

*Figure 9–12.   Logical Partitions for a Three-Item Set. (Burling, p. 21)*

There are 124 ways in which a set of four terms can be discretely but non-redundantly apportioned into cells by the application of binary components, and various additional complicating factors are suggested: (1) homonymy; (2) empty semantic spaces; (3) nonbinary components; (4) parallel components; and (5) redundant solutions.

Burling (1964, pp. 24–27) concludes that logical indeterminacy negates claims that componential accounts explicate the rules which native speakers use for grouping social and genealogical criteria into concepts (e.g., Wallace, 1962). There are several objections to this argument. First, rather than reckoning with linguistic complementarity and indeterminacy, Burling (1964) merely provides a numerical measure of the latter, and suggests that that measure provides a proof of the insolubility of the former. This solution fails to cope with the sources of indeterminacy, and evidences an unawareness of the range of ethnographic solutions, or signals from various cultural contexts that may be deployed in limiting—ethnographically or ethnologically—the selection of dimensions and logical operators. Consider Hymes' (1964, pp. 116–119) perceptive critique of Burling's argument.

The notion "total number of logical possibilities is relevant only if all solutions, or forms of dimensional sorting have an equal chance of being arrived at " (Hymes, 1964, p. 116). When analysis is rigorously dependent on determining the questions native speakers ask in categorizing experience (e.g., Frake, 1964, p. 132), then the critical assignment problem becomes one of determining culturally relevant solutions, of choosing dimensions and logical operators that generate "productive statements about the relevant relationships obtaining among locally defined categories and contexts (of objects and events) within a given social matrix" (Conklin, 1964, p. 25), rather than an enumeration of the total number of logical possibilities.

It is absolutely essential to distinguish an appropriate sorting for the members of sets, and an appropriate assignment of semantic features to the dimensions of the sorting (Hymes, 1964, p. 117). "The notion of logically possible solutions applies only to the former, which can be formal and cognitively empty. Given a set, the possible sortings, and the possible pertinent semantic features, are both finite in number; and one sorting usually will eliminate some features as possible, while particular features will eliminate some sortings" (Hymes, 1964, p. 117). Hymes (1964, p. 117) suggests that the distinction between sorting and assignment is a surface reflection, so to speak, of a more basic underlying distinction: (i) *Sorting* is a model that accounts for the way in which a set is organized; (ii) *Assignment* is an explanation that is involved in the prediction of naming, and, consequently, makes the "reported organization" of a set intelligible or motivated.

To predict naming is to treat the analysis as generative, as accounting for the acceptability and nonacceptability of acts of naming, including, by implication, acts of naming novel objects. To predict the naming of novel objects introduces the possibility, indeed necessity, of discriminating among alternative solutions in terms of the semantic features validly pertinent to designating an item $x$, $y$, or not in the set (Hymes, 1964, p. 117).

Once the right assignment of semantic features to the dimensions of the sorting (Hymes, 1964, p. 117) has been made, semantic transformation rules can be enumerated for semantically ambiguous, although grammatically and morphosyntactically identical, statements in two languages. By way of example, consider a situation that Conklin (1962, pp. 125–127) encountered during the course of field work in the Philippines.

1. A woman, whose brother (*x*) and husband (*y*) are both named Juan, has a son who is also named Juan (*z*) and a daughter who has a son named Pedro (*P*) (Conklin, 1962, p. 125).
2. There are two fluent speakers of English who know Pedro and the members of his family. One (*F*) is a Filipino, whose first language was Tagalog; the other (*A*), a native speaker of American-English.
3. Assume that one of the Juans (*x*, *y*, or *z*) has died and this information is available only to *A* (or *F*) who wishes to relate this information to his friend *F* (or *A*) (Conklin, 1962, p. 125).
4. Depending on the circumstances, either: (i) Pedro's *Grandfather* Juan died, or (ii) Pedro's *Uncle* Juan died. If *A* uses (i), *F* may ask *Which grandfather*?; if *F* uses (ii), *A* may ask *Which uncle*? Conklin (1962, p. 127) illustrates the semantic distinction between *A*'s usage of (i and ii) and *F*'s usage of (i and ii).

| *Sentence* | *Kin Term Used* | *Kin Type(s) Included*[1] |
|---|---|---|
| A1 | Grandfather | *y* (Pr Fa) |
| F1 | Grandfather | *x* and *y* (Pr Fa, Pr Pr Br) |
| A2 | Uncle | *x* and *z* (Pr Br, Pr Pr Br) |
| F2 | Uncle | *z* (Pr Br) |

[1] Pr = parent's.

The semantic transformations that "underlie" these usages and that allow us to decode them are a reflection of two complementary principles (Conklin, 1962, p. 127):

| *Systems* | *Semantic Principles* |
|---|---|
| 1. Central Philippine systems of kinship classification. | Universal terminological recognition of generation. |
| 2. North American systems of kinship classification. | Universal terminological recognition of degree of collaterality. |

The complementarity principles that underlie the obligatory semantic distinction between Central Philippine systems of kinship classification and North American systems of kinship classification may be generalized from an ethnographic to an ethnological (comparative) context. (See Buchler, 1964).

The general issue of "psychological reality" as previously mentioned is addressed by Romney and D'Andrade's (1964a, p. 154) consideration of the "selection of behavioral measures that would be affected if a componential analysis were isomorphic with cognitive structure." In developing behavioral measure of individual cognitive operations, several techniques are employed (Romney and D'Andrade, 1964a, p. 154): (i) A listing of kin terms in free recall; (ii) the semantic differential; and (iii) direct judgments of similarity and difference with the triad method. (See Chapter Eight.)

"The general prediction we have made from componential analysis to cognitive measures is that the more components any two terms have in common, the greater will be the similarity of response to these terms. This prediction is derived from the assumption that the components of a term constitute the meaning of that term for an individual; hence, the more components which are shared, the more similar the meaning" (Romney and D'Andrade, 1964a, p. 154, and see Chapter Eight).

The foregoing formulation (i.e., assumption) blurs the distinction between psychological reality and analytic validity. It would seem more appropriate to pose as a hypothesis an equation between sharing of analytically derived components, on the one hand, and similarity of meaning on the other. That the components of a term constitute the meaning of that term for an individual would then be a testable theorem, derived from the preceding hypothesis or postulate, rather than an assumption.

## TYPOLOGIES

Typological orderings are based on extrinsically defined attribute dimensions in which the cells represent subpartitions of an "attribute space" (Conklin, 1964, p. 40; Greenberg, 1957). In a sense, typologies are the converse of paradigms (Conklin, 1964, p. 40): 1. *Paradigm:* entities to be classified provide the necessary contrasts from which relevant and defining attributes are derived; 2. *Typology:* essentially arbitrary contrasts are derived from attribute combinations.

For example, two dichotomies lead to the fourfold table shown in Figure 9–13 (Lazarsfeld, 1961, p. 111):

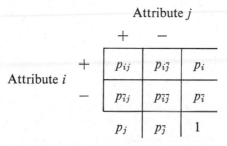

Figure 9–13. A Typological Ordering.

in which (1) "observations" are arbitrarily designated as (+) and (−), (2) the corresponding frequencies are designated $p_i$ and $p_{\bar{\imath}}$, respectively, and

$p_i + p_{\bar{i}} = 1$. The joint frequency is $p_{ij}$ for the "response pattern" $++$, and $p_{i\bar{j}}$ for the response pattern $+-$, and so on. All items are numbered and listed in an arbitrary sequence (Lazarsfeld, 1961, p. 172).

## TAXONOMIES

The constituent entities of a taxonomic hierarchy are vertically ordered by nondimensional class inclusion (Conklin, 1964, p. 39; cf. Gregg, 1954; Frake, 1961; Simpson, 1961; Durbin, 1966), or "inclusion of reference" (Kay, 1966, p. 21). "Hierarchic positions in a taxonomy—biological or otherwise—are not permutable, and so far as folk taxonomies are concerned, the definition and arrangement of included taxa are nonarbitrary" (Conklin, 1964, pp. 39–40).

If we define a taxonomy as a system of contrast sets related by vertical class inclusion, then a structure of this type need not have a unique beginner or segregate that includes all other segregates: it is only necessary that the segregate at the most general or inclusive level form a demonstrable contrast set (Frake, 1962, p. 80). Such a structure, or lexical hierarchy has two axes: (1) horizontal differentiation of coordinate categories; and (2) vertical increase of generalization or specification (Conklin, 1962, p. 128). Within taxonomic structures, there are often subhierarchies of varying depths. Indeed, the "embedding of shallow subhierarchies within increasingly deeper ones is characteristic of many systems of folk classification" (Conklin, 1962, p. 128).

Conklin (1962, p. 128) outlines four specific requirements for model taxonomic systems. 1. There is only one maximal or unique taxon, which includes all other taxa or segregates in the system, at the highest level; 2. The number of levels is uniform and finite throughout the system; 3. Taxa at the same level are always mutually exclusive; There are theorems for these specific requisites, as well as for other properties of taxonomic systems.

*Theorem* 1. Every taxonomic system has a unique beginner.

For all $z$, if $(z \epsilon T \subset S)$ then there is an $x$ such that $(X = B'z)^2$ (Gregg, 1954, p. 48).

*Theorem* 2. Every member of the field of a taxonomic system is included in either the beginner of the system or is related to a segregate at the most inclusive level by vertical inclusion.

For all $z$, if $(z \epsilon T \subset S)$ then, for all $x$, if $(x \epsilon \text{FIELD}'z)$ then $(x \subset B'z)^3$ (Gregg, 1954, p. 50).

---

[2] Where (1) $z \epsilon T \subset S(=)z$ is a member of the taxonomic system, and (2) $B'z$ is the set of all beginners of $z$.

[3] Where $X \subset B'z$ is to be read $x$ is included in the set of all beginners $z$.

| | | | | Son | Daughter | Grandson | Grand-daughter | Father | Mother | Grand-father | Grand-mother | Father-in-law | Mother-in-law | Son-in-law | Daughter-in-law | Sister-in-law | Brother-in-law |
|---|---|---|---|---|---|---|---|---|---|---|---|---|---|---|---|---|---|
| Relative | Blood Relative | Non-lineal | Consan-guineals | Child | | Grandchild | | Parent | | Grandparent | | In-Law | | | | | |
| | | | | Descendant | | | | Ancestor | | | | | | | | | |

*Figure 9–14. A Partial Taxonomic Diagram of One Dialect of American-English Kinship Terminology (Kay, 1966, p. 21).*

*Theorem* 3. There are two types of relations within taxonomic systems: (1) horizontal differentiation of contrastive but coordinate categories; and (2) vertical increase of generalization or specification (Conklin, 1962, p. 128). Put more abstractly, if $z$ is a taxonomy, and $x$ and $y$ are members of the taxonomy, then $y$ is included in $x$ or $x$ is included in $y$, or $x$ and $y$ are mutually exclusive.

For all $z$, if $(z \in T \subset S)$ then, for all $x$ and all $y$, if $(x \in \text{FIELD}'z)$ and $(y \in \text{FIELD}'z)$ then $y \subset y$ or $(x \subset y)$ or $(z \cap y = EM)$ (Gregg, 1954, p. 51). The partial kinship taxonomy (Kay, 1966, p. 21) shown in Figure 9–14 should be referred to in terms of the preceding and following discussion.

Let us now consider several frequently encountered problems in the analysis of folk taxonomies (Conklin, 1962, pp. 129–130). (1) *Multiple and Interlocking Hierarchies:* Folk segregates may belong simultaneously to several distinct hierarchies and the depth of their embedding within subhierarchies may vary as a function of underlying principles of taxonomic ordering; for example, formal properties, on the one hand, and functions or cultural treatment on the other. Further, subhierarchies may be interarticulated in numerous ways "and there is always the potentiality of partial inclusion or domain overlap" (Conklin, 1962, p. 129). (2) *Extrahierarchic Relations:* Folk categories need not be related by either class inclusion or contrast. The analytic difficulties that must be reckoned with if lexemes designate separate ontogenetic stages of members of particular segregates are not restricted to botanical and zoological taxonomies. In "kinship taxonomies," ontogenetic stages are often marked by synonymous usage. For example, the referential synonyms (my) *infant, baby, child,* and *son* (or *daughter*) may designate separate ontogenetic levels *as well as* class inclusion relations. In a similar manner, the referential kin terms *father, dad,* and *daddy,* which are frequently cited in discussions of synonymy as possible examples of equivalent terms in different age, sex, and social-class languages, may also be regarded as separate ontogenetic stages of a specific segregate. (3) *Types of Contrast:* In addition to binary, segregate opposition (antonymy), segregates may be contrasted in serial and discontinuous arrays.

## COVERT CATEGORIES

Up to this point, we have assumed that a system of segregates related by hierarchic inclusion must be monolexemically labelled. It has recently been demonstrated, however, that many culturally revealing categories related by class inclusion are not monolexemically labelled (Berlin, Breedlove, and Raven, 1967). To be somewhat more specific, there appear to many taxonomic structures with neither a unique beginner nor completely labelled midlevel nodes. Covert midlevel categories that may be analytically derived suggest interesting methodological problems. If these unnamed taxa are not taken into account, axiomatic distinctions between paradigms and taxonomies are somewhat blurred (Werner, n. d., 1 and 2). Two interesting and interrelated questions follow closely: (1) How do we demonstrate the presence of covert categories and (2) what analytic tests may be employed to demonstrate their presence?

If the presence of covert categories can be demonstrated, then lower level subsets of terms, within named contrast sets or paradigms, might be expected to be conceptually grouped together: these covert subsets could have a high information value with considerable psychological relevance (Berlin *et al.*, 1967, p. 5). These unnamed subsets may be revealed by (1) having informal discussions, which may suggest that some named categories in the same contrast set are more closely related cognitively than others, thus providing a partial demonstration of higher level covert categories governing this ordering; (2) determining the extent to which informants subdivide lists of named categories within the same contrast set; (3) investigating the conceptual features of covert categories with the triad test; a procedure requiring informants to specify which term in a set of three is "most different" from the others; and (4) by presenting informants with a set of named categories and having them construct a folk key. Consequently, an informant is required to verbalize the full array of conceptual distinctions that have been used in making divisions. Finally, by the use of paired comparisons, an informant may be requested to compare logical pairs of named categories in terms of relevant similarities and differences (Berlin *et al.*, 1967).

It is of considerable interest that, at the very least, some of these procedures are employed in distinguishing paradigms from taxonomies and both from taxonomies embedded within larger taxonomic structures. Once these types of semantic structures are carefully distinguished, we may state with some degree of confidence their axiomatic properties (Werner, n. d. 2, pp. 3–6).

There are three axioms or requirements for a taxonomic relation (Werner, n. d. 2, pp. 3–4). Consider the partial taxonomy for American-English kinship terms in reference to these requirements.

**1.** A taxon cannot be in a taxonomic relationship with itself.
**2.** A taxon cannot be at the same time a dominating and a subordinate taxon.
**3.** A subordinate of a subordinate taxon is a subordinate taxon.

The following theorem holds for a system of semantic relations that satisfies these axioms.

*Theorem 1. The necessary and sufficient condition that the three foregoing requirements hold is that the graph of the taxonomy be free of cycles* (i.e., that the graph of every taxonomy is a tree) (Werner, n. d. 2, p. 4).

From the transitive properties of taxonomic relations, Werner (n. d. 2, p. 46) derives a theorem that is relevant to our discussion of covert categories:

*Theorem 2. The nodes on a path from the origin F of a taxonomy are completely connected.*

For a three-level taxonomy see Figure 9–15.

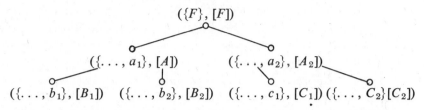

$(\{F\}, [F])$

$(\{\ldots, a_1\}, [A])$   $(\{\ldots, a_2\}, [A_2])$

$(\{\ldots, b_1\}, [B_1])$   $(\{\ldots, b_2\}, [B_2])$   $(\{\ldots, c_1\}, [C_1])$ $(\{\ldots, C_2\}[C_2])$

*Figure 9–15.   Completely Connected Path Rules for a Three-Level Taxonomy.*

Werner (n. d. 1, pp. 47–48) illustrates that the path from $F$, $a_1$ to $F$, $a_1$, $b_1$, $c_1$ may be drawn as the sides of a square in which the combined graph of

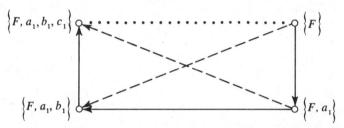

*Figure 9–16.   A Completely Connected Graph for Taxonomic Orderings.*

solid and dotted lines represents a completely connected graph (Werner, n. d. 1, p. 48). Two nontrivial generalizations about taxonomies follow closely: (1) the transitive properties of taxonomies affect the nature of definitions, and (2) informants tend to agree on the most general and most specific (terminal) nodes, whereas knowledge of midlevel nodes may vary greatly (Werner, n. d. 1, p. 48). As long as there is knowledge of terminal and general nodes, communication will be possible, as "there will always be a path from the most specific node to the most general node regardless of their disagreement on the depth (number of levels) of intermediate or intervening classifications" (Werner, n. d. 1, p. 48) (see Figure 9–16).

Now consider a somewhat more formal axiomatic approach to paradigmatic structures and the implications of this approach for the formal semantic analysis of American-English kinship terminology. All definitions and theorems derive from studies by O. Werner (n. d. 1, p. 2).

## DEFINITIONS

First, a paradigm is not a relation. In a sense, then, the relation between the descriptive units of a paradigm are the converse of taxonomic relations, which are of the form $aRb$, where $R$ is an arbitrary relation such as "kind of," "stage of," "larger than," "superordinate to," "consists of," and so on. Consider a set $U$ of the components that make up a paradigm, which is then partitioned into mutually exclusive subsets called dimensions $D_i$ whose sum is $U$. Dimensions $D_i \neq 0$, such that $\bigwedge_{i=1}^{n} D_i = \emptyset$, (i.e., the intersection of all dimensions is the empty set) and $\bigcup\limits_{i=1}^{n} D_i = U$ (i.e., a set of disjoint nonempty subsets whose union is $U$). That is, the intersection of all dimensions is the null or empty set, and the union of all dimensions, or a set of disjoint nonempty subsets is the set $U$ (Werner, n. d. 2, pp. 4–5; n. d. 1, p. 24).

A definition of a paradigm follows closely from these properties:

*Definition. A paradigm is the set of all subsets $C_i$ of U containing exactly one element from each dimension* (Werner, n. d. 2, p. 5; n. d. 1, p. 24).

*Theorem 2. A paradigm cannot be represented by a graph* (Werner, n. d. 2, p. 5).

A graph can be most generally represented as an ordered pair $(P, R)$, where $P$ is the set of all elements of the graph and $R$ is a binary relation that holds between the elements of that set. A binary relation $R$ requires that at least two elements of $P$ should be ordered. It can be easily seen that this contradicts the definition of a paradigm (Werner, n. d. 2, p. 5).

Werner's (n. d. 1, pp. 26–33) formal distinction between taxonomies and paradigms appears to be similar to Wallace and Atkins' (1960, p. 71) distinction between Nonorthospace Type II and orthogonal spaces. Like "deep taxonomies," symmetrical paradigms appear to be characteristic of certain domains (e.g., pronominal sets). They are not "empirically rare" in the same sense as asymmetric exchange systems.

An asymmetrical or incomplete paradigm may be represented by a mapping of dimensions onto a nonorthogonal class-product space. In somewhat more general terms (Werner, n. d. 2, pp. 27–28):

1. *A symmetrical paradigm is the semantic representation of a single-level taxonomy.*
2. *An asymmetrical paradigm is the semantic representation of a single-level taxonomy, plus "conditions of neutralization."*

The neutralization of a dimension $S_i$ of a paradigm $(P)$ is total if $D_i \Rightarrow \emptyset$, and partial if $S_i \Rightarrow S_i{}'$, where $S_i{}'$ is similar to $S_i$, although one or more contrasts between the elements in $S_i$ are neutralized.

## CONCLUSIONS

In order to apply some of the methods and constructs reviewed in this chapter, let us represent Kay's (1966, p. 21; see page 210) partial taxonomy of American-English kinship terminology in the form of a tree graph or decision tree as shown in Figure 9–17.

We can easily see that the depth of subhierarchies within this tree graph are not constant. The multiple paths from terminal nodes to the cover label "Blood Relative" includes a greater number of decision points than the paths from terminal nodes to the cover label "In-law." The depth of the embedding and type of contrast within subhierarchies is in part a function of the analyst's decision to exclude referential synonyms from the tree graph. For example, the decision node that is labelled "Child" and the terminal

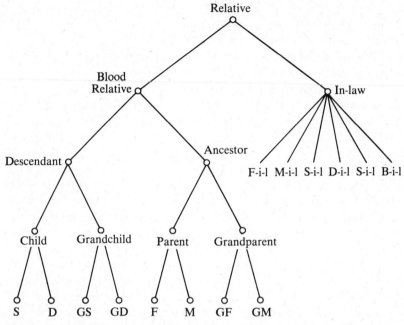

*Figure 9–17. A Partial Tree Graph of American-English Kinship Terminology (cf. Kay, 1966, p. 21)*

nodes that are related to this node by vertical class inclusion might be alternatively represented as shown in Figure 9–18.

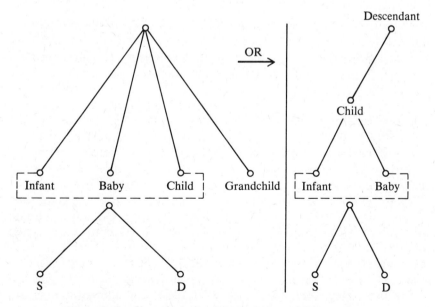

*Figure 9–18. Partial Tree Graphs with Referential Synonyms.*

As an exercise, the reader might find it profitable to derive a set of queries that would produce the alternative responses, types of contrast, and forms of embedding that are represented within these subhierarchies. It is only through a consideration of various types of assignments that one can pass from the formalism of taxonomic orderings to the possible decision processes underlying adequate sortings. It may also be useful to finish drawing in the affinal section of the tree graph. If "the reader finds a solution that satisfies his intuitions concerning the notion 'level of contrast,' he will probably also find that it is based explicitly or implicitly on the feature definitions (componential definitions) of the lexemes. The relations of inclusion of reference alone do not in general solve the level of contrast problem" (Kay, 1966, p. 21). Finally, it might prove instructive to draw a graph of a complete set of American-English kinship terms, which derives from a solution that includes covert categories on midlevel nodes. Note that Werner's (n. d. 1, p. 46) second theorem for taxonomic orderings does not say that all nodes will be labelled or that there will be general agreement on the depth of intermediate classifications: only that the nodes on a path are completely connected.

We should make it clear in conclusion that the anthropologist's interest in componential analysis, taxonomic orderings, and other approaches to structural semantics derives from a more basic interest in decision processes in culture, choice behavior, principles of classification and related processes, rather than in kinship terminologies or any other domain as a "thing" in itself. A good deal of literature on choice behavior, cognition, simulation of intellectual processes (artificial intelligence), and various other topics that we have not reviewed, are therefore directly relevant to the central, although often implicit, concerns of this chapter (e.g., Miller, Galanter, and Pribram, 1960; Bruner, Goodnow, and, Austin, 1962; Feigenbaum and Feldman, 1963).

Finally, let us outline what the act of rendering classes of things equivalent does for the organism: the achievements of categorizing (Bruner *et al.*, 1962, pp. 11–15). (1) By categorizing as equivalent discriminably different events, persons, or things in the natural, supernatural, and social world, the organism reduces the complexity of its environment. (2) Categorization allows us to identify the objects of the world about us. (3) When a category based on a set of defining attributes is established, the necessity of constant learning is greatly reduced. "For the abstraction of defining properties makes possible future acts of categorizing without benefit of further learning" (Bruner *et al.*, 1962, p. 12). (4) Categorizing channels instrumental activity. To know what an object is, that a man is a brother, uncle, or priest, is to know in advance what actions are appropriate and what actions are inappropriate in reference to the categorized object. Categorizing and, in particular, the achievement of categories, is directly related to the issue of jural rules as constraints on choice behavior, as well as the development of measures for testing the adequacy of productive ethnographic statements. (5) Categorizing allows the organism to order and relate classes of events. This achievement of categorizing clearly indicates, we think, why taxonomies and the rule systems that allow us to shift from one taxonomy to another are of intrinsically greater interest than paradigmatic orderings.

"We map and give meaning to our world by relating classes of events rather than by relating individual events. 'Matches' the child learns, will 'cause' a set of events called 'fires'. The meaning of each class of things placed in quotation marks—matches, causes, and fires—is given by the imbeddedness of each class in such relationship maps. The moment an object is placed in a category, we have opened up a whole vista of possibilities for 'going beyond' the category by virtue of the superordinate and causal relationships linking this category to others" (Bruner, Goodnow, and Austin, 1962, p. 13).

# Chapter
# Ten
# Iroquois
# Systems
# of
# Kinship
# Terminology

As we stressed in the previous chapter, formal techniques are useful and important because they permit us insights into the form of institutions. By their nature, they are algorithms that will reduce redundancy and complexity in systematic relations to comprehensible principles. They are of intrinsic importance in comparative research—that "butterfly collecting" which Radcliffe-Brown pursued with zeal, and Leach disparaged. What we propose to do in the next two chapters is to explore the form of certain system categories (such as "Iroquois systems" and "Omaha systems"). We examine the theoretical concepts utilized in the past to characterize these systems (concepts like "cross/parallel distinction," "generational terminology," and "generational skewing") in order to show two things, (1) that the range of empirical variation that has been labelled by these category words is very great, and (2) that with the use of formal techniques the variation can be described in detail. The variation can be subsequently reduced to a set of formal principles that are logically related, parsimonious, and predictive in that they will generate all and only the systems which we have labelled as "Iroquois" or "Omaha" or whatever. On the way we hope to be able to review the theoretical concepts that have been useful in the past in explaining the form of the systems. We hope that the reader's reaction at the end of this exploration will be, "I never knew the systems were so variable, nor that they could be made to look so simple, in principle." And to reassure the reader who has not been accustomed to formal analyses in the past, we would also like to point out that there is nothing magical, or even difficult, about them. They do require a bit of perseverance from time to time, but in fact they are merely restatements of what we knew all the time, although we perhaps didn't know we knew it.

Iroquois kinship terminologies, like many other comparative (ethnological) concepts (e.g., patrilineal descent systems, asymmetric exchange systems), include a rather heterogeneous assortment of structures. The concept of an Iroquois-type system is of value in isolating and drawing attention to certain terminological features, which are shared by practically all systems of this sort: (1) a generation type classification in all generations (Morgan, 1870, p. 141; Dumont, 1953a, p. 34, 1957, p. 26); (2) a pervasive elder-younger age distinction within certain generations (Morgan, 1871, pp. 145–146; Dumont, 1953a, p. 34, 1957, p. 26); and (3) a distinction between "cross" and "parallel" relatives (Morgan, 1870, p. 145; Lounsbury, 1964b; Kay, 1965). The latter is criterial and will therefore receive particular attention in this chapter. Attempts to explain or account for these regularities fall into two general categories: (1) explanations that purport to demonstrate causal or functional relations between principles of terminological classification, on the one hand, and social groups and/or marriage rules, on the other; and (2) structural explanations that attempt to satisfy explicitly the criteria of adequacy and parsimony, and at the same time account for Iroquois forms of classification in terms of certain underlying regularities, and principles. The latter form of explanation is the particular concern of this chapter. It is not that we are uninterested in the relationship of Iroquois terminologies to various principles of social organization or to other cultural variables; the extent of this interest, and the more general theoretical problems which such functional relations raise, only serve to emphasize the importance of formal analysis as a kind of direction indicator in getting functional analyses profitably oriented (Lounsbury, 1964a, p. 352). Our concern will be, simply, to perform a formal analysis of "Iroquois." But before considering the rewrite rules that produce Iroquois-type classifications, we must be prepared to answer two basic questions: (1) *How* do Iroquois systems differ from one another (2) *How much* do Iroquois systems differ from one another? These questions seem so obvious that it might be thought that social anthropology would have supplied the answers many years ago. This is not the case. In logic, our task is to structure the variability between Iroquois terminologies, and to construct a developmental typology from the resultant scale. A scale of this type will allow us to measure the structural relations between all Iroquois systems. The scale types that are produced by our analysis can be regarded as strictly logical in nature; numerical positions that provide the minimal information that will allow us to differentiate Iroquois systems from one another. The method that we use is economical and explicit: it is known as scalogram analysis. (See Chapter Eight.)

## A SCALOGRAM ANALYSIS OF IROQUOIS TERMINOLOGICAL SYSTEMS

The first problem concerns the universe of phenomena which we wish to examine: the universe of "Iroquois systems." Using as a guide Murdock

(1949) and the Ethnographic Atlas, a list was prepared of all reported Iroquois terminologies. As many sources as possible were located, all those where the information was adequate were used. Data were sufficient for a total of 41 systems. We then look at the kinship terminology of each of these societies and write out all the equations (mergings), that take place in each terminology. Having written out the terminological equations the algorithm of scalogram analysis rank orders the kinship terminologies by scale steps. Note that this is an empirical process that assumes two things: (1) that the construct Iroquois system is unitary and (2) that the rank order of systems that emerges is the best reflection of the logical development of the construct "Iroquois system." Those mergings that are found in all 41 systems (there are four of them) will be our *threshold variables*, and will constitute, for our purposes, the minimal criteria by virtue of which we will call a system Iroquois. In more familiar terms we can say that all the Iroquois systems represented (1) merge cross cousins, while differentiating them from parallel cousins and (2) merge patrilateral female cross cousins with same sex siblings, and matrilateral male cross cousins with same sex siblings. This is expressed by the format of the threshold variables that state

| | |
|---|---|
| 1. FZS = MBS | 3. FBD = Z |
| 2. FZD = MBD | 4. MZS = B. |

The rank order of variables that will yield the highest coefficient is

| | |
|---|---|
| **1.** FZS = MBS | **4.** FBD = Z |
| **2.** FZD = MBD | **5.** MZS = B |
| **3.** FBS = B | **6.** MZD = Z |

7. All male and female bilateral consanguineal relatives of zero degree of collaterality, and of the second ascending generation, are equated with either a male or a female bilateral consanguineal relative of first degree of collaterality, of the second ascending generation.
8. All male and female bilateral consanguineal relatives of zero degree of collaterality, and of the second descending generation, are equated with either a male or a female bilateral consanguineal relative of the second descending generation (i.e., all collaterals of $-2$ generation are merged with lineals).
9. F = FB                     10. M = MZ

This rank order of variables yields the following scale types, remembering that the highest-order variable present defines the scale type.

There are nineteen scale errors (omitting the nonscalable equations as we stated we would). The coefficient of reproducibility is 0.955 (see Table 10–1). From a knowledge of the presence of a higher order variable, we may derive

### Table 10–1.  A Scalogram Analysis of Iroquois Terminological Systems

| System No. | Scale type | 1 | 2 | 3 | 4 | 5 | 6 | 7 | 8 | 9 | 10 |
|---|---|---|---|---|---|---|---|---|---|---|---|
| 1 | 4 | + | + | + | + | − | − | 0 | 0 | − | − |
| 2 | 4 | + | + | + | + | − | − | − | − | − | − |
| 3 | 5 | + | + | + | − | + | − | − | − | − | − |
| 4 | 6 | + | + | + | + | + | + | 0 | 0 | − | − |
| 5 | 6 | + | + | + | + | + | + | − | − | − | − |
| 6 | 6 | + | + | + | + | + | + | 0 | 0 | − | − |
| 7 | 8 | + | + | + | + | + | + | + | + | − | − |
| 8 | 8 | + | + | + | + | + | + | + | + | − | − |
| 9 | 8 | + | + | + | + | + | + | + | + | − | − |
| 10 | 8 | + | + | + | + | + | + | + | + | − | − |
| 11 | 8 | + | + | + | + | + | + | + | + | − | − |
| 12 | 8 | + | + | + | + | + | + | − | + | − | − |
| 13 | 8 | + | + | − | − | − | − | + | + | − | − |
| 14 | 8 | + | + | − | − | + | + | − | + | − | − |
| 15 | 9 | + | + | + | + | + | + | 0 | 0 | + | − |
| 16 | 10 | + | + | + | + | + | + | + | + | + | + |
| 17 | 10 | + | + | + | + | + | + | + | + | + | + |
| 18 | 10 | + | + | + | + | + | + | + | + | + | + |
| 19 | 10 | + | + | + | + | + | − | − | + | + | + |
| 20 | 10 | + | + | + | + | + | + | + | + | + | + |
| 21 | 10 | + | + | + | + | + | + | + | − | + | + |
| 22 | 10 | + | + | + | + | + | + | + | + | + | + |
| 23 | 10 | + | + | + | + | + | + | + | − | + | + |
| 24 | 10 | + | + | + | + | + | + | + | + | + | + |
| 25 | 10 | + | + | + | + | + | + | + | + | + | + |
| 26 | 10 | + | + | + | + | + | + | − | + | + | + |
| 27 | 10 | + | + | + | + | + | + | + | 0 | + | + |
| 28 | 10 | + | + | + | + | + | + | 0 | + | + | + |
| 29 | 10 | + | + | + | + | + | + | 0 | + | + | + |
| 30 | 10 | + | + | + | + | + | + | + | + | + | + |
| 31 | 10 | + | + | + | + | + | + | 0 | + | + | + |
| 32 | 10 | + | + | + | + | + | + | 0 | 0 | + | + |
| 33 | 10 | + | + | + | + | + | + | 0 | − | + | + |
| 34 | 10 | + | + | + | + | + | + | − | − | + | + |
| 35 | 10 | + | + | + | + | + | + | 0 | − | + | + |
| 36 | 10 | + | + | + | + | + | + | 0 | + | + | + |
| 37 | 10 | + | + | + | + | + | + | + | + | + | + |
| 38 | 10 | + | + | + | + | + | + | + | + | + | + |
| 39 | 10 | + | + | + | + | − | − | 0 | 0 | + | + |
| 40 | 10 | + | + | + | + | + | + | 0 | 0 | + | + |
| 41 | 10 | + | + | + | + | + | + | + | 0 | + | + |

Coefficient of reproducibility = 0.955.

| Terminological Systems | Scale Types | Terminological Systems | Scale Types |
|---|---|---|---|
| **1.** Ittik | 4 | **21.** Kurtatchi | 10 |
| **2.** Kapauku | 4 | **22.** Mappila | 10 |
| **3.** Maria Gond | 5 | **23.** Iroquois | 10 |
| **4.** Tukina | 6 | **24.** Yekuana | 10 |
| **5.** Bacairi | 6 | **25.** Jicarilla Apache | 10 |
| **6.** Havasupai | 6 | **26.** Plains Cree | 10 |
| **7.** Tanaina (Illiamma) | 6 | **27.** Black Carib | 10 |
| **8.** Sinhalese | 8 | **28.** Toda | 10 |
| **9.** Kutubu | 8 | **29.** Camayura | 10 |
| **10.** Vedda | 8 | **30.** Nambicuara | 10 |
| **11.** Ojibwa | 8 | **31.** Ila | 10 |
| **12.** Lau | 8 | **32.** Aueti | 10 |
| **13.** Garo | 8 | **33.** Calapalo | 10 |
| **14.** St. Lawrence Island | | **34.** Zulu | 10 |
| (Sivokakmeit) | 8 | **35.** Iwalapeti | 10 |
| **15.** Guahibo | 8 | **36.** Paressi | 10 |
| **16.** Naidjbeedj | 9 | **37.** Piaroa | 10 |
| **17.** Lesu | 10 | **38.** Fort Jameson Ngoni | 10 |
| **18.** Dobu | 10 | **39.** Bora-Bora | 10 |
| **19.** Hottentot | 10 | **40.** Mander | 10 |
| **20.** Navaho | 10 | **41.** Maw | 10 |

lower order variables in accordance with the rule which we have already formulated: when a $\pm$ is preceded by a 0 or a $\pm$, predict downward, filling in the terminological equation that is located on the axis which is denoted by the 0 or $\pm$ in question.

All terminological assignments that are (1) not ethnographically recorded, and (2) that are located on an axis which has scored in the positive category for the system in question may be generated.

| Systems and Unrecorded Scale Variables | | Scale Type |
|---|---|---|
| **1.** | *Naidjbeedj:* | 7,8 | 9 |
| **2.** | *Calapalo:* | 7 | 10 |
| **3.** | *Camayura:* | 7 | 10 |
| **4.** | *Aueti:* | 7,8 | 10 |
| **5.** | *Black Carib:* | 8 | 10 |
| **6.** | *Guahibo:* | 8,9 | 10 |
| **7.** | *Iwalapeti:* | 7 | 10 |
| **8.** | *Nambicuara:* | 7 | 10 |
| **9.** | *Paressi:* | 7 | 10 |
| **10.** | *Toda:* | 8 | 10 |
| **11.** | *Maw:* | 8 | 10 |
| **12.** | *Bora-Bora:* | 7,8 | 10 |
| **13.** | *Mander:* | 7,8 | 10 |

To sum up: the variability between 41 Iroquois systems has been structured with a Guttman scale.

Despite the very great range of variation between Iroquois subtypes (or scale types), the very high coefficient of reproducibility enables one to say that the concept is unidimensional.

The next problem is to discuss the question as to *what* each Iroquois-type system is. Remembering that we are not asking what it "does" (a functional account), nor how it came to be (a historical account), but merely asking what it looks like. What are its formal properties? The rewrite rules that will generate the scale steps can now be formulated.

We may now briefly review the various graphic conventions that have been previously specified and indicate some additional ones that will be used in formulating the rewrite rules and corollaries.

1. *Primary kin types:*

F = father     S = son
M = mother    D = daughter
B = brother    H = husband
Z = sister      W = wife.

2. *Relative products:* Secondary and more genealogically distant kin types are written by placing the symbols for primary kin types in juxtaposition. For example,

ZS = sister's son
MZD = mother's sister's daughter
FMBS = father's mother's brother's son.

3. *Sex designators:* Mars ($\male$) and Venus ($\female$) symbols are used for designating the sex of the propositus (Ego), a kinsman or a linking kinsman (Lounsbury, 1964a, p. 358).
For example,

$\male$ = male (Ego, linking kinsman, or kinsman)
$\female$ = female (Ego, linking kinswoman, or kinswoman).

Preposing the sex designators to the relative products yields the following abbreviations:

$\male$MB = any male person's mother's brother
$\female$ZS = any female person's sister's son.

To discuss the formal properties of Iroquois (or any kinship terminological) systems, we utilize transformational analysis, which permits us to state in the most economical terms the formal characteristics of terminological systems. The *rewrite rules* that are the end result of a transformational account of a terminological system are the most economical form of expressing the structural characteristics of the system.

## THE RULES AND COROLLARIES

I. *Half-sibling Rule.* Lounsbury's (1964a, p. 361) half-sibling rule expresses, in formal terms, the absence of an obligatory distinction between full and half siblings. It is written

$$\text{Half-sibling Rule: } FS \rightarrow B; \quad MS \rightarrow B;$$
$$FD \rightarrow Z; \quad MD \rightarrow Z.$$

*Let one's parent's child be considered to be one's sibling* (Lounsbury, 1964a, p. 360).

II. *Basic Iroquois Rule.* The basic Iroquois transformation rule cycles cross kin types through their denotative range, and underlies the Iroquois opposition between cross and parallel kin types. It is written

$$\text{Transformation Rule (Iroquois Type I): } FZ \ldots \rightarrow MB \ldots$$

This is to be read: *Let the kin type* FATHER'S SISTER, *whenever it occurs as a link between Ego and any other relative, be regarded as structurally equivalent to the kin type* MOTHER'S BROTHER *in that context.*

III. *Iroquois Merging Rules.* Lounsbury's (1964a, p. 357) merging rule "expresses the formal equivalence, in specified contexts, between siblings of the same sex." An adequate account of Iroquois systems necessitates the formulation of other types of merging rules. If these rules express the formal equivalence between lineal and first-degree collaterals, other than mother's sister and father's brother, then these rules are referred to as "stronger" merging rules. The general notion that Iroquois systems classify by generation, is expressed by the following rules:

$$\text{Merging Rule: } \male B \ldots \rightarrow \male \ldots ; \text{ and } \female Z \ldots \rightarrow \female \ldots$$

*Let any person's sibling of the same sex as himself (or herself), when a link to some other relative, be regarded as equivalent to that person himself (or herself) directly linked to said relative* (Lounsbury, 1964a, p. 360).

$$\text{Corollary: } \ldots \male B \rightarrow \ldots \male ; \text{ and } \ldots \female Z \rightarrow \ldots \female.$$

*Any linking relative's sibling of the same sex as himself (or herself) is to be regarded as equivalent to that linking relative* (Lounsbury, 1964a, p. 360).

IV. The "stronger" merging rules are written

$$\text{Merging Rule (Stronger Form I): } \ldots \male FZ \rightarrow \ldots \male M.$$

This is to be read: *Any male linking relative's* FATHER'S SISTER *is to be regarded as equivalent to that male linking relative's* MOTHER.

If this rule is operative, then its corollary specifies an equivalence between reciprocals of the kin types covered by the rule.

$$\text{Corollary: } \female BS \ldots \rightarrow \female S \ldots ; \text{ and } \female BD \ldots \rightarrow \female D \ldots$$

This is to be read: *Let a woman's* BROTHER'S CHILD (BROTHER'S SON *or* BROTHER'S DAUGHTER), *as linking relative be regarded as structurally equivalent to that woman's* CHILD (SON *or* DAUGHTER, *respectively*) *in that context.*

$$\text{Merging Rule (Stronger Form II): } \ldots \varphi MB \rightarrow \ldots \varphi F.$$

This is to be read: *Any female linking relative's* MOTHER'S BROTHER *is to be regarded as equivalent to that female linking relative's* FATHER.

The corollary of this rule specifies an equivalence between the reciprocals of the kin types covered by the rule.

$$\text{Corollary: } \male ZS \ldots \rightarrow \male S \ldots \text{; and } \male ZD \ldots \rightarrow \male D \ldots$$

This is to be read: *Let a man's* SISTER'S CHILD (SISTER'S SON *or* SISTER'S DAUGHTER) *as a linking relative, be regarded as structurally equivalent to that man's* CHILD (SON *or* DAUGHTER, *respectively*), *in that context.*

The Iroquois transformation rule may be rewritten

$$\begin{bmatrix} + \text{ mas.} \\ + \text{ g.r.} \\ + \text{ sen.} \\ + \text{ con.} \end{bmatrix} \begin{bmatrix} - \text{ mas.} \\ - \text{ g.r.} \\ - \text{ sen.} \\ + \text{ con.} \end{bmatrix} \rightarrow \begin{bmatrix} - \text{ mas.} \\ + \text{ g.r.} \\ + \text{ sen.} \\ + \text{ con.} \end{bmatrix} \begin{bmatrix} + \text{ mas.} \\ - \text{ g.r.} \\ - \text{ sen.} \\ + \text{ con.} \end{bmatrix} \text{ in env. } \underline{\hspace{2cm}} X.$$

The merging rules reducing sibling of same sex (when a link) to Ego (Lounsbury 1964a, p. 360) may be rewritten

(a)
$$\begin{bmatrix} + \text{ mas.} \\ - \text{ g.r.} \\ - \text{ sen.} \\ + \text{ con.} \end{bmatrix} \rightarrow \begin{bmatrix} \emptyset \end{bmatrix} \text{ in env. } [+ \text{ mas.}] \underline{\hspace{2cm}} X.$$

and

(b)
$$\begin{bmatrix} - \text{ mas.} \\ - \text{ g.r.} \\ - \text{ sen.} \\ + \text{ con.} \end{bmatrix} \rightarrow \begin{bmatrix} \emptyset \end{bmatrix} \text{ in env. } [- \text{ mas.}] \underline{\hspace{2cm}} X.$$

The corollaries (any linking relative's sibling of the same sex is to be regarded as equivalent to that linking relative) are

(a)
$$\begin{bmatrix} + \text{ mas.} \\ - \text{ g.r.} \\ - \text{ sen.} \\ + \text{ con.} \end{bmatrix} \rightarrow \begin{bmatrix} \emptyset \end{bmatrix} \text{ in env. } X [+ \text{ mas.}] \underline{\hspace{2cm}} .$$

(b) $\begin{bmatrix} - \text{ mas.} \\ - \text{ g.r.} \\ - \text{ sen.} \\ + \text{ con.} \end{bmatrix} \rightarrow \begin{bmatrix} \ \\ \ \\ \ \end{bmatrix} \varnothing$   in env. $X$ $[-\text{ mas.}]$ _____ .

The two merging rules may be combined

$\begin{bmatrix} \alpha \text{ mas.} \\ - \text{ g.r.} \\ - \text{ sen.} \\ + \text{ con.} \end{bmatrix} \rightarrow \begin{bmatrix} \ \\ \ \\ \ \end{bmatrix} \varnothing$   in env. $[\alpha \text{ mas.}]$ _____ $X$.

(noting that $\alpha$ takes the same value in both the expression and in the limiting condition.)

The corollaries may be combined

$\begin{bmatrix} \alpha \text{ mas.} \\ - \text{ g.r.} \\ - \text{ sen.} \\ + \text{ con.} \end{bmatrix} \rightarrow \begin{bmatrix} \ \\ \ \\ \ \end{bmatrix} \varnothing$   in env. $X$ $[\alpha \text{ mas.}]$ _____ .

IV.  The "stronger" merging rule (Form I) may be rewritten

$\begin{bmatrix} + \text{ mas.} \\ + \text{ g.r.} \\ + \text{ sen.} \\ + \text{ con.} \end{bmatrix} \begin{bmatrix} - \text{ mas.} \\ - \text{ g.r.} \\ - \text{ sen.} \\ + \text{ con.} \end{bmatrix} \rightarrow \begin{bmatrix} - \text{ mas.} \\ + \text{ g.r.} \\ + \text{ sen.} \\ + \text{ con.} \end{bmatrix}$   in env. $X$ $[+\text{ mas.}]$ _____ .

The corollaries are

(a) $\begin{bmatrix} + \text{ mas.} \\ - \text{ g.r.} \\ - \text{ sen.} \\ + \text{ con.} \end{bmatrix} \begin{bmatrix} + \text{ mas.} \\ + \text{ g.r.} \\ - \text{ sen.} \\ + \text{ con.} \end{bmatrix} \rightarrow \begin{bmatrix} + \text{ mas.} \\ + \text{ g.r.} \\ - \text{ sen.} \\ + \text{ con.} \end{bmatrix}$   in env. $[-\text{ mas.}]$ _____ $X$.

(b) $\begin{bmatrix} + \text{ mas.} \\ - \text{ g.r.} \\ - \text{ sen.} \\ + \text{ con.} \end{bmatrix} \begin{bmatrix} - \text{ mas.} \\ + \text{ g.r.} \\ - \text{ sen.} \\ + \text{ con.} \end{bmatrix} \rightarrow \begin{bmatrix} - \text{ mas.} \\ + \text{ g.r.} \\ - \text{ sen.} \\ + \text{ con.} \end{bmatrix}$   in env. $[-\text{ mas.}]$ _____ $X$.

The "stronger" merging rule (Form II) may be rewritten

$\begin{bmatrix} - \text{ mas.} \\ + \text{ g.r.} \\ + \text{ sen.} \\ + \text{ con.} \end{bmatrix} \begin{bmatrix} + \text{ mas.} \\ - \text{ g.r.} \\ - \text{ sen.} \\ + \text{ con.} \end{bmatrix} \rightarrow \begin{bmatrix} + \text{ mas.} \\ + \text{ g.r.} \\ + \text{ sen.} \\ + \text{ con.} \end{bmatrix}$   in env. $X$ $[-\text{ mas.}]$ _____ .

The corollaries are

(a)
$$\begin{bmatrix} - \text{mas.} \\ - \text{g.r.} \\ - \text{sen.} \\ + \text{con.} \end{bmatrix} \begin{bmatrix} + \text{mas.} \\ + \text{g.r.} \\ - \text{sen.} \\ + \text{con.} \end{bmatrix} \rightarrow \begin{bmatrix} + \text{mas.} \\ + \text{g.r.} \\ - \text{sen.} \\ + \text{con.} \end{bmatrix} \text{ in env. } [+ \text{mas.}] \text{_____} X.$$

(b)
$$\begin{bmatrix} - \text{mas.} \\ - \text{g.r.} \\ - \text{sen.} \\ + \text{con.} \end{bmatrix} \begin{bmatrix} - \text{mas.} \\ + \text{g.r.} \\ - \text{sen.} \\ + \text{con.} \end{bmatrix} \rightarrow \begin{bmatrix} - \text{mas.} \\ + \text{g.r.} \\ - \text{sen.} \\ + \text{con.} \end{bmatrix} \text{ in env. } [+ \text{mas.}] \text{_____} X.$$

The "stronger" merging rules (Forms I and II) may be combined

$$\begin{bmatrix} \alpha \text{ mas.} \\ + \text{g.r.} \\ + \text{sen.} \\ + \text{con.} \end{bmatrix} \begin{bmatrix} -\alpha \text{ mas.} \\ - \text{g.r.} \\ - \text{sen.} \\ + \text{con.} \end{bmatrix} \rightarrow \begin{bmatrix} -\alpha \text{ mas.} \\ + \text{g.r.} \\ + \text{sen.} \\ + \text{con.} \end{bmatrix} \text{ in env. } X \, [\alpha \text{ mas.}] \text{_____} .$$

The four corollaries may be combined

$$\begin{bmatrix} - \text{g.r.} \\ - \text{sen.} \\ + \text{con.} \end{bmatrix} \begin{bmatrix} + \text{g.r.} \\ - \text{sen.} \\ + \text{con.} \end{bmatrix} \rightarrow \begin{bmatrix} + \text{g.r.} \\ - \text{sen.} \\ + \text{con.} \end{bmatrix} \text{ in env. } [\alpha \text{ mas.}] \text{_____} X.$$

And so, with six sets of matrices, we can give an account of (1) the half-sibling rule, (2) the Iroquois transformation rule, (3) the merging rules, (4) the "stronger" merging rules, and the corollaries of all of these. We have gone from 15 separate rules to six matrices—which means nothing more than that we have achieved a good deal of economy. The following matrices include all the necessary instructions for generating Iroquois-type systems.

$$\begin{bmatrix} + \text{g.r.} \\ + \text{sen.} \\ + \text{con.} \end{bmatrix} \begin{bmatrix} \alpha \text{ mas.} \\ + \text{g.r.} \\ - \text{sen.} \\ + \text{con.} \end{bmatrix} \rightarrow \begin{bmatrix} \alpha \text{ mas.} \\ - \text{g.r.} \\ - \text{sen.} \\ + \text{con.} \end{bmatrix}, \text{ where } \alpha = \pm.$$

$$\begin{bmatrix} + \text{mas.} \\ + \text{g.r.} \\ + \text{sen.} \\ + \text{con.} \end{bmatrix} \begin{bmatrix} - \text{mas.} \\ - \text{g.r.} \\ - \text{sen.} \\ + \text{con.} \end{bmatrix} \rightarrow \begin{bmatrix} - \text{mas.} \\ + \text{g.r.} \\ + \text{sen.} \\ + \text{con.} \end{bmatrix} \begin{bmatrix} + \text{mas.} \\ - \text{g.r.} \\ - \text{sen.} \\ + \text{con.} \end{bmatrix} \text{ in env. } \text{_____} X.$$

$$\begin{bmatrix} \alpha \text{ mas.} \\ - \text{g.r.} \\ - \text{sen.} \\ + \text{con.} \end{bmatrix} \rightarrow \begin{bmatrix} \\ \emptyset \\ \\ \end{bmatrix} \text{ in env. } [\alpha \text{ mas.}] \text{_____} X.$$

$$\begin{bmatrix} \alpha \text{ mas.} \\ - \text{ g.r.} \\ - \text{ sen.} \\ + \text{ con.} \end{bmatrix} \rightarrow \begin{bmatrix} \emptyset \\ \\ \end{bmatrix} \text{ in env. } X [\alpha \text{ mas.}] \underline{\hspace{2cm}} .$$

$$\begin{bmatrix} \alpha \text{ mas.} \\ + \text{ g.r.} \\ + \text{ sen.} \\ + \text{ con.} \end{bmatrix} \begin{bmatrix} -\alpha \text{ mas.} \\ - \text{ g.r.} \\ - \text{ sen.} \\ + \text{ con.} \end{bmatrix} \rightarrow \begin{bmatrix} -\alpha \text{ mas.} \\ + \text{ g.r.} \\ + \text{ sen.} \\ + \text{ con.} \end{bmatrix} \text{ in env. } X [\alpha \text{ mas.}] \underline{\hspace{2cm}} .$$

$$\begin{bmatrix} - \text{ g.r.} \\ - \text{ sen.} \\ + \text{ con.} \end{bmatrix} \begin{bmatrix} + \text{ g.r.} \\ - \text{ sen.} \\ + \text{ con.} \end{bmatrix} \rightarrow \begin{bmatrix} + \text{ g.r.} \\ - \text{ sen.} \\ + \text{ con.} \end{bmatrix} \text{ in env. } [\alpha \text{ mas.}] \underline{\hspace{2cm}} X.$$

Now that some of the formal properties of the calculus have been explored, consider the manner in which the calculus operates on Iroquois forms of classification.

### Scale Variables

$$\text{FZS} \rightarrow \text{MBS} \quad \text{(by Transformation Rule I)} \tag{1}$$
$$\rightarrow \text{FZS} \quad \text{( by a second application).}$$

Similarly, a FZD is transformed into a MBD, and a MBD is transformed into a FZD, by reversing the direction of the algebraic formulation (by reversing the arrow, and by letting three dots [. . .] follow the kin type MB).

3,4,5,6 $\qquad$ $$\text{FBS} \rightarrow \text{FS} \quad \text{(by Merging Rule)} \tag{2}$$
$$\rightarrow \text{B} \quad \text{(by Half-sibling Rule).}$$

The same rules generate variables three, four, five, and six.

| | | | |
|---|---|---|---|
| 7 | FFB → FF | (by Merging Rule Corollary) | (3) |
| 7 | FMB → FF | (by Merging Rule—Stronger Form II) | (4) |
| 7 | MFZ → MM | (by Merging Rule—Stronger Form I) | (5) |
| 8 | FZSSS → FSSS | (by Merging Rule—Stronger Form II Corollary) | (6) |
| | → BSS | (by Half-sibling Rule) | |
| | → SS | (by Merging Rule—Stronger Form I Corollary) | |
| 8 | MBDSD → MDSD | (by Merging Rule—Stronger Form II Corollary) | (7) |
| | → ZSD | (by Half-sibling Rule) | |
| | → SD | (by Merging Rule—Stronger Form II Corollary) | |
| 8 | FBSSS → FSSS | (by Merging Rule) | (8) |
| | → BSS | (by Half-sibling Rule) | |
| | → SS | (by Merging Rule—Stronger Form I Corollary) | |

8        MZDDD → MDDD    (by Merging Rule)                                    (9)
          → ZDD        (by Half-sibling Rule)
          → DD         (by Merging Rule Corollary—
                        Stronger Form II).

Similarly, all bilateral, consanguineal relatives of either sex, and of second degree of collaterality, of the second descending generation, are given a zero-degree collateral assignment.

9        FB → F        (by Merging Rule)                                       (10)
10       MZ → M        (by Merging Rule).                                      (11)

One of the problems that has to be considered in the formal analysis of Iroquois systems is the distinction between cross and parallel relatives, which is a classic distinction in anthropology. Recent attempts to formalize the terms of the construct *cross* and *parallel* have provoked discussion, and it will be interesting to pursue the work in this area in order to show the complexities of the constructs. First we shall take an example from Kapauku terminology (Pospisil, 1960) and see how more distant kin-type strings can be reduced by the reverse application of the expansion rules formulated in the earlier part of this chapter. We take kin-type strings (quinaries, i.e., made up of 5 biological kin types) and reduce them to their kernel, or base form for cross types (examples 1 and 2), and parallel types (examples 3 and 4). We will examine the kin-type strings, and pose the question, "By what criteria have we made the decision that (1) those terms which reduce to *cross types* are in fact *cross terms*, and (2) those terms which reduce to parallel types are in fact *parallel terms*?"

The Kapauku kin-type strings are

FFZDS → FFDS    (by Merging Rule Corollary—Stronger
                Form II)                                             (1)
    → FZS       (by Half-sibling Rule)
FMBDD → FMDD    (by Merging Rule—Stronger Form II
                Corollary)                                           (2)
    → FZD       (by Half-sibling Rule)
FMBSD → FMSD    (by Merging Rule—Stronger Form I
                Corollary)                                           (3)
    → FBD       (by Half-sibling Rule)
    → FD        (by Merging Rule)
    → Z         (by Half-sibling Rule)
FFZSS → FFSS    (by Merging Rule—Stronger Form II
                Corollary)                                           (4)
    → FBS       (by Half-sibling Rule)
    → FS        (by Merging Rule)
    → B         (by Half-sibling Rule).

This family of reductions illustrates that the distinction between cross and parallel kin types is a function of the sexes of the initial terminus and the immediate linking relative in a genealogical chain (Pospisil, 1960). When the sexes are opposite, then the final terminus in a genealogical chain is a cross kin type. For example, FFZDS and FMBDD are second cross cousins (terminologically equivalent to FZS and FZD, respectively), as, in both cases, the sexes of the initial terminus and the immediate linking kinsmen are opposite ($\overline{FF}Z\overline{D}S$ and $\overline{FM}B\overline{D}D$), respectively. The sexes of the ancestral siblings (the intervening links), although different, are not of taxonomic significance in distinguishing cross from parallel kin types. This is best demonstrated by considering two parallel kin types (terminologically equivalent to siblings and paternal parallel cousins): FMBSD and FFZSS. The sexes of the ancestral siblings, in both cases, are different ($FM\overline{B}SD$ and $FF\overline{Z}SS$), whereas the sexes of the initial terminus and the immediate linking kinsmen in· the genealogical chain are the same ($\overline{FMB}SD$ and $\overline{FFZ}SS$, respectively). Similarly, MFBDS is a parallel kin type, not because of the sexes of the ancestral siblings ($M\overline{F}BDS$), but because of the sexes of the initial and the linking kinsmen in the genealogical chain ($\overline{M}FB\overline{D}S$).

Certain assignments in Lesu terminology (Powdermaker, 1933) are clarified by the taxonomic diagnostic that Pospisil (1960) has introduced. For example, although the sex of the ancestral siblings would suggest that FMBD is a cross kin type, the new diagnostic suggests that FMBD is a parallel kin type: FMBD is, in fact, terminologically equivalent to MZ. Let us conclude this section by considering two other approaches to the cross/parallel distinction.

I. In his analysis of the Seneca system, Lounsbury (1964b) defines the cross/parallel distinction in terms of six componential features as follows. (1) $L=$ inheres "in any kin type in which *the sex of the designated kin is the* SAME *as that of the first link*"; (Lounsbury 1964b: 1081) (2) $L\neq$ inheres "in any kin type in which *the sex of the designated kin is* OPPOSITE *to that of the first link*" (Lounsbury, 1964b, p. 1078); (3) $\lrcorner=$ inheres "in any kin type in which *the sex of the last link is the* SAME *as that of the propositus*" (*Ibid.,* p. 1081); (4) $L\neq$ inheres "in any kin type in which *the sex of the last link is* OPPOSITE *to that of the propositus*" (*Ibid.,* p. 1081); (5) $\Lambda=$ inheres in any kin type in which *the sex of the last link is the* SAME *as that of the first link*" (*Ibid.,* p. 1082); (6) $\Lambda\neq$ inheres in any type "*in which the sex of the last link is* OPPOSITE *to that of the first link*." The cross/parallel distinction is generalized from these features: a relationship is parallel if it is characterized by the features $L=$, and $L=$ and $\Lambda=$; and cross if it is characterized by the features $L\neq$, $L\neq$, and $\Lambda\neq$ (*Ibid.,* p. 1083).

To sum up: the principle operative in the reckoning of bifurcation in Iroquois terminologies is *not* solely a function of the sexes of the intervening links in a genealogical chain. In Lounsbury's (1964b, p. 1079) terminology, the reckoning of bifurcation—the distinction between cross and parallel kin—is a function of (1) the relationship between the sex of the designated kin and that of the first link; (2) the relationship between the sex of the last link and that of the propositus; (3) the relationship between the sex of the last link and that of the first link. If relations (1, 2, 3) are of the form "same as," then parallel. If relations (1, 2, 3) are of the form "different than," then cross.

II. Kay (1965) has recently attempted to generalize the cross/parallel distinction to the total range of consanguineal relationships in unilineal descent systems. A system of algebraic notation, introduced by Romney (Romney and D'Andrade, 1964a), is employed in which (1) $m$ and $f$ denote male and female nodes, (2) the symbol $a$ denotes a node of either sex, (3) the symbols $+$ and $-$ denote vertical genealogical bonds traced upward and downward, respectively, and (4) the symbol 0 denotes a sibling bond. In Romney's notation, the kin type FZDS (m.s.) may be translated into the algebraic string $m + m\,0f - f - m$. Kay (1965, p. 32) refers to symbols of the opposite sex of the descent rule ($m$ with matrilineal descent and $f$ with patrilineal descent) as $\bar{d}$ symbols, and defines the cross/parallel distinction in terms of a function $g$, "which gives for any string the total number of $\bar{d}$ symbols immediately preceded by $+$ and $\bar{d}$ symbols immediately followed by $-$." The cross/parallel distinction is defined (Kay, 1965, p. 32), "For any string, if the value of $g$ is an even number, the relation is parallel; if the value of $g$ is an odd number, the relation is cross."

In the string $(m + m\,0f - f - m)$, $g = 2$ under patrilineal descent and $g = 1$ under matrilineal descent; the relation is parallel under patrilineal descent ($g$ is an even number) and cross under matrilineal descent ($g$ is an odd number).

Consider Kay's (1965, p. 32) definition of the cross/parallel distinction in terms of the function $g$ in reference to several Kapauku categories previously discussed. Let us begin by translating three kin type strings, (1) FFZDS (m.s.), (2) FMBDD (m.s.), (3) FMBSD (m.s.), into Romney's algebraic notation: (1) $m + m + m\,0f - f - m$, (2) $m + m + f\,0m - f - f$, (3) $m + m + f\,0m - m - f$. The value of the function $g$ for these strings under patrilineal descent (Kapauku) is (1) $g = 2$, (2) $g = 2$, (3) $g = 2$. That is, strings (1), (2), and (3) are defined as parallel kin types (even) by Kay's formal definition of the cross/parallel distinction. Pospisil's (1960) diagnostic indicates, however, that strings (1) and (2) are cross kin types, whereas string (3) is a parallel kin type (cf. foregoing). Further, if we define Kapauku kin types in reference to the function $g$, then the string $m + m\,0f - f$ (FZD — m.s.) represents a cross relation (1 is an odd number); the strings $m + m + f\,0m - f - f$ ($g = 2$) and $m + m\,0f - f$ ($g = 1$) are, however, terminologically equivalent kin types to opposite categories (e.g., FMBDD/parallel and FZD/cross; FMBSD/cross and FBS/parallel). Kay's generalization of the cross/parallel distinction appears to be applicable only to moiety systems or systems predicted on an implicit moiety-type reckoning.[1] The discussion of Kariera terminology (a Dravidian system) with reference to a four-section mode of reckoning, provides an example of a system of this type.

### DRAVIDIAN TERMINOLOGY

It is necessary, at the outset, to distinguish Dravidian terminology from the classic Iroquois type. Iroquois terminologies, on the one hand, and the terminology of symmetric marriage systems (Dravidian terminology), on the other, are widely different things, except for superficial terminological resemblances. Classified on a functional level, in terms of the type of exchange of women which they ensure within the group, they have nothing in common, except that their terminology is symmetrical. The basic formal distinction between symmetric systems on the one hand, and Iroquois systems, on the other, is clear: there are no distinct affinal assignments (e.g., H, W) in Dravidian (symmetric) systems. Conversely, virtually all Iroquois systems have terminologically distinct affinal assignments. This distinction may be formulated in somewhat different terms and on a functional level as follows:

1. The Dravidian terminology consistently and explicitly distinguishes "prohibited" women (nonmarriageable categories) from "lawful" women (genealogically or categorically defined affines). Such systems have positive marriage rules in the sense that Dumont (1953a) (see Chapter Six) uses the term.
   Whereas,
2. The classic Iroquois terminology defines only what is prohibited (nonmarriageable categories); the exchange of women is governed by other institutions. There is no positive marriage rule.

Further, in Iroquois systems we discussed the notion of a structural opposition between certain classes of persons, between "fathers" and "mother's brothers," "mothers" and "father's sisters," "cross and parallel cousins." It has been suggested, however, that there is an implicit misconception in the assumption of a cross/parallel opposition in systems of the Dravidian type (Dumont, 1953a; 1957, pp. 24–27). The opposition between cross and parallel classes in Iroquois systems is based upon the principle of bifurcation (Murdock, 1949, p. 104). A classic anthropological notion is that consanguines are bifurcated into cross and parallel classes as a function of the sex of the intervening relative (ancestral siblings). The formula is same sex = parallel kin (FB ____, MZ ____); opposite sex = cross kin (MB ____, FZ ____). As we have seen (cf. Pospisil, 1960), the distinction between cross

---

[1] But see final section for a more extended discussion of this problem, particularly in the light of Tyler's (1966) criticisms, and Kay's reformulation.

and parallel kin types is a function of the sexes of the initial terminus and the immediate linking relative, rather than of the sexes of all intervening links, as in the Dravidian terminology (Lounsbury, 1964b, p. 1079).

In Iroquois systems, the consanguineal content of cross kin classes is primary; the affinal content is clearly derivative. It is contingent upon the marriage of a "cross cousin." In Dravidian systems, the converse of this formulation is relevant: the affinal content of "cross" kin categories is primary; the consanguineal content is derivative. Once we attempt to explain the terminology on a functional level, the superficial similarities between these systems give way to a clearer understanding of their basic differences. Although they "swim in the same water," they are as different as a whale is from a fish.

A brief explanation of the foregoing remarks is in order. The "meaning" of MB in Iroquois systems is consistently cognatic; in the Dravidian terminology, the cognatic "meaning" of MB is a derivative of the affinal meaning: father's affine (Dumont, 1966). It follows that MB does not become "father's affine" as a result of marriage: marriage is generated by affinity. Further, we may postulate a prior genealogical definition whereby MB "means" father of marriageable female and subsequently WF. It is, thus, inappropriate to say that one marries a cross cousin: one marries the daughter of an affine. As affinity assumes a diachronic dimension, the daughter of an affine is "ipso facto" an affine (Dumont, 1957, p. 24). The Dravidian terminology is divided into affinal terms and kin terms (cognates): the rules of affinal exchange are terminologically encoded (cf. Yalman, 1962, p. 556; Dumont, 1957).

To sum up: (1) the basic principle of opposition in Dravidian systems is between cognates and affines, rather than between cross and parallel relatives. (2) Marriage exchanges are governed by an affinal code, which is transmitted through the medium of the terminological system, and (3) enduring alliances between categories of affines are independent of lineality of descent: they are governed by structural principles of their own, which are not a function of descent reckoning. The formal and functional distinctions between Iroquois and Dravidian systems may be summarized in terms of two dimensions, (a) principles of terminological opposition, and (b) principles of marriage exchange, as follows:

|  | Principles of terminological opposition | Principles of marriage exchange |
|---|---|---|
| **Dravidian terminology** | **Cognates/Affines** | **Governed by the terminological code** |
| **Iroquois terminology** | **Cross kin/Parallel kin** | **Governed by various social institutions** |

Marriage exchanges that occur either between exogamous descent groups (Lévi-Strauss, 1949), or within bilateral, endogamous kindreds (Yalman, 1962, p. 548), may be considered "signals," which can be decoded only through an understanding of the formal rules that underlie this behavior and serve as a basis for the cryptanalyst.

The foregoing theoretical assumptions suggest that our first task is to formulate the coding rules that regulate "exchange events" in Dravidian systems, whether these events involve the actual exchange or the retention of women (Yalman, 1962), within endogamous kindreds.

We call rewrite rules that are written in "Dravidian fashion" *hereditary affinity rules:* they express, in formal terms, Dumont's (1953a, 1957, 1966) notion that affinity, in Dravidian systems, is transmitted from generation to generation.

Let us illustrate the logic underlying the reckoning of bifurcation in Dravidian terminologies by accounting, for the "marriageable" category in two Dravidian-type systems: Kariera and Njamal.

In his classic report on Kariera kinship and social organization, Radcliffe-Brown (1930, p. 47) lists the denotative range of Kariera kin classes in the following manner:

1. FF; with his brothers, husbands of the father's mother's sisters, and the brothers of the mother's mother: FFB, FMZH, MMB.
2. FM; with her sisters, wives of the father's father's brothers, and sisters of the mother's father: FMZ, FFBW, MFZ.
3. MF; with his brothers, husbands of the mother's mother's sisters, and brothers of the father's mother: MFB, MMZH, FMB.
4. MM; with her sisters, wives of the mother's father's brothers, and sisters of the father's father: MMZ, MFBW, FFZ.
5. F including own father, father's brother, mother's sister's husband, father's father's brother's son, mother's mother's brother's son, etc.: FB, MZH, FFBS, MMBS.
6. M including own mother, mother's sisters, father's brother's wife, mother's mother's sister's daughter, etc.: MZ, FBW, MMZD, etc.
7. MB including the brother of any woman called "mother" and the husband of the sister of any man called "father": FZH.
8. FZ including the sister of any man called "father" and the wife of any man called "mother's brother": MBW.
9. "older brother"
10. "younger brother"
11. "older sister"
12. "younger sister"
13a. *Marriageable category* (male ego): FZD, MBD, FFZSD, FMBSD, MFZDD, MMBDD, etc.
13b. *Marriageable category* (female ego): FZS, MBS, FFZSS, FMBSS, MFZDS, MMBDS, etc.

**14.** "son"
**15.** "daughter"
**16.** "sister's son"
**17.** "sister's daughter"

In the five generations there are twenty classes of relatives, two of which (brother and sister) are further subdivided on the basis of age within the generation. There are, however, only eighteen terms for these twenty-two kinds of relatives by reason of the terms for grandparents being used reciprocally for grandchildren (Radcliffe-Brown, 1930, p. 48).

Our first rule is an "opposite sex" version of Lounsbury's half-sibling rule:

I. Hereditary Affinity Rule I:

$$FS \ldots \rightarrow Z \ldots ; \qquad MS \ldots \rightarrow Z \ldots ;$$
$$FD \ldots \rightarrow B \ldots ; \qquad MD \ldots \rightarrow B \ldots$$

This is to be read: *Let one's parent's child, when a link to some other relative, be regarded as equivalent to one's sibling of opposite sex.*

*Hereditary Affinity Rule I* is mapped onto distinctive features in the following manner:

$$FS \ldots \rightarrow Z \ldots ,$$

$$\begin{bmatrix} +\text{mas.} \\ +\text{g.r.} \\ +\text{sen.} \\ +\text{con.} \end{bmatrix} \begin{bmatrix} +\text{mas.} \\ +\text{g.r.} \\ -\text{sen.} \\ +\text{con.} \end{bmatrix} \rightarrow \begin{bmatrix} -\text{mas.} \\ -\text{g.r.} \\ -\text{sen.} \\ +\text{con.} \end{bmatrix} \text{ in env. } \underline{\qquad} X.$$

$$FD \ldots \rightarrow B \ldots ,$$

$$\begin{bmatrix} +\text{mas.} \\ +\text{g.r.} \\ +\text{sen.} \\ +\text{con.} \end{bmatrix} \begin{bmatrix} -\text{mas.} \\ +\text{g.r.} \\ -\text{sen.} \\ +\text{con.} \end{bmatrix} \rightarrow \begin{bmatrix} +\text{mas.} \\ -\text{g.r.} \\ -\text{sen.} \\ +\text{con.} \end{bmatrix} \text{ in env. } \underline{\qquad} X.$$

$$MS \ldots \rightarrow Z \ldots ,$$

$$\begin{bmatrix} -\text{mas.} \\ +\text{g.r.} \\ +\text{sen.} \\ +\text{con.} \end{bmatrix} \begin{bmatrix} +\text{mas.} \\ +\text{g.r.} \\ -\text{sen.} \\ +\text{con.} \end{bmatrix} \rightarrow \begin{bmatrix} -\text{mas.} \\ -\text{g.r.} \\ -\text{sen.} \\ +\text{con.} \end{bmatrix} \text{ in env. } \underline{\qquad} X.$$

$$MD \ldots \rightarrow B \ldots ,$$

$$\begin{bmatrix} -\text{mas.} \\ +\text{g.r.} \\ +\text{sen.} \\ +\text{con.} \end{bmatrix} \begin{bmatrix} -\text{mas.} \\ +\text{g.r.} \\ -\text{sen.} \\ +\text{con.} \end{bmatrix} \rightarrow \begin{bmatrix} +\text{mas.} \\ -\text{g.r.} \\ -\text{sen.} \\ +\text{con.} \end{bmatrix} \text{ in env. } \underline{\qquad} X.$$

The rules may be combined

$$
\begin{bmatrix} + \text{ g.r.} \\ + \text{ sen.} \\ + \text{ con.} \end{bmatrix}
\begin{bmatrix} + \text{ g.r.} \\ - \text{ sen.} \\ + \text{ con.} \end{bmatrix}
\rightarrow
\begin{bmatrix} - \text{ g.r.} \\ - \text{ sen.} \\ + \text{ con.} \end{bmatrix} \text{ in env. } \underline{\hspace{2cm}} X.
$$

First the Kariera. Romney and Epling (1958, pp. 62–63) indicate that the relationally defined kin types which a male Ego may marry include FZD, MBD, FFZSD, FMBSD, MFZDD, MMBDD, and so on.

|  |  |  |
|---|---|---|
| FFZSD → FFSD | (by Merging Rule—Stronger Form II Corollary) | (1) |
| → FZD | (by Half-sibling Rule—Modified Form) | |
| → MBD | (by Transformation Rule I) | |
| FMBSD → FMSD | (by Merging Rule—Stronger Form I Corollary) | (2) |
| → FZD | (by Half-sibling Rule—Modified Form) | |
| → MBD | (by Transformation Rule I) | |
| MFZDD → MFDD | (by Merging Rule—Stronger Form II Corollary) | (3) |
| → MBD | (by Half-sibling Rule—Modified Form) | |
| → FZD | (by Transformation Rule I) | |
| MMBDD → MMDD | (by Merging Rule—Stronger Form I Corollary) | (4) |
| → MBD | (by Half-sibling Rule—Modified Form) | |
| → FZD | (by Transformation Rule I). | |

Similarly for the Njamal:

|  |  |  |
|---|---|---|
| MMBDS → MMDS | (by Merging Rule—Stronger Form I Corollary) | (1) |
| → MBS | (by Half-sibling Rule—Modified Form) | |
| → FZS | (by Transformation Rule I) | |
| FFZSS → FFSS | (by Merging Rule—Stronger Form I Corollary) | (2) |
| → FZS | (by Half-sibling Rule—Modified Form) | |
| → MBS | (by Transformation Rule I). | |

The terminal step in the above derivations is written in "Dravidian fashion": FZD → W, MBD → W, MBS → H, FZS → H.

Consider the final derivation (2). FFZSS is reduced, in Dravidian fashion, to MBS; an Iroquois-type reduction of the same kin type follows (cf. Kapauku analysis):

$$\text{FFZSS} \rightarrow \text{FFSS} \quad \text{(by Merging Rule Corollary—}$$
$$\text{Stronger Form II)}$$
$$\rightarrow \text{FBS} \quad \text{(by Half-sibling Rule)}$$
$$\rightarrow \text{FS} \quad \text{(by Merging Rule)}$$
$$\rightarrow \text{B} \quad \text{(by Half-sibling Rule).}$$

Although the intervening links ($\overline{\text{FF}}\text{ZSS}$) are not of relevance in the reckoning of bifurcation in Iroquois systems, they are of relevance in the reckoning of bifurcation in Dravidian systems. The formula is: opposite sex = affines ("cross"); same sex = cognates ("parallel"). Bifurcation, in Dravidian terminologies, is a function of the sex, in a genealogical chain, of the ancestral siblings.

Other Kariera assignments are accounted for by the following rules:

II.  Half-parent Rule: $MH \rightarrow F$.

This is to be read: *Let one's* MOTHER'S HUSBAND *be considered to be one's* FATHER.

Corollary: $FW \rightarrow M$.

This is to be read: *Let one's* FATHER'S WIFE *be considered to be one's* MOTHER.

Mapped onto distinctive features, these transformations are written:

Rule:

$$\begin{bmatrix} - \text{ mas.} \\ + \text{ g.r.} \\ + \text{ sen.} \\ + \text{ con.} \end{bmatrix} \begin{bmatrix} + \text{ mas.} \\ - \text{ g.r.} \\ - \text{ sen.} \\ - \text{ con.} \end{bmatrix} \rightarrow \begin{bmatrix} + \text{ mas.} \\ + \text{ g.r.} \\ + \text{ sen.} \\ + \text{ con.} \end{bmatrix}$$

Corollary:

$$\begin{bmatrix} + \text{ mas.} \\ + \text{ g.r.} \\ + \text{ sen.} \\ + \text{ con.} \end{bmatrix} \begin{bmatrix} - \text{ mas.} \\ - \text{ g.r.} \\ - \text{ sen.} \\ - \text{ con.} \end{bmatrix} \rightarrow \begin{bmatrix} - \text{ mas.} \\ + \text{ g.r.} \\ + \text{ sen.} \\ + \text{ con.} \end{bmatrix}$$

These may be combined into a single "alpha rule":

$$\begin{bmatrix} \alpha \text{ mas.} \\ + \text{ g.r.} \\ + \text{ sen.} \\ + \text{ con.} \end{bmatrix} \begin{bmatrix} -\alpha \text{ mas.} \\ - \text{ g.r.} \\ - \text{ sen.} \\ - \text{ con.} \end{bmatrix} \rightarrow \begin{bmatrix} -\alpha \text{ mas.} \\ - \text{ g.r.} \\ + \text{ sen.} \\ + \text{ con.} \end{bmatrix}$$

III. Sex-Reversal Rule (Form I): MM . . . ♂ → FF . . . ♂.

> This is to be read: *Let the kin type* MOTHER'S MOTHER, *whenever it occurs as a link between Ego and any male relative, be regarded as structurally equivalent to the kin type* FATHER'S FATHER *in that context.*

> Corollary: FF . . . ♀ → MM . . . ♀.

> This is to be read: *Let the kin type* FATHER'S FATHER, *whenever it occurs as a link between Ego and any male relative, be regarded as structurally equivalent to the kin type* MOTHER'S MOTHER *in that context.*

IV. Sex-Reversal Rule (Form II): MF . . . ♀ → FM . . . ♀.

> This is to be read: *Let the kin type* MOTHER'S FATHER, *whenever it occurs as a link between Ego and any female relative, be regarded as structurally equivalent to the kin type* FATHER'S MOTHER *in that context.*

> Corollary: FM . . . ♂ → MF . . . ♂.

> This is to be read: *Let the kin type* FATHER'S MOTHER, *whenever it occurs as a link between Ego and any male relative, be regarded as structurally equivalent to the kin type* MOTHER'S FATHER *in that context.*

These rules are mapped onto distinctive features:

Sex Reversal Rule (Form I):

$$
\begin{bmatrix} - \text{mas.} \\ + \text{g.r.} \\ + \text{sen.} \\ + \text{con.} \end{bmatrix}
\begin{bmatrix} - \text{mas.} \\ + \text{g.r.} \\ + \text{sen.} \\ + \text{con.} \end{bmatrix}
\rightarrow
\begin{bmatrix} + \text{mas.} \\ + \text{g.r.} \\ + \text{sen.} \\ + \text{con.} \end{bmatrix}
\begin{bmatrix} + \text{mas.} \\ + \text{g.r.} \\ + \text{sen.} \\ + \text{con.} \end{bmatrix}
$$

in env. _____ $X$ [+ mas.].

Corollary:

$$
\begin{bmatrix} + \text{mas.} \\ + \text{g.r.} \\ + \text{sen.} \\ + \text{con.} \end{bmatrix}
\begin{bmatrix} + \text{mas.} \\ + \text{g.r.} \\ + \text{sen.} \\ + \text{con.} \end{bmatrix}
\rightarrow
\begin{bmatrix} - \text{mas.} \\ + \text{g.r.} \\ + \text{sen.} \\ + \text{con.} \end{bmatrix}
\begin{bmatrix} - \text{mas.} \\ + \text{g.r.} \\ + \text{sen.} \\ + \text{con.} \end{bmatrix}
$$

in env. _____ $X$ [− mas.].

Sex Reversal Rule (Form II):

$$
\begin{bmatrix} - \text{mas.} \\ + \text{g.r.} \\ + \text{sen.} \\ + \text{con.} \end{bmatrix}
\begin{bmatrix} + \text{mas.} \\ + \text{g.r.} \\ + \text{sen.} \\ + \text{con.} \end{bmatrix}
\rightarrow
\begin{bmatrix} + \text{mas.} \\ + \text{g.r.} \\ + \text{sen.} \\ + \text{con.} \end{bmatrix}
\begin{bmatrix} - \text{mas.} \\ + \text{g.r.} \\ + \text{sen.} \\ + \text{con.} \end{bmatrix}
$$

in env. _____ $X$ [− mas.].

Corollary:

$$
\begin{bmatrix} + \text{ mas.} \\ + \text{ g.r.} \\ + \text{ sen.} \\ + \text{ con.} \end{bmatrix}
\begin{bmatrix} - \text{ mas.} \\ + \text{ g.r.} \\ + \text{ sen.} \\ + \text{ con.} \end{bmatrix}
\rightarrow
\begin{bmatrix} - \text{ mas.} \\ + \text{ g.r.} \\ + \text{ sen.} \\ + \text{ con.} \end{bmatrix}
\begin{bmatrix} + \text{ mas.} \\ + \text{ g.r.} \\ + \text{ sen.} \\ + \text{ con.} \end{bmatrix}
$$

in env. _____ $X$ [+ mas.].

These rules and corollaries may be combined into a single rule:

$$
\begin{bmatrix} + \text{ g.r.} \\ + \text{ sen.} \\ + \text{ con.} \end{bmatrix}
\begin{bmatrix} + \text{ g.r.} \\ + \text{ sen.} \\ + \text{ con.} \end{bmatrix}
\rightarrow
\begin{bmatrix} + \text{ g.r.} \\ + \text{ sen.} \\ + \text{ con.} \end{bmatrix}
\begin{bmatrix} + \text{ g.r.} \\ + \text{ sen.} \\ + \text{ con.} \end{bmatrix}
$$

in env. _____ $X$ [$\alpha$ mas.].

The derivations follow

| | | |
|---|---|---|
| FFB → FF | (by Merging Rule) | (1) |
| FMZH → FMH | (by Merging Rule) | (2) |
| → FF | (by the Half-Parent Rule) | |
| MMB → FFB | (by the Sex-Reversal Rule—Form I) | (3) |
| → FF | (by the Merging Rule) | |
| FMZ → FM | (by the Merging Rule) | (4) |
| FFBW → FFW | (by the Merging Rule) | (5) |
| → FM | (by the Half-Parent Rule Corollary) | |
| MFZ → FMZ | (by the Sex-Reversal Rule—Form II) | (6) |
| → FM | (by the Merging Rule) | |
| MFB → MF | (by the Merging Rule) | (7) |
| MMZH → MMH | (by the Merging Rule) | (8) |
| → MF | (by the Half-Parent Rule) | |
| FMB → MFB | (by the Sex Reversal Rule—Form II Corollary) | (9) |
| → MF | (by the Merging Rule) | |
| MMZ → MM | (by the Merging Rule) | (10) |
| MFBW → MFW | (by the Merging Rule) | (11) |
| → MM | (by the Half-Parent Rule—Corollary) | |
| FFZ → MMZ | (by the Sex Reversal Rule—Form I—Corollary) | (12) |
| → MM | (by the Merging Rule). | |

In conclusion, let us consider Kay's (1965, p. 34) theorem for four-section systems in relation to the foregoing derivations:

*Theorem 3. In a four-section system,*

  i. *A relation describes a member of Ego's section if and only if the relation is parallel under both patri- and matri-descent.*
 ii. *A relation describes a member of Ego's spouse's section if and only if the relation is cross under both patri- and matri-descent.*
iii. *A relation describes a member of Ego's father's section if and only if it is parallel under patri-descent and cross under matri-descent.*
 iv. *A relation describes a member of Ego's mother's section if and only if it is parallel under matri-descent and cross under patri-descent.*

First we list the foregoing kin types and their translation into Romney's algebraic notation:

| *Kin types* | *Algebraic Strings* |
|---|---|
| (1) FFZSD (m.s.) | $m + m + m\,0\,f - m - f$ |
| (2) FMBSD (m.s.) | $m + m + f\,0\,m - m - f$ |
| (3) MFZDD (m.s.) | $m + f + m\,0\,f - f - f$ |
| (4) MMBDD (m.s.) | $m + f + f\,0\,m - f - f$ |
| (5) MMBDS (f.s.) | $f + f + f\,0\,m - f - m$ |
| (6) FFZSS (f.s.) | $f + m + m\,0\,f - m - m.$ |

The foregoing strings give the following values for the function $g$ under patrilineal and matrilineal descent:

  (1) patri-descent: $g = 1$; matri-descent: $g = 3$
  (2) patri-descent: $g = 1$; matri-descent: $g = 3$
  (3) patri-descent: $g = 3$; matri-descent: $g = 1$
  (4) patri-descent: $g = 3$; matri-descent: $g = 1$
  (5) patri-descent: $g = 3$; matri-descent: $g = 1$
  (6) patri-descent: $g = 1$; matri-descent: $g = 3.$

All of the foregoing relations are members of Ego's spouse's section (cross under both patri- and matri-descent) as specified by Kay's (1965, p. 34) *Theorem 3*. Similarly, the following Njamal kin types are assigned to Ego's father's section (parallel under patri-descent and cross under matri-descent):

| *Kin types* | *Algebraic Strings* |
|---|---|
| (1) FFBS (m.s.) | $m + m + m\,0\,m - m$ |
| (2) FMZS (m.s.) | $m + m + f\,0\,f - m$ |
| (3) MMBS (m.s.) | $m + f + f\,0\,m - m.$ |

These strings give the following values for the function $g$:

  (1) patri-descent: $g = 0$; matri-descent: $g = 3$
  (2) patri-descent: $g = 2$; matri-descent: $g = 1$
  (3) patri-descent: $g = 2$; matri-descent: $g = 1.$

Let us now extend the cross/parallel distinction to affinal relations in four-section (Kariera) systems by (1) introducing a symbol ($=$) which represents a marriage bond, (2) defining a function $g^1$ which gives for any string (a) the total number of $\bar{d}$ symbols immediately preceded by $+$, (b) $\bar{d}$ symbols immediately followed by $-$, (c) $m$ symbols followed by $=$ and $f$ symbols preceded by $=$ under patrilineal or matrilineal descent. The cross/parallel distinction is defined in terms of the function $g^1$: For any string, if the value of $g^1$ is an even number, the relation is parallel; if the value of $g^1$ is an odd number, the relation is cross (Kay, 1965, p. 32). We now consider certain Njamal kin types that are assigned to Ego's section under Kay's (1965, p. 34) *Theorem 3* (iii): (1) FFB (m.s.), (2) MMB (m.s.), (3) MFWB (m.s.), and (4) MMZH. These kin types are translated into algebraic strings and the value of function $g^1$ under patrilineal and matrilineal descent is given as follows:

(1) $m + m + m\ 0\ m$     patri-descent: $g = 0$;   matri-descent: $g = 2$
(2) $m + f + f\ 0\ m$       patri-descent: $g = 2$;   matri-descent: $g = 0$
(3) $m + f + m = f\ 0\ m$ patri-descent: $g^1 = 2$; matri-descent: $g = 2$
(4) $m + f + f\ 0\ f = m$ patri-descent: $g^1 = 2$; matri-descent: $g^1 = 0$.

In this section we have followed Kay's (1965, p. 43) suggestion by examining a generalization of the cross/parallel distinction in a restricted area of the semantic space of a terminological system and have extended this distinction to "affinal" relations in Kariera systems. In the foregoing example, all relations are assigned to Ego's section (parallel under both patri- and matri-descent).

## A FURTHER NOTE ON THE CROSS/PARALLEL DISTINCTION

In an evaluation of cross/parallel definitions, Tyler (1966) demonstrates (1) logical inconsistencies in the derivation of the theorems, (2) empirical inconsistencies, and (3) the relevance of the issues involved in the cross/parallel controversy for alternative interpretations of the "nature of kinship reckoning."

Tyler (1966, pp. 419–422) suggests that there is no necessary relation between Kay's (1965, p. 30) definition of the cross/parallel distinction and his first theorem.

Kay states his theorem as follows: For any kin relation, if it is deducible from the principle of lineage exogamy alone that a person standing in that relation to Ego is in Ego's lineage, then the relation is parallel; if it is similarly deducible that a person standing in the relation is not in Ego's lineage, the relation is cross (Kay, 1965, p. 33).

If it can be demonstrated that *Theorem 1* accounts only for situations in which assignment to a cross or parallel class is determined by categorical membership in descent groups, and consequently bears no necessary relation to the dimensional properties of intervening consanguineal links, then *Theorem 1* is directly relevant to the position that kinship reckoning is based on classification in reference to "social grouping" rather than "natural" genealogical linkage (Leach, 1958; Needham, 1962b). Tyler (1966, p. 420) contends that when there is more than one $f$ link and more than two inter-marrying lineages, "the relation between the theorem and the definition is either indeterminate or contradictory."

This can be easily shown by translating the string $m + f + m\, 0f - f - m$ (MFZDS: m.s.) in a patridescent system (alter is a cross relative: $g = 3$) to show lineage affiliation where there are five lineages, according to the following conventions: (1) upper case letters are substituted for males, lower case letters for females; (2) parentheses indicate permutational possibilities; and (3) subscript letters $i, j \ldots$ represent restrictions "where permutational possibilities of one slot in a string are governed by descent group membership (the rules of exogamy) of preceding slots" (Tyler, 1966, p. 417).

The string $B + a + A\, 0\, a - B - B$ for the genealogical representation

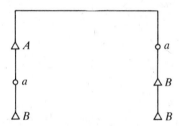

of a patrilineal moiety system may be permuted to $A + A\, 0\, a - \begin{pmatrix} B \\ C \end{pmatrix}$, which will generate $A + A\, 0\, a - B$ *and* $A + A\, 0\, a - C$, which indicates that the descent group membership of alter may be either $B$ or $C$ in a patrilineal system without moieties (Tyler, 1966, p. 417). And

$$A + \begin{pmatrix} b \\ c \end{pmatrix}_i + \begin{pmatrix} b \\ c \end{pmatrix}_j 0 \begin{pmatrix} B \\ C \end{pmatrix}_k - A,$$

where $i \neq j$ and $j = k$. The constraints imposed by the subscript letters allow us to generate from the above string $A + b + c\, 0\, C - A$, and $A + c + b\, 0\, B - A$; but not $A + b + b\, 0\, C - A$, $A + c + c\, 0\, C - A$, $A + b + c\, 0\, B - A$, and so on (cf. Tyler, 1966, pp. 417–418).

Now it can be easily seen that the string $m + f + m\, 0f - f - m$ can be translated, so to speak, to show lineage affiliation in a "five lineage system," to the "set of strings"

$$
A + \begin{pmatrix} b \\ c \\ d \\ e \end{pmatrix}_i + \begin{pmatrix} B \\ C \\ D \\ E \end{pmatrix} 0 \begin{pmatrix} b \\ c \\ d \\ e \end{pmatrix}_k - \begin{pmatrix} a \\ b \\ c \\ d \\ e \end{pmatrix}_l - \begin{pmatrix} A \\ B \\ C \\ D \\ E \end{pmatrix}_m ,
$$

where $i = j = k$; $K \neq l$; $l \neq m$ (Tyler, 1966, p. 421).

In this case *Theorem 1* holds as both ego and alter are parallel relatives on the basis of common lineage membership. It is important to note that the relationship holds only in the case where both ego and alter are $(A)$. "Thus the theorem directly contradicts the definition. The reason for this is simple: *the designation (same lineage, different lineage) has no necessary relation to the sex of constituent links in a string*" (Tyler, 1966, p. 421), it is a function of the marriage link between alter's father and mother.

Empirical applications of the cross/parallel definitions yield the following results. (1) An application of Kay's *Theorem 1* and definition to a system of exogamous patrilineal sibs organized into five exogamous phratries (Koya) yields incorrect predictions and clearly indicates that the theorem directly contradicts the definition (Tyler, 1966, pp. 424–426). (2) Lounsbury's definition adequately partitions the consanguineal domain of one matrilineal moiety system (Seneca Iroquois) in terms of the cross/parallel distinction. Kay's (1965, p. 34) *Theorem 2* (In a system of exogamous moieties [two-section system], a relation between ego and a kinsman is parallel if and only if the kinsman is in ego's moiety, and the relation is cross if and only if the kinsman is in the other moiety) is consistent with the definition, but both the theorem (2) and the definition yield inaccurate predictions (Tyler, 1966, pp. 424–425). (3) In a similar fashion, neither Kay's definition nor *Theorem 1* will produce satisfactory results for a matrilineal clan system (White Mountain Apache), whereas modified versions of Lounsbury's cross/parallel rules partition the consanguineal domain (Tyler, 1966, pp. 425–428). Finally, Kay's definition—but not *Theorem 1*—adequately partitions the consanguineal domain of the Brahman Telugu system.

A recent note by Kay (1967, pp. 83–85) provides a clearer formal basis for differentiating Iroquois distinction(s) from the Dravidian distinction(s) and implicitly counters aspects of the criticisms directed against his implied universal general cross/parallel distinction. In fact, Dravidian systems classify kin types in very much the same way as the Iroquois-type was imagined to do. The Dravidian and Iroquois forms of classification are rarely distinguished in the anthropological literature, although "they are systems premised on very different principles of reckoning . . ." (Lounsbury, 1964b, p. 1079, fn. 4).

In defining general Iroquois cross/parallel, Kay (1967, p. 84) defines a function $h$. The domain of this function is the set of all nonlineal kin types;

the range of $h$ is the set of integers $-1, 0, 1, 2, \ldots$ . The function $h$ is defined for the set of all nonlineal kin types, or the set of strings $s$ containing (1) the sibling bond 0 following the $i$th node, and (2) $n$ nodes, by the equation (Kay, 1967, p. 84):

**1.** $h(s) = \begin{cases} i - 2 & \text{when } i \leq (n - i), \quad \text{and} \\ n - i - 2 & \text{when } i > (n - i). \end{cases}$

Iroquois cross/parallel is then defined in terms of the function $h$.

**2.** Definition: For any string $s$,
  **i.** $s$ is *Iroquois-cross* if and only if:
    **a.** $s$ is in the domain of $h$, and
    **b.** the $(i - h)$th node of $s$ and the $(i + 1 + h)$th node of $s$ are of opposite sex;
  **ii.** otherwise $s$ is *Iroquois-parallel*.

A less general form of Iroquois cross/parallel is obtained from definition (2) by inserting appropriate generation restrictions. This is of relevance for Seneca cross/parallel as "Lounsbury restricts the universe of kin-types over which the distinction is defined to ego's own and the two adjacent generations" (Kay, 1967, p. 84). Initially, Kay (1967, p. 84) summarizes the appropriate generation restrictions by defining the generational removal of a string.

**3.** Definition: For any string $s$, the *generational removal of $s$*, $Gr(s)$, is the absolute value of the difference of the number of $+$'s in $s$ and the number of $-$'s in $s$.

Seneca cross/parallel is then defined as a special case of Iroquois cross/parallel.

**4.** Definition: For any string $s$ such that $Gr(s) \leq 1$
  **i.** $s$ is *Seneca-cross* if and only if:
    **a.** $s$ is in the domain of $h$, and
    **b.** the $(i - h)$th node of $s$ and the $(i + 1 + h)$th node of $s$ are of opposite sex;
  **ii.** otherwise $s$ is *Seneca-parallel*.

Kay (1967, p. 84) clearly indicates that the Dravidian cross/parallel distinction is actually two distinctions, one for each possible descent rule. Two functions are then defined, $g_{mat}$ (matrilineal) and $g_{pat}$ (patrilineal), "for each of which the domain is the set of all strings and the range is the set of all nonnegative integers" (Kay, 1967, p. 84).

**5.** Definition: For any string $s$,
  **i.** $g_{mat}(s)$ is the total number $+m$ and $m-$ sequences occurring in $s$.
  **ii.** $g_{pat}(s)$ is the total number of $+f$ and $f-$ sequences occurring in $s$.

**6.** Definition: For any string $s$,

    **i.** $s$ is *Dravidian matri-cross* if and only if $g_{mat}(s)$ is odd, and is *Dravidian matri-parallel* if and only if $g_{mat}(s)$ is even.

    **ii.** $s$ is *Dravidian patri-cross* if and only if $g_{pat}(s)$ is odd, and is *Dravidian patri-parallel* if and only if $g_{pat}(s)$ is even.

## CONCLUSION

The productivity of formal analysis can be seen in the way it led to the posing and partial resolution of a number of problems, which had been either unnoticed, or covertly ignored in the past. The first problem approached was the nature of an Iroquois system. We indicated that the diversity in empirical systems could be reduced by a series of formal steps to an ordered scale, and a set of transformational matrices that displayed the logical relations between the empirical systems. The second problem that arose out of the examination of Iroquois systems was the notion of *cross* versus *parallel*, terms that had been more or less taken for granted by most social anthropologists for many years. They turned out, upon inspection, to be highly complex constructs, which, however valid, were sources of much confusion. Through the medium of formalized kinds of analysis we were able to clear away some of the confusion, and establish the difficulties implicit in the distinction between "Iroquois" systems and "Dravidian" systems.

# Chapter Eleven

# Omaha and Miwok-Type Kinship Terminologies

The principles governing the development—or evolution—of Omaha kinship terminologies, and the relationship of these principles to residence rules, corporate kin groups, and asymmetric marriage systems, has been the subject of considerable theoretical interest and analysis (e.g., Lowie, 1930; White, 1939, 1959b; Murdock, 1949; Lane and Lane, 1959; Eyde and Postal, 1961; Moore, 1963). At the outset of this chapter we consider some theories on the sociological determinants of kinship terminologies and suggest the inadequacies in this approach. The "sociological-determinant" theory is evaluated in the light of the criteria that we have enumerated in the discussion of transformational analysis: (1) explicitness, (2) economy, and (3) descriptive adequacy. Discussions of the determinants of kinship terminologies take place under three major headings: (1) terminology is determined by marriage form; (2) terminology is determined by universal sociological principles; and (3) terminology is determined by the constitution of kin and residential groups.

## KINSHIP TERMINOLOGY AND MARRIAGE FORMS

Under the influence of Kohler, various marriage rules, often in combination with other institutional variables, have been suggested as determinants of kinship terminology. The form of the kinship terminology has been said to be determined by: (1) the sororate and levirate (Sapir, 1916; Lowie, 1919, pp. 33–34); (2) secondary cross-generational marriages (Rivers, 1914, 1924, pp. 70, 191; Gifford, 1916; Lesser, 1929; Lowie, 1930, pp. 104–105, 107–108; 1932; 1947, p. 37; Aginsky, 1935); (3) symmetric and/or asymmetric cross-cousin marriage (Rivers, 1914, p. 27; Lowie, 1947, p. 37; Lane and Lane,

[247]

1959; Eyde and Postal, 1961); and (4) oblique (cross-generational) and asymmetrical cross-cousin marriages (Moore, 1963).

Let us begin by defining the various marriage rules just listed: (1) the *sororate* is a cultural rule that favors the marriage of a man and the sister of his deceased wife, (2) the *levirate* is the logical converse of the sororate: a cultural rule that favors the marriage of a widow and her deceased husband's brother (Murdock, 1949, p. 29). A secondary marriage is any union that follows an individual's first marriage. (3) A *secondary cross-generation marriage* is the secondary marriage of individuals belonging to different generations, genealogically, and/or categorically defined. (4) *Asymmetric/ symmetric cross-cousin marriage* is a cultural rule that prescribes the marriage of a man with a woman who is a member of a specified category (which for the sake of brevity we sometimes misleadingly label MBD, or MBD = FZD. See Chapters Four and Five for full discussion). Murdock (1949, p. 123) has summarized the theoretical notion that kinship terminology of the bifurcate merging type (F = FB; M = MZ) may be derived from sororate and levirate marriages. The argument is worth quoting in detail as it is characteristic, in principle, of marriage determinant theories of kinship classification: if Ego's mother normally marries the father's brother when the father dies, there will be a tendency to employ the same terms for Fa and FaBr, for Br and FaBrSo, for Si and FaBrDa, for So and BrSo, and for Da and BrDa because to Ego such persons are likely to play similar family or kinship roles. In the same way the sororate would equate MoSi with Mo, MoSiSo with Br, MoSiDa with Si, and a woman's sister's children with her own (Murdock, 1949, p. 123).

The three basic objections to all of the foregoing interpretations are related to both the descriptive and the functional adequacy of these theoretical notions.

The specified causal relations between secondary marriage forms (levirate, sororate, or cross-generational) and kinship terminology can, at best, provide only a partial enumeration of the terminology of any system of kinship classification. The explanation of bifurcate merging terminology, as derived from the sororate or levirate, is an excellent example. As the rules that produce classifications of the bifurcate merging type also generate other assignments in any terminological system of this sort, the specified causal relationship between marriage rules and principles of kinship classification is (a) logically redundant and (b) descriptively inadequate. Secondary marriages can occur only in a fraction of all unions and are, consequently, unlikely to significantly influence kinship usages (cf. Murdock, 1949, pp. 123–124). Here we assume that statistically marginal events (secondary marriages) will have a negligible effect upon the cultural codes underlying systems of kinship classification. Once the coding principles have been adequately described, in a parsimonious fashion, then the relationship of these principles to social structural variables may be tested with some degree of confidence.

So far as theories that relate asymmetric marriage to the form of the kinship terminology are concerned, any theory that attempts to relate asymmetric alliance to the development of Omaha and/or Crow terminology fails to account for the differential functions which terminological systems perform. For example, Omaha terminologies, on the one hand, and the terminology of asymmetric marriage systems, on the other, are, in fact, different things, except for superficial terminological (i.e., formal) resemblances (Lévi-Strauss, 1951). Classified on a functional level, in terms of the type of exchange of women which the terminological codes insure within the group, they have nothing in common, except that their terminology is asymmetrical (cf. Buchler, 1966b). The basic formal distinction between asymmetric and Omaha (or Crow) systems is clear: there are no distinct affinal assignments in most asymmetric systems. Conversely, virtually all Omaha (and Crow) systems have terminologically distinct affinal assignments. In sum, a failure to differentiate the Crow-Omaha type from the Miwok (asymmetric) type may lead to rather serious interpretive errors, for "the important point with the Crow-Omaha type is not that two kinds of cross-cousins are classified in different generation levels, but rather that they are classified with consanguineous kin instead of with affinal kin as it occurs, for instance, in the Miwok system" (Lévi-Strauss, 1951, p. 162).

The "distinctive features" of asymmetrical systems are—in a sense—the converse of the features that define "Crow-Omaha systems" (see Alliance Chapters, Five and Six). By inverting criterial phrases in the formulae that define asymmetrical systems, formulae that define the "Crow-Omaha type" (Lévi-Strauss, 1965, pp. 19–20) are generated. Examples of these formulae follow:

I. A generalized definition of an *asymmetric system* may be formulated by saying that whenever a descent line is picked up to provide a mate, all individuals belonging to that line *are defined as potential mates* for the first lineage, during a period covering several generations.

II. The "generalized definition of a *Crow-Omaha system* may, conversely, best be formulated by saying that whenever a descent line is picked up to provide a mate, all individuals belonging to that line *are excluded from the range of potential mates* for the first lineage, during a period covering several generations" (Lévi-Strauss, 1965, p. 19).

III. An *asymmetrical system* "transforms" *kinsmen into affines* (Lévi-Strauss, 1965, p. 19), and conversely

IV. A *Crow-Omaha system* "transforms" *affines into kinsmen* (Lévi-Strauss, 1965, p. 19).

V. The "aim" of the coding rules underlying this type of transformation in *asymmetric systems* is to make possible—or compulsory—*the retention of matrimonial alliances within the circle of kin* (Lévi-Strauss, 1965, p. 19).

VI. The "aim" of the coding rules underlying this type of transformation in *Crow-Omaha systems* is to make it possible—or compulsory—

for *kinship and affinity to become mutually exclusive ties* (Lévi-Strauss, 1965, p. 19).

Formulations V–VI account for the strategic position that is assigned to Crow-Omaha systems in the theory of kinship and marriage.

For they provide the hinge which articulates elementary structures [whose perfect expression can be found in (asymmetric systems)], with complex structures [which find their perfect expression in (Crow-Omaha systems)]. In fact the Crow-Omaha systems still belong to the elementary structures from the point of view of the marriage prohibitions they frame in sociological terms, but they already belong to the complex structures from the point of view of the probabilist alliance network which they produce. In my terminology, they use a negative, mechanical model at the level of the norms, to generate a positive, statistical model at the level of the facts (Lévi-Strauss, 1965, p. 19; cf. Lévi-Strauss, 1965, p. 18).

With Lévi-Strauss (1965) we can amplify the distinctions using his (1949, 1953) distinctions between (1) elementary and complex structures, (2) mechanical and statistical models. The distinction between elementary structures and complex structures is not isomorphic with the distinction between "prescriptive systems" and "preferential systems." A spouse, in an elementary structure, is selected "for the reason that he or she belongs to a particular social group or to a given category of kinship; in other words, because the relationship between the intermarrying pair is defined in terms pertaining to the social structure" (Lévi-Strauss, 1965, p. 18). Conversely, the reason for the preference *or* the prescription, in a complex structure, is not derived from or defined in terms of the social structure.

It can be stated—following Lévi-Strauss—(a) that the notions "elementary structures" and "complex structures" are purely heuristic, and (b) that the distinction between elementary structures, on the one hand, and complex structures and Crow-Omaha systems, on the other, may be defined in terms of both the elementary core, and the alliance network that is produced (in the case of the second type). The "elementary" core of *"elementary structures"* may be formulated as a *positive, mechanical model*; the elementary core of *Crow-Omaha systems*, and of *"complex structures"* may be formulated as a negative, *mechanical model*.

At the level of the facts (alliance links), these elementary cores generate (1) a positive, statistical model (Crow-Omaha systems), (2) a positive, statistical model (complex structures), and (3) a positive, mechanical model (asymmetrical systems). This characterization of the level of the facts describes model networks. For probabilistic alliance networks (1 and 2) have mechanical dimensions, derived, on the one hand (1), from structural properties, and, on the other (2), from "nonstructural" properties; whereas mechanically defined alliance networks (3) have statistical components, derived from the freedom of choice that invariably overrides the "positive constraints" defined by the "elementary core."

## SOCIOLOGICAL PRINCIPLES

Various sociological principles were first introduced into kinship studies in contradistinction to the view (Morgan, 1877) that the kinship terminology of the Australian tribes had its origin in a prior condition of group marriage and was not correlated with existing social institutions (Radcliffe-Brown, 1930, p. 426). The "classificatory principle" in terminology, as well as the levirate, was accounted for by a single sociological principle: "The principle of the social equivalence of brothers" (Radcliffe-Brown, 1930, p. 429), or the "unity of the sibling group" (Radcliffe-Brown, 1959, p. 64). This last principle refers to the unity of the sibling group as viewed by a person who is both outside it and connected with it by a kin relationship to one of its members (Radcliffe-Brown, 1959, p. 64). For example, this notion of the unity of the sibling group is used to account for the terminological merging of F and FB, M and MZ (and in certain systems, MB), S and BS, D and BD, FF and FFB (Radcliffe-Brown, 1959, pp. 65–66). It was suggested (Radcliffe-Brown, 1930, p. 428) that this principle was present in all classificatory systems. Similarly, variations between types of systems were explained in terms of the different ways in which this extension of the basic classificatory principle can be applied (Radcliffe-Brown, 1959, p. 66). All other attempts to account for kinship systems (in terms of secondary marriages, exogamous moieties, and so on) either were consigned to "conjectural history" or were rejected for completely tangential reasons (Radcliffe-Brown, 1959, p. 61). As was noted in Chapter Four, derivative principles, e.g., the structural principle of the unity of the lineage group (Radcliffe-Brown, 1959, pp. 70–79), were used to account for Omaha and Crow systems. It was suggested that a limited number of structural principles govern various types of generational skewing and that these principles underlie both the terminological system and the social structure (Radcliffe-Brown, 1959, p. 75). The principle of the unity of the lineage group specifies that a person who is connected with a lineage by some significant kin or affinal bond will terminologically merge lineage members who belong to various "natural" generations. Similarly, this principle may govern the unitary classification of clan members (Radcliffe-Brown, 1959, pp. 70–71), and is said to account for the following forms of Omaha generational skewing: (1) MB = MBS, MBSS, MBSSS; (2) MZ = MBD, MBDD, MBDDD; (3) B = MBDS, MBDDS; (4) F = FMBDS, FMBSDS, FMBSSDS; (5) FM = FMBD, FMBSD; (6) FMB = FMBS, FMBSS. Variations in the development of the principle of the unity of the lineage group were used to explain the extension of terminological principles from the genealogical lineage to the clan. In sum, the ordering of persons within kinship terminologies is derived from the application of specified structural principles to either patrilineal or matrilineal lineages (Radcliffe-Brown, 1959, p. 78): kinship terminology directly reflects principles of social organization and regulates social behavior (Radcliffe-Brown, 1959, pp. 68–75, *passim*).

There are a number of objections to the foregoing interpretations that can be reviewed. As the suggested sociological principles, or laws, are common to all "classificatory systems"—or unilineal descent systems—they cannot account for terminological variations between these systems. As they fail to account for the variation between systems, they certainly cannot account for underlying similarities. Their predictive value is negated by the very fact of variation; a unitary principle would be expected to produce a common effect (cf. Lowie, 1937, pp. 224–225; Murdock, 1949, p. 121; Lévi-Strauss, 1953, pp. 542–543). Consider Radcliffe Brown's (1959, p. 78) notion that Crow and Omaha systems are produced by the application of a single structural principle to matrilineal and patrilineal lineages, respectively: that the meaning of the kin terms in Crow and Omaha systems are adequately explained by propositions that state an invariant relationship between lineage membership and terminological classification. Let us parallel Lounsbury's (1964a, p. 355) critique of these notions. In reference to Fox terminology (an Omaha system) (Tax, in Eggan, 1937), Radcliffe-Brown (1959, p. 72) notes "that a man calls his mother's father 'grandfather,' but calls all the males of the lineage in the three succeeding generations 'mother's brother' (MB)." An examination of Fox terminology indicates that the meaning of the mother's brother term in this Omaha system cannot be *a male member of my mother's patrilineage*, for (a) there are male members of mother's patrilineage who are not members of the mother's brother's class (MF) and (b) there are "mother's brothers" who are not members of mother's patrilineage: for example, MMZS, MMZSS, and MMBDS. Patrilineage membership is neither a necessary nor a sufficient condition for assignment to the mother's brother's kin class in this Omaha system. Further, Radcliffe-Brown's conceptions fail to provide any general explanation for Omaha- and Crow-type classifications when these systems are not associated with patrilineal or matrilineal lineages, or when Omaha and Crow are found in inappropriate combinations (e.g., Omaha-matrilineages; Crow-patrilineages). Radcliffe-Brown's formulations cannot cope with the very considerable variation between kinship terminologies which fall within any given structural type (Omaha, Crow, and so on).

## THE CONSTITUTION OF KIN AND RESIDENTIAL GROUPS

Theories that account for kinship systems in terms of the constitution of kin and local groups have, for nearly a century, exerted a dominant influence in kinship studies (Tylor, 1889, p. 261; Rivers, 1914, pp. 70–72; 1924, pp. 58, 67–68; Lowie, 1915, pp. 223, 226; 1919, p. 29; 1929, pp. 380–383; Kroeber, 1917, pp. 86–87; Lesser, 1929, p. 722; White, 1939, p. 569; 1959, p. 133; Murdock, 1947, pp. 57–58; 1949, pp. 124–125, 148–156, 161–171, *passim*).

For example, various theorists (White, 1939, 1959b; Murdock, 1949) have suggested that Iroquois terminology is a "base form" from which Omaha and Crow systems have evolved, with the development of sib organization and/or various preferential marriage rules. Rules of residence and descent, and the alignments of kinsmen which they produce, are said to be the independent variable; kinship terminology is said to be the dependent variable. The evolutionary choice between the Omaha/Crow alternative is said to be a function of lineality of descent. A society that develops "strongly" corporate, patrilineal descent groups, will, it is suggested, often develop Omaha kinship terminology. Conversely, the development of strongly corporate matrilineal descent groups will often result in the development of Crow kinship terminology. Alternatively, it has been suggested that asymmetric marriage rules and residence rules "precondition" the social groups which determine Omaha and Crow systems (Lane and Lane, 1959, pp. 262–264).

One of the inadequacies of theories of this sort is that they purport to provide a general explanation for the development of various types of kinship terminologies without first describing, with some economical and explicit set of operations, the explained regularities. Once a set of developmental regularities have been comprehensively described, then a theoretical analysis of these regularities may be more feasibly undertaken. One cannot really expect that the notion of a "strongly" corporate patrilineal descent group will satisfactorily account for the development of Omaha kinship terminologies, unless we have previously been provided with some precise, and operationally explicit, explanation of what, in fact, a strongly developed kin group is. Our method for measuring the development of Omaha terminologies, for assigning logical priority to certain terminological equations, is known as scalogram analysis.

## A SCALOGRAM ANALYSIS OF OMAHA TERMINOLOGICAL SYSTEMS

The rank order of terminological equations on the Omaha scale is as follows:

1. MBS = MB
2. MBSS = MB
3. MBD = M or MZ
4. FZD = D or ZD

5. MMBD = MM
6. FZDS = SS
7. MFZD = Z.

In Wintu terminology, FZDS = SS (Du Bois, 1935). This is a scale error. The coefficient of reproducibility is computed as follows:

$$1 - \frac{1}{7 \times 14} = 0.99.$$

Following is the rank order of Omaha systems and their associated scale types (cf. Scale I);

| Systems | Scale Types |
|---|---|
| 1. Wintu (Du Bois, 1935) | 2 |
| 2. Dorobo (Huntingford, 1942, 1951, 1954) | 4 |
| 3. Tokelau (Macgregor, 1937) | 4 |
| 4. Chahar (Vreeland, 1953) | 4 |
| 5. Bari (Seligman, 1932) | 4 |
| 6. Lango (Driberg, 1923, 1932) | 4 |
| 7. Arapesh (Mead, 1942) | 5 |
| 8. Kalmuk (Aberle, 1953) | 5 |
| 9. Amba (Winter, 1956) | 6 |
| 10. Tzeltal (Sousberghe and Uribe, 1962) | 6 |
| 11. Fox (Tax, in Eggan, 1937) | 7 |
| 12. Nyoro (Beattie, 1957–1959) | 7 |
| 13. Omaha (Dorsey, 1881–1882) | 7 |
| 14. Northern Pomo (Gifford, 1922) | 7 |

### Table 11–1.  A Scalogram Analysis of Omaha Terminological Systems

| System no. | Scale type | Scale variables | | | | | | |
|---|---|---|---|---|---|---|---|---|
| | | 1 | 2 | 3 | 4 | 5 | 6 | 7 |
| 1 | 2 | + | + | − | − | 0 | + | 0 |
| 2 | 4 | + | + | + | + | − | − | − |
| 3 | 4 | + | + | + | + | − | − | − |
| 4 | 4 | + | + | + | + | − | − | − |
| 5 | 4 | + | + | + | + | − | − | − |
| 6 | 4 | + | + | + | + | − | − | − |
| 7 | 5 | + | + | + | + | + | − | − |
| 8 | 5 | + | + | + | + | + | − | − |
| 9 | 6 | + | + | + | + | + | + | − |
| 10 | 6 | + | + | + | + | + | + | − |
| 11 | 7 | + | + | + | + | + | + | + |
| 12 | 7 | + | + | + | + | + | + | + |
| 13 | 7 | + | + | + | + | + | + | + |
| 14 | 7 | + | + | + | + | + | + | + |

Coefficient of Reproducibility = 0.99.

## A TRANSFORMATIONAL ANALYSIS OF OMAHA KINSHIP TERMINOLOGIES

A scalogram analysis of Omaha kin terms (Table 11–1) provides the minimal structural information that will allow us to differentiate Omaha systems from one another; an analysis of this sort, however, fails to account for those kin class assignments which are not of significance in measuring the logical development of Omaha terminologies. A sufficient account (i.e., a complete enumeration) of the assignments of biological kin types in the consanguineal domain to kinship terms is produced by a formalization of the classificatory logic that underlies Omaha systems: Lounsbury's Omaha rules. Lounsbury has three types of Omaha systems which he discriminates on the basis of the three *skewing rules* that generate the appropriate kin class assignments for each system.

They are as follows:

$$\text{Type One: } FZ \ldots \rightarrow Z \ldots$$

*Let the kin type, FATHER'S SISTER, whenever it occurs as a link between Ego and any other relative, be regarded as structurally equivalent to the kin type, SISTER, in that context* (Lounsbury, 1964a p. 359).

If this rule is applicable, the corollary specifies an equivalence between the kin types covered by the rule.

$$\text{Corollary: } \ldots \female BS \rightarrow \ldots \female B; \text{ and } \ldots \female BD \rightarrow \ldots \female Z.$$

This is to be read: *One's female linking relative's BROTHER'S CHILD (BROTHER'S SON or BROTHER'S DAUGHTER) is to be regarded as structurally equivalent to that female linking relative's SIBLING (BROTHER or SISTER, respectively.)* (Lounsbury, 1964a p. 360.)

Skewing Rule—Omaha Type I may be written

$$\begin{bmatrix} + \text{ mas.} \\ + \text{ g.r.} \\ + \text{ sen.} \\ + \text{ con.} \end{bmatrix} \begin{bmatrix} - \text{ mas.} \\ - \text{ g.r.} \\ - \text{ sen.} \\ + \text{ con.} \end{bmatrix} \rightarrow \begin{bmatrix} - \text{ mas.} \\ - \text{ g.r.} \\ - \text{ sen.} \\ + \text{ con.} \end{bmatrix} \text{ in env. } \underline{\hspace{2cm}} X.$$

The corollaries are

(a)
$$\begin{bmatrix} + \text{ mas.} \\ - \text{ g.r.} \\ - \text{ sen.} \\ + \text{ con.} \end{bmatrix} \begin{bmatrix} + \text{ mas.} \\ + \text{ g.r.} \\ - \text{ sen.} \\ + \text{ con.} \end{bmatrix} \rightarrow \begin{bmatrix} + \text{ mas.} \\ - \text{ g.r.} \\ - \text{ sen.} \\ + \text{ con.} \end{bmatrix} \text{ in env. } X \, [- \text{ mas.}] \underline{\hspace{1.5cm}}.$$

(b)
$$\begin{bmatrix} + \text{ mas.} \\ - \text{ g.r.} \\ - \text{ sen.} \\ + \text{ con.} \end{bmatrix} \begin{bmatrix} - \text{ mas.} \\ + \text{ g.r.} \\ - \text{ sen.} \\ + \text{ con.} \end{bmatrix} \rightarrow \begin{bmatrix} - \text{ mas.} \\ - \text{ g.r.} \\ - \text{ sen.} \\ + \text{ con.} \end{bmatrix} \text{ in env. } X \, [- \text{ mas.}] \underline{\hspace{1.5cm}}.$$

Omaha skewing rule Type I reduces all members of the "uncle" class to the genealogical kernel MB, and the corollary reduces all members of the "nephew" and "niece" class (FBDS, FBDD, FZS, FZD) to the kernels ZS and ZD, respectively, as well as having consequences for innumerable other kin types. Consider Lounsbury's (1964a, p. 361) reductions for the "uncle" class (*nehcihsaha*) in Fox terminology. First we assign the terms to their generational levels, and then they are reduced.

$$G^2: \text{MMFZS}$$
$$G^1: \text{MB, MFBS, MMZS}$$
$$G^0: \text{MBS, MFBSS, MMZSS, MMBDS}$$
$$G^{-1}: \text{MBSS}$$
$$G^{-2}: \text{MBSSS}$$

| | | | |
|---|---|---|---|
| MMFZS | → MMZS | (by Skewing Rule) | (1) |
| | → MMS | (by Merging Rule) | |
| | → MB | (by Half-sibling Rule) | |
| MMZSS | → MMSS | (by Merging Rule) | (2) |
| | → MBS | (by Half-sibling Rule) | |
| | → MB | (by Skewing Rule Corollary) | |
| MMBDS | → MMZS | (by Skewing Rule Corollary) | (3) |
| | → MMS | (by Merging Rule) | |
| | → MB | (by Half-sibling Rule) | |
| MBSSS | → MBSS | (by Skewing Rule Corollary) | (4) |
| | → MBS | (by a second application of same) | |
| | → MB | (by a third application of same). | |

So for Omaha Type I we can reduce the kin types to kernels that are isomorphic with the terms by a set of four rewrite rules. We use this set of rewrite rules as the criteria to designate our system Omaha Type I.

Lounsbury (1964a, p. 362) notes that all terminological extensions reduce to the primary meaning of the appropriate conceptual classes and that no hierarchical order of preference need be assigned to the reduction rules: the rules constitute an unordered set. This is a point that Lévi-Strauss (1949) made two decades ago. But Lounsbury was dealing with a "pocket version" of an Omaha system, restricting the universe of kin types which he considered for his analysis. However much it may be desirable to retain an unordered set of rules (i.e., an instruction that reads, apply any rule at any time, just so long as it applies), it seems that if one is to undertake an analysis of the Fox system *in toto*, then one has to first create new rewrite rules, and second, order the application of the rules. This results in a loss of economy, but a gain in the sense that we can begin to have some notion of the logical and historical priority of one transformational operation over another. Bright and Minnick (1966) have carried out this fuller analysis, and their results can be briefly reviewed here.

In their analysis the rules and corollaries are formulated to account for certain aspects of the grandparental and grandchild terminology in the Fox system. The first rule is designated as a *cross sibling rule*, and, it is suggested that Lounsbury's merging rule may be more appropriately labelled as a *parallel sibling rule*.

Cross Sibling Rule: ... MB → ... F; and ... FZ → ... M.

*Let any linking relative's* MOTHER'S BROTHER *or* FATHER'S SISTER *be regarded as equivalent to that linking relative's* FATHER *or* MOTHER, *respectively* (Bright and Minnick, 1966, p. 382).

Corollary: ♂ZS ... → ♂S ... ; ♂ZD ... → ♂D ... ; ♀BS ... → ♀S ... ;
♀BD ... → ♀D ...

*Let a man's* SISTER'S *or a woman's* BROTHER'S CHILDREN (SON *or* DAUGHTER), *as linking relatives, be regarded as equivalent to his or her own children* (SON *or* DAUGHTER, *respectively*) (Bright and Minnick, 1966, p. 382).

The second rule, and its corollary, belongs to the same general category as Lounsbury's skewing rules, although its range of operation is more restricted. It operates between ascending or descending generations and affects mothers and mother's kin in the same way, whereas Lounsbury's skewing rules equate Ego's terminological generation with ascending and descending generations (Bright and Minnick, 1966, pp. 383–384). This rule is designated a *minor lineal rule* and it is suggested that Lounsbury's skewing rule may be labelled as the *major lineal rule*.

Minor Lineal Rule: SS ... → S ... ; SD ... → S ... ; DS ... → D ... ;
DD ... → D ...

*One's* CHILD'S CHILD, *as linking relative, is to be regarded as equivalent to one's* CHILD (Bright and Minnick, 1966, p. 383).

Corollary: ... FF → ... F; ... FM → ... M; ... MF → ... F;
... MM → ... M.

*One's linking relative's* PARENT'S PARENT *is to be regarded as equivalent to that linking relative's* PARENT (Bright and Minnick, 1966, p. 383).

Although Lounsbury's notational system includes a symbol to indicate that linking kin must be involved (. . .), the converse of this symbol—that linking kin must not be involved—is not explicitly introduced in the initial Crow-Omaha paper (Lounsbury, 1964a). Consequently, ♀Z might mean a female linking kinsman's sister or a female Ego's sister, and the sister could be either the designated kin or a link to some other kin (Bright and Minnick, 1966, p. 384). This distinction may be explicitly accounted for by (1) a single dot, which indicates an initial or terminal element, as in Romney's (1965, p. 136) *Special collateral descendant rule* (.a 0 a— → .a − a−); (2) a vertical line, which indicates terminal position only, as in Lounsbury's (1965, p. 168) *Spouse-identification* (Crow) *rule*

$$|\sigma BW| \rightarrow |\sigma B|, \text{ and reciprocally, } | \varphi HB| \rightarrow |\sigma B|$$
$$| \varphi ZH| \rightarrow | \varphi Z|, \text{ and reciprocally, } |\sigma WZ| \rightarrow | \varphi Z|.$$

or (3) the rewritten version of Bright and Minnick's (1966, p. 384) *cross sibling rule*: ... MB# → ... F#; ... FZ# → ... M#.

Alternatively, inaccurate reductions may be eliminated by prescribing an order of precedence among rules. For Fox, such an ordering takes the following form (Bright and Minnick, 1966, p. 386):

| | |
|---|---|
| **1.** Major lineal rule  } | in that order |
| **2.** Parallel sibling rule } | |
| **3a.** Minor lineal rule  } | after rules 1 and 2, but unordered |
| **3b.** Cross sibling rule  } | with respect to each other |
| **x.** Half-sibling rule | unordered with respect to all others |

When necessary, the ordering of descriptive rules seems to us to be of potentially greater theoretical value than boundary markers, in view of the important hypothesis that such an ordering may reflect historical order of development.

With reference to the Fox system and Central Algonkian systems in general, there is a relevant observation by Hockett (1964, p. 247) to the effect that "the extension of 'father' and 'mother' to 'parallel-uncle' and 'parallel-aunt' ... seems to be relatively recent." Because this extension of terms is accounted for by the parallel sibling rule, the fact that this rule has a lower priority than the major lineal rule may be a descriptive reflection of its historical recency. If such correlations can be shown in a sufficient number of cases, we will clearly have a powerful tool for reconstructing prehistoric developments in kinship organization (Bright and Minnick, 1966, p. 387).

For Omaha Type II we are presented with a different set of correspondences and therefore new rewrite rules are composed that will serve to distinguish this type of Omaha system from all others.

Skewing Rule (Omaha Type II): First Stronger Form:

$$FZ \rightarrow Z.$$

*Let the kin type* FATHER'S SISTER *be equivalent to the kin type* SISTER (Lounsbury, 1964a, p. 369).

The rule's corollary specifies an equivalence between the kin types covered by the rule.

$$\text{Corollary: } \varphi BS \rightarrow \varphi B; \text{ and } \varphi BD \rightarrow \varphi Z.$$

*Let a woman's BROTHER'S CHILD be equivalent to that woman's sibling* (Lounsbury, 1964a, p. 370).

This rule (Omaha Type II) is a "stronger" version of Omaha Type I; the rule now applies to FZ, and its corollary to ♀BS and ♀B, in whatever context they occur. Tzeltal (Sousberghe and Uribe, 1962) is an example of a system of this type (Table 11–1).

$$\begin{bmatrix} + \text{ mas.} \\ + \text{ g.r.} \\ + \text{ sen.} \\ + \text{ con.} \end{bmatrix} \begin{bmatrix} - \text{ mas.} \\ - \text{ g.r.} \\ - \text{ sen.} \\ + \text{ con.} \end{bmatrix} \rightarrow \begin{bmatrix} - \text{ mas.} \\ - \text{ g.r.} \\ - \text{ sen.} \\ + \text{ con.} \end{bmatrix}$$

The corollaries are

$$\begin{bmatrix} + \text{ mas.} \\ - \text{ g.r.} \\ - \text{ sen.} \\ + \text{ con.} \end{bmatrix} \begin{bmatrix} + \text{ mas.} \\ + \text{ g.r.} \\ - \text{ sen.} \\ + \text{ con.} \end{bmatrix} \rightarrow \begin{bmatrix} + \text{ mas.} \\ - \text{ g.r.} \\ - \text{ sen.} \\ + \text{ con.} \end{bmatrix} \text{ in env. } [- \text{ mas.}] \underline{\qquad}.$$

and,

$$\begin{bmatrix} + \text{ mas.} \\ - \text{ g.r.} \\ - \text{ sen.} \\ + \text{ con.} \end{bmatrix} \begin{bmatrix} - \text{ mas.} \\ + \text{ g.r.} \\ - \text{ sen.} \\ + \text{ con.} \end{bmatrix} \rightarrow \begin{bmatrix} - \text{ mas.} \\ - \text{ g.r.} \\ - \text{ sen.} \\ + \text{ con.} \end{bmatrix} \text{ in env. } [- \text{ mas.}] \underline{\qquad}.$$

The second stronger form may be written

$$\begin{bmatrix} - \text{ mas.} \\ - \text{ g.r.} \\ - \text{ sen.} \\ + \text{ con.} \end{bmatrix} \rightarrow \begin{bmatrix} - \text{ mas.} \\ + \text{ g.r.} \\ - \text{ sen.} \\ + \text{ con.} \end{bmatrix} \text{ in env. } X \, [+ \text{ mas.}] \underline{\qquad}.$$

Its corollary is

$$\begin{bmatrix} + \text{ mas.} \\ - \text{ g.r.} \\ - \text{ sen.} \\ + \text{ con.} \end{bmatrix} \rightarrow \begin{bmatrix} + \text{ mas.} \\ + \text{ g.r.} \\ + \text{ sen.} \\ + \text{ con.} \end{bmatrix} \text{ in env. } X \, [- \text{ mas.}] \underline{\qquad}.$$

Skewing Rule (Omaha Type III): Second Stronger Form

$$\ldots \male Z \rightarrow \ldots \male D \, .$$

*Let a man's SISTER, as linking relative, be regarded as equivalent to that man's DAUGHTER as linking relative* (Lounsbury, 1964a, p. 372).

The corollary of the rule specifies an equivalence between the kin types covered by the rule.

Corollary: ... ♀B → ... ♀F.

*Let any female linking relative's BROTHER be regarded as equivalent to that female linking relative's FATHER (Lounsbury, 1964a, p. 372).*

Skewing Rule III transforms a FZS, FZD, and so on, into a "grandchild" (e.g., Khalkha).

$$\begin{array}{llr} \text{FZS} \rightarrow \text{FDS} & \text{(Skewing Rule III)} & \\ \rightarrow \text{ZS} & \text{(Half-sibling Rule)} & (5) \\ \rightarrow \text{DS} & \text{(Skewing Rule III).} & \end{array}$$

The corollary of Skewing Rule III generates the terminological assignments of Omaha systems (e.g., Khalkha, Wintu), in which MB, MBS, MBSS, and so on, are given a second ascending generation classification.

$$\begin{array}{llr} \text{MBSS} \rightarrow \text{MBS} & \text{(Skewing Rule I Corollary)} & \\ \rightarrow \text{MB} & \text{(by a second application of same)} & (6) \\ \rightarrow \text{MF} & \text{(Skewing Rule III Corollary).} & \end{array}$$

Using Lounsbury's rules, we reduce a number of expanded kin types *to the genealogically closer kin types to which they are structurally equivalent.* The scale variables that are accounted for by each reduction series are noted.

| *Scale Variables* | | *Reduction Series* | |
|---|---|---|---|
| 1,2 | MBSS → MBS | (by Skewing Rule I Corollary) | (7) |
| | → MB | (by a second application of same) | |
| 3 | MBD → MZ | (by Skewing Rule I Corollary) | (8) |
| | → M | (by Merging Rule) | |
| 4 | FZD → ZD | (by Skewing Rule I) | (9) |
| 5 | MMBD → MMZ | (by Skewing Rule I Corollary) | (10) |
| | → MM | (by Merging Rule) | |
| 6 | FZDS → ZDS | (by Skewing Rule I). | (11) |

Scale variable six equates a grandchild (SS) with a FZDS. In many Omaha systems FZDS is also equated with ZDS; zero and first degree collaterals of the second descending generation are not differentiated. Consequently, an additional taxonomic distinction (lineal vs. collateral) must be introduced. SS and ZDS may be glossed "lineal grandson" and "collateral grandson," respectively. These kin types, in turn, are members of the superclass "grandchild," which may include kin types such as (e.g., Fox) FFZSS, FFZSD, FFZDS, FFZDD, MZSSS, and FZSSS.

$$\begin{array}{llr} \text{MFZD} \rightarrow \text{MZD} & \text{(by Skewing Rule I)} & (12) \\ \rightarrow \text{MD} & \text{(by Merging Rule)} & \\ \rightarrow \text{Z} & \text{(by Half-sibling Rule).} & \end{array}$$

## RANK AND LINEAL FORMS OF CLASSIFICATION

The three major criterial properties of Omaha systems (Lounsbury, 1964a; Romney, 1965) are (1) the merging of relatives in the mother's line (MB, MBS, and so on); (2) the merging of children of one's own line (FFZS, FZS, ZS); and (3) the terminological separation of lines (1) and (2). The variation in Omaha systems is usually related to whether second ascending generation relatives are terminologically distinguished from "lower generation" relatives in the mother's line, "and the reciprocal classification of the second descending generation children of own line (namely, Br Da Ch)" (Romney, 1965, pp. 139–140).

Lounsbury's (1964a) classification of Omaha systems is based upon two basic dimensions: (1) the merging and differentiation of second ascending generation relatives and their reciprocals in the mother's line; and (2) the merging or differentiation of females across generation boundaries within own line (cf. Romney, 1965, p. 140).

If we let (+) represent merging and (−) differentiation, then the fourfold classification may be summarized in Figure 11–1.

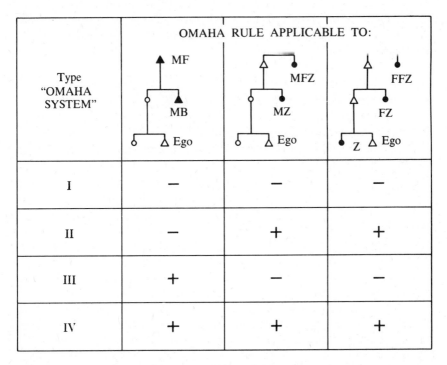

| Type "OMAHA SYSTEM" | OMAHA RULE APPLICABLE TO: | | |
|---|---|---|---|
| | MF / MB / Ego | MFZ / MZ / Ego | FFZ / FZ / Ego |
| I | − | − | − |
| II | − | + | + |
| III | + | − | − |
| IV | + | + | + |

*Figure 11–1. The Subvarieties of "Omaha-Type" Systems of Terminology on the Basis of Generation Skewing in the Consanguineal Domain (cf. Lounsbury, 1964a; Romney, 1965).*

Romney (1965) has suggested that a lineal type of Omaha classification, as exemplified by Kalmuk Mongol, should be distinguished from Lounsbury's "rank" type systems. The distinction between rank and lineal forms of Omaha classification centers on the classification of "remote lines" (Lines other than one's own patriline [Romney, 1965, pp. 140–141]):

| Variables | Coding Rules | |
|---|---|---|
| | *Lineal forms of classification* | *Rank forms of classification* |
| **A.** *Ascending lines:* | | |
| A.1: Mother's line | A.1, A.2, A.3 | A.1: One dimension underlying |
| A.2: Mother's mother's line | are merged | Lounsbury's classification of |
| A.3: Father's mother's line | | Omaha systems. |
| **B.** *Line children of ascending lines:* | | |
| B.1:  Children of (A.1) | B.1, B.2, B.3 | B.1: Merged with sibling class |
| B.2:  Children of (A.2) | are merged | B.2: Merged with mother's line |
| B.3:  Children of (A.3) | | B.3: Merged with first generation relatives of own line |

In general terms, rank systems merge the line children of mother's line with relatives in one's own patriline; lineal system differentiate own line from all other lines.

## RANGE REDUCTION RULES

In order to consider, in somewhat greater detail, Romney's (1965) rules for a lineal type of Omaha classification (Kalmuk Mongol), let us review Romney's method of "range reduction."

Firstly, all geneological kin types are listed in Romney's (Romney and D'Andrade, 1964a) notational system. In addition to the symbols that we have already introduced, an additional one must be added: ( ) represents an expansion. Further, in the Kalmuk Mongol analysis, superscripts represent numbers of expansions and subscripts represent sex correspondences. Secondly, the denotative range of each kin term is reduced to a single notational expression. Romney (1965, p. 129) equates the latter step to the reduction of allophones to a phoneme. Finally, components are defined in terms of significant and minimal differences among reduced ranges. There are four range reduction rules (Romney, 1965, pp. 130–133).

Rule 1. *Rule of minimal difference within range.* Where two kin types within a range are identical except for a difference in sex markers in the same position, the two kin types may be written as one with the symbol for "person of either sex" (a) in the contrasting position. Rule 1 is to be applied before all others (Romney, 1965, p. 130). For example:

$$\left. \begin{array}{l} \text{1. MMB (m.s.) } m + f + f\, 0\, m \\ \text{2. FMB (m.s.) } m + m + f\, 0\, m \end{array} \right\} \rightarrow m + a + a\, 0\, m$$

Rule 2. *Rule of sequence difference within range.* Where any two expressions are identical except for one additional "link" (i.e., a pair consisting of one sex and one relation marker), the "link" may be written in parentheses. The parentheses indicate an optional expansion. This rule must be labelled with a superscript indicating number of reductions made (Romney, 1965, p. 131).

In this range reduction rule, "parentheses indicate optional inclusion of the enclosed link, and the superscripts indicate number of applications of options" (Romney, 1965, p. 131). An "Omaha-type range" may be used to exemplify this rule:

1. MB (m.s.) $m + f\,0\,m$
2. MBS (m.s.) $m + f\,0\,m - m$ $\Big\} \rightarrow m + f\,0\,(m-)^{0,\,1,\,2}m.$
3. MBSS (m.s.) $m + f\,0\,m - m - m$

Rule 3. *The rule of paired sequence difference within range.* Rule 3 is an extension of Rule 2. Where any two expressions are identical within a range except for "paired links," the "paired links" may be written in parentheses. For example:

1. FBS (or D:m.s. or f.s.) $a + m\,0\,m - a$
2. MZS (or D:m.s. or f.s.) $a + f\,0\,f - a$ $\Big\} \rightarrow a(+a_i)^x\,0\,(a_i-)^y a.$
3. S (or D:m.s. or f.s.) $a\,0\,a$

where $x = y = 0, 1$; and subscript $i$ indicates that whatever sex appears in the first parenthesis, appears again in the second.

Rule 4. *The rule of reciprocals within range.* Where any two kin types differ only by the fact that they are complete reciprocals of one another, either expression may be written between slashes and be taken to represent both (Romney, 1965, p. 132).

In Romney's (1965, p. 132) notational system, a reciprocal of any kin type is found by writing the expression in reverse order and changing all $+$'s to $-$'s and vice-versa, without changing 0 and $=$ links. Romney (1965, pp. 132–133) illustrates the operation of the range reduction rules in reference to the denotative range of the Kalmuk Mongol kin term /Nahcaha/.

1. MMB $\rightarrow a + f + f\,0\,m$
2. FMB $\rightarrow a + m + f\,0\,m$
3. MFB $\rightarrow a + f + m\,0\,m$
4. MMBS $\rightarrow a + f + f\,0\,m - m$
5. FMBS $\rightarrow a + m + f\,0\,m - m$
6. MFBS $\rightarrow a + f + m\,0\,m - m$
7. MB $\rightarrow a + f\,0\,m$
8. MBS $\rightarrow a + f\,0\,m - m$
9. MBSS $\rightarrow a + f\,0\,m - m - m$
10. MBSSS $\rightarrow a + f\,0\,m - m - m - m$

Examining the kin type strings that are designated by the algebraic expressions to the right, we proceed to apply rule one, which specifies that where two expressions are identical in form except that one has the male node ($m$) and the other the female ($f$), we may combine the two by rewriting them as $a$.

Thus expressions 1 and 2 can be rewritten

*Summary String*

$$\left. \begin{array}{l} \text{1. } a+f+f\,0\,m \\ \text{2. } a+m+f\,0\,m \end{array} \right\} \rightarrow a+a+f\,0\,m \text{ (I).}$$

Expressions 4 and 5 can be rewritten in the same manner:

$$\left. \begin{array}{l} \text{4. } a+f+f\,0\,m-m \\ \text{5. } a+m+f\,0\,m-m \end{array} \right\} \rightarrow a+a+f\,0\,m-m \text{ (II).}$$

Scanning the remaining kin type strings, we can see, by inspection, that there are no further expressions in which we can apply the rule of minimum difference within the range. It is instructive to note the restrictions on the application of this rule. For example, it appears at first sight as though string 6 could be merged into summary string II by the substitution of an $a$.

*Summary String*

$$\left. \begin{array}{ll} \text{1. Summary string II} & a+a+f\,0\,m-m \\ \text{6. (string 6)} & a+f+m\,0\,m-m \end{array} \right\} \rightarrow a+a+a\,0\,m-m^*.$$

The expression $a$ can be rewritten as $f$ or $m$, and therefore it would seem to include the $f$ which is the second node in kin string 6. But, in fact, the nodes have to be mutually and exclusively contrastive. If we were to write out the denotative range of summary string $a+a+a\,0\,m-m$, we would generate the following:

1. $a+m+m\,0\,m-m$
2. $a+f+f\,0\,m-m$
3. $a+m+f\,0\,m-m$
4. $a+f+m\,0\,m-m$.

And by inspecting the strings of the actual denotative range of the kin term /Nahcaha/ we will find that (1) does not occur, and therefore our rewrite rule is generating a term that does not appear in the original denotative range, and is incorrect.

Rule two states that optional expansions from a base expression can be rewritten as parentheticals, with a superscript to indicate the number of permissible expansions. (Rule of sequence difference within range.) In an Omaha system where characteristically we have kin terms extended across generational lines, this rule is widely applicable. Note that our first summary string and kin type string number 7 may be reduced

Summary String

1. (summary string I) $a + a + f\,0\,m$
2. (string 7) $\qquad a + f\,0\,m$
$\left.\right\}\to a + (a+)^{0,\,1}f\,0\,m$ (III).

Note as well, that our second summary form from the application of rule two, can be combined with string 8 in the same manner.

Summary String

1. (summary string II) $a + a + f\,0\,m - m$
2. (string 8) $\qquad a + f\,0\,m - m$
$\left.\right\}\to a + (a+)^{0,\,1}f\,0\,m - m$ (IV).

Note that strings 7, 8, 9, 10 can be combined by rule two

Summary String

7. $a + f\,0\,m$
8. $a + f\,0\,m - m$
9. $a + f\,0\,m - m - m$
10. $a + f\,0\,m - m - m - m$
$\left.\right\}\to a + f\,0\,(m-)^{0,\,1,\,2,\,3}m$ (V).

Summary strings III and IV can be similarly reduced:

Summary String

1. Summary string III $a + (a+)^{0,\,1}f\,0\,m$
2. Summary string IV $a + (a+)^{0,\,1}f\,0\,m - m$
$\left.\right\}\to a + (a+)^{0,\,1}f\,0\,(m-)^{0,\,1}m$

(VI)

Similarly, the two remaining strings (3 and 6) can be rewritten with a single expansion expression:

3. $a + f + m\,0\,m$
6. $a + f + m\,0\,m - m$
$\left.\right\}\to a + f + m\,0\,(m-)^{0,\,1}m.$

This leaves us with three summary strings (V, VI, VII). These are

$$(\text{V})\ a + f\,0\,(m-)^{0,\,1,\,2,\,3}m.$$
$$(\text{VI})\ a + (a+)^{0,\,1}f\,0\,(m-)^{0,\,1}m.$$
$$(\text{VII})\ a + f(+m)^{0,\,1}\,0\,(m-)^{0,\,1}m.$$

Summary strings V, VI, and VII can be reduced by the use of superscripts to formulate one expression that will generate all and only the biological kin types covered by the term /Nahcaha/.

VIII. $a(+a)^{i} + f(+m)^{j}\,0\,(m-)^{k}m$
$\qquad$ [$i + j = 0, 1;\ k = 0, 1, 2, 3$ and if $i$ or $j = 1$, then $k = 0, 1$].

In this way all the denotative ranges of the kinship terms of Kalmuk Mongol are reduced to their core expressions, and from these core expressions are deduced a set of five rewrite rules that provide us with a structural summary of the "skewing" and "merging" characteristics of this highly developed Omaha system. The rewrite rules for the Kalmuk Mongol form of lineal (Omaha) classification are

Rule 1. *Patri-parallel expansion rule* (Romney, 1965, p. 136):

$$0 \rightarrow +m\ 0\ m-.$$

This rule may be applied 0, 1, 2, or 3 times.

Rule 2. *Special collateral descendant rule* (Romney, 1965, p. 136):

$$.a\ 0\ a- \rightarrow .a - a-.$$

where . indicates either an internal or terminal element.

Rule 3. *Patrilineal merging rule* (Romney, 1965, p. 137):

$$+f\ 0 \rightarrow +f + m\ 0 \text{ and/or } +f\ 0\ m-.$$

*Corollary.*

$$0f- \rightarrow 0\ m - f- \text{ and/or } +m\ 0f-.$$

Rule 4. *Ascending and descending merging rules* (Romney, 1965, p. 137):

$$a + f \ldots \rightarrow a + a + f \ldots \text{ and/or } a + f + a \ldots .$$

*Corollary.*

$$\ldots f - a - a \rightarrow \ldots f - a.$$

where ... represent noninitial or nonterminal elements.

Rule 5. *Patrilineal ascending and descending rules* (Romney, 1965, p. 137):

$$+m\ 0\ a. \rightarrow +m + m\ 0\ a.$$
$$+m + m \ldots \rightarrow +m + m + m \ldots .$$

*Corollaries.*

$$.a\ 0\ m - m- \rightarrow .a\ 0\ m - m - m-$$
$$\ldots m - m- \rightarrow \ldots m - m - m-.$$

   In this section, then, we have attempted to show two approaches to a formal analysis of Omaha systems. In the end it is a matter of taste and background as to whether one takes the Romney approach, or the Lounsbury. Both systems allow us to view the underlying principles of kin-class assignment in any kinship system, and given the same system, both should arrive at the same solution. Romney's method is preferable in that it allows one to see the explicit steps by which analysis is carried out. The intuitive leaps whereby rewrite rules are arrived at are eliminated in favor of a step-by-step approach utilizing the ordered reduction rules. Perhaps, as well, his system is more manipulatable, once the notational system is thoroughly digested; and it has the added advantage of reducing the number of primitives in the notational system from eight to three, while explicating the operators that are contained within the primitives in the more traditional (Lounsbury) notational system.

In this final section we would like to consider asymmetric systems. By utilizing the techniques of formal analysis we would like to demonstrate a number of things. First, it becomes clear that a formal analysis is both more adequate, and accounts for more asymmetric terminologies, than the contextual (total structural) analysis of Needham. Second the use of formal analysis enables us to see the alternatives that are semantically implicit in the systems of classification themselves. Lastly we would like to show how these semantic alternatives (polysemy) differentiate asymmetric (Miwok) type systems from Omaha systems, which we have described up to here.

## ASYMMETRIC EXCHANGE TERMINOLOGIES

The distinction between Omaha and asymmetric exchange terminologies (or "Miwok type systems") has been discussed on (1) a formal level and (2) a functional level. That is (1) in terms of "categorical" differences in ordering affines and consanguines within the terminological set; and (2) with respect to the marriage regulatory entailments of the genealogical code. Omaha systems have terminologically distinct affinal assignments; asymmetrical exchange systems do not. The institutional expression of this logic is manifest in affinal alliances, of a political and economic nature (Leach, 1951), between lineal descent groups. Some of the more superficial formal (terminological) similarities between Omaha and asymmetric exchange terminologies are as follows: MB = MBS, MF (Purum, Vaiphei; Needham, 1958b, 1959a); FZS = ZS, SS and FZD = ZD, SD (Purum); MBD = M (Mapuche; Faron, 1956); MBD = MM (Vaiphei). In many asymmetric exchange terminologies, however, genealogically defined affines are assigned to consanguineal categories; for example, WB = MBS, BW = MBD, WF = MB.

In this section we are concerned with the genealogical principles that order the categories of an asymmetric system with particular reference to Purum relationship terminology (Das, 1945; Needham, 1958b). We begin this analysis by presenting extensional definitions [by listing the *denotata* of thirteen Purum lexemes which are actually radicals, isolated by Needham (1964, p. 1378) on the basis of a comparative study of their languages and societies]. We then proceed from a set of extensional definitions to what Lounsbury (1964b, p. 1088) has referred to as *basic member definitions* and supplementary *rules of extension*; or generative rules. Here the formal status of differences of genealogical degree within each class of denotata of a term is explicitly recognized. The extensional definitions are followed by Needham's (Table 11–2) ordering of the Purum categories of descent and alliance.

*Purum Kin Terms: Extensional Definitions*

1. *pu*: FF, MF, MB, WF, MBS, WB, WBS
2. *pi*: FM, MM, MBW, WM, WBW
3. *pa*: F, FB, MZH
4. *nu*: M, MZ, FBW
5. *ni*: FZ
6. *rang*: FZH
7. *ta*: eB, FBSe, MZSe
8. *u*: eZ, FBDe, MZDe
9. *hau*: yB, FBSy, MZSy, yZ, MZDy, MB, BW, WBD
10. *sar*: Z
11. *mau*: SW
12. *sha*: S, BS, WZS, D, BD, WZD
13. *tu*: FZS, ZH, FZD, ZS, DH, ZD, SS, SD, DSW, DS, SDH, DD.

### Table 11–2.  Purum Categories of Descent and Alliance

| f. | m. | ← f. | m. | ← f. | m. | ← f. |
|----|----|----|----|----|----|----|
| | | | *pu* | *pi* | *pu* | *pi* |
| | *rang* | *ni* | *pa* | *nu* | *pu* | *pi* |
| | | *u* | *ta* | | | |
| *tu* | *tu* | *sar* | (ego) | *nau* | *pu* | *pi* |
| | | *nau* | *nau* | | | |
| *tu* | *tu* | *sha* | *sha* | *nau* *mau* | *pu* | |
| *tu* | *tu* | *tu* | *tu* | | | |

(After Needham, 1962a, p. 76.)

A basic dimension of the tripartite categorization of the social order is the Purum division of the total society into (1) wife-giving groups, (2) wife-taking groups, and (3) lineally related descent groups (Needham, 1962a, p. 78). These constructs may include several descent groups relative to any specified descent group. The men of a wife-giving group are *pu*; their wives are *pi*: the denotative ranges of these two categories are (a) FF, MF, MB, WF, MBS, WB, WBS, and (b) FM, MM, MBW, WM, WBW, respectively. The basic functional dimension of the system is defined by the opposition of the categories *pu/tu*. This crucial opposition between wife-giving and wife-taking categories is the governing principle of the Purum terminology of social classification (Needham, 1964, p. 1380). Governing the categorization of the men of a wife-giving group is Hereditary Affinity Rule I.

Hereditary Affinity Rule I: W . . . → M . . . .

This is to be read: *Let one's WIFE, as linking relative, be regarded as equivalent to one's MOTHER, as linking relative.*

A second Hereditary Affinity Rule must be introduced to account for the classification of the wives of the men of a wife-giving group: i.e., the denotata of the term *pi*. The rule is written as follows:

Hereditary Affinity Rule II . . . ♀BW → . . . ♀M

This is to be read: *Let any female linking relative's BROTHER'S WIFE be regarded as equivalent to that female linking relative's MOTHER.*

We can now derive core expressions for the men and women of wife-giving groups.

e.g.,

| | | | |
|---|---|---|---|
| WBW | → MBW | (Hereditary Affinity Rule I) | (1) |
| | → MM | (Hereditary Affinity Rule II) | |
| | → WM | (Hereditary Affinity Rule I), | |

and

| | | | |
|---|---|---|---|
| WBS | → MBS | (Hereditary Affinity Rule I) | (2) |
| | → MB | (Skewing Rule I Corollary) | |
| | → MF | (Skewing Rule III Corollary) | |
| | → WF | (Hereditary Affinity Rule I) | |
| | → WB | (Skewing Rule III Corollary). | |

Two denotative types are not accounted for in the foregoing derivations: FF and FM. A transformation rule of the form M . . . → F . . . would have to be formulated to account for these types. However, a rule of this type would assign various denotata to Purum categories of which they are not empirically members.

Now a rule must be formulated which expresses the formal equivalence between "half-parents" and "full-parents."

Half-parent Rule: FW → M; MH → F.

This is to be read: *Let one's parent's (FATHER or MOTHER) spouse (WIFE or HUSBAND) be considered to be one's parent (MOTHER or FATHER, respectively).*

In formal terms, the "half-parent rule" should be written as rule and corollary.

We continue with the derivations for Purum terminology:

| | | | |
|---|---|---|---|
| MZH → MH | (Merging Rule) | | (3) |
| → F | (Half-parent rule) | | |
| FBW → FW | (Merging Rule) | | (4) |
| → M | (Half-parent rule) | | |
| FBeS → FSe | (Merging Rule) | | (5) |
| → eB | (Half-sibling rule) | | |
| MZeS → MSe | (Merging Rule) | | (6) |
| → eB | (Half-sibling rule) | | |
| FBeD → FDe | (Merging Rule) | | (7) |
| → eZ | (Half-sibling rule) | | |
| MZeD → MDe | (Merging Rule) | | (8) |
| → eZ | (Half-sibling rule). | | |

A further rule must be introduced to account for a terminological assignment which Needham (1962a, p. 78) indicates is an "infraction of one of the cardinal rules of matrilateral terminologies, viz., that marriageable women must be distinguished from prohibited women."

Affinal Merging Rule I:  . . . ♀BD → . . . ♀D.

This is to be read: *One's female linking relative's* BROTHER'S DAUGHTER *is to be regarded as equivalent to one's female linking relative's* DAUGHTER.

| | | |
|---|---|---|
| WBD → MBD | (Hereditary Affinity Rule I) | (9) |
| → MD | (Affinal Merging Rule I) | |
| → yZ | (Half-sibling rule). | |

The implications of the foregoing derivation are sufficiently interesting to consider in some detail. It is important to note that a reduction rule that accounts for the formal equivalence of MBD and yZ merely provides a description of one of the principles governing the social classification of marriageable women; it fails to provide any general explanation of the terminological equation in the social context of an asymmetric alliance system. Let us consider Needham's "contextual" explanation. Needham (1962a, 1964, pp. 1379, 1380) draws an implicit distinction between the social category marriageable women and the term that denotes this category (*Ka-nau-nu/nau*; reduced by Needham to the radical *nau*). Put somewhat differently, Needham argues that assignment to the kin class by which Purum denote marriageable women is a necessary, but not a sufficient condition for assignment to the social category "marriageable women." The necessary and sufficient conditions for assignment to the latter category include (a) kin class membership and (b) membership in a category of wife-giving descent groups (*pu*), rather than solely in the mother's brother's descent group. The meaning of "marriageable women" in the Purum terminology of social classification is *a same generation, female member of a wife-giving (pu) descent group.* In sum, Needham uses the contextual variable of descent group membership to sort denotative types into wife-giving, wife-taking, and lineal kin categories congruent with an asymmetric alliance system. If this explanation of the ordering principles governing the opposition between wife-givers and wife-takers is considered adequate, then it must be similarly applicable to the Lamet and Chawte (e.g., 1960c) kinship lexicons, for here too we encounter the equation MBD = Z in the context of asymmetric alliance. These modes of classification must be accounted for in the context of the systems in which they occur; they can scarcely be considered a disquieting anomaly (Needham, 1960b, p. 102). Similarly, Needham (1959a, p. 399) has suggested that the assignment of MBD, in the Vaiphei system, to a second ascending generation, zero-degree collateral class, is mistaken. But all of the assignments of this "problematic class" are generated by previously formulated rules:

$$MBD \rightarrow MZ \quad \text{(Skewing Rule I Corollary)} \qquad (10)$$
$$\rightarrow MM \quad \text{(Skewing Rule III Corollary)}$$
$$MBW \rightarrow MM \quad \text{(Hereditary Affinity Rule II)}. \qquad (11)$$

The introduction of the third affinity rule changes the rules from an unordered to an ordered set. The ordering principle is formulated as follows; Hereditary Affinity Rule III will always precede Hereditary Affinity Rule I in a reduction derivation.

Hereditary Affinity Rule III: WZ ... → B ... .

This is to be read: *Let one's wife's sister, as linking relative, be regarded as equivalent to one's* BROTHER, *as linking relative.*

$$WZS \rightarrow BS \quad \text{(Hereditary Affinity Rule III)} \qquad (12)$$
$$WZD \rightarrow BD \quad \text{(Hereditary Affinity Rule III)}. \qquad (13)$$

An additional taxonomic distinction must be introduced (lineal vs. collateral) to differentiate "lineal sons and daughters" (S, D) from "collateral sons and daughters" (BS, BD). "Collateral sons and daughters" are further differentiated by the sex of the initial link in the genealogical chain: when the link is male, they are assigned to the category *sha*; when the link is female (ZS, ZD), they are assigned to the wife-taking category (*tu, maksa*) which, in the Purum dualistic system of symbolic classification, is associated with the inferior feminine cycle, left, *Nangan* division, affines, evil spirits, and so on (Needham, 1962a, pp. 95–96). An additional rule, and the corollary of H. A. Rule I are formulated to "produce" the designatum (the class of all possible denotata) of the term that defines Purum wife-takers.

Corollary: Hereditary Affinity Rule I:   ... H → ... S.

This is to be read: *One's linking relative's* HUSBAND *is to be regarded as equivalent to one's linking relative's* SON.

$$
\begin{array}{lll}
\text{FZS} \rightarrow \text{ZS} & \text{(Skewing Rule I)} & (14) \\
\quad\rightarrow \text{DS} & \text{(Skewing Rule III)} & \\
\quad\rightarrow \text{DH} & \text{(Corollary, Hereditary Affinity Rule I)} & \\
\quad\rightarrow \text{ZH} & \text{(Skewing Rule III)} & \\
\text{FZD} \rightarrow \text{ZD} & \text{(Skewing Rule I)} & (15) \\
\quad\rightarrow \text{DD} & \text{(Skewing Rule III)}. &
\end{array}
$$

The various rules that have been formulated to account for the genealogical principles underlying the analytic encoding of relatives in the kinship terminology of an asymmetric system may be mapped on distinctive features.

I. Hereditary Affinity Rule I:

$$
\begin{bmatrix} -\text{ mas.} \\ -\text{ g.r.} \\ -\text{ sen.} \\ -\text{ con.} \end{bmatrix} \rightarrow \begin{bmatrix} -\text{ mas.} \\ +\text{ g.r.} \\ +\text{ sen.} \\ +\text{ con.} \end{bmatrix} \text{ in env. } \underline{\hspace{2cm}} X.
$$

Corollary:

$$
\begin{bmatrix} +\text{ mas.} \\ -\text{ g.r.} \\ -\text{ sen.} \\ -\text{ con.} \end{bmatrix} \rightarrow \begin{bmatrix} +\text{ mas.} \\ +\text{ g.r.} \\ -\text{ sen.} \\ +\text{ con.} \end{bmatrix} \text{ in env. } X \underline{\hspace{2cm}}.
$$

II. Hereditary Affinity Rule II:

$$
\begin{bmatrix} +\text{ mas.} \\ -\text{ g.r.} \\ -\text{ sen.} \\ +\text{ con.} \end{bmatrix} \begin{bmatrix} -\text{ mas.} \\ -\text{ g.r.} \\ -\text{ sen.} \\ -\text{ con.} \end{bmatrix} \rightarrow \begin{bmatrix} -\text{ mas.} \\ +\text{ g.r.} \\ +\text{ sen.} \\ +\text{ con.} \end{bmatrix} \text{ in env. } X\,[-\text{ mas.}]\,\underline{\hspace{1.5cm}}.
$$

III. Half-parent Rule:

$$
\begin{bmatrix} +\text{ mas.} \\ +\text{ g.r.} \\ +\text{ sen.} \\ +\text{ con.} \end{bmatrix} \begin{bmatrix} -\text{ mas.} \\ -\text{ g.r.} \\ -\text{ sen.} \\ -\text{ con.} \end{bmatrix} \rightarrow \begin{bmatrix} -\text{ mas.} \\ +\text{ g.r.} \\ +\text{ sen.} \\ +\text{ con.} \end{bmatrix}
$$

Corollary:

$$
\begin{bmatrix} -\text{ mas.} \\ +\text{ g.r.} \\ +\text{ sen.} \\ +\text{ con.} \end{bmatrix} \begin{bmatrix} +\text{ mas.} \\ -\text{ g.r.} \\ -\text{ sen.} \\ -\text{ con.} \end{bmatrix} \rightarrow \begin{bmatrix} +\text{ mas.} \\ +\text{ g.r.} \\ +\text{ sen.} \\ +\text{ con.} \end{bmatrix}
$$

IV. Affinal Merging Rule I:

$$\begin{bmatrix} + \text{ mas.} \\ - \text{ g.r.} \\ - \text{ sen.} \\ + \text{ con.} \end{bmatrix} \begin{bmatrix} - \text{ mas.} \\ + \text{ g.r.} \\ - \text{ sen.} \\ + \text{ con.} \end{bmatrix} \rightarrow \begin{bmatrix} - \text{ mas.} \\ + \text{ g.r.} \\ - \text{ sen.} \\ + \text{ con.} \end{bmatrix} \text{ in env. } X\,[- \text{ mas.}]\underline{\qquad}.$$

V. Hereditary Affinity Rule III:

$$\begin{bmatrix} - \text{ mas.} \\ - \text{ g.r.} \\ - \text{ sen.} \\ - \text{ con.} \end{bmatrix} \begin{bmatrix} - \text{ mas.} \\ - \text{ g.r.} \\ - \text{ sen.} \\ + \text{ con.} \end{bmatrix} \rightarrow \begin{bmatrix} + \text{ mas.} \\ - \text{ g.r.} \\ - \text{ sen.} \\ + \text{ con.} \end{bmatrix} \text{ in env. } \underline{\qquad}\;X.$$

[II] and [III] may be reduced to:

$$\begin{bmatrix} + \text{ mas.} \\ - \text{ g.r.} \\ - \text{ sen.} \\ + \text{ con.} \end{bmatrix} \begin{bmatrix} - \text{ mas.} \\ \alpha \text{ g.r.} \\ - \text{ sen.} \\ \beta \text{ con.} \end{bmatrix} \rightarrow \begin{bmatrix} - \text{ mas.} \\ + \text{ g.r.} \\ \alpha \text{ sen.} \\ + \text{ con.} \end{bmatrix} \text{ in env. } X\,[- \text{ mas.}]\underline{\qquad}.$$

Similarly, the half-parent rule and its corollary are reduced:

$$\begin{bmatrix} \alpha \text{ mas.} \\ + \text{ g.r.} \\ + \text{ sen.} \\ + \text{ con.} \end{bmatrix} \begin{bmatrix} \beta \text{ mas.} \\ - \text{ g.r.} \\ - \text{ sen.} \\ - \text{ con.} \end{bmatrix} \rightarrow \begin{bmatrix} \alpha \text{ mas.} \\ + \text{ g.r.} \\ + \text{ sen.} \\ + \text{ con.} \end{bmatrix}$$

Let us now consider an application of Romney's (1965) method of range reduction to a selected segment of the kinship lexicon of an asymmetric exchange system: the "genealogical range" of the Purum category *pu*; the men of wife-giving groups.

I. The first step is to write the genealogical range of this category in Romney's (Romney and D'Andrade, 1964a; Romney 1965) notation system.

*Lexeme: pu*

1. FF (m.s.)    $m + m + m$
2. MF (m.s.)    $m + f + m$
3. MB (m.s.)    $m + f\,0\,m$
4. WF (m.s.)    $m = f + m$
5. MBS (m.s.)   $m + f\,0\,m - m$
6. WB (m.s.)    $m = f\,0\,m$
7. WBS (m.s.)   $m = f\,0\,m - m.$

Rule 1. By rule 1, expressions (1 and 2) reduce to $m + a + m$.
Rule 2. By rule 2, expressions (6 and 7) reduce to $m = f\,0\,(m-)^{0,1}m$, and (3 and 5) reduce to $m + f\,0\,(m-)^{0,1}m$.

We now have

1. $m + a + m$
2. $m + f 0 (m-)^{0,1}m$
3. $m = f + m$
4. $m = f 0 (m-)^{0,1}m.$

According to Romney (1965, p. 133), the next step is to state the contingencies among options with superscripts on the parentheses. For the expressions:

1. $a(+a)^{0,1} + f 0 (m-)^{0,1}m$
2. $a + f(+m)^{0,1} 0 (m-)^{0,1}m$
3. $a + f 0 (m-)^{0,1,2,3}m$
4. $a(+a)^i + f(+m)^j 0 (m-)^k m.$

This is done as follows (Romney, 1965, p. 133): where $i + j = 0$ or 1, and $k = 0, 1, 2,$ or 3, and if either $i$ or $j = 1$, then $k = 0$ or 1.

The "reduced" expression (4), "together with the statement of the contingent values of $i, j,$ and $k$, is defined as an *extended kernel*" (Romney, 1965, p. 133). This type of formulation is particularly useful as a "loosening" of the contingency statements or values of $i, j,$ and $k$, and allows one to account for categories that are defined by recursive functions. On the level of surface data, such categories are often analytically marked by appending an *etc.* to a list of kin types. In this case, we would like to suggest a somewhat different, and more intuitive, range reduction or terminal "factoring operation" that illustrates some of the interesting criterial properties of asymmetric or Miwok exchange terminologies.[1] On a formal plane, these reductions to an extended kernel of the Purum category $pu$ are suggested by an implicit rule for relation marker reductions in the first set of (4) expressions. These expressions are initially reduced to:

$$m \begin{bmatrix} + a + m \\ + f 0 (m-)^{0,1}m \\ = f + m \\ = f 0 (m-)^{0,1}m \end{bmatrix} \qquad (1)$$

$$m \begin{bmatrix} \begin{pmatrix} + a \\ = f \end{pmatrix} m \\ \begin{pmatrix} + \\ = \end{pmatrix} f 0 (m-)^{0,1}m \end{bmatrix} \qquad (2)$$

$$m \begin{bmatrix} \begin{pmatrix} + \begin{pmatrix} m \\ f \end{pmatrix} \end{pmatrix} + \\ = f \\ (\pm) f 0 (m-)^{0,1} \end{bmatrix} \qquad (3)$$

[1] We are indebted to Nicholas A. Hopkins for his helpful suggestions on these derivations.

$$\begin{bmatrix} (\pm) f+ \\ (\pm) f\,0\ (m-)^{0,\,1} \\ +\ m+ \end{bmatrix} m \tag{4}$$

$$\begin{bmatrix} +\ a+ \\ =\ f+ \\ (\pm) f\,0\ (m-)^{0,\,1} \end{bmatrix} m. \tag{5}$$

Aspects of derivation (4) $\begin{bmatrix} (\pm) f+ \\ (\pm) f \end{bmatrix}$ are directly relevant to one of Lévi-Strauss' (1965, p. 19) axioms for asymmetric systems: *asymmetrical exchange terminologies transform kinsmen into affines.* The relation markers $(\pm)$ pre-posing $f+$ and $f\,0\ (m-)^{0,\,1}$ may be intuitively interpreted as a product of the latent ambiguity of a notational system that assigns a positive value to the consanguineal content of affinal categories. Although kinsmen are trans-formed into affines, consanguineal properties are consistently imposed, so to speak, on an essentially affinal grid.

Our analysis of Purum relationship terminology has been concerned with determining the formal consequences of a set of primitive statements (axioms) and with specifying the rules and logical procedures for deriving theorems (kin class assignments) from these statements. Rather than defining kin classes conjunctively—by isolating shared values on a denumerable set of dimensions as in componential solutions in which the members of a class are assigned the same structural description, regardless of degree of genea-logical distance, our account takes the form of a set of rules, which derive "genealogically closer" kin types from the genealogical chains to which they are structurally equivalent.

This account provides a formal specification of Lévi-Strauss' (1951, p. 162; cf. 1949, pp. 444–458) conception that the important point with the asymmetric terminological type (as distinguished from the Omaha type) is that cross cousins are classified with affinal rather than consanguineal kin. A set of rules are formulated which transform genealogically derived "affines" into consanguines; as in Dravidian systems, these coding rules imply "that affinity is transmitted from one generation to the next just as consanguinity ties are" (Dumont, 1957, p. 24; 1953a). The category, but not the group, "wife-givers" is entailed by the terminologically encoded marriage regula-tion: the "prescription" to marry a nau (*ka-nau-nu/nau*) applies to the category of wife-giving groups (*pu*) rather than to only the mother's brother's descent group (Needham, 1964b, p. 1380). In the Purum case, this is clearly shown in Needham's (1962a, p. 79, Table 5) analysis and tabulation of fifty-four marriages from the villages of Khulen, Tampak, and Changning-long; 48.1 per cent are not with women of the mother's clan. On the level of the "facts," the system is clearly preferential, and can only be accounted for by probabilistic formulations.

On several occasions, Needham (e.g., 1962a, p. 85, 87; 1962b, p. 259) has argued for the necessity of the study of systems of prescriptive alliance through an "imaginative apprehension" of their system of social categories and has suggested that attempts to construe such classifications in a genealogical framework invariably distort the indigenous idealogy, and fail to take into account the pervasive conceptual order to which the social and symbolic orders (we fail to understand the distinction) are integrally related as part to whole. However, in the analysis of the ordering of relatives within the terminology of a system of prescriptive alliance, genealogically defined equations are invariably resorted to in demonstrating a matrilateral prescription (e.g., Needham, 1962a, p. 77), and although genealogical connection may be disregarded in ritually assimilating a woman into a marriageable (from a nonmarriageable) category (Needham, 1962a, p. 87), a property of the definition of both appropriate and inappropriate marriage categories is consistently genealogical. A point of radical analytic importance, therefore, is that a strictly formal account of the coding rules underlying the genealogical ordering of relatives within kinship terminologies need not be construed as antithetical to the contextual analysis of the "more abstract structural principles" underlying a culture's social and symbolic structure. Even in the initial definition of status differentials between wife-givers and wife-takers, inferences from genealogical considerations play a significant analytic role; for example, the association of wife-givers with senior lineal kinsmen (FF, MF) and wife-takers with junior lineal kin (DS, SS) (Needham, 1962a, p. 84).

## CONCLUSION

Let us summarize the contents of this chapter. Omaha systems have been a subject of great interest for anthropologists for very nearly a century. The kin-class assignments of an Omaha system, and in particular the overriding of the inherent distinction of generation (Murdock, 1949, p. 134), merging up to four generations in the same line into one kin class has seemed intrinsically so "different" or "exotic" that it begged for solutions. It was as if anthropologists were saying, "Solve the Crow-Omaha systems, and the rest of the systems will be simple." A great deal of effort has been put into "solving the Omaha problem," or in better terms, searching for the determinants of Omaha systems. In the first part of this chapter the major attempts were reviewed, and criticized.

The next question posed was the same as in the previous chapter concerning the construct *Iroquois system*. We asked, given a universe of 14 Omaha systems, what the minimum structural information was that differentiated empirical systems. The method of scalogram analysis was used to differentiate, by a series of scale steps, what the minimum criteria of differentiation were, and in what manner the systems could be rank-ordered so as to yield the highest coefficient of reproducibility. The next step was to "fit" the scale types to structural types utilizing the technique of transformational analysis.

Rewrite rules were developed, following Lounsbury (1964a, b), and the scale steps were matched to them. It was then possible to compare two approaches to typology, the scalogram method, which generates an ordinal measure, and the transformational approach, which generates a structural typology derived from principles of classification underlying genealogical codes.

Then, as a methodological exercise with a highly developed Omaha system (Kalmuk Mongol), we applied the converse of Lounsbury's approach: Romney's approach. We compared Lounsbury's intuitive procedure for deriving generative rules with Romney's explicit and clearly formulated algorithm.

Finally we returned to a problem that had been raised in Chapters Five and Six, namely, the distinctions that are made both intuitively and formally between Crow-Omaha systems, and systems of asymmetric alliance. It was found that formal analysis was of great utility in an examination of asymmetric systems in that it allowed greater generality, greater flexibility, and minimal redundancy in the statement of the underlying coding principles. It was shown that the Romney algorithm was directly relevant to aspects of the Miwok problem.

Our original problems (the determinants of Omaha, and by inference, Crow systems) were not those with which we finished. What we have done is performed (after others) a necessary prolegomenon to the study of the sociological determinants of kinship systems. Through the medium of formal analyses (scalogram, transformational, componential accounts) we are now in a position to state in generalized form the nature of the phenomenon under observation. Before the work of Lounsbury and Romney, itself based on the work of countless predecessors, we were not even able to state that. Work in the future can take two directions. Some will wish to refine and develop the methodological apparatus of formal analysis in order to find solutions of a greater elegance, and generality. But also, now that the universe of discourse is "under control," as it were, now that we know what we are talking *about* when we utilize the constructs Iroquois, Omaha, Crow, and so on, it will be possible to focus sociological work more finely than before, and control correlational work to a much greater degree.

# Chapter Twelve

# Information Theory and Social Organization

That information theory—or "the mathematical theory of communication" —poses problems of significant methodological and theoretical interest for social anthropology was suggested well over a decade ago by C. Lévi-Strauss when he outlined the utility of the path of classical analysis in the study of marriage systems:

This outlook [the increasing consolidation of social anthropology, economics, and linguistics into one field, that of communication] should open the study of kinship and marriage to approaches directly derived from the theory of communication. In the terminology of this theory it is possible to speak of the information of a marriage system by the number of choices at the observer's disposal to define the marriage status of an individual. Thus the information is unity for a dual exogamous system, and, in an Australian kind of kinship typology, it would increase with the logarithm of the number of matrimonial classes. A theoretical system where everybody could marry everybody would be a system with no redundancy, since each marriage choice would not be determined by previous choices, while the positive content of marriage rules constitutes the redundancy of the system under consideration. By studying the percentage of "free" choices in a matrimonial population (not absolutely free, but in relation to certain postulated conditions); it would thus become possible to offer numerical estimates of its entropy, both absolute and relative (Lévi-Strauss, 1953, p. 538).

In terms of Lévi-Strauss' suggestion, we must, at the outset, pose and seek an answer to the following question: *How does one measure amount of information?* In the mathematical theory of communication, "amount of information" is measured by the logarithm of the number of available choices. For reasons that will become apparent in a later section of this chapter it is convenient to use logarithms to the base 2, rather than common or Briggs' logarithm to the base 10 (Weaver, 1962, p. 100). If there are only two available choices (from the viewpoint of the observer), as in a "two-section system," then information is unity: the logarithm of 2 to the base 2. If one has 32 alternative categories, or messages among which he is equally free to choose, then since $32 = 2^5$ so that $\log_2 32 = 5$, one says that this situation is characterized by 5 bits[1] of information.

The quantity which uniquely meets the natural requirements that one sets up for "information" turns out to be exactly that which is known in thermodynamics as *entropy* (Weaver, 1962, p. 103).

In the physical sciences, the entropy associated with a situation is a measure of the degree of randomness, or of "shuffled-ness" if you will, in the situation . . . (Weaver, 1962, p. 103).

That information be measured by entropy is, after all, natural when we remember that information, in communication theory, is associated with the amount of freedom of choice we have in constructing messages. Thus for a communication source one can say, just as he would also say it of a thermodynamic ensemble, "This situation is highly organized, it is not characterized by a large degree of randomness or of choice—that is to say, the information (or the entropy) is low" (Weaver, 1962, p. 103).

In the "analyses" of section systems that follow,[2] a distinction is made between maximum and relative entropy. The *maximum entropy* of a system is the logarithm to the base 2 of the number of kinship terms; the *actual entropy* is the logarithm to the base 2 of the categories upon which these kin terms are mapped: sections or subsections. On a preliminary basis, let us merely assume that these are the number of choices at the observer's disposal to define the marriage status of an individual. The *relative entropy* is the ratio of the actual to the maximum entropy. The *redundancy* of a system is one minus the relative entropy. The higher the redundancy,[3] the more efficient the recoding operations that map kinship terms on sections. To be somewhat more explicit, if we attempt to measure the information of a marriage system by the number of choices at our disposal to define the marriage status of an individual, then redundancy measures the fraction of the "message," or maximum entropy that is unnecessary, repetitive, or redundant, if we had access to the additional information provided by the actual entropy.[4] Here actual entropy is equated with the number of choices at our disposal to define

---

[1] *Bit* is a condensation of binary digit.

[2] For biological and psychological applications of information theory, cf. McCulloch and Pitts, 1943; Miller, 1953, 1956; Quastler, 1953, 1955; Rapaport, 1955; for anthropological applications: Wallace, 1961; Buchler, 1967a; Buchler and Selby, 1968.

[3] Conversely, the lower the relative entropy, the more efficient the recoding process.

[4] I.e., mapping on sections, or subsections.

the marriage status of an individual, *given the additional information that kin terms are mapped on sections or subsections*. Following the methodological path that Lévi-Strauss has suggested, we demonstrate that section systems may be rank-ordered; this rank ordering is of ordinal strength: the scale orders section systems in terms of their "recoding efficiency."

To place the present discussion in historical context, let us review–in a schematic manner—explanations of class, or section systems.

## SECTION SYSTEMS[5]

Section systems have typically been represented in the anthropological literature as double descent systems, although in most cases this interpretation requires the posited existence of one of the lines as "submerged" or "implicit" (Radcliffe-Brown, 1927, 1929, 1930, 1951; Seligman, 1927; Lawrence, 1937; Murdock, 1940, 1949; Lane, 1961; Lane and Lane, 1962). For example, in a recent publication the Lanes assert that "Through much of the questionable area in Australia, localized patrilineal sibs are bisected by implicit but unrecognized matrilineal moieties" (1962, p. 46). This is a position not substantially different from that taken over sixty years earlier by Galton (1889b) and Durkheim (1897), who viewed four-class systems as the result of a combination of matrilineal moieties and patrilineal local groups (Goody, 1961, p. 6). Following Durkheim, Radcliffe-Brown maintained that "In Australian tribes with four sections or eight sub-sections every person belongs to one of a pair of matrilineal moieties and one of a pair of patrilineal moieties" (1929, p. 199), a statement followed by the assertion that "It is important to note that moieties exist in every section system whether they are named or not" (1930, p. 39). Lawrence came to a similar conclusion: "Four divisions, called 'sections' if they bear names, are found because the patrilineal moieties and the matrilineal moieties bisect each other" (1937, p. 324). Murdock also characterized section systems as double descent systems, "a combination of co-existing matrilineal and patrilineal modes of affiliation" (1940, p. 559). In a 1951 statement, Radcliffe-Brown reiterated his earlier position: "The kinship system of an Australian tribe is usually one of double descent, patrilineal and matrilineal" (1951, p. 40).

However, with all respect for the logic behind a half-century's analyses of section systems, Goody has rather clearly shown that these systems are *not* characterized by double descent (1961). Posited "anonymous" moieties (Lawrence, 1937) or "implicit" descent lines, although of analytic and theoretic value to the anthropologists who have utilized them in their analyses, do not account for the facts in the sense of double descent. "'Classes' and 'marriage sections' do *not* necessarily presuppose the existence of both patrilineal and matrilineal descent groups" (Goody, 1961, p. 9). An alliance

---

[5] We are indebted to Richard A. Thompson for his contributions to this section of the discussion.

theorist, Dumont, has taken the argument one step further (1966), attempting to show that "classes" and "marriage sections" in Australian-type systems do not necessarily presuppose *descent* groups. He has further suggested that the alternating generation feature of section systems represents a form "more primitive than a continuous flow of generations" (Dumont, 1966, p. 238). To Dumont, *descent* is an apparent misnomer in the case of section systems.

But why, then, if the double descent model is viewed as incorrect by both a descent theorist (Goody) and an alliance theorist (Dumont), has it been supported with such tenacity over the years? Partly this is due to Mrs. Seligman's early and almost imperceptible shift from a discussion of matrimonial classes to descent groups (1927); on the one hand, she discussed marriage classes, on the other, she discussed descent groups, concluding that "Marriage classes . . . may be regarded . . . as groups or groupings resulting from the recognition of bilateral descent" (1927, p. 374). With this conceptual step, marriage in section systems was logically reduced to a role as "the negative residue of real or hypothetical unilineal transmission of membership in holistic descent groups" (Dumont, 1966, p. 249), a role rather consistently accepted by most descent theorists.

It is curious to note that descent theorists, accustomed as they are to constructing models directly from concrete reality, have seen the necessity for utilizing as an element in their models a totally nonempirical element—the "anonymous" bisecting moiety or descent line. In defense of this, they have been forced back through a sort of infinite regress into the position of making statements of this type: "With small, relatively stable residential groups based on a unilocal principle, or with localized lineages, certain types of marriage regulations automatically create dual divisions of the society of opposed linearity to that given recognition through residence and/or descent" (Lane, 1961, p. 16). Although Josselin de Jong warned of the danger of confusing overt and latent structural features (1952), and Lévi-Strauss pointed out the pitfalls of attempting to explain cross-cousin marriage in terms of double descent (1949), a number of descent theorists (e.g., the Lanes) continue to reify the concept of latent descent lines to support their double descent model for section systems.

This is again a *logical* position only, not one in general supported by available data. Descent theorists have traditionally and uncritically accepted the double descent model from Radcliffe-Brown (and Durkheim) to the present (excepting Goody). Seligman clarified the model by conveniently translating "marriage classes" into "descent lines," thus plugging the most glaring logical hole in the model and facilitating its continued acceptance. To call this acceptance *uncritical* is not too strong, for even the alliance theorist Lévi-Strauss has shown a tendency to accept the interpretations of Radcliffe-Brown and Lawrence, even though these interpretations violate his warning on cross-cousin marriage (Dumont, 1966, p. 234). Among descent theorists, Goody stands practically alone in rejecting the double descent hypothesis for section systems (1961). Among alliance theorists, Dumont has apparently indicated the future direction for the controversy in rejecting section systems as descent systems at all (1966).

Explanations of class or section systems may now be summarized with fuller bibliographic reference:

I. *Morgan and Howitt*[6]: *Survivals.* Sections, subsections, or marriage classes were said to be a survival of a prior custom of group marriage.

II. *Galton,*[7] *Durkheim,*[8] *Deacon,*[9] *Radcliffe-Brown,*[10] *B. Seligman,*[11] *Lawrence,*[12] *Murdock,*[13] *the Lanes*[14]: *Implicit and Explicit Moieties.* Four-section systems are said to be produced by the "intersection" of male and female descent lines; subsection systems "are formed where the mother's potential line is also recognized in order to prevent marriage with these relatives" (Service, 1960, p. 421). Where moieties are implicit, unnamed, or "analytically derived," positive marriage rules[15] are accounted for in terms of groups which do not exist, or of which "the people" are not conscious (cf. Dumont, 1966).

III. *Dumont: "Alliance Theory"; Positive Marriage Rules.*[16] L. Dumont (1966) has recently reviewed "the spell of underlying descent" in the analysis of section, or subsection systems. Dumont (1966, p. 232) reminds us that the moieties—the intersection or crosscutting of which have been said to "generate" or "explain" sections or classes—are, in fact, often either nonexistent or unnamed.

To explain groups and arrangements (positive marriage rules) that consciously exist by groups which do not exist, or of which the people are not conscious, may seem a dubious procedure unless one recognizes the advantages involved in terms of general anthropological theory (Dumont, 1966, p. 232).

Dumont (1966, p. 235) continues to differentiate (i) what is "given," ethnographically, from (ii) what has been construed by various theorists.

i. a. Named sections or subsections;
  b. Rules of intermarriage between these [a] elements;
  c. Rules determining the section membership of children for each "type" of intermarriage.

| | | |
|---|---|---|
| [6] 1877, 1889 | [9] 1927 | [12] 1937 |
| [7] 1889b | [10] 1927, 1930, 1951 | [13] 1940, 1949 |
| [8] 1897 | [11] 1927 | [14] 1961, 1962 |

[15] There is much less difference between the sections than between the marriage rules with which they are associated (Josselin de Jong, 1952, p. 15); consequently, the sections cannot, in the strictest sense, be said to determine the choice of a spouse, although they do have the function of limiting the choice to a specific category (cf. Josselin de Jong, 1952, p. 16).

[16] Cf. Lévi-Strauss, 1949.

**ii.** [c] has been construed as "rules of filiation," or "descent," and [a, b, c] is explained as "a system based on the unilineal transmission of qualities from an individual to his children" (Dumont, 1966, p. 236).

In Australia, there is, Dumont argues (1966, p. 237), an alternation of two kinds of generations; rather than a unilineal group, line, or a collective unity, "there is a whole based on the opposition between its two complementary parts, i.e., a structure" (Dumont, 1966, p. 237).

Dumont's (1966, pp. 239–249) analysis of Kariera, Aranda, Ambrym, and Murngin section systems follows closely from his emphasis on intermarriage between sections as a positive link which, with the paternal pairing, unites sections into a whole in terms of complementary relations, rather than construing intermarriage "as the negative residue of real or hypothetical unilineal transmission of membership in holistic descent groups" (Dumont, 1966, p. 249).

IV. *Warner, Elkin, Radcliffe-Brown, Service: Regrouping and "generalizing" the "kinship system."* Finally, it has been suggested that section terms are (a) signposts for certain types of social relations (e.g., Elkin, 1954), or (b) "sociocentric nomenclature" (Service, 1960) that regroup kinship terms (Warner, 1958).

## KARIERA: INFORMATION MEASURES

I. There are eighteen "kinship terms," although there are twenty classes of relatives, two of which (B and Z) are further subdivided on the dimension of relative age, as grandparental terms are used reciprocally for grandchildren (Radcliffe-Brown, 1930, p. 48).

II. These terms are "assigned" to one of four sections. Radcliffe-Brown (1930, p. 38) represents these sections, or "the system of marriage and descent" by means of the diagram in Figure 12–1.

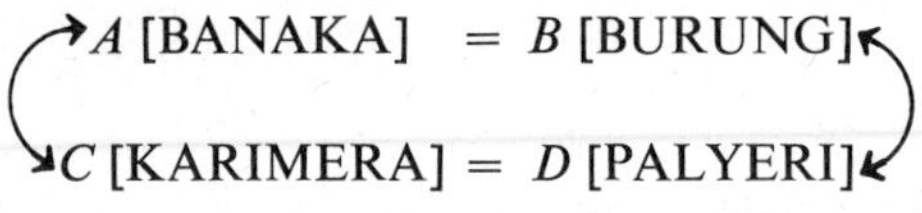

$$A \text{ [BANAKA]} \quad = \quad B \text{ [BURUNG]}$$
$$C \text{ [KARIMERA]} = D \text{ [PALYERI]}$$

*Figure 12–1. Representation of Kariera Section System (Radcliffe-Brown, 1930).*

in which the sign = connects the two sections that intermarry, and the arrow sign connects the section of a mother with that of her child.

To be somewhat more precise, the arrows denote "cycles" (*ACA, BDB*) or matrilineal filiation (Dumont, 1966, p. 239). In 1913, Radcliffe-Brown linked the patrilocally paired sections (couples) with diagonal arrows; in the 1930 representation, the patrilineal arrows disappeared.

This change underlies the paradox of Radcliffe-Brown's attitude as a whole. On the one hand he insisted on the basic group being the patrilocal horde; on the other, when diagramming the section system, he chose to stress increasingly the hypothetical matrilineal aspect (Dumont, 1966, p. 239).

In Lawrence's (1937) representation (Figure 12–2), (a) the patrilocal "couples" are brought on a horizontal line and linked with arrows; and (b) the patrilineal moieties are labelled by $X$ and $Y$; the "hypothetical" matri-moieties by $A$ and $B$. In this representation the vertical dimension clearly does not correspond to generation differences, and the patrimoieties denote two kinds of local groups.

*Figure 12–2. Representation of Kariera Section System (Lawrence, 1937).*

In Dumont's (1966, pp. 239–240) symbolization,

**i.** $A$ and $B$ are two kinds of local groups that are
**ii.** divided into two generation sections: $A1$ and $A2$; $B1$ and $B2$, where
**iii.** $[=]$ denotes reciprocal intermarriage between sections and their patrilocal couples.

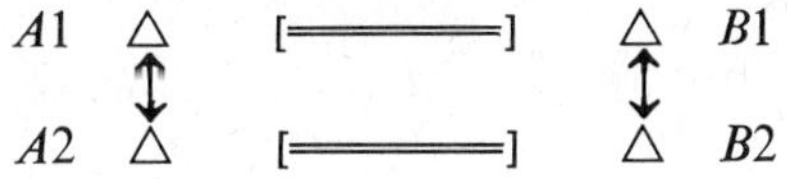

$$A1 \quad \triangle \qquad [\!=\!\!=\!\!=\!] \qquad \triangle \quad B1$$
$$\updownarrow \qquad\qquad\qquad\qquad \updownarrow$$
$$A2 \quad \triangle \qquad [\!=\!\!=\!\!=\!] \qquad \triangle \quad B2$$

*Figure 12–3. Representation of Kariera Section System (Dumont, 1966).*

Figure 12–3 is a representation, close to the Kariera idea (intermarriage between sections) and practice (patrilocal residence), of the tribe as a whole. We should bear in mind that a symbol such as $A1$ does not represent the local group of a section, but rather the whole section as dispersed into a number of local groups.

Following Lévi-Strauss' (1963a, p. 299) suggestion, we take a numerical estimate of the system's entropy, both absolute and relative. The *relative entropy* is the ratio of the actual to the maximum entropy (Weaver, 1962, p. 104). We first consider the percentage of "free choices" in the matrimonial population. These choices are absolutely free; we postulate no conditions that constrain individual choice. Thus,

**1.** $\log_2 Z \ (= -\log_2 1/Z)$ is taken as the asymptote of all possible estimates of the free choices (absolute) in a matrimonial system, where
**2.** $Z$ = the number of mutually exclusive classes in a kinship lexicon. For Kariera, this gives

$$\text{(maximum entropy)} \qquad \log_2 Z = 4.17, \text{ where} \qquad (1)$$
$$Z = 18, \text{ and}$$

**3.** $\log_2 E \ (= -\log_2 1/E)$ is taken as the asymptote of all possible estimates of the actual entropy, where
**4.** $E =$ the number of matrimonial sections.
For Kariera, this gives

(actual entropy) $\qquad \log_2 E = 2.0$, where $\qquad\qquad$ (2)
$$E = 4.$$

The *relative entropy*—the ratio of the actual to the maximum entropy—then, is .47. And the *redundancy*—one minus the *relative* entropy—is .53.

## ARANDA: INFORMATION MEASURES

I. Although forty terms of relationship are used by males, the "number is reduced first by the fact that the same terms are used for grandparents and for grandchildren, secondly by the use of the same term for certain male relatives and for their sisters, thirdly by the existence of certain self reciprocal terms" (Radcliffe-Brown, 1930, p. 51). For comparative purposes—in terms of quantitive estimates of redundancy and relative entropy—the numerical ratio of the Kariera and Aranda kinship lexicons is of primary interest. We therefore set the number of Aranda kin classes at thirty-six (cf. explanation of Aranda kinship chart; Radcliffe-Brown, 1930).

II. These terms are "assigned" to one of eight "subdivisions." The rules of marriage and descent in the system of eight *subsections* are represented in Figure 12–4 (Radcliffe-Brown, 1930, p. 39)[17]:

Figure 12–4.   Representation of Aranda Section System (Radcliffe-Brown, 1930).

The irregular form of these "couples" ($A1\,D2$, $A2\,D1$, and so on) is enough to condemn the formulation. The ordinary meaning of the vertical dimension in such figures is jeopardized, and the only intimation that the system is a holistic or closed one lies in the circular form of the "matrilineal cycles" (Dumont, 1966, p. 240).

Subsequently, Lawrence (1937) modified this formulation by

**i.** bringing each patrilocal couple of sections on one horizontal line;
**ii.** calling the putative matrimoieties $A$ and $B$; and
**iii.** designating the local groups $P$, $Q$, $R$, $S$ (Dumont, 1966, p. 241).

[17] More recently, Lévi-Strauss and G. Th. Guilbaud (Lévi-Strauss, 1966, p. 83) have represented the regulation of marriage by eight subsections among the Aranda in the form of annulus.

The four kinds of local groups (*P, Q, R, S*) are bisectioned into generation sections by the operation of matrilineal descent (see Figure 12–5).

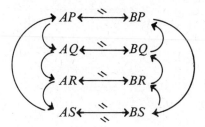

*Figure 12–5. Representation of Aranda Section System (Lawrence, 1937, p. 326).*

In Dumont's (1966, p. 241) formulation,

**i.** *A, B, C, D* designate the four kinds of local groups;
**ii.** 1 and 2 distinguish the opposed generations; and
**iii.** *A*1, *A*2, *B*1, *B*2, and so on represent the eight Aranda sections.

Dumont (1966, p. 243) represents the alternation of intermarriage in alternate generations in the form of a parallelogram, where the two horizontal planes correspond to the generations and the four local groups are labelled *P*1 − 2, *Q*1 − 2, *R*1 − 2, *S*1 − 2 (see Figure 12–6).

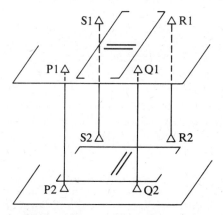

*Figure 12–6. Aranda Section System: Alternation of Intermarriage in Alternate Generations (Dumont, 1966, p. 243).*

Indeed, Dumont's (1966) solution within the frame of reference of intermarriage, the "conception of a whole in terms of complementary relations," allows him to derive logical transformation rules that govern the transition from four- to eight-section systems.

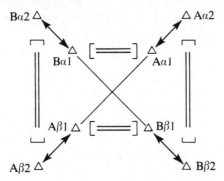

*Figure 12–7.  Aranda Section System: Transition from Kariera to Aranda (Dumont, 1966, p. 243).*

*Aa*, *AB* and *Ba*, *BB* represent the dichotimization of different kinds of patrilocal groups.

In terms of intermarriage, the difference with Kariera "consists in the fact that the two generation sections of one local group *marry not in the same, but in two different kinds of local group*" (Dumont, 1966, p. 241). The Aranda system links, by symmetrical intermarriage, four kinds of local groups.[18]

**Table 12–1.   Representation of Aranda Section System**

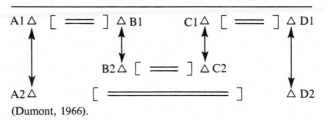

(Dumont, 1966).

Alliance theory takes a unified view of section and subsection systems "by regarding them as holistic systems of intermarriage between generation sections paired in patrilocal groups" (Dumont, 1966, p. 241). Conversely, double descent theory

considers the whole system exclusively in terms of hypothetical moieties, and consequently it views intermarriage not as an effective link between sections, but only as the negative corollary of descent; not as a positive rule, but as the residue of negative rules (Dumont, 1966, pp. 241–242).

For "descent" theorists, intermarriage is a derivative, secondary phenomena; a "shadowy" and negative consequence of rules, groups, and categories whose very existence is invoked to account for the observable functions of intermarriage.

[18] Kariera links two kinds of local groups.

Kay's (1965) formal axiomatization of some principles of classification in eight-section systems are relevant to our discussion of the Aranda system. Consider, for example, Lemma 1 and Theorem 5 (Kay, 1965, pp. 36–37).

*Lemma 1.* In an eight-section system, all kin relations between ego and a member of his own matrimoiety are parallel under matri-descent, and all kin relations between ego and a member of the other matrimoiety are cross under matri-descent.

Kay's theorem for four-section systems[19] and Lemma 1 imply Theorem 5.

*Theorem 5.* In an eight-section system, all relations between ego and a member of his own section are parallel under both rules of descent, and all relations between ego and a member of his spouse's section are cross under both rules of descent (Kay, 1965, p. 37).

Consider Theorem 5 in reference to Radcliffe-Brown's (1930, p. 56) chart of the distribution of relatives through eight subsections in the Aranda system

*Aranda Type: Eight Subsections*
*Ego is $A^1$*

| $[A_1]$ | $[B_1]$ |
|---|---|
| FF | FMB |
| B | MMBDS |
| SS | ZSS |
| $[A_2]$ | $[B_2]$ |
| MMB | MF |
| MMBSS | MBS |
| ZDS | DS |
| $C_1$ | $D_1$ |
| FMBS | MMBS |
| ZS | MBDS |
| $[C_2]$ | $[D_2]$ |
| MB | F |
| MBSS | S |

Let us (1) translate a number of kin types into Romney's (1965) notation, and (2) derive values of these kin types under patri- and matri-descent, as

---

[19] Reviewed in the section of the "Iroquois" chapter that deals with Dravidian forms of classification.

an application of Theorem 5, as well as values of selected kin types under matri-descent, as a somewhat restricted application of Lemma 1 (see Table 12–2.)

**Table 12–2.  Kin Types and Descent Rules**

| | Kin types | Descent rule | Value of function $g$ | |
|---|---|---|---|---|
| 1) FF | m + m + m | patri- | $g = 0$ | |
| | | matri- | $g = 2$ | |
| 2) SS | m − m − m | patri- | $g = 0$ | parallel |
| | | matri- | $g = 2$ | |
| 3) FMB | m + m + f 0 m | patri- | $g = 1$ | |
| | | matri- | $g = 1$ | |
| 4) MMBDS | m + f + f 0 m − f − m | patri- | $g = 3$ | |
| | | matri- | $g = 1$ | cross |
| 5) ZSS | m 0 f − m − m | patri- | $g = 1$ | |
| | | matri- | $g = 1$ | |

Strings [1] and [2] are members of Ego's section: they are parallel (even) under patri- and matri-descent. Strings [3]–[5] are members of Ego's spouse's section: they are cross (odd) under both rules of descent.

| | Kin types | Descent rule | Value of function $g$ | |
|---|---|---|---|---|
| 1) FF | m + m + m | matri- | $g = 2$ | |
| 2) MMBSS | m + f + f 0 m − m − m | matri- | $g = 2$ | |
| 3) FMBS | m + m + f 0 m − m | matri- | $g = 2$ | parallel |
| 4) MBSS | m + f 0 m − m − m | matri- | $g = 2$ | |
| 5) MMBDS | m + f + f 0 m − f − m | matri- | $g = 1$ | |
| 6) DS | m − f − m | matri- | $g = 1$ | |
| 7) MBDS | m + f 0 m − f − m | matri- | $g = 1$ | cross |
| 8) F | m + m | matri- | $g = 1$ | |

Strings [1]–[4] are parallel (even) under matri-descent: they are members of Ego's own matrimoiety $[A_1, A_2, C_1, C_2]$. Strings [5]–[8] are cross (odd) under matri-descent: they are members of the opposite matrimoiety $[B_1, B_2, D_1, D_2]$.

For the Aranda kinship lexicon, the value of $\log_2 Z$ gives (maximum entropy) $\log_2 Z = 5.17$, where (1)

$$Z = 36, \text{ and}$$

(actual entropy) $\quad\quad \log_2 E = 3.00, \text{ where} \quad\quad\quad (2)$

$$E = 8.$$

The relative entropy (=) 0.57. The redundancy is 0.43.

At this point, we may summarize these numerical estimates as shown in Table 12–3.

#### Table 12–3.  Information Measures

| Measures | Systems | |
|---|---|---|
| | Kariera | Aranda |
| Maximum entropy | 4.17 | 5.17 |
| Actual entropy | 2.00 | 3.00 |
| Relative entropy | 0.47 | 0.57 |
| Redundancy | 0.53 | 0.43 |

## DISCUSSION

What—in reference to the Kariera and Aranda "analyses"—is the significance of measures such as entropy—maximum, actual, and relative—and redundancy?

We initially assume that the kin classes for any section system are known, or have been determined. This assumption allows us to bypass the initial level in our hierarchy of questions and measures. We may then proceed to the decision processes—of the observer—involved in the recoding operation that maps kin classes on sections. Following Lévi-Strauss' (1963a, p. 299) suggestion, we then measure the "information of a marriage system by the number of choices at the observer's disposal to define the marriage status of an individual." And in this regard, there are *no constraints* placed on the selection of a marriage partner. We assume complete ignorance to several very basic questions; for example: (1) Are there "incest taboos" on the marriage of primary relatives? (2) Is the "selection" of a marriage partner constrained by the bisexual nature of reproduction? Like Lévi-Strauss' (1963a, p. 212) archaeologists of the future coming from another planet, our uncertainty is reduced by the testing of a series of rather tenuous hypotheses.

The parlor game of "Twenty Questions" is a useful illustration of gradual uncertainty-reduction (Bendig, 1953; Attneave, 1959, pp. 2–7).

One of the players announces, "I am thinking of something 'Animal'" (or "Vegetable," or "Mineral," as the case may be), and the others proceed to ask him questions to which he can answer "Yes" or "No." Their goal is to discover what he has in mind by asking not more than twenty such questions (Attneave, 1959, p. 2).

Let us consider a simplified form of this game in which the thing being thought of—the "kin class" into which an individual may marry—is a particular square on a checkerboard, and the task of the observer—or questioner—is to discover which of the eighteen possible squares (kin classes) it is. It is easy to show that exactly five questions, *properly asked*, are always necessary and sufficient to locate that square, as $\log_2 Z = 4.17$ (maximum entropy). These questions might take the following form (Table 12–4; cf. Attneave, 1959, p. 3):

**1.** Is it one of the nine on the left half of the board? (Yes)
**2.** Is it one of the three in the upper third of the nine remaining? (No)
**3.** Is it one of the three in the middle third of the six remaining? (No)
**4.** Is it one of the two in the right two thirds of the three remaining? (Yes)
**5.** Is it the left one of the two remaining? (Yes)

**Table 12–4.   An Illustration of Gradual Uncertainty-Reduction: Kariera Kin Classes**

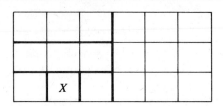

If the observer always attempts to define the marital status of an individual by asking the same questions, any sequence of five *Yes*'s and *No*'s will yield a unique cell (Attneave, 1959, p. 3). Letting 1 mean *Yes* and 0 mean *No*, 10011 will represent the cell illustrated in Table 12–4: five binary digits are needed to specify one alternative out of 18. In the binary number system a single digit (*bit*) specifies a choice from 2 alternatives, two digits specify one of $2^2$ or 4 alternatives, and so on. The uncertainty involved in the question, "Which square on the checkerboard may individual X marry?" amounts to six bits of information.

When the observer maps the kin classes on sections, the information necessary to define the marriage status of an individual in the Kariera system is radically reduced. This may be most obviously illustrated by using, once again, the checkerboard example:

**Table 12–5.   An Illustration of Gradual Uncertainty-Reduction: Kariera Sections**

|       |       |
|:-----:|:-----:|
| α | γ |
| β | δ |

It is easy to show that exactly two questions, *properly asked*, are always necessary and sufficient to define the marriage status of an individual, as $\log_2 E = 2.0$ (actual entropy). These questions might take the following form:

**1.** Is it one of the two on the right side of the board? (No)
**2.** Is it the upper one of the two remaining? (Yes)

As in the previous example, any sequence of two *Yes*'s and *No*'s will yield a unique cell: 01 will represent the cell illustrated in Table 12–5: two bits of information are needed to specify one alternative out of 4. In the binary number system, questions (1)–(2), asked in the same way, will yield 00, 11, and 10, for $\beta$, $\gamma$, and $\delta$, respectively. From this discussion, two points follow closely.

**1.** From a knowledge of the sequences of binary digits that yield various cells on our checkerboard matrix, it is possible to derive the form— although not the content—of ethnographic queries.
**2.** The binary number system is uniquely applicable to ethnological theories concerned with enumerating the distinctive features that underlie cultural systems.[20] Given this interest in an infrastructure that "unfolds" in the permutation and transformation of a set of dichotomous scales, the binary number system is of particular interest in the formulation of "statistical models." The binary number system has the same general properties as the decimal system, with which we are more familiar, but it uses only two different symbols (zero and one) instead of ten.

In the decimal system, one digit is necessary to specify one alternative out of $10^1$ or 10, two to specify one alternative out of $10^2$ or 100, three to specify one alternative out of $10^3$ or 1000, and so on. Likewise, in binary numbers, a single digit specifies a choice from two alternatives, two digits specify one of $2^2$ or 4 alternatives . . . (Attneave, 1959, p. 3).

## GENEALOGICAL QUERIES

Let us now attempt to derive entropy measures for the Kariera matrimonial population, using Romney and Epling's (1958, p. 69) diagram (Table 12–6), and questions based on genealogical criteria rather than paradigmatic assumptions, as in the "twenty questions" example.

It is easy to show that five "correct" questions are always necessary and sufficient to locate the unique cell that defines the marriage status of a given individual. With sole reference to Kariera kin classes—rather than sections— questions might take the following form:

**1.** Is it male? (No)
**2.** Is it lineal? (No)
**3.** Is it own generation? (Yes)
**4.** Is it older? (No)
**5.** Is it younger? (No)

[20] Lévi-Strauss, 1945, 1949, 1963a, 1964, 1966.

## Table 12–6. Kariera Kinship Model

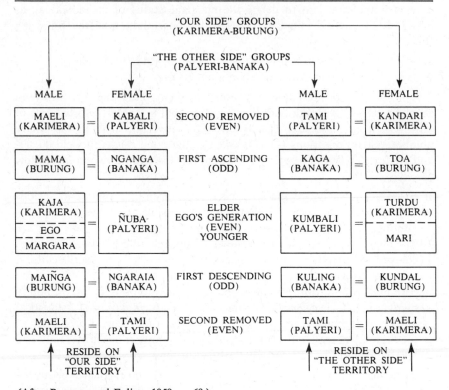

"OUR SIDE" GROUPS
(KARIMERA-BURUNG)

"THE OTHER SIDE" GROUPS
(PALYERI-BANAKA)

| MALE | FEMALE | | MALE | FEMALE |
|---|---|---|---|---|
| MAELI (KARIMERA) = | KABALI (PALYERI) | SECOND REMOVED (EVEN) | TAMI (PALYERI) = | KANDARI (KARIMERA) |
| MAMA (BURUNG) = | NGANGA (BANAKA) | FIRST ASCENDING (ODD) | KAGA (BANAKA) = | TOA (BURUNG) |
| KAJA (KARIMERA) --- EGO --- MARGARA = | ÑUBA (PALYERI) | ELDER EGO'S GENERATION (EVEN) YOUNGER | KUMBALI (PALYERI) = | TURDU (KARIMERA) --- MARI |
| MAIÑGA (BURUNG) = | NGARAIA (BANAKA) | FIRST DESCENDING (ODD) | KULING (BANAKA) = | KUNDAL (BURUNG) |
| MAELI (KARIMERA) = | TAMI (PALYERI) | SECOND REMOVED (EVEN) | TAMI (PALYERI) = | MAELI (KARIMERA) |

RESIDE ON "OUR SIDE" TERRITORY

RESIDE ON "THE OTHER SIDE" TERRITORY

(After Romney and Epling, 1959, p. 69.)

NOTE. Each cell represents a class of individuals. The first term in each is the vocative term and the second is the section term.

Everyone is assumed to be married. The equal sign signifies marriage.

A male Karimera Ego is assumed.

"Our side" is exogamous.

Generations are endogamous.

Close vs. distant distinction is not represented in the table.

Sex is ignored in second removed generation when person is younger than Ego.

The reader may easily determine that, under the assumption of binary choice, the foregoing questions are the only ones that may be asked. For example, the query—Is it collateral?—is inappropriate, as a *Yes* response will generate a new set of queries: Is it a first degree collateral? Is it a second degree collateral? and so on.

Once again, letting 1 mean *Yes* and 0 mean *No*, 00100 will represent the marriageable category *ñuba* in the Romney-Epling diagram (Table 12–6). When the observer maps Kariera kin classes onto sections, the information necessary to define the marriage status of an individual is reduced to two bits of information. For example,

1. Is it Banaka or Karimera? (No)
2. Is it Palyeri? (Yes)

Or, taking Romney and Epling (1958) as given,

1. Is it our side? (No)
2. Is it Palyeri? (Yes)

In a binary number system questions one and two will yield 01. 01 represents the marriage section Palyeri in the same diagram.

The same procedures may be used to illustrate the derivation of the entropy measures for the Aranda matrimonial population. Exactly six questions, properly asked, are always necessary and sufficient to locate the unique cell that defines the marriage status of a given individual. In the Aranda case, the questions might take the following form (cf. Table 12–7):

1. Is it one of the eighteen on the left half of the board? (No)
2. Is it one of the nine in the upper half of the eighteen remaining? (Yes)
3. Is it one of the three in the upper third of the nine remaining? (No)
4. Is it one of the three in the bottom half of the six remaining? (No)
5. Is it one of the two in the left two thirds of the three remaining? (Yes)
6. Is it the left one of the two remaining? (No)

Letting 1 mean *Yes* and 0 mean *No*, 010010 will represent the cell illustrated in Table 12–7.

**Table 12–7. An Illustration of Gradual Uncertainty-Reduction: Aranda Kin Classes**

Given, as input, the numerical dimension of Aranda kin classes, six bits of information are processed in producing the desired output—the marriage status of a given individual. The maximum entropy, $\log_2 Z = 5.17$.

When the observer maps Aranda kin classes on eight sections, the information necessary to define the marriage status of an individual is specified by three binary digits, or questions that involve a binary choice. These questions might take the following form (see Table 12–8):

1. Is it one of the four on the left hand side of the board? (Yes)
2. Is it one of the upper two of the four remaining? (Yes)
3. Is it the left one of the two remaining? (No)

**Table 12–8.   An Illustration of Gradual Uncertainty-Reduction: Aranda Sections**

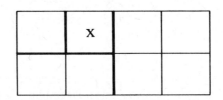

In comparing the recoding processes implicit in mapping Kariera and Aranda kin classes on sections, the summarized measures indicate that the Kariera mapping is somewhat more "efficient" than the Aranda mapping. This conclusion is easily derived by comparing the *relative entropy* and *redundancy* measures. The redundancy measure is higher for Kariera, the relative entropy measure is lower; the recoding operation is, therefore, more "efficient."

The "southern part" of the Aranda "tribe," in which there are four sections, rather than eight subsections, may be compared with the foregoing analyses (Radcliffe-Brown, 1930, p. 57).

As the "kinship system" is the same as in the northern part of the tribe, it follows that each of these four sections contains the relatives who are divided between two subsections in the north (Radcliffe-Brown, 1930, p. 57). Thus, for S. Aranda, the value of $\log_2 Z$ gives

(maximum entropy)      $\log_2 Z = 5.17$, where      (1)
            $Z = 36$, and

(actual entropy)      $\log_2 E = 2.0$, where      (2)
            $E = 4$, and

i. *Relative entropy* = 0.37
ii. *Redundancy* = 0.63.

Summarizing, we have Table 12–9.

Table 12–9.   Information Measures: Australian Section Systems

| Measures | Systems | | |
|---|---|---|---|
| | Kariera | Aranda | S. Aranda |
| Maximum entropy | 4.17 | 5.17 | 5.17 |
| Actual entropy | 2.00 | 3.00 | 2.00 |
| Relative entropy | 0.47 | 0.57 | 0.37 |
| Redundancy | 0.53 | 0.43 | 0.63 |

# MURNGIN: INFORMATION MEASURES[21]

In Lévi-Strauss' (1949) terminology, the Murngin system is bilineal (disharmonic) and asymmetric.[22] The section system, it has been suggested (Josselin de Jong, 1952, p. 37), is the product of the intersection of two unnamed matrilineal moieties and two named patrilineal moieties. Each of the four sections includes two named subsections as shown in Table 12–10.

Table 12–10.   Sections and Moieties in Murngin

| | Patrimoiety I | Patrimoiety II |
|---|---|---|
| Matrimoiety A | Ngarit | Warmut |
| | Bulain | Karmarung |
| Matrimoiety B | Bangardi | Balang |
| | Kaijark | Buralang |

(After Josselin de Jong, 1952, p. 37.)

There are seventy-one "kinds of relatives" (Warner, 1958, p. 57): "the Murngin exchange system requires or at least accounts for a kinship terminology embracing 5 generations and 6 sibling groups in each generation" (Josselin de Jong, 1952, p. 49).

For the Murngin system, we derive two sets of information measures: (1) the first accounts for the *named eight subsections;* (2) the second for the *functionally defined "marriage sections."*

[21] Cf. Radcliffe-Brown, 1930; Elkin, 1933, 1953; Lawrence, 1937; Lévi-Strauss, 1949; Lawrence and Murdock, 1949; Leach, 1951; Radcliffe-Brown, 1951; Josselin de Jong, 1952; Berndt, 1955.

[22] The "Murngin controversy" is not reviewed here, see Chapter Six.

For the Murngin kinship lexicon, the value of $\log_2 Z$ gives

$$\text{(maximum entropy)} \quad \log_2 Z = 6.14, \text{ where} \tag{1}$$
$$Z = 71, \text{ and}$$

$$\text{(actual entropy)} \quad \log_2 E = 3.00, \text{ where} \tag{2}$$
$$E = 8, \text{ for the } \textit{named subsections}, \text{ and}$$

**i.** *Relative entropy* $= 0.48$
**ii.** *Redundancy* $= 0.52$, and

$$\text{(actual entropy)} \quad \log_2 E = 2.00, \text{ where} \tag{3}$$
$$E = 4, \text{ for the } \textit{``marriage sections,''} \text{ and}$$

**i.** *Relative entropy* $= 0.32$
**ii.** *Redundancy* $= 0.68$.

We are now in a position to rank-order these systems; the ordering is of ordinal strength,[23] and ranks section systems in terms of the efficiency of their recoding processes (mapping kin terms on sections). As the magnitude of the redundancy measure increases, and that of the relative entropy measure decreases, the efficiency of the recoding processes increases. The operation of rank ordering that is a product of the application of this principle generates the scale shown in Table 12–11.

**Table 12–11.  Efficiency Scale: Australian Section Systems**

| Measures | Systems | | | | |
|---|---|---|---|---|---|
| | Aranda | Murngin[a] | Kariera | S. Aranda | Murngin[b] |
| Maximum entropy | 5.17 | 6.14 | 4.17 | 5.17 | 6.14 |
| Actual entropy | 3.00 | 3.00 | 2.00 | 2.00 | 2.00 |
| Relative entropy | 0.57 | 0.48 | 0.47 | 0.37 | 0.32 |
| Redundancy | 0.43 | 0.52 | 0.53 | 0.63 | 0.68 |

increasing efficiency →

[a]Named subsections.
[b]"Marriage sections."

Table 12–12 includes two-section and six-section systems, as well as the four- and eight-section systems that we have analyzed previously:

[23] An ordinal scale has the structure of an isotonic or order-preserving group; this group includes transformations by all increasing monotonic functions (Stevens, 1962, p. 26).

#### Table 12–12. Efficiency Scale: Section Systems

| Measures | Systems | | | | | | | | | |
|---|---|---|---|---|---|---|---|---|---|---|
| | Arabana[a] | Karadjeri[b] | Aranda | Ambrym[c] | Murngin[d] | Pakala[e] | Kariera | "S. Aranda" | Murngin[f] | Canella[g] |
| Maximum entropy | 4.24 | 3.70 | 5.17 | 4.70 | 6.14 | 4.24 | 4.17 | 5.17 | 6.14 | 4.58 |
| Actual entropy | 3.00 | 2.58 | 3.00 | 2.58 | 3.00 | 2.00 | 2.00 | 2.00 | 2.00 | 1.00 |
| Relative entropy | 0.70 | 0.67 | 0.57 | 0.54 | 0.48 | 0.47 | 0.47 | 0.37 | 0.32 | 0.22 |
| Redundancy | 0.30 | 0.33 | 0.43 | 0.46 | 0.52 | 0.53 | 0.53 | 0.63 | 0.68 | 0.78 |

increasing efficiency $\longrightarrow$

NOTE. [a]Elkin, 1937.
[b]Elkin, 1954.
[c]Deacon, 1927.
[d]Named subsections.
[e]Elkin, 1937.
[f]"Marriage sections."
[g]Nimuendaju and Lowie, 1937.

Lévi Strauss (1966, p. 4?) has suggested that "primitive classifications"

are evidence of thought which is experienced in all the exercises of speculation and resembles that of the naturalists and alchemists of antiquity and the middle ages: Galen, Pliny, Hermes Trismegistus, Albertus Magnus . . .

Further,

Native classifications are not only methodical and based on carefully built up theoretical knowledge. They are also at times comparable from a formal point of view, to those still in use in zoology and botany (Lévi-Strauss, 1966, p. 43).

In this chapter we have followed a methodological path suggested by Lévi-Strauss: the informational analysis of recoding processes in culture. Psychologists speak of these processes—in reference to memory span—in terms of grouping an input sequence into units or chunks (Miller, 1965, p. 261). In communication theory, the process of recoding takes the following form. An input

is given in a code that contains many chunks with few bits per chunk. The operator recodes the input into another code that contains fewer chunks with more bits per chunk. There are many ways to do this recoding, but probably the simplest is to group the input events, apply a new name to the group, and then remember the new name rather than the original input events (Miller, 1965, p. 261).

From whatever other perspective they are considered, the recoding implications of Australian section systems should not be neglected. *The Savage
Mind* (Levi-Strauss, 1965) is as consistently concerned with processes of
this type as are communication engineers, experimental psychologists and
linguists. And all of this merely serves to re-emphasize that the kind of logic
in "primitive thought" "is as rigorous as that of modern science, and that the
difference lies, not in the quality of the intellectual process, but in the nature
of the things to which it is applied" (Lévi-Strauss, 1963a, p. 230).

If, as Kroeber (1952, p. 218) suggested, "traits of formal social organization"—such as sections and subsections—are the product of unconscious
experiment and play of fashion, then it is of some theoretical interest that
this unconscious experimentation "attempted" to reverse, on an intellectual
plane, the second law of thermodynamics—the law that entropy always
increases.

## KINSHIP LEXICONS: MEASURES OF INFORMATION PROCESSING CAPACITY

In a recent study, Wallace (1961, p. 458) attempts to resolve the "paradoxical" nonassociation between basic patterns of kinship terminology and
evolutionary position (Service, 1960). His (Wallace, 1961, p. 464) solution is
a general one, formulated on the level of the intellect: "It seems likely that
the primitive hunter and the urban technician live in cognitive worlds of
approximately equal complexity and crowdedness."

Wallace (1961, pp. 459–460) introduces a measure of semantic complexity,
based upon the Shannon information measure, that depends upon a method
we discussed in an earlier section: componential analysis. Consider Wallace's
(1961, p. 459) measure of the semantic complexity of a single term in reference
to the componential paradigm of "selected" American-English consanguine
kinship terms (Wallace, 1961, p. 460; Wallace and Atkins, 1960).

A measure of the semantic complexity of a single term can be done quite precisely,
by counting the number of cells ($N_t$) occupied by the term, and dividing that number
by the number of cells ($N_s$) in the taxonomic space. The fraction $N_t/N_s$, or a function thereof, will be a measure of the semantic complexity of the term in question.
If one wishes to measure the semantic complexity of the whole taxonomic lexicon,
one may calculate the mean semantic complexity of the several terms. This last
operation will yield a value for mean $N_t/N_s$ which cannot be larger than $I/L$, where
$L$ is the number of terms in the lexicon (Wallace, 1961, p. 459).

Formulated in logarithmic (and testable) terms,

1. $\log_2 L$ $(= -\log_2 I/L)$ is taken as the asymptote of all possible estimates
   of the semantic complexity of a terminological system, where
2. $L =$ the number of mutually exclusive terms in a lexicon, and
3. the functions $\log_2 L$, $-\log_2 N_t/N_s$ (the antilogarithm), and $-\log_2$ (mean
   $N_t/N_s$) are denoted by $H_{sem}$.

The numerical value of the logarithm $\log_2 L$ ($= -\log_2 I/L$) "also indicates the minimum number of binary dimensions necessary to the construction of a taxonomic space adequate to contain all the terms of the lexicon, and, again, its anti-logarithm is the maximum number of entities in the lexicon" (Wallace, 1961, p. 460).

The absence of any necessary relationship between the size and the technological level of a society, on the one hand, and the complexity of the kinship terminology system is illustrated by computing the value of $H_{sem}$ for kinship terms in six cultures as shown in Table 12–13.

**Table 12–13. The Minimum Mean Semantic Information Quantity ($H_{sem}$) for Kinship Terms in Six Cultures**

| Society and locality | Number of terms | Minimum $H_{sem}$ | Order of societal population | Technological level |
|---|---|---|---|---|
| Kariera (Australia) | 23 | 4.52 | Hundreds | Hunting and gathering |
| Comanche (Southwest U.S.) | 37 | 5.21 | Hundreds | Hunting and gathering |
| Könkämä Lapps (European Arctic) | 49 | 5.64 | Hundreds | Nomadic reindeer herding |
| Truk (Micronesia) | 14 | 3.82 | Thousands | Horticulture and fishing |
| Japan | 39 | 5.29 | Millions | Modern industrial |
| United States | 37 | 5.21 | Millions | Modern industrial |

(From Wallace 1961, p. 461, Table II.)

From a consideration of segmental phonemes in natural languages, verb paradigms, and various types of games and status hierarchies (as well as kinship terminologies), Wallace[24] (1961, p. 462) derives the "$2^6$ Rule":

irrespective of race, culture, or evolutionary level, culturally institutionalized folk taxonomies will not contain more than $2^6$ entities and consequently will not require more than six orthogonally related binary dimensions for the definitions of all of the terms.

Further,

*the evolution of cultural complexity is limited, in so far as folk taxonomies are concerned, by the two-to-the-sixth-power rule.* (Wallace, 1961).

[24] Wallace's use of the Shannon-Weiner measure is inappropriate as the condition of equiprobability is not met. The condition is met in the preceding analysis of section systems and in the discussion below. Wallace's application was the first explicit use of the theory of selective information in social anthropology. For this reason it is reviewed.

What is limited is the complexity of the taxonomies which are components of the various cultural sub-systems (Wallace, 1961, p. 462). Such a rule reflects a cognitive limit, constant for human populations, on the complexity of semantic spaces with which all but a few individuals in any society can reliably and comfortably function (Wallace, 1961, p. 463).

And from experimental psychology we have Miller's (1965) review of studies concerned with absolute judgments of unidimensional and multidimensional stimuli: the experimental results appear to lend support to Wallace's hypothecated "information channel capacity." Indeed, Miller speaks of limitations built into us by learning or our nervous systems that constrain channel capacities (1965, p. 250), a *span of absolute judgment* that limits the accuracy with which we can absolutely identify the magnitude of a unidimensional stimuli variable (1965, p. 256), as *span of perceptual dimensionality* (1965, p. 257).

Despite these important results, the "numerical complexity" of other folk taxonomies must be accounted for in some theoretically relevant manner.

The "threshold problem" has been anticipated by Lévi-Strauss (1966, p. 154):

In the present state of knowledge, the figure of two thousand appears to correspond well, in order of magnitude, to a sort of threshold corresponding roughly to the capacity of memory and power of definition of ethnozoologies or ethnobotanies reliant on oral tradition. It would be interesting to know if this threshold has any significant properties from the point of view of Information Theory.

Consider, for example, some of the examples adduced by Lévi-Strauss (1966):

1. The botanical vocabulary of the Hanunóo approaches two thousand (Conklin, 1954, pp. 115–117, 162).
2. Six hundred named plants have been recorded among the Pinatubo (Fox, 1953, p. 179).
3. A single Seminol informant could identify two hundred and fifty species and varieties of plants (Sturtevant, 1960).

This seeming paradox may be resolved by considering in quantitative terms the decision processes underlying terminological hierarchies (Buchler, 1967a, p. 27). A problem that originated in a consideration of the evolutionary implications of basic patterns of kinship terminology suggests a somewhat more general theoretical interpretation. And this interpretation is suggested by Wallace's (1961) formalization: by defining a hypothesis (rule or law) as an equation ($\log_2 L = -\log_2 I/L$; $\log_2 L = 7 \pm 2$; and $L = 2^6$), in which the variables are formulated in terms (operationally) that indicate what is to be measured and how the law may be tested (Rapaport, 1957,

p. 147; cf. Buchler, 1967a, pp. 23, 25, 26, 29), Wallace's equations suggest manipulations that will yield a more general formulation. Further, the equations admit the possibility of negative results, for if "certain measurements do *not* yield certain quantities, the law can be said not to hold or not to apply in the situation examined" (Rapaport, 1957, p. 147).

A generalization of Wallace's (1961) hypothesis must be prefaced by the point that the "$2^6$" rule applies only (in the examples cited) to terminal taxa, rather than to a folk taxonomy. These terminal taxa constitute a paradigm "wherein (a) the meaning of every (linguistic) form has a feature in common with the meaning of all other forms of the set, and (b) the meaning of every form differs from that of every other form of the set by one or more additional features" (Lounsbury, 1964b, p. 1073).

In attempting to reformulate the "$2^6$" rule we must account for the numerical complexity (a) of numerous paradigmatic subsystems as well as (b) folk taxonomies. A relatively simple (in a numerical sense) example may clarify the problem.

Consider a folk taxonomic hierarchy of Nuer "spirits of the above" and "spirits of the below" (Evans-Pritchard, 1953a, 1953b; c.f. Buchler, 1966c, pp. 10–13).

I. Spirits of the above

    **1a.** Spirits of the air
      A.1 *deng*
       a *dayim*
       b *dhol*
      B.1 *teny*
      C.1 *rangdit*
       c *mabith*
      D.1 *din*
      E.1 *win*
    **2a.** *Colwic* spirits

II. Spirits of the below

    **1b.** Totemic spirits
    **2b.** Totemistic spirits
    **3b.** Fetishes
    **4b.** Mature sprites
      A.2 *biel pam* (the meteorite sprite)
      B.2 *bel yier* (the river sprite)
      C.2 *biel jiath* (the tree sprite)
      D.2 *biel real* (the termite mound sprite)
      E.2 *kwoth juaini* (the sprite of the grasses)

Table 12–14.   A Folk Taxonomic Hierarchy of Nuer Spirits of the Above and Spirits of the Below (cf. Buchler, 1966c, p. 33)

| Kwoth (= spirit: the root of the paradigm) | | | | | | | | | | | | | |
|---|---|---|---|---|---|---|---|---|---|---|---|---|---|
| I | | | | | | | | II | | | | | |
| 1a | | | | | 2a | 1b | 2b | 3b | 4b | | | | |
| A.1 | B.1 | C.1 | D.1 | E.1 | | | | | | | | | |
| a | b | | c | | | | | | A.2 | B.2 | C.2 | D.2 | E.2 |

"Once a taxonomic partitioning has been worked out it can be tested systematically for terminological contrast with frames such as 'Is that an *X*?' with an exception of a negative reply" (Frake, 1962, pp. 81–82). For example, an ethnographer might ask the following questions about the "son of a river spirit" (*deng*):

1. "Is he a Spirit of the below?"
2. "Is he a *colwic* spirit?"
3. "Is he *teny*?"
4. "Is he *dhol*?"

The respective replies would generate the taxonomy of "Nuer spirits":

1. "No, he is a Spirit of the above."
2. "No, he is a Spirit of the air."
3. "No, he is a son of *deng*."
4. "No, he is *dayim*."

This series of queries and replies isolates the following levels and principles of contrast and class inclusion:

SPIRITS of the ABOVE—contrasts with—SPIRITS of the BELOW

SPIRITS of the AIR—contrasts with—COLWIC SPIRITS

SON of DENG—contrasts with—TENY

DAYIM—contrasts with—DHOL

Using the Shannon information measure—$\log_2$ of the number of available choices—the amount of information that is processed by our hypothesized native speaker may be measured for each level of the taxonomic hierarchy:

   **i.** *Level* 1: $\log_2 2 = 1.0 \ (2 = 2^1)$
   **ii.** *Level* 2: $\log_2 2 = 1.0 \ (2 = 2^1)$
   **iii.** *Level* 3: $\log_2 5 = 2.32 \ (5 = 2^{2.32})$
   **iv.** *Level* 4: $\log_2 2 = 1.0 \ (2 = 2^1)$.

The basic rule for transforming the decision processes "underlying" folk taxonomic hierarchies into bits of information is very simple: every time the number of alternative taxa on any level increases by a factor of two, one bit of information is added (Miller, 1965). There are, then, 3.459 bits of information that are processed in the foregoing series of replies. Like Wallace's (1961) measure of semantic complexity, this is merely a descriptive statement. However, if this descriptive measure can be generalized to other culturally institutionalized taxonomies, then (a) a rule, or hypothesis, similar in form to the $2^6$ rule may be formulated, which specifies certain limits on the amount of information that may be processed in "descending" from the most general to the most specific level of folk hierarchies, and (b) the relative importance of taxonomies, within a given domain, may be determined by the Shannon information measure ("the greater the number of distinct social contexts in which information about a particular phenomenon must be communicated, the greater the number of different levels of contrast into which that phenomenon is categorized," Frake, 1961, p. 121). Although the alternative classifications on any level may be rather numerous, prior questions and responses often limit the conceptually distinct categories from which a choice is made (on lower levels; e.g., that of terminal taxa), to a limited set of culturally appropriate responses. For example, on Level [3], the prior series of questions and replies limits appropriate responses to five alternatives, whereas there are ten conceptually distinct categories on this level.

In this application of the Shannon information measure to the decision processes underlying folk taxonomies,

1. $\log_2 D_{th} \ (= -\log_2 I/D_{th})$ is taken as the asymptote of all possible estimates of the decision processes underlying folk taxonomies, where
2. $D_{th}$ = the conceptually distinct categories from which choices are made in "descending" from the most "general" to the terminal level of a taxonomy.
3. The rule, or hypothesis, is $D_{th} = \log_2 11 \pm 2 \ (1)$.

The "threshold problem" posed by Lévi-Strauss (1966, p. 154) must be resolved on a somewhat more abstract and theoretic plane. Let us first suggest a formal solution; then an interpretation of this solution.
[1.] Maximally, a taxonomy with a slightly higher numerical threshold than

what Lévi-Strauss suggests[25] will be "eleven levels deep." To be somewhat more precise, if each taxon is successively partitioned by a "binary operator" on each subordinate level, then the numerical distribution of "lexemes" might be

| Level | Lexemes |
|-------|---------|
| 1 | 1 |
| 2 | 2 |
| 3 | 4 |
| 2 | 8 |
| 5 | 16 |
| 6 | 32 |
| 7 | 64 |
| 8 | 128 |
| 9 | 256 |
| 10 | 512 |
| 11 | 1024 |

Level [1] is the "root" of the taxonomy: a common feature of meaning. Level [11] comprises all terminal taxa. If we are concerned with computing logarithmic measures of the "decision processes" "underlying" culturally institutionalized folk taxonomies, then the properties of the suggested numerical threshold—from the point of view of Information Theory—may be derived.

[2.] Schematically, a taxonomy that comprises 2,047 folk taxa—given the principle of binary partition—might be structured in the following manner:

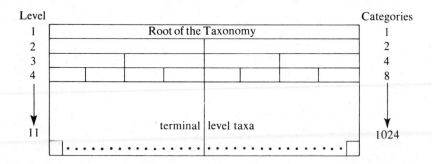

[3.] Within the frame of reference of gradual-uncertainty reduction, consider a logarithmic measure of the information that might be processed—by a hypothetical informant—in locating a (any) terminal level taxa. We consider only terminal taxa as they represent a maximum estimate, so to speak, of the decision processes underlying taxonomies.

[25] On the one hand, 2,000; 2,047 on the other.

The following queries might be posed in attempting to "key out" a terminal taxon.

*Queries:*

1. "Is it some kind of A?"
2. "Is it some kind of C?"
3. "Is it some kind of E?"
4. "Is it some kind of G?"
5. "Is it some kind of I?"
6. "Is it some kind of K?"
7. "Is it some kind of M?"
8. "Is it some kind of O?"
9. "Is it some kind of Q?"
10. "Is it some kind of S?"

The responses that these queries might elicit are

1. "No, it's some kind of B."
2. "Yes, it's some kind of C."
3. "No, it's some kind of F."
4. "No, it's some kind of H."
5. "No, it's some kind of J."
6. "No, it's some kind of L."
7. "No, it's some kind of N."
8. "No, it's some kind of P."
9. "No, it's some kind of R."
10. "No, it's some kind of T."

We are now in a position to summarize (a) the amount of information—in bits—that are processed on each level of our theoretic taxonomy, and (b) the manner in which our queries reduce uncertainty by "halfing"—on each level—the number of categories under consideration.

| Level | Choices | Bits of information | "Deleted taxa" | Remaining taxa |
|---|---|---|---|---|
| 1 | 0 | 0 | 1 | 2046 |
| 2 | 2 | 1 | 1024 | 1022 |
| 3 | 2 | 1 | 512 | 510 |
| 4 | 2 | 1 | 256 | 254 |
| 5 | 2 | 1 | 128 | 126 |
| 6 | 2 | 1 | 64 | 62 |
| 7 | 2 | 1 | 32 | 30 |
| 8 | 2 | 1 | 16 | 14 |
| 9 | 2 | 1 | 8 | 6 |
| 10 | 2 | 1 | 4 | 2 |
| 11 | 2 | 1 | 1 | 1 |

In eliciting the internal structure or sequences of complimentary relations of a taxonomy that is partitioned, on each level, by a binary operator, 4.32 bits of information are processed. On the basis of this formal test, we may revise hypothesis (1) to read

$$D_{th} = \log_2 18 \pm 2 \tag{2}$$

It might be suggested that the "Threshold Effect" to which Lévi-Strauss (1966, p. 154) has referred reflects constraints on channel capacity—in particular, span of perceptual dimensionality—as well as power of definition.

From the point of view of Information and Taxonomic Theory, it is clear that "number of choices" or bits of information remain constant on all levels, as taxa are "eliminated from" consideration: as uncertainty is reduced.

Our final rule, then, defines—in maximal terms—the information "underlying" the numerical threshold.

It is evident that the "numerical complexity" of folk taxonomies need not trouble us, as long as we construe the decision-processes "underlying" taxonomic structures within the framework of gradual uncertainty-reduction, rather than on an empirical plane.

Let us now attempt to provide a somewhat more general interpretation of these results in terms of some recent "explorations" in cognitive psychology (Miller, Galanter, and Pribram, 1960).

The general notion of a search plan—searching for an object in the physical environment—serves as a model for certain cognitive processes that would not ordinarily be thought of as a type of searching, but which "have all the formal characteristics of search except that the object sought is not located in spatial coordinates" (Miller, *et al.*, 1960, p. 161). For example, a concept-learning task that is often employed in experimental studies of thinking and the behavior of the scientist can be described in the same terms that are used for perceptual search problems. Like the scientist or a subject in a concept-learning experiment, the ethnographer's informant searches through a set of possible solutions, which may be regarded as possible hypotheses about a particular concept, rather than objects that can be seen. In the information processing games that we have presented in this chapter, our hypothetical informant, in helping the ethnographer to find an appropriate label for a marriageable category, a spirit, or any other "kind of thing" that may be ordered within a taxonomic field, produces information that allows us to reduce, at each taxonomic node, our set of possible hypotheses or alternative solutions. We think that it is reasonable to assume that decision trees similar to the ones that we have discussed, are replicated in natural settings.

Now it might be argued that our use of elementary information theory concepts, in particular $\log_2$, implies a digital mechanism—which represents all input, including continuous variation, in terms of discretely different states, whereas "the savage mind" is a highly complex mechanism that integrates digital and analogue processes on multidimensional scales. Here we can only suggest that perceptual mechanisms provide an analogue-to-digital input for the higher mental processes, allowing persons to deal "digitally" with analogue as well as digital processes (Miller *et al.*, 1960, pp. 90–91). All of this would tend to support Lévi-Strauss' and Jakobson's use of a binary logic in the analysis of myths, phonemic systems, and other products of the intellect.

Finally, what about Wallace's $2^6$ rule and Miller's similar, but experimentally derived, magical number seven?

What about the seven wonders of the world, the seven seas, the seven deadly sins, the seven daughters of Atlas in the Pleiades, the seven ages of man, the seven levels of hell, the seven primary colors, the seven notes of the musical scale, and the seven days of the week? What about the seven-point rating scale, the seven categories for absolute judgement, the seven objects in the span of attention, and the seven digits in the span of immediate memory? For the present I propose to withhold judgement. Perhaps there is something deep and profound behind all these sevens, something just calling out for us to discover it. But I suspect that it is only a pernicious, Pythagorean coincidence (Miller, 1956, p. 96).

# Chapter

# Thirteen

# Conclusions

Although it has been well over two decades since the first publication of von Neumann and Morgenstern's classic *Theory of Games and Economic Behavior* (4th ed., 1964), the limitations of the objectives that they outline (1964, pp. 6–7), are remarkably relevant to anthropological studies as they approach a new phase of conceptualization:

The great progress in every science came when, in the study of problems which were modest as compared with ultimate aims, methods were developed which could be extended further and further. The free fall is a very trivial physical phenomenon, but it was the study of this exceedingly simple fact and its comparison with the astronomical material, which brought forth mechanics.

It seems to us that the same standard of modesty should be applied in economics [and the behavioral sciences in general]. It is futile to try to explain—and "systematically" at that—everything economic. The sound procedure is to obtain first utmost precision and mastery in a limited field, and to proceed to another, somewhat wider one, and so on.

It would be pretentious and misleading to assert that modern anthropology has achieved *utmost precision and mastery* in even the most limited fields; but aspects of the wide and important study of kinship and social organization appear to be on the threshold of the development of a theory based on an analysis of the interpretation of "ethnological facts." This stage will ultimately be marked by the transition from unmathematical plausibility considerations to the formal procedures of mathematics, and "the theory finally obtained must be mathematically rigorous and conceptually general" (von Neumann and Morgenstern, 1964, p. 7).

[311]

A partial and tentative example of this transition may be exemplified by some of the formal languages that were reviewed in the preceding chapters, and by other formal languages that are applicable to a variety of more complex situations in the general field of social organization.

Consider transformational analysis—an elementary algebraic language that has been applied to the analysis of kinship terminologies. The primitives or symbol tokens (kin types) that are embedded in the axiom set may be expressed in any form of symbolic notation and may denote referents that are not contained within a genealogical grid. Further, the language is formal, and therefore perfectly general, and may consequently be applied to a wide variety of domains (myth, economics, and so on): the language is conceptually general. Applications thus far have served to corroborate the "theory," although analysts have mistakenly assumed that applications yield results for more complex situations (the nature of kinship extensions, the universality of the nuclear family) that lead beyond the familiar and the obvious.

We can state with some degree of confidence that any theory purporting to explain even a segment of the topics reviewed in this text will be a mosaic of theories developed in other fields, that have been, for the most part, diligently ignored by social anthropologists.

For example, although students of social organization have manifested considerable interest and developed ingenious "theories" to explain various forms of exchange in human societies, they have virtually ignored the theory of games, which was designed to account for the interlinked decision processes and utility scales underlying systems of exchange (Buchler and Nutini, 1968), as well as related approaches such as linear programming. The general field of social organization is essentially concerned with choice variables, rational decision rules, and related topics, and consequently must ultimately come to grips with the formal languages that are usually subsumed under the general label of *decision theory*. The literature on primitive social organization persistently skips around discussions of optimization processes, and yet refuses to confront the formal languages designed to explain these processes such as linear and dynamic programming.

The literature on kinship and social organization is, to a considerable extent, a series of polemical and highly redundant dialogues on definitional criteria for low-level theoretical constructs that are unlikely to lead to conceptually general formulations or lend themselves to formal mathematical procedures. That this trend is difficult to reverse is well illustrated by Lévi-Strauss' (1949) attempt to isolate the forms of reciprocity underlying various "types" of exchange systems. Despite this innovative methodological reorientation, subsequent discussions have floundered about such topics as the prescriptive/preferential "opposition," causal explanations based upon affective considerations, and so on. By choosing the middle ground, anthropological science has, with certain notable exceptions, paid mere lip service to the epistemological foundations upon which any decisive break must depend, and to the general processes underlying low-level theoretical concepts. By reviewing and attempting to synthesize the contemporary literature, we hope that we have cleared the field for progress *more mathematico*. To translate von Neumann and Morgenstern (1964, p. 4) on an anthropological plane: the anthropological problems were not initially clearly formulated and are quite often stated in such vague terms as to make mathematical treatment a priori appear hopeless, because it is quite uncertain what the problems really are. One thing, however, is clear: progress does not lie on the road of more refined typologies, definitional considerations, and theoretical formulations that exclude choice variables. Descriptive work that construes jural rules as absolute constraints on behavior and ignores probability considerations at the outset is likely to stifle theory construction and confuses the basic epistemological distinction (the bifurcation of nature) between the immediately sensed and the postulated but not sensed. An example from Chapters Five and Six is instructive.

A large segment of the literature on Australian section systems is implicitly or explicitly concerned with essentially typological problems and explanatory issues that are constrained by these typological concerns: How many sections, descent lines, and so on, characterize various systems? What are the analytic or social processes that generate these systems? How are these systems related on a developmental plane? These are all legitimate endeavors, particularly within an eighteenth-century Linnaean framework; none, however, develop measures for the processes underlying these systems of exchange and communication. Consider an example.

In many Australian systems (e.g., the Tiwi of Melville and Bathurst Islands), it is perfectly clear that men attempt to maximize the objective function "number of wives," and, at the same time, attempt to minimize a cost function involved in the acquisition of wives. Although anthropologists have not recognized it as such, the decision processes underlying the maximization of this function is a linear programming problem of the general form (cf. Buchler and McKinlay, 1968)

$$Z = \sum_{j=1}^{n} C_j X_j \qquad (j = 1, 2, \ldots, n),$$

subject to restraints of the form

$$\sum_{j=1}^{n} a_{ij} \left( \begin{matrix} \leq \\ = \\ \geq \end{matrix} \right) b_i \qquad (i = 1, 2, \ldots, m),$$

and

$$x_i \geq 0 \qquad (j = 1, 2, \ldots, n),$$

where

$x_j$ = the quantity of the $j$th variable of interest to the decision maker, where there are $n$ variables being considered: $x_j$ is either an integer 1, if and only if individual $j$ obtains a wife, and $x = 0$ if individual $j$ does not.

$c_j$ = the per unit contribution to the objective function (profit or cost) of the $j$th variable, where there are $n$ variables: the qualification of individual $j$ in terms of political debts outstanding to him. Political debts refer to "women owed or outstanding."

$z$ = the objective function to be maximized or minimized.

$a_i$ = the exchange coefficient of the $j$th variable in the $i$th restraint where there are $m$ restraints and $n$ variables.

$b_j b_i$ = the $ij$th requirement where there are $m$ requirements in all.

An approach of this sort assumes neither that the exchange of women is a strictly determined outcome of a set of jural rules, nor that these rules are an outcome of a statistical trend in spouse-seeking political behavior. If, on the other hand, we are concerned with statistical trends in individual choice behavior, beyond the trivial assertion that jural rules are an emergent phenomena of these trends, quite simple probability models derived from population genetics (Dahlberg, 1948, pp. 91–92), as well as simulation techniques, which account for fluctuations in demographic parameters, rates of realization of ideal patterns and other types of indeterminacies (Kunstadter et al., 1963; Gilbert and Hammel, 1966), provide interesting opportunities for testing the degree of isomorphism between the calculus of probability and a particular collection of empirical events (Buchler, 1967a).

In the preceding chapter, we assumed the "rule-constrained position" and measured the decision processes underlying the choice of a marriage partner. This analysis may be interpreted on two interrelated levels: analytic or developmental. The decision processes may approximate a query-response set employed by an ethnologist or a child in learning a system's marriage rules, or alternatively, may be regarded as a measure of the information content of the system. The information processing model approximates a *numerical machine*, "where the data are represented by a set of choices among a number of contingencies, and the accuracy is determined by the sharpness with which the contingencies are distinguished, the number of alternative contingencies presented at every choice, and the number of choices given" (Wiener, 1965, p. 117). Although we employed a numerical machine constructed on the binary scale, analyses of information processing systems in other domains may find *analogy machines*, where the data are represented by measurements on some continuous scale (cf. Leach, 1964), or numerical machines constructed on "nonbinary" scales, of greater relevance.

What, then is the relevance of this analysis to the classic study of Australian section systems? The answer is quite simple: none. We have posed the problem on a deeper level (and in somewhat different terms), as it is on this level, rather than in reference to "observed" constructs such as descent group, descent line, and so on (cf. Leach, 1961b, pp. 2–3, 12), that universals may be sought. These universals relate to channel capacity, recoding structure, and information processing systems in culture, and are based on adequate measures. This notion of universals is analogous, in certain respects, to Chomsky's (1965, p. 6) notion of a universal grammar. Information processing universals account for the "creative" aspect of cultural systems. An essential property of "culture" is that it provides the means for the "appropriate" processing of a wide variety of information in an indefinite range of new situations. The notion "indefinite range" refers to capacity rather than actual performance. The fundamental descriptive inadequacy of "particular cultural grammars" can be overcome only by universal statements of the invariants governing information processing, channel capacity, and recoding structures. As these deep-seated regularities are universals, they are omitted from "particular grammars" (cf. Chomsky, 1965, p. 6). It is our thesis that this path toward the intellect, which at first may appear alien to the goals of modern anthropology, is the only certain path to a mature stage of conceptualization, and, at the same time, poses a series of criteria, questions, and problems that are not suggested by studies formulated on an empirical plane.

Finally, we would like to argue for the necessity of a change in terminological usage that is related to the foregoing discussion and that appears to be of quite general significance. We refer to the now engraved distinction between mechanical and statistical models. As all models are mechanisms of one sort or another, a distinction between deterministic and stochastic models would appear to be more appropriate and in line with current thought. Leaving aside the interrelated problems of discovery procedures and the passage between levels, the essential distinction between these mechanisms might be formulated in terms of the transition probabilities governing the movement from one state to the other.

Just as there is a hierarchy of codes and criteria of adequacy, a partial hierarchy of models might be formulated.

Stochastic (with transition probabilities unspecified)

*stochastic* (= performance models), where the transition probabilities are given by /0.98/0.0/0.01/, or /0.99/ 0.01/0.0/ ... /0/, and so on.

*deterministic* (= competence models), where the transition probabilities are given by /0.0/1.00/0.0/ ... /0/, and so on.

This partial hierarchy is relevant not only to social anthropology, but also to history, sociology, and ethnography. We may, therefore, recall Lévi-Strauss' (1963, p. 286) mechanical/statistical distinction which generates the following formula:

|  | History | Sociology | Ethnography | Social Anthropology |
|---|---|---|---|---|
| Mechanical/ Statistical | − | − | + | + |

(where + refers to the assignment of mechanical, and − to the assignment of statistical to the category of analysis.)

Substituting the deterministic/stochastic opposition for Lévi-Strauss' terms, we characterize the products of research (not the initial stage of research) by a formulation which summarizes the relevance of both models to all four subject areas.

|  | History | Sociology | Ethnography | Social Anthropology |
|---|---|---|---|---|
| Stochastic/ Deterministic | ± | ± | ± | ± |

It can be seen that the criterial attributes that distinguish the two model types lie not at the level of features, but rather are embedded in the transition probabilities.

Essentially this means that if models and forms of explanation are mapped over tree graphs, *stochastic-type* processes generate outcomes that are partially predictable; *deterministic-type* processes generate outcomes that are completely predictable. This distinction is equivalent to the strategy rule/ ground rule opposition. A central problem in social anthropology and linguistics is the formulation of correspondence rules (stochastic or deterministic) that relate these forms of explanation to one another. Although we have continually emphasized the importance of the ground rule/strategy rule opposition, much of the text has been concerned with a discussion, synthesis, and formalization of ground rules. With certain notable exceptions, there are few ethnographies that will permit one to formalize adequately the strategic continua underlying cultural systems. In this sense, we can conclude by echoing the melancholy note that Lévi-Strauss (1953) sounded over a decade ago:

When we come to realize not only what should be done but also what we should be in a position to do, and when we make at the same time an inventory of our material, we cannot help feeling in a disheartened mood. It looks almost as if cosmic physics were to work with Babylonian observations. The celestial bodies are still there, but unfortunately the native cultures from which we used to gather our data are rapidly disappearing and that which they are being replaced by can only furnish data of a very different type. To adjust our techniques of observation to a theoretical framework which is far more advanced is a paradoxical situation, quite opposite to that which has prevailed in the history of sciences. Nevertheless, such is the challenge to modern anthropology.

# Bibliography

**Aberle, D.** (1953) *The Kinship System of the Kalmuk Mongols*, Albuquerque, New Mexico: University of New Mexico Publications in Anthropology, No. 8.

**Ackerman, C.** (1964) Structure and Statistics: The Purum Case, *American Anthropologist* **66**, 53–67.

**Ackerman, C.** (1965) Structure and Process: The Purum Case, *American Anthropologist* **67**, 83–91.

**Adams, R. N.** (n.d.) Personal Communication.

**Adams, R. N.** (1960) An Inquiry into the Nature of the Family, in Dole, Gertrude E., and Robert L. Carneiro (eds.), *Essays in the Science of Culture*, New York: Thomas Crowell Co.

**Aginsky, B.** (1935) Kinship Systems and the Forms of Marriage, *Memoirs of the American Anthropological Association*, XLV.

**Aoki, H.** (1966) Nez Perce and Proto-Sahaptian Kinship Terms, *International Journal of American Linguistics* **32**, 357–368.

**Appell, G. N.** (1967) Observational Procedures for Identifying Kindreds: Social Isolates among the Rungus of Borneo, *Southwestern Journal of Anthropology* **23**, 192–207.

**Arensberg, C. M.**, and **S. T. Kimball** (1940) *Family and Community in Ireland*, Cambridge, Mass.: Harvard University Press.

**Atkins, J.**, and **L. Curtis** (1968) Game Rules and the Rules of Culture, in *Game Theory in the Behavioral Sciences*, Buchler, I. R., and H. G. Nutini (eds.), Pittsburgh: University of Pittsburgh Press.

**Attneave, F.** (1959) *Applications of Information Theory to Psychology*, New York: Holt.

[319]

**Bachofen, J. J.** (1861) *Das Mutterrecht*, Stuttgart, Germany.

**Barker, Roger W.,** and **Herbert F. Wright** (1954) *Midwest and Its Children*, Evanston, Ill.: Row Peterson.

**Barnes, J. A.** (1949) Measures of Divorce Frequency in Simple Societies, *Journal of the Royal Anthropological Institute* **89,** 37–62.

**Barnes, J. A.** (1960) Marriage and Residential Continuity, *American Anthropologist* **62,** 850–866.

**Barnes, J. A.** (1961) Physical and Social Kinship, *Philosophy of Science* **28,** 296–299.

**Barnes, J. A.** (1962) African Models in the New Guinea Highlands, *Man* **62,** 5–9.

**Barnes, J. A.** (1964) Physical and Social Facts in Anthropology, *Philosophy of Science* **31,** 294–297.

**Barth, F.** (1966) Models of Social Organization, *Occasional Papers of the Royal Anthropological Association* No. **23.**

**Beattie, J. H. M.** (1957–58) Nyoro Kinship, Marriage and Affinity, *Africa* 27–28, 317–340, 1–22.

**Beattie, J. H. M.** (1964) Kinship and Social Anthropology, *Man* **130.**

**Befu, H.** (1965) Social Organization, in *Biennial Review of Anthropology*, Siegel, B. J. (ed.), Stanford: Stanford University Press.

**Bendig, A. W.** (1953) Twenty Questions: An Informational Analysis, *Journal of Experimental Psychology* **46,** 345–348.

**Berge, C.** (1966) *The Theory of Graphs*, New York: John Wiley & Sons, Inc.

**Berlin, B., D. F. Breedlove,** and **P. H. Raven** (1966) Folk Taxonomies and Scientific Classification, *Science* **154** (3746), 273–275.

**Berlin, B., D. F. Breedlove,** and **P. H. Raven** (1968) Covert Categories and Folk Taxonomies, *American Anthropologist* (in press).

**Berndt, R.** (1955) Murngin (Wulamba) Social Organization, *American Anthropologist* **57,** 84–106.

**Berting, J.,** and **H. Philipsen** (1960) Solidarity, Stratification and Sentiments: The Unilateral Cross-Cousin Marriage According to the Theories of Lévi-Strauss, Leach, and Homans and Schneider, *Bijdragen tot de Taal-, Land-, en Volkenkunde* **116,** 55–80.

**Bishop, Barbara M.** (1951) Mother-Child Interaction and the Social Behavior of Children, *Psychological Monographs* **65,** No. 11.

**Blake, Judith** (1962) *Family Structure in Jamaica: The Social Context of Reproduction*, New York: The Free Press.

**Blehr, O.** (1963) Action Groups in a Society with Bilateral Kinship: A Case Study from the Faroe Islands, *Ethnology* **2,** 269–275.

**Bohannon, Laura** (1952) A Genealogical Charter, *Africa* **22,** 301–315.

**Bohannon, Laura,** and **Paul Bohannon** (1953) *The Tiv of Central Nigeria*, London: Oxford University Press.

**Bohannon, Paul** (1954a) Expansion and Migration of the Tiv, *Africa* **24,** 2–16.

Bohannon, Paul (1954b) *Tiv Farm and Settlement*, London: HMSO.

Bohannon, Paul (1958) *Justice and Judgement Among the Tiv*, London: Oxford University Press.

Bohannon, Paul (1963) *Social Anthropology*, New York: Holt Rinehart.

Braithwaite, R. B. (1955) *Scientific Explanation: A Study of the Function of Theory, Probability and Law in Science*, Cambridge: Cambridge University Press.

Braithwaite, R. B. (1963) *Theory of Games as a Tool for the Moral Philosopher*, Cambridge: Cambridge University Press.

Briffault, R. (1927) *The Mothers*, New York.

Bright, W., and J. Minnick (1966) Reduction Rules in Fox Kinship, *Southwestern Journal of Anthropology* 22, 381–388.

Brookfield, H. C., and Paula Brown (1963) *Struggle for Land*, Melbourne: Oxford University Press.

Brown, Paula (1962) Non-Agnates among the Patrilineal Chimbu, *Journal of the Polynesian Society* 71, 57–69.

Brown, Roger (1965) *Social Psychology*, New York: The Free Press.

Bruner, J., J. Goodnow, and G. Austin (1962) *A Study of Thinking*, Cambridge, Mass.: Harvard University Press.

Buchler, I. R. (1964) A Formal Account of the Hawaiian- and Eskimo-Type Kinship Terminologies, *Southwestern Journal of Anthropology* 20, 286–318.

Buchler, I. R. (1966a) On Physical and Social Kinship, *Anthropological Quarterly* 39, 17–25.

Buchler, I. R. (1966b) Measuring the Development of Kinship Terminologies: Scalogram and Transformational Accounts of Omaha-Type Terminologies, *Bijdragen tot de Taal-, Land-, en Volkenkunde* 122, 36–63.

Buchler, I. R. (1966c) Semantique Descriptive des Catégories Religieuses Nuer, *L'Homme* 6, 35–58.

Buchler, I. R. (1967a) Rules, Laws and Probabilities in Social Anthropology, in *Research Methods in Comparative Social Anthropology*, Paris: Mouton. (in press)

Buchler, I. R. (1967b) Analyse Formelle des Terminologies de Parenté Iroquoises, *L'Homme* 7, 5–31.

Buchler, I. R., and R. M. McKinlay (1968) Decision Processes in Culture: A Linear Programming Analysis, in *Game Theory in the Behavioral Sciences*, Buchler, I. R., and H. G. Nutini (eds.), Pittsburgh: University of Pittsburgh Press.

Buchler, I. R., and H. G. Nutini (1968a) Introduction, *Game Theory in the Behavioral Sciences*, Pittsburgh: University of Pittsburgh Press.

Buchler, I. R., and H. G. Nutini (1968b) *Game Theory in the Behavioral Sciences*, Pittsburgh: University of Pittsburgh Press.

Buchler, I. R., and H. A. Selby (1968) Animal, Vegetable or Mineral? in *Festchrift for Claude Lévi-Strauss*, Pouillon, J., and P. Maranda (eds.), Paris: Mouton.

Burling, R. (1964) Cognition and Componential Analysis: God's Truth or Hocus-Pocus? *American Anthropologist* **66**, 20–28.

Bush, R. R. (1963) An Algebraic Treatment of Rules of Marriage and Descent, Appendix II, in *An Anatomy of Kinship* (H. C. White), Englewood-Cliffs, N. J.: Prentice-Hall.

Cancian, Francesca (1963) Family Interaction in Zinacantan, Unpub. Ph.D. Thesis, Cambridge, Mass.: Harvard University.

Cancian, Francesca (1964) Interaction Patterns in Zinacanteco Families, *American Sociological Review* **29**, 540–550. [also in Vogt, E. (ed.) *Los Zinacantecos* (Mexico City, Instituto Nacional Indigenista, 1966)].

Chafe, W. L. (1965) Meaning in Language, *American Anthropologist* **67**, (No. 5, part 2), 23–36.

Chomsky, N. (1957) *Syntactic Structures*, The Hague: Mouton.

Chomsky, N. (1964) A Review of B. F. Skinner's *Verbal Behavior* in *The Structure of Language*, Fodor, J. A., and J. J. Katz (eds.), Englewood-Cliffs, N. J.: Prentice-Hall.

Chomsky, N. (1965) *Aspects of the Theory of Syntax*, Cambridge, Mass.: M.I.T. Press.

Clarke, Edith (1957) *My Mother who Fathered Me: A Study of the Family in Three Selected Communities in Jamaica*, London: Ruskin House.

Coale, Ansley J. (1965) Appendix: Estimates of Average Size of Household, in *Aspects of the Analysis of Family Structure*, Coale *et al.*, Princeton: Princeton University Press.

Cohen, Yehudi A. (1956) Structure and Function: Family Organization and Socialization in a Jamaican Community, *American Anthropologist* **58**, 664–686.

Colby, B. (1966) Ethnographic Semantics, A Preliminary Survey, *Current Anthropology* **7**, 3–32.

Coleman, J. (1957) *Introduction to Mathematical Sociology*, Glencoe, Ill., The Free Press of Glencoe.

Conklin, H. C. (1954) The Relation of Hanunóo Culture to the Plant World, Unpublished Ph.D. Dissertation, Yale University.

Conklin, H. C. (1962) Lexicographical Treatment of Folk Taxonomies, in *Problems in Lexicography*, Householder, F. W., and S. Saporta (eds.), Bloomington, Indiana: University of Indiana Press.

Conklin, H. C. (1964) Ethnogenealogical Method, in *Explorations in Cultural Anthropology*, Goodenough, W. H. (ed.), New York: McGraw-Hill.

Coult, A. D. (1962) An Analysis of Needham's Critique of the Homans and Schneider Theory, *Southwestern Journal of Anthropology* **18**, 317–335.

Coult, A. D. (1963) Causality and Cross-Sex Prohibitions, *American Anthropologist* **65**, 266–277.

Coult, A. D., and R. W. Habenstein (1964) Exogamy and American Kinship, *Social Forces* **41**, 174–180.

Cowgill, G. L. (1964) Statistics and Sense: More on the Purum Case, *American Anthropologist* **66**, 1358–1365.

**Cumming, Elaine,** and **D. M. Schneider** (1961) Sibling Solidarity: A Property of American Kinship, *American Anthropologist* **63,** 498–507.

**Dahlberg, G.** (1948) *Mathematical Methods for Population Genetics,* Basle: S. Karger.

**Das, T. C.** (1945) *The Purums: An Old Kuki Tribe of Manipur,* Calcutta.

**Davenport, W.** (1959) Nonunilinear Descent and Descent Groups, *American Anthropologist* **61,** 557–572.

**Davenport, W.** (1960) Jamaican Fishing: A Game Theory Analysis, *Yale University Publications in Anthropology* **59,** 3–11.

**Davenport, W.** (1961) The Family System of Jamaica, *Social and Economic Studies* **10,** 420–454.

**Davenport, W.** (1963) Social Organization, in *Biennial Review of Anthropology,* Siegel, B. J. (ed.), Stanford: Stanford University Press.

**Davis, K.,** and **W. L. Warner** (1937) Structural Analysis of Kinship, *American Anthropologist* **39,** 291–313.

**Deacon, A. B.** (1927) The Regulation of Marriage in Ambrym, *Journal of the Royal Anthropological Institute,* 325–342.

**Dorsey, J. O.** (1881–82) *Omaha Sociology,* Washington: Smithsonian Institution, Bureau of Ethnology. **Third Annual Report** 205–307.

**Driberg, J. H.** (1923) *The Lango,* London.

**Driberg, J. H.** (1932) Some Aspects of Lango Kinship, *Sociologus* **8,** 44–61.

**Drucker, P** (1951) *The Northern and Central Nootkan Tribes,* Wash., D. C. Smithsonian Institution, Bureau of American Ethnology. **Bull. No. 144,** U. S. Government Printing Office.

**DuBois, Cora** (1935) Wintu Ethnography, *University of California Publications in American Archaeology and Ethnology* **36,** 1–148.

**Dumont, L.** (1950) Kinship and Alliance Among the Pramalai Kallar, *Eastern Anthropologist* **4,** 3–26.

**Dumont, L.** (1953a) The Dravidian Kinship Terminology as an Expression of Marriage, *Man* **53,** 34–39.

**Dumont, L.** (1953b) Dravidian Kinship Terminology, *Man* **53,** Art 54.

**Dumont, L.** (1957) Hierarchy and Marriage Alliance in South Indian Kinship, *Occasional Paper of the Royal Anthropological Institute,* No. **12.**

**Dumont, L.** (1966) Descent or Intermarriage? A Relational View of Australian Descent Systems, *Southwestern Journal of Anthropology* **22,** 231–250.

**Durbin, M.** (1966) The Goals of Ethnoscience, *Anthropological Linguistics* **8,** 22–41.

**Durkheim, E.** (1897) La prohibition de l'inceste et ses origines, *L'Année Sociologique* **1,** 1–70.

**Durkheim, E.** (1947) *The Division of Labor in Society,* Glencoe, Illinois: The Free Press.

**Eggan, F.** (ed.) (1937) *Social Anthropology of the North American Tribes,* Chicago: University of Chicago Press. (2nd ed., 1955).

**Eggan, F.** (1950) *Social Organization of the Western Pueblos,* Chicago: University of Chicago Press.

Eggan, F. (1954) Social Anthropology and the Method of Controlled Comparison, *American Anthropogloist* **56**, 743–763.

Eggan, F. (1955) *Social Anthropology of the North American Tribes*, enlarged ed., Chicago: University of Chicago Press.

Elkin, A. P. (1933) Marriage and Descent in East Arnhem Land, *Oceania* **3**, 412–415.

Elkin, A. P. (1937) Kinship in South Australia, *Oceania* **8**, 419–452.

Elkin, A. P. (1953) Murngin Kinship Re-Examined and Remarks on Some Generalizations, *American Anthropologist* **55**, 412–419.

Elkin, A. P. (1954) *The Australian Aborigines*, 3rd ed., London: Angus and Robertson.

Emmeneau, M. B. (1941) Language and Social Forms. A Study of Toda Kinship Terms and Dual Descent, in *Language, Culture and Personality: Essays in Memory of Edward Sapir*, Spier, Leslie, A. Irving Hallowell and Stanley Newman (eds.), Menasha, Wisconsin: Sapir Memorial Publication Fund.

Evans-Pritchard, E. E. (1929) The Study of Kinship in Primitive Societies, *Man* **29**, 190–193.

Evans-Pritchard, E. E. (1932) The Nature of Kinship Extensions, *Man* **32**, 12–15.

Evans-Pritchard, E. E. (1940) *The Nuer*, London: Oxford University Press.

Evans-Pritchard, E. E. (1951) *Kinship and Marriage Among the Nuer*, London: Oxford University Press.

Evans-Pritchard, E. E. (1953a) The Nuer Conception of Spirit in Its Relation to the Social Order, *American Anthropologist* **55**, 201–214.

Evans-Pritchard, E. E. (1953b) Nuer Spear Symbolism, *Anthropological Quarterly* **26**, 1–19.

Eyde, D. B., and P. M. Postal (1961) Avunculocality and Incest: The Development of Unilateral Cross-Cousin Marriage and Crow-Omaha Kinship Systems, *American Anthropologist* **63**, 747–771.

Fallers, L. A. (1957) Some Determinants of Marriage Stability in Busoga: A Reformation of Gluckman's Hypothesis, *Africa* **27**, 106–121.

Faron, L. C. (1956) Araucanian Patri-Organization and the Omaha System, *American Anthropologist* **58**, 435–456.

Fathauer, G. H. (1962) Trobriand, in Schneider, D. M., and Kathleen Gough (eds.) (1961).

Feigenbaum, E. A., and Feldman J. (eds.) (1963) *Computers and Thought*, New York: McGraw-Hill.

Firth, Raymond (1930) Marriage and the Classificatory System of Relationship, *Journal of the Royal Anthropological Institute* **60**, 235–268.

Firth, Raymond (1951) *Elements of Social Organization*, London: Watts.

Firth, Raymond (1957) A Note on Descent Groups in Polynesia, *Man* **57**, 2.

Firth, Raymond (1963) Bilateral Descent Groups: An Operational Viewpoint, in *Studies in Kinship and Marriage*, Schapera, I. (ed.) Occasional Paper of the Royal Anthropological Institute, No. **16**.

Fischer, J. L. (1958) The Classification of Residence in Censuses, *American Anthropologist* **60**, 508–517.

Fischer, J. L. (1964) Solutions for the Natchez Paradox, *Ethnology* **3**, 53–65.

Fison, L. (1880) *Kamilaroi and Kurnai*, Melbourne.

Fodor, J. A. (1966) How to Learn to Talk: Some Simple Ways, in *The Genesis of Language: A Psycholinguistic Approach*, Smith, F., and G. A. Miller (eds.), Cambridge, Mass.: The M.I.T. Press.

Fortes, M. (1935) *Marriage Law Among the Tallensi*, Gold Coast: Government Press.

Fortes, M. (1936) Ritual Festivities and Social Cohesion in the Hinterland of the Gold Coast, *American Anthropologist* **38**, 590–604.

Fortes, M. (1940) The Political Systems of the Tallensi in the Northern Territories of the Gold Coast, in Fortes, M., and E. E. Evans-Pritchard (eds.) (1940).

Fortes, M. (1944) Descent in the Social Structure of the Tallensi, *Africa* **14**, 362–385.

Fortes, M. (1945) *The Dynamics of Clanship Among the Tallensi*, London: Oxford University Press.

Fortes, M. (1949a) *The Web of Kinship Among the Tallensi*, London: Oxford University Press.

Fortes, M. (1949b) Time and Social Structure: An Ashanti Case Study, in *Social Structure*, Fortes, M (ed.), London: Oxford University Press, 54–84.

Fortes, M. (1951) Social Anthropology, in Heath, A. E. (ed.) (1951).

Fortes, M. (1953) The Structure of Unilineal Kin Groups, *American Anthropologist* **55**, 17–41.

Fortes, M. (1958) Introduction, in Goody, J. (ed.) (1958).

Fortes, M. (1959) Descent, Filiation, and Affinity, *Man*, Nos. **309, 331.**

Fortes, M., and E. E. Evans-Pritchard (eds.) (1940) *African Political Systems*, London: Oxford University Press.

Fortune, R. (1933) A Note on Some Forms of Social Organization, *Oceania* **4**, 1–9.

Fox, R. B. (1953) The Tinutubo Negritos: Their Useful Plants and Material Culture, *Philippine Journal of Science*, Vol. **80**, Nos. 3 and 4.

Frake, C. O. (1961) The Diagnosis of Disease Among the Subanum of Mindanao, *American Anthropologist* **63**, 113–132.

Frake, C. O. (1962) The Ethnographic Study of Cognitive Systems, in *Anthropology and Human Behavior*, Gladwin, T., and W. C. Sturtevant (eds.), Washington, D. C.: The Anthropological Society of Washington.

Frake, C. O. (1964) Notes on Queries in Ethnography, *American Anthropologist* **66**, 132–145.

Frazer, J. G. (1910) *Totemism and Exogamy*, London.

Frazier, E. Franklin (1957) Introduction, in *Caribbean Studies: A Symposium*, Rubin, Vera (ed.), Jamaica: Institute of Social and Economic Research, pp. v–viii.

**Freeman, J. D.** (1961) On the Concept of the Kindred, *Journal of the Royal Anthropological Institute* **91**, 192–220.

**Freeman, J. D.** (1962) The Family System of the Iban of Borneo, in Goody, J. (ed.) (1962), 15–52.

**Freilich, Morris** (1961) Serial Polygyny, Negro Peasants and Model Analysis, *American Anthropologist* **63**, 955–975.

**Fried, M. H.** (1957) The Classification of Corporate Unilineal Descent Groups, *Journal of the Royal Anthropological Institute* **87**, 1–30.

**Fulkerson, D. R.** (1965) Upsets in Round Robin Tournaments, *Canadian Journal of Mathematics* **17**, 957–969.

**Fustel de Coulanges, N.-D.** (1864) *La Cité Antique; étude sur le culte, le droit, les institutions de la Grèce et de Rome*, Paris: Durand.

**Galton, F.** (1889a) (in E. B. Tylor) On a Method of Investigating the Development of Institutions Applied to the Laws of Marriage and Descent, *Journal of the Royal Anthropological Institute* **18**, 272.

**Galton, F.** (1889b) Note on Australian Marriage Systems, *Journal of the Royal Anthropological Institute* **18**, 70–72.

**Gellner, E.** (1957) Ideal Language and Kinship Terms, *Philosophy of Science* **24**, 235–243.

**Gellner, E.** (1960) The Concept of Kinship, *Philosophy of Science* **27**, 187–204.

**Gellner, E.** (1963) Nature and Society in Social Anthropology, *Philosophy of Science* **30**, 236–251.

**Geohegan, W. H.,** and **P. Kay** (1964) More Structure and Statistics: A Critique on C. Ackerman's Analysis of the Purum, *American Anthropologist* **66**, 1351–58.

**Gibbs, J. L.** (1965) *Peoples of Africa*, New York: Holt, Rinehart and Winston.

**Gifford, E. W.** (1916) Miwok Moieties, *University of California Publications in American Archeology and Ethnology* **12**, 139–194.

**Gifford, E. W.** (1922) California Kinship Terminologies, *University of California Publications in American Archeology and Ethnology* **18**, 1–285.

**Gifford, E. W.** (1940) A Problem in Kinship Terminology, *American Anthropologist* **42**, 190–194.

**Gilbert, J. P.,** and **E. A. Hammel** (1966) Computer Simulation and the Analysis of Problems in Kinship and Social Structure, *American Anthropologist* **68**, 71–93.

**Gilbert, W. H.** (1937) Eastern Cherokee Social Organization, in Eggan, F. (ed.), 1937, 285–316.

**Gilbert, W. H.** (1955) Eastern Cherokee Social Organization, in *Social Anthropology of North American Tribes*, Eggan, F. (ed.). Enlarged Edition. Chicago: University of Chicago Press, 285–338.

**Glasse, R. M.** (1959) The Huli Descent System, *Oceania* **29**, 171–184.

**Glick, Paul G.** (1957) *American Families*, New York: John Wiley & Sons.

**Gluckman, Max** (1950) Kinship and Marriage Among the Lozi of Northern Rhodesia and the Zulu of Natal, in *African Systems of Kinship and Mar-*

*riage*, Radcliffe-Brown, A. R., and Daryll Forde (eds.), Oxford University Press for the International African Institute, 166–206.

Goldberg, S. (1958) *Introduction to Difference Equations*, New York: John Wiley & Sons.

Goodenough, W. H. (1951) *Property, Kin and Community on Truk*, New Haven: Yale University Press. Yale University Publications in Anthropology, No. **46**.

Goodenough, W. H. (1955) A Problem in Malayo-Polynesian Social Organization, *American Anthropologist* **57**, 71–83.

Goodenough, W. H. (1956a) Componential Analysis and the Study of Meaning, *Language* **32**, 195–216.

Goodenough, W. H. (1956b) Residence Rules, *Southwestern Journal of Anthropology* **12**, 22–37.

Goodenough, W. H. (1961) *Review* of G. P. Murdock (ed.) *Social Structure in South East Asia*, *American Anthropologist* **63**, 1341–1347.

Goodenough, W. H. (1962) Kindred and Hamlet in Lakalai, New Britain, *Ethnology* **1**, 5–12.

Goodenough, W. H. (1964) Introduction, in *Explorations in Cultural Anthropology*, Goodenough, W. H. (ed.), New York: McGraw-Hill.

Goodenough, W. H. (1965a) Yankee Kinship Terminology: A Problem in Componential Analysis, in Hammel, E. A. (ed.) (1965), 259–287.

Goodenough, W. H. (1965b) Rethinking "Status" and "Role," in *The Relevance of Models for Social Anthropology*, Banton, Michael (ed.), New York: Frederick A. Praeger, 1–24.

Goody, J. (ed.) (1958) The Developmental Cycle in Domestic Groups. *Cambridge Papers in Social Anthropology*, No. 1. Cambridge University Press. England.

Goody, J. (1959) The Mother's Brother in West Africa, *Journal of the Royal Anthropological Institute*, **89**, 61–88.

Goody, J. (1961) The Classification of Double Descent Systems, *Current Anthropology* **2**, 3–12.

Gough, Kathleen (1959a) The Nayars and the Definition of Marriage, *Journal of the Royal Anthropological Institute* **89**, 23–34.

Gough, Kathleen (1959b) *Review* of L. Dumont, *Un Sous-Caste de l'Inde*, *Man* **59**, 202–203.

Gough, Kathleen (1961) The Nayar: Central Kerala; The Nayar: North Kerala, in *Matrilineal Kinship*, Schneider, D. M., and Kathleen Gough (eds.), Berkeley and Los Angeles: University of California Press.

Green, B. F. (1954) Attitude Measurement, in *Handbook of Social Psychology*, Lindzey, G. (ed.) Vol. **1**, 335–370.

Greenberg, J. (1957) The Nature and Uses of Linguistic Typologies, *International Journal of American Linguistics* **23.2**, 68–77.

Gregg, J. R. (1954) *The Language of Taxonomy: An Application of Symbolic Logic to the Study of Classificatory Systems*, New York: Columbia University Press.

Gregor, A. J. (n.d.) Political Science and the Uses of Functional Analysis, Ms. University of California, Berkeley.

Guttman, L. (1944) A Basis for Scaling Qualitative Data, *American Sociological Review*, **9**, 139–150.

Guttman, L. (1945) A Basis for Analyzing Test-Retest Reliability, *Psychometrika* **10**, 255–282.

Guttman, L. (1946) The Test-Retest Reliability of Qualitative Data, *Psychometrika*, **11**, 81–95.

Guttman, L. (1950a) The Basis for Scalogram Analysis, in *Studies in Psychology in World War II*, Stouffer, S. A. (ed.) Vol. **IV**, 60–90.

Guttman, L. (1950b) Problems in Reliability, in *Studies in Psychology in World War II*, Stouffer, S. A. (ed.) Vol. **4**, 277–312.

Guttman, L. (1950c) The Principal Components of Scale Analysis, in *Studies in Psychology in World War II*, Stouffer, S. A. (ed.) Vol. **4**, 312–362.

Haddon, A. C. (1910) *History of Anthropology*, New York.

Hallowell, A. I. (1960) The Beginnings of Anthropology in America, in de Laguna, F. (ed.) (1960) 1–90.

Hammel, E. A. (1961) The Family Cycle in a Coastal Peruvian Slum and Village, *American Anthropologist* **63**, 989–1005.

Hammel, E. A. (1965a) A Transformational Analysis of Comanche Kinship Terminology, in Hammel, E. A. (ed.) (1965b).

Hammel, E. A. (ed.) (1965b) *Formal Semantic Analysis*. Special Publication of the American Anthropologist, Vol. **65**, No. 5, Part 2. Menasha, Wisconsin: American Anthropological Association.

Harary, F., R. Z. Norman, and D. Cartwright (1965) *Structural Models: An Introduction to the Theory of Directed Graphs*, New York: John Wiley & Sons.

Hart, C. W. (1943) A Reconsideration of Natchez Social Structure, *American Anthropologist* **45**, 374–386.

Heath, A. E. (1951) *Scientific Thought in the Twentieth Century*, London.

Held, D. J. (1957) *The Papuas of Waropen*, The Hague: Nijhoff.

Herskovits, M. J., and Frances S. (1947) *Trinidad Village*, New York: Alfred A. Knopf.

Hertz, H. R. (1894) *Die Prinzipien der Mechanik*, Leipzig.

Hocart, A. M. (1937) Kinship Systems, *Anthropos* **32**, 545–551.

Hockett, C. F. (1964) The Proto Central Algonquian Kinship System, in *Explorations in Cultural Anthropology*, Goodenough, W. H. (ed.), New York: McGraw-Hill, 239–258.

Hoffmann, H. (1965) Formal vs. Informal Estimates of Cultural Stability, *American Anthropologist* **67**, 110–115.

Hoffmann, H. (n.d.) Markov Chains in Ethiopia. (forthcoming in Kay, P. [ed.]), *Explorations in Mathematical Anthropology*.

Hogbin, H. I. (1930) The Study of Kinship in Primitive Societies, *Man* **30**, 114–115.

Hogbin, H. I. (1939) *Experiments in Civilization*, London: Routledge.

Homans, G. C. (1950) *The Human Group*, New York: Harcourt, Brace and World.

Homans, G. C. (1962) *Sentiments and Activities*, Glencoe, Ill.: The Free Press.

Homans, G. C., and D. Schneider (1955) *Marriage, Authority and Final Causes: A Study of Unilateral Cross-Cousin Marriage*. Glencoe, Ill.: The Free Press.

Howitt, A. W. (1889) Further Notes on the Australian Class Systems, *Journal of the Anthropological Institute* 18, 31–68.

Howitt, A. W. (1906) The Native Tribes of South-East Australia, *Folklore* 17.

Huntingford, G. W. B. (1942) The Social Organization of the Dorobo, *African Studies* 1, 183–200.

Huntingford, G. W. B. (1951) The Social Institutions of the Dorobo, *Anthropos* 46, 1–48.

Huntingford, G. W. B. (1954) The Political Organization of the Dorobo, *Anthropos* 49, 123–148.

Hymes, D. (1964) Discussion of Burling's Paper, *American Anthropologist* 66, 116–119.

Jakobson, R. (1962) *Selected Writings*, Vol. I: Phonology, 's-Gravenhage, Mouton.

Jakobson, R., and M. Halle (1956) *Fundamentals of Language*, Janua Linguarum 1, 's-Gravenhage, Mouton.

Jakobson, R., G. Fant, and M. Halle (1961) *Preliminaries to Speech Analysis: The Distinctive Features and Their Correlates* (4th Printing), Cambridge, Mass.: The M.I.T. Press.

de Josselin de Jong, J. P. B. (1952) *Lévi-Strauss' Theory of Kinship and Marriage*, Leiden, Holland: Rijksmuseum voor Volkenkunden.

Kay, P. (1964) A Guttman Scale of Tahitian Consumer Behavior, *Southwestern Journal of Anthropology* 20, 160–167.

Kay, P. (1965) A Generalization of the Cross/Parallel Distinction, *American Anthropologist* 67, 30–43.

Kay, P. (1966) Comment on Colby (1966).

Kay, P. (1967) On the Multiplicity of Cross/Parallel Distinctions, *American Anthropologist* 69, 83–85.

Keesing, R. (1966) Comment on Colby (1966).

Keesing, R. (1967) Statistical Models and Decision Models of Social Structure: A Kwaio Case, *Ethnology* 4, 1–16.

Kelly, George (1955) *The Psychology of Personal Constructs*, New York: W. W. Norton.

Kemeny, J. G., J. L. Snell, and G. L. Thompson (1962a) *Introduction to Finite Mathematics*, Englewood Cliffs, N. J.: Prentice-Hall.

Kemeny, J. G., J. L. Snell, and G. L. Thompson (1962b) *Mathematical Models in the Social Sciences*, Boston: Ginn & Co.

Kemeny, J. G., J. L. Snell, and G. L. Thompson (1965) *Introduction to Finite Mathematics*, Englewood Cliffs, N. J.: Prentice-Hall.

Kohler, J. (1884) Studien uber Frauengemeinschaft, Frauenraub und Frauenkauf, *Zeitschrift fur vergleichende Rechtswissenschaft* V.

Kroeber, A. L. (1909) Classificatory Systems of Relationship, *Journal of Royal Anthropological Institute* 39, 77–84.

Kroeber, A. L. (1917) California Kinship Systems, *University of California Publications in American Archaeology and Ethnology* 12.

Kroeber, A. L. (1936) Kinship and History, *American Anthropologist* 38, 338–341.

Kroeber, A. L. (1938) Basic and Secondary Patterns of Social Structure, *Journal of the Royal Anthropological Institute* 67, 299–310.

Kroeber, A. L. (1952) *The Nature of Culture*, Chicago: University of Chicago Press.

Kunstadter, P. (1963) A Survey of the Consanguine or Matrifocal Family, *American Anthropologist* 65, 56–66.

Kunstadter, P., R. Buhler, F. F. Stephan, and C. F. Westoff (1963) Demographic Variability and Preferential Marriage Patterns, *American Journal of Physical Anthropology* 21, 511–519.

de Laguna, Frederica (1960) *Selected Papers from the American Anthropologist, 1888–1920*, Evanston, Ill.: Row Peterson.

Landau, H. G. (1951) On Dominance Relations and the Structure of Animal Societies: Effect of Inherent Characteristics, *Bulletin of Mathematical Biophysics* 13, 1–19.

Lane, R. B. (1961) Comment on Goody (The Classification of Double Descent Systems), *Current Anthropology* 2, 15–17.

Lane, R. B., and B. S. Lane (1959) On the Development of Dakota-Iroquois and Crow-Omaha Kinship Terminologies, *Southwestern Journal of Anthropology* 15, 254–265.

Lane, R. B., and B. S. Lane (1962) Implicit Double Descent in Southeast Australia and the Northeastern New Hebrides, *Ethnology* 1, 46–52.

Lawrence, W. E. (1937) Alternating Generations in Australia, in *Studies in the Science of Society*, Murdock, G. P. (ed.), New Haven: Yale University Press.

Lawrence, W. E., and G. P. Murdock (1949) Murngin Social Organization, *American Anthropologist* 53, 37–55.

Lazarsfeld, P. (1961) The Algebra of Dichotomous Systems, in *Studies in Item Analysis and Prediction*, Solomon, H. (ed.), Stanford: Stanford University Press.

Leach, E. R. (1945) Jinghpaw Kinship Terminology, *Journal of the Royal Anthropological Institute* 75, 59–72.

Leach, E. R. (1950) Social Research in Sarawak, *Colonial Research Studies*, I, 1–93, London: HMSO.

Leach, E. R. (1951) The Structural Implications of Matrilateral Cross-Cousin Marriage, *Journal of the Royal Anthropological Institute* 81, 23–55.

Leach, E. R. (1954) *Political Systems of Highland Burma*, Cambridge, Mass.: Harvard University Press.

Leach, E. R. (1957) Aspects of Bridewealth and Marriage Stability Among the Kachin and Lakher, *Man* 57, 59.

Leach, E. R. (1958) Concerning Trobriand Clans and the Kinship Category "Tabu", in *The Developmental Cycle in Domestic Groups*, Goody, Jack (ed.), Cambridge, England: Cambridge University Press.

Leach, E. R. (1960) The Sinhalese of the Dry Zone of Northern Ceylon, in *Social Structure in Southeast Asia*, Murdock, G. P. (ed.), London: Tavistock Publications, 116–126.

Leach, E. R. (1961a) *Pul Eliya*, Cambridge, England: Cambridge University Press.

Leach, E. R. (1961b) *Rethinking Anthropology*, London School of Economics Monographs on Social Anthropology, No. 22. London: The Athlone Press.

Leach, E. R. (1962) Notes on Some Unconsidered Aspects of Double Descent Systems, *Man* 62, 214.

Leach, E. R. (1963) Determinants of Cross-Cousin Marriage, *Man* 63, 76–77.

Leach, E. R. (1964) Anthropological Aspects of Language: Animal Categories and Verbal Abuse, in *New Directions in the Study of Language*, Lenneberg, E. H. (ed.), Cambridge, Mass.: The M.I.T. Press.

Leach, E. R. (1965) Review of *Mythologiques: Le Cru et le Cuit. American Anthropologist* 67, 775 780.

Le Play, F. (1884) *L'Organization de la Famille*, Paris: Dentu, Libraire.

Lesser, A. (1929) Kinship Origins in the Light of Some Distributions, *American Anthropologist* 31, 710–730.

Lévi-Strauss, C. (n.d.) Préface a la Deuxième Édition de *Les Structures Élémentaires de la Parenté*. Ms. Facsimile.

Lévi-Strauss, C. (1936) Contributions a l'Étude de l'Organization Sociale des Indiens Bororo, *Journal de la Société des Américanistes* 28, 269–304.

Lévi-Strauss, C. (1945) L'Analyse Structurale en Linguistique et en Anthropologie, *Word* 1, 1–21.

Lévi-Strauss, C. (1949) *Les Structures Élémentaires de la Parenté*, Paris: Presses Universitaires de France.

Lévi-Strauss, C. (1950) Introduction, in Mauss, M. *Sociologie et Anthropologie*, Paris. Presses Universitaires de France.

Lévi-Strauss, C. (1951) Language and the Analysis of Social Laws, *American Anthropologist* 53, 155–163.

Lévi-Strauss, C. (1953) Social Structure, in *Anthropology Today*, Kroeber, A. L. (ed.), Chicago: University of Chicago Press, 524–554.

Lévi-Strauss, C. (1955) The Structural Study of Myth, *Journal of American Folklore* 78, 428–444.

Lévi-Strauss, C. (1956) Les Organizations Dualistes Existent-Elles? *Bijdragen tot de Taal-, Land-, en Volkenkunde* 112, 99–128.

Lévi-Strauss, C. (1960a) On Manipulated Sociological Models, *Bijdragen tot de Taal-, Land-, en Volkenkunde* 116, 45–54.

Lévi-Strauss, C. (1960b) The Family, in *Man, Culture, and Society*, Shapiro, Harry L. (ed.), New York: Oxford University Press. (First published 1956.)

Lévi-Strauss, C. (1961) Comment on Goody (1961).

Lévi-Strauss, C. (1963a) *Structural Anthropology*, tr. Claire Jacobson and Brook Grundfest Schoepf, New York: Basic Books.

Lévi-Strauss, C. (1963b) The Bear and the Barber, *Journal of the Royal Anthropological Institute* **93**, 1–11.

Lévi-Strauss, C. (1963c) *Totemism* (translated from the French by Rodney Needham), Boston: Beacon Press.

Lévi-Strauss, C. (1964) *Mythologiques: Le Cru et le Cuit*, Paris: Plon.

Lévi-Strauss, C. (1965) The Future of Kinship Studies, *Proceedings of the Royal Anthropological Institute* (1965).

Lévi-Strauss, C. (1966) *The Savage Mind*, Chicago: University of Chicago Press. (originally published 1962)

Lévi-Strauss, C. (1967) *Mythologiques: Du Miel Aux Cendres*. Paris: Plon.

Lewis, I. M. (1965) Problems in the Comparative Study of Unilineal Descent, in *The Relevance of Models for Social Anthropology*, Banton, Michael (ed.) New York: Praeger, 87–112.

Linton, R. (1936) *The Study of Man*, New York: Appleton-Century.

Livingstone, F. B. (1959) A Further Analysis of Purum Social Structure, *American Anthropologist* **61**, 1084–1087.

Livingstone, F. B. (1965) Mathematical Models of Marriage Systems, *Man* **65**, 149–152.

Livingstone, F. B. (1968) The Application of Structural Models to Marriage Systems in Anthropology, in Buchler, I. R., and H. G. Nutini (eds.) (1968).

Longbaugh, Richard (1963) A Category System for Coding Interpersonal Behavior, *Sociometry* **26**, 319–344.

Lounsbury, F. G. (1956) A Semantic Analysis of the Pawnee Kinship Usage, *Language* **32**, 158–194.

Lounsbury, F. G. (1964a) A Formal Account of the Crow- and Omaha-Type Kinship Terminologies, in *Explorations in Cultural Anthropology*, Goodenough, W. H. (ed.), New York: McGraw-Hill.

Lounsbury, F. G. (1964b) The Structural Analysis of Kinship Semantics, in *Proceedings of the Ninth International Congress of Linguists*, Lunt, Horace G. (ed.), The Hague: Mouton, 1073–1093.

Lounsbury, F. G. (1965) Another View of Trobriand Kinship Categories, in *Formal Semantic Analysis*, Hammel, E. A. (ed.), Menasha, Wisc.: 142–185.

Lowie, R. H. (1915) Exogamy and the Classificatory Systems of Relationship, *American Anthropologist* **17**, 223–239.

Lowie, R. H. (1916) Historical and Sociological Interpretation of Kinship Terminologies, *Holmes Anniversary Volume*, 298–300.

Lowie, R. H. (1919) The Matrilineal Complex, *University of California Publications in American Archaeology and Ethnology* **16**, 29–45.

Lowie, R. H. (1920) *Primitive Society*, New York.

Lowie, R. H. (1928) A Note on Relationship Terminologies, *American Anthropologist* **30**, 263–267.

Lowie, R. H. (1929) Relationship Terms, *Encyclopedia Britannica* (14th ed.) London.

Lowie, R. H. (1930) The Omaha and Crow Kinship Terminologies, *Verhandlungen des Internationalen Amerikanisten Kongresses* **24**, 102–108.

Lowie, R. H. (1932) Kinship, *Encyclopedia of the Social Sciences* **VIII**, 570.

Lowie, R. H. (1937) *History of Ethnological Theory*, New York: Holt, Rinehart and Winston.

Lowie, R. H. (1947) *Primitive Society*, New York (2nd ed).

Lowie, R. H. (1948) *Social Organization*, New York: Holt, Rinehart and Winston.

Lubbock, J. (1892) *The Origin of Civilization and the Primitive Condition of Man* (5th ed.) New York.

Macgregor, G. (1937) Ethnology of the Tokelau Islands, *Bulletin of the Bernice P. Bishop Museum* **39**, 127–147.

Maine, Sir Henry (1871) *Ancient Law*, London.

Malinowski, B. (1913) *The Family Among the Australian Aborigines*, London: Hodder. Reprinted with an Introduction by J. A. Barnes, New York: Schocken Books, 1963.

Malinowski, B. (1927) *Sex and Repression in Savage Society*, London: Routledge.

Malinowski, B. (1929) *The Sexual Life of Savages*, London: Routledge.

Malinowski, B. (1930) Kinship, *Man* **30**, 19–29.

Malinowski, B. (1932) *The Sexual Life of Savages*, London: Routledge.

Mauss, M. (1923–24) Essai sur le Don, *L'Année Sociologique* (2ᵉ série). (*The Gift*. Trans. I. Cunnison. Glencoe, Ill. 1954)

Mauss, M. (1950) *Sociologie et Anthropologie*, Paris: Presses Universitaires de France.

Maybury-Lewis, D. (1960) The Analysis of Dual Organizations: A Methodological Critique, *Bijdragen tot de Taal-, Land-, en Volkenkunde* **116**, 2–44.

Maybury-Lewis, D. (1965) Prescriptive Marriage Systems, *Southwestern Journal of Anthropology* **21**, 207–230.

Mayer, P. (1949) *The Lineage Principle in Gusii Society*, International African Institute, Memorandum No. 24.

McAllister, J. Gilbert (1935) *Kiowa-Apache Social Organization*. (Unpub. Ph.D. thesis, University of Chicago, Chicago).

McAllister, J. Gilbert (1937) Kiowa-Apache Social Organization, in Eggan, F. (ed.), 1937, 99–106.

McCulloch, W. S., and W. A. Pitts (1943) A Logical Calculus of the Ideas Immanent in Nervous Activity, *Bulletin of Mathematical Biophysics* **5**, 115–133.

McLennan, J. F. (1886) *Studies in Ancient History*, London.

**McNeill, D.** (1966) Developmental psycholinguistics, in *The Genesis of Language: A Psycholinguistic Approach*. F. Smith and G. A. Miller (eds.), Cambridge, Mass.: The M.I.T. Press.

**Mead, M.** (1942) The Mountain Arapesh, *Anthropological Papers of the American Museum of Natural History* **40**, 163–233.

**Meggitt, M.** (1958) The Enga of the New Guinea Highlands, *Oceania* **28**, 253–330.

**Meggitt, M.** (1965) *The Lineage System of the Mae-Enga of New Guinea*, New York: Barnes and Noble.

**Mehler, J.** (1963) Some effects of grammatical transformations on the recall of English sentences. *Journal of Verbal Learning and Verbal Behavior* **2**, 346–351.

**Mencher, Joan P.,** and **Helen Goldberg** (1967) Kinship and Marriage Regulations Among the Namboodiri Brahmans of Kerala, *Man* n.s. **2**, 87–106.

**Merton, R.** (1957) *Social Theory and Social Structure*, Glencoe, Ill.: Free Press.

**Metzger, D.,** and **G. E. Williams** (1962) Tenejapa Medicine II. Sources and Harbingers of Illness, *Stanford University. Anthropology Research Reports*, Preliminary Report 14.

**Metzger, D.,** and **G. E. Williams** (1963a) A Formal Ethnographic Study of Tenejapa Ladino Weddings, *American Anthropologist* **65**, 1076–1101.

**Metzger, D.,** and **G. E. Williams** (1963b) Tenejapa Medicine I: The Curer, *Southwestern Journal of Anthropology* **19**, 216–234.

**Metzger, D.,** and **G. E. Williams** (1966) Some Procedures and Results in the Study of Native Categories: Tzeltal "Firewood," *American Anthropologist* **68**, 389–407.

**Miller, F.** (1964) Tzotzil Domestic Groups, *Journal of the Royal Anthropological Institute* **94**, 172–182.

**Miller, G. A.** (1953) What is Information Measurement? *American Psychologist* **8**, 3–11.

**Miller, G. A.** (1956) The Magical Number Seven, plus or Minus Two: Some Limits on our Capacity for Processing Information, *Psychological Review* **63**, 81–97.

**Miller, G. A.** (1965) The Magical Number "Seven" plus or Minus Two, in *Readings in the Psychology of Cognition*, Anderson, R. C., and D. P. Ausubel (eds.), New York: Holt, Rinehart and Winston.

**Miller, G. A., E. Galanter,** and **K. Pribram** (1960) *Plans and the Structure of Behavior*, New York: Henry Holt & Co.

**Mitchell, J. Clyde** (1956) *The Yao Village: A Study in the Social Structure of a Nyasaland Tribe*, Manchester: University of Manchester Press.

**Mitchell, W. E.** (1963) Theoretical Problems in the Concept of the Kindred, *American Anthropologist* **65**, 343–354.

**Mitchell, W. E.** (1965) The Kindred and Baby-Bathing in Academe, *American Anthropologist* **67**, 977–985.

**Moon, J. W.** (1963) An Extension of Landau's Theorem on Tournaments, *Pacific Journal of Mathematics* **13**, 1343–1345.

Moore, S. F. (1963) Oblique and Asymmetrical Cross-Cousin Marriage and Crow-Omaha Terminology, *American Anthropologist* **65**, 296–312.

Morgan, L. H. (1870) *Systems of Consanguinity and Affinity of the Human Family*, Smithsonian Contributions to Knowledge, XVII, 1–590.

Morgan, L. H. (1877) *Ancient Society*, New York.

Morris, C. W. (1946) *Signs, Language and Behavior*, Englewood Cliffs, N. J.: Prentice-Hall.

Muller, E. W. (1964) Structure and Statistics: Some Remarks on the Purum Case, *American Anthropologist* **66**, 1377–1386.

Murdock, G. P. (1940) Double Descent, *American Anthropologist* **42**, 555–561.

Murdock, G. P. (1947) Bifurcate Merging, *American Anthropologist* **49**, 56–69.

Murdock, G. P. (1949) *Social Structure*, New York: Macmillan.

Murdock, G. P. (1951) British Social Anthropology, *American Anthropologist* **53**, 465–473.

Murdock, G. P. (1957) World Ethnographic Sample, *American Anthropologist* **59**, 664–687.

Murdock, G. P. (1959) *Africa: Its Peoples and their Culture History*, New York: McGraw-Hill.

Murdock, G. P. (1960) Cognatic Forms of Social Organization, in *Social Structure in Southeast Asia*, Murdock, G. P. (ed.), 1–14.

Murdock, G. P. (1964) The Kindred, Brief Communication in *American Anthropologist* **66**, 129–132.

Nagel, E. (1961) *The Structure of Science*, New York: Harcourt Brace.

Naroll, R. (1961) Two Solutions to Galton's Problem, *Philosophy of Science* **28**, 16–39.

Naroll, R. (1964) A Fifth Solution to Galton's Problem, *American Anthropologist* **66**, 863–867.

Naroll, R., and R. G. D'Andrade (1963) Two Further Solutions to Galton's Problem, *American Anthropologist* **65**, 1053–1067.

Needham, R. (1954) The Systems of Teknonyms and Death–Names of the Penan, *Southwestern Journal of Anthropology* **10**.

Needham, R. (1958a) The Formal Analysis of Prescriptive Patrilateral Cross-Cousin Marriage, *Southwestern Journal of Anthropology* **14**, 199–219.

Needham, R. (1958b) A Structural Analysis of Purum Society, *American Anthropologist* **60**, 75–101.

Needham, R. (1959a) Vaiphei Social Structure, *Southwestern Journal of Anthropology* **15**, 396–406.

Needham, R. (1959b) Mourning Terms, *Bijdragen tot de Taal-, Land-, en Volkenkunde* **115**.

Needham, R. (1960a) Descent Systems and Ideal Language, *Philosophy of Science* **27**, 96–101.

Needham, R. (1960b) A Structural Analysis of Aimol Society, *Bijdragen tot de Taal-, Land-, en Volkenkunde* **116**.

**Needham, R.** (1960c) Chawte Social Structure, *American Anthropologist* **62**, 236–253.

**Needham, R.** (1961) Notes on the Analysis of Asymmetric Alliance, *Bijdragen tot de Taal-, Land-, en Volkenkunde* **117**.

**Needham, R.** (1962a) *Structure and Sentiment: A Test Case in Social Anthropology*, Chicago: University of Chicago Press.

**Needham, R.** (1962b) Genealogy and Category in Wikmunkan Society, *Ethnology* **1**, 225–264.

**Needham, R.** (1963) Symmetry and Asymmetry in Prescriptive Alliance, *Bijdragen tot de Taal-, Land-, en Volkenkunde* **119**.

**Needham, R.** (1964) Explanatory Notes on Prescriptive Alliance and the Purum, *American Anthropologist* **66**, 1377–1386.

**Needham, R.** (1966) Comments on the Analysis of Purum Social Structure, *American Anthropologist* **68**, 171–177.

**Nimuendajú, C.,** and **R. H. Lowie** (1937) The Dual Organization of the Ramkokamekra (Canella) of Northern Brazil, *American Anthropologist* **39**, 565–582.

**Nutini, H. G.** (n.d.) On the Concepts of Epistemological Ordering and Co-ordinative Definitions. Ms. University of Pittsburgh.

**Nutini, H. G.** (1965) Some Considerations on the Nature of Social Structure and Model Building: A Critique of Claude Lévi-Strauss and Edmund Leach, *American Anthropologist* **67**, 707–731.

**Nutini, H. G.** (1967) Lévi-Strauss' Conception of Science, in *Festschrift for Claude Lévi-Strauss*, Pouillon, J., and P. Maranda (eds.), Paris: Mouton. (forthcoming).

**O'Nell, C.,** and **H. A. Selby** (1968) Sex Roles and the Incidence of *Susto* in two Zapotec Indian Communities, *Ethnology* **7**, 95–105.

**Opler, M. E.** (1937a) Apache Data Concerning the Relation of Kinship Terminology to Social Classification, *American Anthropologist* **39**, 201–212.

**Opler, M. E.** (1937b) An Outline of Chiricahua Apache Social Organization, in Eggan, F. (ed.), 1937, 173–214.

**Otterbein, K. F.** (1963a) The Family Organization of the Andros Islanders: A Case Study of the Mating System and Household Composition of a Community in the Bahama Islands. Unpublished Ph.D. dissertation. University of Pittsburgh.

**Otterbein, K. F.** (1963b) The Household Composition of the Andros Islanders. *Social and Economic Studies* **12**, 78–83.

**Otterbein, K. F.** (1965) Caribbean Family Organization: A Comparative Analysis, *American Anthropologist* **67**, 66–81.

**Park, G. K.** (1962) Sons and Lovers: Characterological Requisites of the Roles in a Peasant Society, *Ethnology* **I**, 412–424.

**Parsons, T.** (1943) The Kinship System of the Contemporary United States, *American Anthropologist* **45**, 22–38.

Parsons, T. (1949) *The Structure of Social Action*, Glencoe, Illinois: The Free Press.

Parsons, T. (1954) The Incest Taboo in Relation to Social Structure and the Socialization of the Child, *British Journal of Sociology* 5, 101–117.

Parsons, T., and Robert F. Bales (1955) *Family, Socialization and Interaction Process*, Glencoe, Illinois: The Free Press.

Pehrson, R. N. (1954) Bilateral Kin Groupings as a Structural Type, *Journal of East Asiatic Studies* 3, 199–202.

Pehrson, R. N. (1957) *The Bilateral Network of Social Relations in Könkämä Lapp District*, Bloomington: Indiana University Research Center in Anthropology, Folklore, and Linguistics.

Peranio, R. (1961) Descent, Descent Line and Descent Group in Cognatic Social Systems, in *Proceedings of the Annual Spring Meeting of the American Ethnological Association*, Garfield, V. E. (ed.), Seattle: University of Washington Press.

Pospisil, L. (1960) The Kapauku Papuans and their Kinship Organization, *Oceania* 30, 188–209.

Pospisil, L., and W. S. Laughlin (1963) Kinship Terminology and Kindred among the Nuniamut Eskimo, *Ethnology* 3, 180–189.

Pouwer, J. (1960) Loosely Structured Societies, in Netherlands New Guinea, *Bijdragen tot de Taal-, Land-, en Volkenkunde* 116, 109–118.

Powdermaker, H. (1933) *Life in Lesu*, Smithsonian Institution, New York.

Quastler, H. (ed.) (1953) *Essays on the Use of Information Theory in Biology*, Urbana, Ill.: University of Illinois Press.

Quastler, H. (1955) *Information Theory in Psychology: Problems and Methods*, Glencoe, Illinois: The Free Press of Glencoe.

Quimby, G. I. (1946) Natchez Social Structure as an Instrument of Assimilation, *American Anthropologist* 48, 134–136.

Radcliffe-Brown, A. R. (1913) Three Tribes of Western Australia, *Journal of the Royal Anthropological Institute* 43, 143–194.

Radcliffe-Brown, A. R. (1924) The Mother's Brother in South Africa, *South African Journal of Science* 21, 542–555.

Radcliffe-Brown, A. R. (1927) The Regulation of Marriage in Ambrym, *Journal of the Royal Anthropological Institute* 57, 343–348.

Radcliffe-Brown, A. R. (1929) Bilateral Descent, *Man* 29, 199–200.

Radcliffe-Brown, A. R. (1930) The Social Organization of the Australian Tribes, *Oceania* 1, 34–63, 206–246, 322–341, 426–456.

Radcliffe-Brown, A. R. (1935a) Kinship Terminologies in California, *American Anthropologist* 37, 530–534.

Radcliffe-Brown, A. R. (1935b) Patrilineal and Matrilineal Succession, *The Iowa Law Review* 20, 286–303.

Radcliffe-Brown, A. R. (1941) The Study of Kinship Systems, *Journal of the Royal Anthropological Institute* 71, 1–18.

Radcliffe-Brown, A. R. (1950) Introduction, in *African Systems of Kinship and*

*Marriage*, Radcliffe-Brown, A. R., and D. Forde (eds.), London: Oxford University Press.

**Radcliffe-Brown, A. R.** (1951) Murngin Social Organization, *American Anthropologist* **53**, 37–55.

**Radcliffe-Brown, A. R.** (1953) Dravidian Kinship Terminology, *Man* **53**, 112.

**Radcliffe-Brown, A. R.** (1959) *Structure and Function in Primitive Society*, Glencoe, Ill.: The Free Press of Glencoe. (2nd ed. 1965).

**Radcliffe-Brown, A. R.** (1964) *Method in Social Anthropology*, Glencoe, Ill.: The Free Press.

**Radcliffe-Brown, A. R., and D. Forde** (eds.) (1950) *African Systems of Kinship and Marriage*, London: Oxford University Press.

**Radin, Paul** (1923) The Winnebago Tribe, 37*th Annual Report, Bureau of American Ethnology* 1915–1916. Washington, D. C.

**Rapaport, A.** (1949) Outline of a Probabilistic Approach to Animal Sociology, *Bulletin of Mathematical Biophysics* **11**, 183–196, 273–281.

**Rapaport, A.** (1955) Application of Information Networks to a Theory of Vision, *Bulletin of Mathematical Biophysics* **17**, 15–33.

**Rapaport, A.** (1957) Comment: The Stochastic and the "Teleological" Rationales of Certain Distributions and the So-Called Principle of Least Effort, *Behavioral Science* **2**, 147–161.

**Rapaport, A.** (1960) *Fights, Games and Debates*, Ann Arbor, Mich.: The University of Michigan Press.

**Rapaport, A.** (1963) Mathematical Models of Social Interaction, in *Handbook of Mathematical Psychology*, Luce, D. R., R. R. Bush, E. Galanter (eds.), New York: John Wiley & Sons.

**Rattray, R. S.** (1932) *Tribes of the Ashanti Hinterland*, 2 Vols. Oxford.

**Richards, Audrey** (1950) Variations in Family Structure among the Central Bantu, in *African Systems of Kinship and Marriage*, Radcliffe-Brown, A. R., and D. Forde (eds.), London: Oxford University Press.

**Rivers, W. H. R.** (1914) *Kinship and Social Organization*, London.

**Rivers, W. H. R.** (1915) Kin, Kinship, *Encyclopedia of Religion and Ethics*, ed., J. Hastings **VII**, 706.

**Rivers, W. H. R.** (1924) *Social Organization*, London: Kegan Paul.

**Robinson, Marguerite S.** (1962) Complementary Filiation and Marriage in the Trobriand Islands: A Re-examination of Malinowski's Material, in *Marriage in Tribal Societies*, Fortes, Meyer (ed.), Cambridge, England: University Press.

**Romney, A. K.** (n.d.) *Social Structure: The Collection and Interpretation of Data*, New York: Holt, Rinehart and Winston. (in press)

**Romney, A. K.** (1961) Social Organization, in *Biennial Review of Anthropology*, Siegel, B. J. (ed.), Stanford: Stanford University Press.

**Romney, A. K.** (1965) Kalmuk Mongol and the Classification of Lineal Kinship Terminologies, in *Formal Semantic Analysis*, Hammel, E. A. (ed.), Menasha, Wisc.: American Anthropological Association.

Romney, A. K., and R. G. D'Andrade (1964a) Cognitive Aspects of English Kin Terms, *American Anthropologist* 66, Part II, No. 3, 146–170.

Romney, A. K., and R. G. D'Andrade (eds.) (1964b) Transcultural Studies in Cognition, Special Issue of the *American Anthropologist* 66, No. 5, Part 2.

Romney, A. K., and P. J. Epling (1958) A Simplified Model of Kariera Kinship, *American Anthropologist* 60, 59–74.

Rudner, R. S. (1966) *Philosophy of Social Science*, Englewood Cliffs, N. J.: Prentice-Hall.

Ryan, D. J. (1959) Clan Formation in the Mendi Valley, *Oceania* 29, 79–90.

Sahlins, M. (1961) The Segmentary Lineage: An Organization of Predatory Expansion, *American Anthropologist* 63, 322–345.

Sahlins, M. (1963a) Remarks on Social Structure in South East Asia, *Journal of Polynesian Society* 72, 39–50.

Sahlins, M. (1963b) Poor Man, Rich Man, Big Man, Chief: Political Types in Melanesia and Polynesia, *Comparative Studies in Society and History* 5, 285–303.

Salisbury, R. F. (1956) Unilineal Descent Groups in the New Guinea Highlands, *Man* 56, 2.

Sapir, E. (1916) Terms of Relationship and the Levirate, *American Anthropologist* 18, 327–337.

Scheffler, H. W. (1965) *Choiseul Island Social Structure*, Berkeley and Los Angeles: University of California Press.

Scheffler, H. W. (1966) Ancestor Worship in Anthropology: Or Observations on Descent and Descent Groups, *Current Anthropology* 7, 541–551.

Scheffler, H. W. (1967) On Scaling Kinship Terminologies, *Southwestern Journal of Anthropology* 23, 159–175.

Schneider, D. M. (1953) A Note on Bride Wealth and the Stability of Marriage, *Man* 53, Article 75.

Schneider, D. M. (1961) The Distinctive Features of Matrilineal Descent Systems, in *Matrilineal Kinship*, Schneider, D. M., and Kathleen Gough (eds.), Berkeley and Los Angeles: University of California Press.

Schneider, D. M. (1964) The Nature of Kinship, *Man* 64, 217.

Schneider, D. M. (1965a) Some Muddles in the Models: Or, How The System Really Works, in *The Relevance of Models for Social Anthropology*, Banton, Michael (ed.), New York: Praeger.

Schneider, D. M. (1965b) American Kin Terms for Kinsmen: A Critique of Goodenough's Componential Analysis of Yankee Kinship Terminology, in *Formal Semantic Analysis*, Hammel, E. A. (ed.). Special edition of the *American Anthropologist* Vol. 67, No. 5, part 2.

Schneider, D. M. (1967) Kinship and Culture: Descent and Filiation as Cultural Constructs, *Southwestern Journal of Anthropology* 23, 65–73.

Schneider, D. M., and Kathleen Gough (eds.) (1961) *Matrilineal Kinship*, Berkeley and Los Angeles: University of California Press.

Schneider, D. M., and G. C. Homans (1955) The American Kinship System, *American Anthropologist* 57, 1194–1208.

Selby, H. A. (1966) Social Structure and Deviant Behavior in Sto. Tomas Mazaltepec. Unpublished Ph.D. Thesis. Stanford, California: Stanford University.

Selby, H. A., and I. R. Buchler (1967) The Mating Game in Mazaltepec: A Game Theoretic and Linear Programming Analysis. Paper read at the Annual Meeting of the American Anthropological Association. Washington, D. C.

Seligman, B. Z. (1927) Bilateral Descent and the Formation of Marriage Classes, *Journal of the Royal Anthropological Institute* 57, 349–375.

Seligman, B. Z. (1929) Incest and Descent, *Journal of the Royal Anthropological Institute* 59, 231–272.

Seligman, C. G. (1932) *Pagan Tribes of the Nilotic Sudan*, London.

Service, E. R. (1960) Sociocentric Relationship Terms and the Australian Class System, in *Essays in the Science of Culture*, Dole, G. E., and R. L. Carneiro (eds.), New York: Thomas Y. Crowell Co.

Service, E. R. (1962) *Primitive Social Organization: An Evolutionary Perspective*, New York: Random House.

Service, E. R., and Helen Service (1954) *Tobati, Paraguayan Town*, Chicago: The University of Chicago Press.

Simpson, G. G. (1961) *Principles of Animal Taxonomy*, New York: Columbia.

Skinner, B. F. (1957) *Verbal Behavior*, New York: Appleton-Century-Crofts.

Smith, M. G. (1962) *West Indian Family Structure*, Seattle: University of Washington Press.

Smith, R. T. (1956) *The Negro Family in British Guiana: Family Structure and Social Status in the Villages*, London: Cambridge University Press.

Smith, R. T. (1957) The Family in the Caribbean, in *Caribbean Studies: A Symposium*, Rubin, Vera (ed.), Jamaica: Institute of Social and Economic Research, 67–75.

Solien, Nancie L. (1959) The Consanguineal Household of the Black Carib of Central America. Unpub. Ph.D. dissertation, University of Michigan.

Solien, Nancie L. (1961) Family Organization in Five Types of Migratory Labor, *American Anthropologist* 63, 1264–1280.

Sousberghe, L. de, and Uribe, C. R. (1962) Nomenclature et Structure de Parenté des Indiens Tzeltal (Mexique), *L'Homme* 2, 102–120.

Stevens, S. S. (1962) Mathematics, Measurement and Psychophysics, in *Handbook of Experimental Psychology*, Stevens, S. S. (ed.), New York: John Wiley & Sons.

Sturtevant, W. (1960) Seminole Medicine Maker, in *In the Company of Man*, Casagrande, J. B. (ed.), New York: Harper and Row.

Swadesh, M. (1946) Chitimacha, in *Linguistic Structures of Native North America*, Hoijer, H. (ed.), New York: Viking Fund.

Swanton, J. R. (1911) Indian Tribes of the Lower Mississippi Valley, *Bulletin of the Bureau of American Ethnology* 43, 1–387.

**Tait, David** (1956) The Family, Household and Minor Lineage of the Konkomba, *Africa* **26,** 219–248; 332–341.

**Tax, S.** (1937) From Lafitau to Radcliffe-Brown: A Short History of the Study of Social Organization, in Eggan, F. (ed.) (1937), 445–481.

**Tax, S.** (1955a) Some Problems of Social Organization, in *Social Anthropology of North American Tribes*, Eggan, F. (ed.). Enlarged Edition. Chicago: University of Chicago Press.

**Tax, S.** (1955b) The Social Organization of the Fox Indians, in *Social Anthropology of North American Tribes*, Eggan, F. (ed.). Enlarged Edition. Chicago: University of Chicago Press.

**Thompson, R. A.** (n.d.) A Programmatic Approach to Formal Elicitation. Ms. University of Texas. Austin, Texas.

**Tyler, S.** (1966) Parallel/Cross: An Evaluation of Definitions, *Southwestern Journal of Anthropology* **22,** 416–432.

**Tylor, E. B.** (1889) On a Method of Investigating the Development of Institutions; Applied to the Laws of Marriage and Descent, *Journal of the Royal Anthropological Institute* **18,** 245–272.

**Tylor, E. B.** (1891) *Review* of: E. Westermarck, The History of Human Marriage, *The Academy* **40,** 288–289.

**Unwin, J. D.** (1929) The Classificatory System of Relationship, *Man* **29,** Art 124.

**Unwin, J. D.** (1930) Kinship, *Man* **30,** Art. 61.

**Van Gennep** (1906) *Mythes et Légendes d'Australie,* Paris.

**Vogt, E.** (ed.) (1965) *Los Zinacantecos.* Mexico City: Instituto Nacional Indigenista.

**von Neumann, J.,** and **O. Morgenstern** (1964) *Theory of Games and Economic Behavior,* Princeton, N. J.: Princeton University Press. 4th Ed.

**Vreeland, A. H.** (1953) *Mongol Community and Kinship Structure,* New Haven: HRAF Press.

**Wallace, A. F. C.** (1961) On Being Just Complicated Enough, *Proceedings of the National Academy of Sciences* **47**(4), 458–464.

**Wallace, A. F. C.** (1962) Culture and Cognition, *Science* **135,** 351–357.

**Wallace, A. F. C.,** and **John Atkins** (1960) The Meaning of Kinship Terms, *American Anthropologist* **62,** 58–80.

**Ward, L. F.** (1921) *Pure Sociology,* 2nd ed., New York.

**Warner, W. L.** (1958) *A Black Civilization,* (rev. ed.), New York: Harper and Bros.

**Weaver, W.** (1962) Recent Contributions to the Mathematical Theory of Communication, in *The Mathematical Theory of Communication,* Shannon, C. E., and W. Weaver (eds.), Urbana, Ill.: University of Illinois Press.

**Webb, T. Theodor** (1933) Tribal Organization in East Arnhem Land, *Oceania* **3,** 406–411.

**Weber, M.** (1949) Objectivity in Social Science and Social Policy, in *On the Methodology of the Social Sciences,* Shils, E. A., and H. A. Finch (tr. and ed.), Glencoe, Illinois: The Free Press of Glencoe.

Weil, A. (1949) On the Algebraic Study of Certain Types of Marriage Laws (Murngin System), in *Les Structures Elémentaires de la Parenté*. C. Lévi-Strauss, Tr. and appended to White, H. (1963), *An Anatomy of Kinship: Mathematical Models for Structures of Cumulated Roles*, Englewood Cliffs, N. J.: Prentice-Hall.

Weinreich, U. (1963) On the Semantic Structure of Language, in *Universals of Language*, J. Greenberg (ed.), Cambridge, Mass.: M.I.T. Press, 114–171.

Werner, O. (n.d.1) Method and Theory in Ethnoscience. 90 pp. Mimeo.

Werner, O. (n.d.2) Taxonomy and Paradigm: Two Semantic Structures. Ms. Northwestern University.

Westermarck, E. (1891) *History of Human Marriage*. London.

White, H. (1963) *An Anatomy of Kinship: Mathematical Models for Structures of Cumulated Roles*, Englewood Cliffs, N. J.: Prentice-Hall.

White, L. A. (1939) A Problem in Kinship Terminology, *American Anthropologist* **41**, 566–573.

White, L. A. (ed.) (1959a) *Lewis Henry Morgan. The Indian Journals* 1859–62, Ann Arbor, Mich.: University of Michigan Press.

White, L. A. (1959b) *The Evolution of Culture*, New York: McGraw-Hill.

Wiener, N. (1965) *Cybernetics: Or Control and Communication in the Animal and the Machine*, Cambridge, Mass.: The M.I.T. Press (2nd ed.).

Wilder, W. (1964) Confusion vs. Classification in the Study of Purum Society, *American Anthropologist* **66**, 1365–1371.

Winter, E. H. (1956) *Bwamba*, Cambridge, Mass.: Harvard University Press.

Worsley, P. M. (1955) The Kinship System of the Tallensi: A Re-evaluation, *Journal of the Royal Anthropological Institute* **86**, 37–75.

Yalman, N. (1962) The Structure of the Sinhalese Kindred: A Re-examination of the Dravidian Terminology, *American Anthropologist* **64**, 548–575.

Zelditch, Morris (1955) Role Differentiation in the Nuclear Family, in T. Parsons, R. Bales, M. Zelditch, and J. Olds, *Family Socialization and Interaction Process*, Glencoe, Ill.: The Free Press.

# Author
# Index

Aberle, D., 254, 319
Ackerman, C., 126, 319
Adams, R. N., 21, 24, 25–26, 319
Aginsky, B., 247, 319
Albertus Magnus, 299
Aoki, H., 166, 171, 173, 319
Appell, G. N., 89, 319
Arensberg, C. M., 28, 319
Aristarchus, 148
Atkins, J., 100, 102, 181, 183–90,
    196, 197, 198–205, 214, 300, 319,
    341
Attneave, F., 291, 292, 293, 319
Austin, G. A., 216, 217, 321

Bachofen, J. J., 29, 320
Bales, R. F., 30, 320, 337
Barker, R. W., 320
Barnes, J. A., 3, 33, 34, 80–81, 99,
    139, 320
Barth, F., 17, 320
Bateson, G., 55
Beattie, J. H. M., 1, 130, 254, 320
Befu, H., 1, 320
Bendig, A. W., 291, 320
Berge, C., 100, 101, 320
Berlin, B., 166, 192, 193, 196, 211–12,
    320

Berndt, R., 297, 320
Berting, J., 126, 320
Blake, J., 24, 320
Blehr, O., 87, 320
Boas, F., 17
Bohannon, L., 77, 78, 133, 320
Bohannon, P., 78, 320, 321
Braithwaite, R. B., 103, 120, 180, 321
Breedlove, D. F., 166, 193, 196,
    211–12, 320
Briffault, R., 2, 321
Bright, W., 256–58, 321
Brookfield, H. C., 77, 79, 321
Brown, P., 77, 78, 79, 81, 321
Brown, R., 182, 183, 321
Bruner, J. S., 216–17, 321
Buchler, I. R., 33, 34, 35, 82, 100,
    102, 153, 169, 179, 207, 249, 280,
    303–304, 312, 313–14, 321, 340
Buhler, R., 158, 330
Burling, R., 136, 205–206, 322
Bush, R. R., 151, 322

Cancian, F., 29–31, 32, 322
Cartwright, N., 162, 164, 328
Chafe, W. L., 199–200, 201, 322
Chomsky, N., 37, 38, 166, 315, 322
Clarke, E., 24, 322

Coale, A. J., 27, 54, 322
Cohen, Y. A., 24, 322
Colby, B., 322
Coleman, J., 83, 322
Conklin, H. C., 7, 89, 192–93, 195,
    196, 206, 207, 208–209, 211, 302,
    322
Copernicus, 148
Coult, A. D., 120, 122–23, 124, 322
Cowgill, U., 126, 322
Cumming, E., 323
Curtis, L., 100–102, 319

D'Andrade, R. G., 136, 181, 182, 183,
    184–90, 197, 198, 207–208, 232,
    262, 273, 335, 339
Dahlberg, G., 314, 323
Das, T. C., 267, 323
Davenport, W., 1, 24, 86, 88, 91, 98,
    153, 323
Davis, K., 58, 323
Deacon, A. B., 283, 299, 323
Dorsey, J. O., 254, 323
Driberg, J. H., 254, 323
Drucker, P., 99, 323
DuBois, C., 253, 254, 323
Dumont, L., 15, 105, 135, 136–39,
    142, 145–47, 220, 233, 234, 235,
    275, 282, 283, 284–88, 323
Durbin, M., 194, 201, 202, 209, 323
Durkheim, E., 2, 15–16, 93, 113, 281,
    282, 283, 323

Eggan, F., 1, 14, 252, 254, 323, 324
Elkin, A. P., 141, 143, 284, 297, 299,
    324
Emmeneau, M. B., 135, 136, 324
Epling, P. J., 136, 145, 148, 237, 293,
    294–95, 339
Evans-Pritchard, E. E., 4–6, 22,
    72–75, 89, 99, 102, 303, 324, 325
Eyde, D. B., 247, 248, 324

Fallers, L. A., 29, 80, 324
Fant, G., 169
Faron, L. C., 267, 324
Fathauer, G. H., 41–42, 324

Feigenbaum, E. A., 216, 324
Feldman, J., 216, 324
Firth, R., 1, 35, 81, 90, 91, 324
Fischer, J. L., 67, 155, 156, 157, 325
Fischer, R. A., 162
Fison, L., 3, 325
Fodor, J., 37, 325
Forde, D., 338
Fortes, M., 1, 53, 55, 56, 58, 69, 70,
    71, 73, 77, 81, 92, 102, 114, 130,
    131–34, 325
Fortune, R., 325
Fox, R. B., 325
Frake, C. O., 196, 206, 209, 304, 305,
    325
Frazer, J. G., 2, 3, 9, 16, 325
Frazier, E. F., 24, 325
Freeman, J. D., 63–67, 87, 89, 98,
    133, 134, 326
Freilich, M., 24, 326
Fried, M. H., 70, 71, 72, 82, 326
Fulkerson, D. R., 159, 326
Fustel de Coulanges, N.-D., 9, 326

Galanter, E., 216, 308, 309, 334
Galen, 299
Galton, F., 181, 281, 283, 326
Gellner, E., 33–35, 326
Geohegan, W. H., 126, 326
Gibbs, J. L., 77, 326
Gifford, E. W., 11, 247, 254, 326
Gilbert, J. P., 158, 314, 326
Gilbert, W. H., 14, 326
Glasse, R. M., 99, 326
Gluckman, M., 29, 80, 81–83, 131,
    326
Goldberg, H., 136, 334
Goldberg, S., 151, 155, 157, 327
Goodenough, W. H., 20, 49, 52, 67,
    68, 81, 86, 88, 89, 90, 91, 92, 93,
    180, 181, 182, 183, 184, 185–87,
    188, 189, 196, 199, 204, 327
Goodnow, J. J., 216–17, 321
Goody, J., 55, 81, 133, 134, 281, 282,
    283, 327
Gough, K., 24, 29, 133, 134, 138, 327,
    339

Green, B. F., 176, 327
Greenberg, J. H., 208, 327
Gregg, J. R., 193, 209, 211, 327
Gregor, A. J., 119, 328
Guilbaud, G. Th., 286
Guttman, L., 83, 174–77, 179, 328

Habenstein, R. W., 322
Haddon, A. C., 328
Halle, M., 169, 170, 329
Hallowell, A. I., 1
Hammel, E. A., 44, 53, 55, 57–58,
    158, 314, 326, 328
Harary, F., 162, 164, 328
Hart, C. W., 156, 328
Heath, A. E., 328
Held, D. J., 81, 328
Hermes Trismegistus, 299
Herskovits, F. S., 24, 328
Herskovits, M. J., 24, 328
Hertz, H. R., 120, 328
Hocart, A. M., 5, 7, 328
Hockett, C. F., 258, 328
Hoffmann, H., 61–63, 67, 328
Hogbin, I., 7, 99, 328, 329
Homans, G. C., 93, 115, 120–23,
    124–25, 163, 329, 340
Hopkins, N. A., 274
Howitt, A. W., 3, 283, 329
Huntingford, G. W. B., 254, 329
Hymes, D., 206, 329

Jakobson, R., 169, 170, 309, 329
de Josselin de Jong, J. P. B., 140, 145,
    147, 282, 283, 297, 329

Kay, P., 126, 181, 193, 194, 195, 196,
    197, 201, 209, 210, 214–16, 220,
    232, 240, 242, 244–45, 289, 326,
    329
Keesing, R., 95, 192, 329
Kelly, G., 189, 329
Kemeny, J. G., 59–61, 151, 153, 163,
    329, 330
Kimball, S. T., 28, 319
Kirchoff, P., 175
Kohler, J., 2, 330

Kroeber, A. L., 5, 6–8, 10, 93, 171,
    182, 252, 300, 330
Kunstadter, P., 24, 158, 314, 330

deLaguna, F., 330
Landau, H. G., 330
Lane, B. S., 247, 253, 281, 282, 283,
    330
Lane, R. B., 247, 253, 281, 282, 283,
    330
Laughlin, W. S., 88, 337
Lawrence, W. E., 140, 141, 145, 281,
    283, 285, 286, 297, 330
Lazarsfeld, P., 208, 209, 330
Leach, E. R., 7, 14, 20, 39–44, 55, 73,
    76, 81, 83–84, 85–86, 87, 91, 92,
    100, 103, 123–24, 126, 131–34,
    153, 154, 156, 160, 169, 180, 219,
    243, 267, 297, 314, 315, 330, 331
Le Play, F., 28, 331
Lesser, A., 247, 252, 331
Lévi-Strauss, C., 2, 15, 16–17, 29,
    31–32, 55, 73, 93, 100, 103,
    105–14, 117–120, 121, 123, 124,
    125, 126, 127, 130, 134, 142–46,
    149, 151, 153, 155, 156, 159, 160,
    169, 235, 249, 250, 252, 256, 275,
    279, 281, 282, 285, 286, 291, 293,
    297, 299, 300, 302, 305, 306, 308,
    309, 312, 316, 331, 332
Levy, M., 27
Lewis, I. M., 82–83, 332
Linton, R., 1, 332
Livingstone, F. B., 126, 151, 159–60,
    161–63, 332
Longbaugh, R., 30, 332
Lounsbury, F., 5, 7, 14, 20, 23, 36–40,
    43–45, 175, 193, 194, 196, 199,
    200, 220, 225, 231, 234, 244, 245,
    252, 254, 256–62, 266–267, 277,
    303
Lowie, R. H., 1, 3, 6, 9–10, 12, 14, 76,
    175, 247, 252, 299, 332, 333, 336
Lubbock, J., 2, 333

MacGregor, G., 254, 333
Maine, H., 70, 333

Malinowski, B., 3–4, 5–7, 23, 34, 37, 39–41, 55, 108, 333
Mauss, M., 2, 15, 16–17, 93, 105, 113, 333
Maybury-Lewis, D., 106, 110–11, 143, 148, 333
Mayer, P., 71, 333
McAllister, J. G., 14, 333
McCulloch, W. S., 280, 333
McKinlay, R. M., 313, 321
McLennan, J. F., 3, 9, 333
McNeill, D., 37, 334
Mead, M., 55, 334
Meggitt, M., 77, 78–79, 80, 99, 254, 334
Mehler, J., 37, 334
Mencher, J. P., 136, 334
Merton, R., 334
Metzger, D., 21–22, 334
Miller, F., 55–56, 68, 216, 334
Miller, G. A., 280, 299, 302, 305, 308, 309, 334
Minnick, J., 256–58, 321
Mitchell, J. C., 53, 89, 334
Mitchell, W. E., 334
Moon, J. W., 159, 334
Moore, S. F., 247, 248, 335
Morgan, L. H., 1, 2, 3–4, 9, 36, 220, 251, 283, 335
Morgenstern, O., 311, 313, 341
Morris, S. F., 182, 335
Muller, E. W., 335
Murdock, G. P., 1, 6, 7, 10–11, 12–13, 14, 19, 20, 22, 23–24, 26, 35, 37, 38, 44, 61, 70–71, 76, 85, 87, 89, 91, 95, 98, 100, 140–41, 145, 175, 233, 247, 248, 252, 253, 276, 281, 297, 330, 335

Nagel, E., 116, 120, 335
Naroll, R., 181, 335
Needham, R., 20, 33, 55, 105, 121, 124–26, 163, 169, 243, 267–68, 269, 270–71, 275–76, 335, 336
Nimuendajú, C., 106, 299, 336
Norman, R. Z., 162, 164
Nutini, H. G., 17, 102, 107, 114, 119, 153, 164, 201, 312, 321, 336

O'Nell, C., 336
Opler, M. E., 11, 14, 336
Otterbein, K. F., 24, 25, 58, 336

Park, G. K., 28, 336
Parsons, T., 336, 337
Pehrson, R. N., 88, 337
Peranio, R., 90, 337
Philipsen, H., 126, 320
Pitts, W. A., 280, 333
Pliny, 299
Pospisil, L., 88, 230, 231, 248, 337
Postal, P. M., 247, 324
Pouwer, J., 81, 337
Powdermaker, H., 231, 337
Pribram, K., 216, 308, 309, 334
Ptolemy, 148

Quastler, H., 280, 337
Quimby, G. I., 156, 337

Radcliffe-Brown, A. R., 2, 4, 10, 12–14, 31, 55, 70–72, 75–76, 85–86, 92, 102, 112, 113, 130, 133, 135–36, 139, 140–43, 145, 149, 219, 235, 236, 251, 252, 281, 282, 283, 284, 286, 289, 296, 337, 338
Radin, P., 107, 338
Rapaport, A., 151, 152, 153–55, 159, 161, 280, 302, 303, 338
Rattray, R. S., 77, 338
Raven, P. H., 166, 192, 193, 196, 211–12, 320
Richards, A., 73, 338
Rivers, W. H. R., 2, 9, 13, 14, 33, 85, 247, 252, 338
Robinson, M. S., 41, 338
Romney, A. K., 1, 5, 20, 21, 48, 136, 145, 148, 181, 182, 183, 184–90, 197, 198, 207–08, 232, 237, 241, 257, 261–67, 273–74, 277, 289, 293, 294–95, 338, 339
Rudner, R. S., 76, 116, 118, 119, 339
Ryan, D. J., 99, 339

Sahlins, M., 72, 81, 98–99, 100, 339
Salisbury, R. F., 81, 339
Sapir, E., 247, 339
Scheffler, H. W., 9, 87, 94, 176, 178, 339
Schneider, D. M., 15, 33, 45, 75, 80, 90, 112, 115, 120–23, 124, 125–26, 129, 134, 163, 199, 323, 329, 339, 340
Selby, H. A., 49, 68, 86, 280, 321, 336, 340
Seligman, B. Z., 4, 6, 281, 282, 283, 340
Seligman, C. G., 254, 340
Service, E. R., 24, 283, 284, 300, 340
Service, H. S., 24, 340
Shannon, C. E., 300, 301, 304, 305
Simpson, G. G., 209, 340
Skinner, B. F., 37, 340
Smith, M. G., 24, 340
Smith, R. T., 24, 53, 340
Snell, J. L., 59–61, 151, 153, 163, 329, 330
Solien, N. L., 24, 25, 340
Sousberghe, L. de, 254, 259, 340
Spier, L., 175
Stephan, F. F., 158, 330
Stevens, S. S., 298, 340
Sturtevant, W., 302, 340
Swadesh, M., 340
Swanton, J. R., 155, 156, 158, 340

Tait, D., 53, 341
Tax, S., 13–14, 252, 254, 341
Thompson, G. L., 59–61, 151, 329, 330
Thompson, R. A., 21, 281, 341
Tyler, S., 233, 242–44, 341
Tylor, E. B., 3, 9, 252, 341

Unwin, J. D., 5, 7, 341
Uribe, C. R., 254, 259, 340

Van Gennep, A., 3, 341
von Neumann, J., 311, 313, 341
Vreeland, A. H., 254, 341

Wallace, A. F. C., 181, 183–90, 196, 197, 198–205, 206, 214, 280, 300, 301–303, 305, 309, 341
Ward, L. F., 2, 341
Warner, W. L., 5, 8, 140–41, 145, 284, 297, 341
Weaver, W., 280, 285, 341
Webb, T. T., 146, 341
Weber, M., 118, 341
Weil, A., 151, 342
Weinreich, U., 200, 342
Werner, O., 212–14, 216, 342
Westermarck, E., 3, 342
Westoff, C. F., 158, 330
White, H., 151, 342
White, L. A., 1, 247, 252, 253, 342
Wiener, N., 314, 342
Wilder, W., 126, 342
Williams, G. E., 21–22, 334
Winter, E. H., 254, 342
Worsley, P. M., 73, 77, 80, 81, 342
Wright, H. F., 320

Yalman, N., 148, 235, 342

Zelditch, Morris, 30, 342

# Subject
# Index

Activity groups, 69, 87
  *See also* Descent groups
Agnatic descent, *See* Patrilineal descent
Alliance theory, 2, 14, Chapters 5, 6
    (105–14)
  Australian section systems and,
    281–84
  concentric structures and, 107–13
  descent theory and, 105, 129–31
  development of, 15–17
  diametric structures, 107–13
  dual organizations and, 106
  ethnographer's objection, 125–27
  interpretive error, 120–23
  Kachin case, 123–24
  *mayu-dama*, 123–24
  Murngin case, 139–45
  positive marriage rules, 114, 137
  positivistic error, 124–25
  preferential/prescriptive distinction,
    102, 125–27
  theory of sentiments, 121–23
  triadism-in-dualism and, 108–12
  Winnebago discrepancy, 107–11
  *See also* Asymmetric exchange;
    Descent theory; Dravidian
    systems; Elementary structures;
    Exchange; Information theory;
    Marriage; Mathematical models;
    Models

Ambilineal groups, 90–91
  localized ramages, 91
  ramages, 91
  *See also* Descent groups
Analog codes, 169
  *See also* Distinctive features
Ancestor-based groups
  ambilineal groups, 90–91
  definitive groups, 90
  descent groups and, 86–87
  nonunilineal, 89–91
  optative groups, 90
  restricted and unrestricted, 90
  unilineal, 90
  *See also* Descent groups
Aranda case, the
  information measures and, 286–91
  *See also* Australian tribes, section
    systems
Assignments, *See* componential analysis
Asymmetric exchange, 110, 111,
    118–25, 132, 134–39
  computer simulations and, 125, 126
  Crow-Omaha systems and, 249–51
  ethnographer's objection, 125–27
  interpretive error, 120–23
  Kachin case, 123–24
  mathematical definition of instability
    in, 154–55
  Omaha systems and, 266–77

Asymmetric exchange (*Cont'd*)
  positivistic error, 124–25
  Purum case, 267–276
  theory of sentiments, 121–23
  *See also* Alliance theory; Australian
    tribes, section systems;
    Elementary structures; Symmetric
    exchange
Australian tribes, 3–4, 10
  alliance theory and, 281–84
  alternate marriage in, 142–49
  couples (descent), 143
  cycles (descent), 143–47
  descent theory, 281–84
  information measure and Aranda,
    286–91
  information measures and Kariera,
    284–86
  information theory and, 279–84
  Kariera case, 235–42
  linear programming and, 313–14
  mathematical properties of, 155–56
  Njamal case, 235, 237–42
  pairs (marriage), 143
  regular marriage and, 145–46
  section systems, 131, 136–48, 281–84
  subsection systems, 140–48
  *See also* Alliance theory; Aranda;
    Asymmetric exchange; Descent
    theory; Dravidian systems;
    Information theory; Kariera;
    Murngin; Symmetric exchange
Autonyms, 170
  *See also* Distinctive features
Avoidance behavior, *see* Evolutionary
    stages (explanations)
Avunuculate, 9


Bales-Longbaugh interaction codings,
    family interaction and, 30
"Big men," 78, 99
  *See also* Descent theory; Group
    formation
Bilateral cross-cousin marriage, *see*
    Alliance theory; Australian tribes;
    Dravidian systems; Exchange;
    Symmetric exchange

Biology and kinship
  extensionist hypothesis, 4–5
  family and, 33–38
  ideal languages, 4
  physiological paternity, 3–4
  sociological parenthood, 3–4,
    69–70
  *See also* Extensionist hypothesis;
    Family; Sociological parenthood
Blood money, 71
Bororo case, the, 106–11
  *See also* Alliance theory
Boundary-setting criteria, *see*
    Componential analysis
Bride price, 71
  Kachin marriage and, 154–56
  marriage stability and, 81–82
British social anthropology
  "Inner circle," 6
  *See also* Alliance theory; Descent
    groups; Descent theory; Descent
    types


Classificatory and descriptive systems,
    4, 6, 8
  *See also* Isolating terminologies;
    Kinship terminology
Complementarism, *see* Componential
    analysis
Complex systems
  conditions for, 117–18
  definition of, 117–18
  distinctive features of, 117–18
  ideal type, 116–18
  *See also* Crow-Omaha systems;
    Elementary structures
Componential analysis, 181–86
  as analytic process, 196–201
  assignments, 206
  boundary-setting criteria, 199
  comparisons of models of, 184–90
  complementarism, 201–204
  connotative meaning, 199
  discovery procedures, 182
  discriminant variables, 187
  eliciting contexts, 205–207
  experimentation and, 189–90

homonyms and metaphors, 199–201, 205

imperfect paradigmatic rules, 202

Kelly triad test and, 189, 208

kernels, 182

logical operators, 201–206

logical space for, 183, 186–88, 196

metaphorical extensions, 200

nonbinary components, 205

noncommutative relational concepts, 204

nonorthogonal spaces, 203–204

of American-English kinship, 183–85

orthogonal spaces, 202–204

paradigms and cognition, 184–87

perfect paradigms, 196–98, 201–204

polysemy, 199

prediction of naming, 206–207

psychological reality and, 204–208

range sets, 189

redundant solutions, 205

regular (vs. irregular) reduction of terms, 201

Romney notational system, 188

semantic differential, 207

semantic dimensions, 181, 196, 38

semantic indeterminacy, 205–6

semantic transformations, 206–207

semological units, 199–201

significata, 182, 196

sortings, 206

substantive results, 181–89

synonymy, 199–201

Trobriand case and, 39–44

See also Extensionist hypothesis; Formal analysis; Linguistic models; Transformational analysis

Computer simulations

asymmetric exchange and, 125, 126

marriage and, 314

parallel cousin marriage and, 158

Conjectural history, 1–3, 8–10

See also Evolutionary stages

Connotative meaning, see Componential analysis

Consanguinity

definition, 3–4

See also Genealogical dimensions

Contrast set, see Linguistic models

Cournot lines, 152

See also Mathematical models; Optimal lines

Covert categories

midlevel nodes and, 211

psychological relevance of, 212

tests for, 212

unique beginner and, 209

See also Linguistic models

Cross-generation marriage, definition of, 248

Cross/parallel distinction, 10

Dravidian systems and, 233–240

Kay's formalization of, 232–33, 242–46

Lounsbury's diagnostic for, 231–32

Pospisil's diagnostic for, 230–31

Romney notation and, 232

Tyler's analysis of, 242–44

See also Dravidian systems; Iroquois systems; Kinship terminology

Crow systems, see Omaha systems

Crow-Omaha systems, 15

asymmetric exchange and, 249–51

definition of, 117

distinctive features of, 117–18, 249–50

ideal types and, 117

kin and residential groups as explanations, 252–53

lineage principles and, 70–71

marriage choice in, 117–18

See also Complex systems; Elementary structures

Davis-Warner approach, see Formal analysis

Decision theory, 312–14, Chapter 4 (69–104), Chapter 7 (151–64)

linear and dynamic programming and, 312–16

See also Descent theory; Information theory; Linguistic models

Descent groups

ancestor-based groups and, 86–87

Descent groups (*Cont'd*)
  compromise kin groups, 71;
    *see also* Residence
  corporate nature of, 70–72
  cosmological ideas and, 73
  Dravidian systems and, 233–40
  fission and, 80–81
  hypergamy and, 83
  hypogamy and, 83
  land tenure and, 79–80
  law and, 74
  lineage, 70–73
  localization and, 72
  'loose structure' and, 79–80
  marital stability, transfer of rights
    and, 80, 83–84
  marriage alliances and, 73
  moieties, 10
  personal kin groups and, 86–88
  polysegmentary systems and, 98–99
  population pressure and, 79–80
  property and, 71, 73
  recruitment and, 78–79
  research strategy and, 74
  segmentary lineages, 72
  sibs, 10
  synthetic analysis and, 74
  *See also* Alliance theory; Australian
    tribes; section systems; Descent
    theory
Descent lines
  ancestor-based groups and, 90–91
  descent theory and, 87
  optation and, 100
  section systems and, 141–48
  *See also* Lines of activation
Descent theory, 2, 8–14, Chapter 4
    (69–104), 249–52
  alliance theory and, 105, 129–31
  "big men, rubbish men" and, 78, 99
  bride-price, marital stability and,
    83–84
  bride-price, rights transfer and,
    83–84
  cognatic/unilineal distinction, 102–104
  correlates of, 10–13
  cross cultural files and, 5–8
  definition, 8–10, 85

descent lines and, 87
descent lines, and anonymous
  moieties, 281–82
domestic relations and, 72–73
double descent and alliance, 281–84
epistemology and, 73–78
-etic level and, 93
feudal political structures and, 83
fission and, 80–81
genealogical charter and, 78–79
Gluckman hypothesis and, 81–82
ground rules and, 100–101
kith and, 87
linear programming and, 91–92
lines of activation, and, 87
local groupings and, 74
local lines and, 99–100
marriage and, 112, 130
nodal kindreds and, 88
non-African models and, 76–81
optation and, 81, 100
personal kindreds and, 86–87
recruitment, ground rules, strategy
  rules and, 99–102
residence and, 77–78
residual lines, 133–34
rules and principles of, 13–14, 70–73,
  76–81, 85–86, 249–53
segmentary principles and, 77–85
selective advantage and, 81–82
stem kindreds, 88
strategy rules and, 91
theory of games and, 91–92
*See also* Alliance theory; Descent
  groups; Gluckman hypothesis;
  Hypergamy; Hypogamy; Omaha
  systems
Descent types
  double descent, 281–84
  matriarchy, 9–10
  matrilineal, 9–10, 73
  matrimoieties, 107
  patriarchy, 9–10
  patrilineal, 9–10, 72–73
  typology and, 73
  *See also* Alliance theory; Descent
    groups; Descent theory; Trobriand
    kinship.

Difference equations, *see* Mathematical models; Natchez class system
Differential equations, 153–57
  *See also* Exchange; Mathematical models
Digital codes, 169
  *See also* Distinctive features; Information theory
Distinctive features
  analog codes, 169
  asymmetric systems, 249–50
  autonyms, 170
  Crow-Omaha systems, 117–18, 249–50
  cultural systems and, 169–70
  of descent systems, 98–99
  digital codes, 169
  of Dravidian transformation rules, 235–42
  in household analysis, 68
  of Iroquois transformation rules, 225–32
  linguistic analysis and, 169–74
  Miwok systems, 249
  mourning terms, 169–71
  necronyms, 160–70
  for Omaha systems, 254–61
  phonemics and, 169–74
  of primary kin types, 171
  teknonyms, 170
  transformation rules and, 169–74
Dravidian systems
  affines in, 233–38
  alliance theory and, 130, 135–39
  bifurcation in, 238
  cognates in, 234–38
  componential analysis and, 136–37
  cross/parallel distinction and, 233–40
  double descent and, 135
  endogamous kindreds and, 235
  exogamous descent groups and, 235
  hereditary affinity rules for, 235–40
  Iroquois terminology and, 233–46
  Kay's formalization of, 240–46
  kinship terminology and, 136–39
  perpetual affinity, 137
  Romney notation and, 241
  section systems and, 139–48
  symmetric exchange and, 233–40

Tyler's analysis of, 242–44
  *See also* Alliance theory; Iroquois systems; Kariera systems
Dual organizations, *see* Alliance theory

Elementary structures, 250
  conditions for, 114
  distinctive features of, 117–18
  ethnographer's objection, 125–27
  as ideal types, 116–17
  interpretive error, 120–23
  Kachin case, 123–24
  patrilateral systems, 124–25
  positivistic error, 124–25
  *See also* Alliance theory; Australian tribes; section systems; Crow-Omaha systems; Dravidian systems
Eliciting contexts, *See* Componential analysis
-Emic level
  level of comparison and, 97
  *See also* Distinctive features; -Etic level
Epistemology of science, 15–17, 116–20, 145–48
  alliance models and, 105–27
  bifurcation of nature and, 313
  competing theories and, 44–45
  correspondence rules, 117–19
  criteria of adequacy, 247–49
  deductive reasoning and, 114–15
  deductive systems, 120–22
  deep structure and, 99
  descent theory and, 74–78, 102–103
  empiricism vs. structuralism, 111–12
  ethnographer's objection, 125–27
  family and, 28
  formal procedures of mathematics and, 311–13
  genetic fallacy, 55
  hierarchy of models and, 315–17
  history of science and, 311
  ideal types, 116–20
  interpretive error, 120–22
  models and, 93, 113–15
  plausibility considerations and, 312–13

Epistemology of science (*Cont'd*)
  positivistic error, 124–25
  simulations and axiomatic
    approaches, 159–61
  surface structure and, 99
  theory of games and, 91
  *See also* Alliance theory; Decision
    theory; Descent theory;
    Information processing;
    Information theory
Equilibrium states
  Alliance theory and, 113
  economic and political, 156–58
  graph theory and, 161–64
  mathematical definition of, 154–55
  Pareto point, 153
  social relations and, 93–94
  *See also* Stochastic processes
Ethnogenealogical method, *see* Kinship
    terminology; Linguistic models;
    Personal kindred
Ethnographic models, 47–48, 88–90,
    92–95, 97–98
  graph theory and, 100–101
Ethnoscience
  definition of domain boundaries, 53
  eliciting frames and, 22–23
  family and, 21–22
  information processing and, 103–104
  personal kindred and, 89
-Etic level
  descent theory and, 93
  kinship distance and, 95–97
  *See also* Distinctive features;
    -Emic level
Evolutionary explanations, *see*
    Avoidance behavior; Classificatory
    and descriptive terms; Descent
    theory; Group formation;
    Hawaiian systems
Evolutionary stages, *See* Conjectural
    history; Father right; Group
    marriage; Mother right;
    Primitive promiscuity
Exchange
  demographic restraints and, 157–58
  differential equations for, 151–64
  échange généralisé, 113, 153

échange restreint, 113, 153
  hypergamy and, 49–52
  marital rights and, 28–29
  mathematical properties of, 153–56
  models of dual organization, 105–27
  nonzero-sum games, 151–53
  positive marriage rules, 113
  positive value of, 105, 113
  prestations, 16, 112–13, 136
  social behavior as, 93–95
  sociology of, 16–17
  symbiotic, 151–52
  transaction theory and, 93, 95
  zero-sum games and, 103, 151
  *See also* Alliance theory; Asymmetric
    exchange; Australian tribes; Crow-
    Omaha systems; Dravidian systems,
    Elementary structures;
    Information theory
Exogamy, 9, 70–71
  *See also* Alliance theory; Asymmetric
    exchange; Descent theory;
    Elementary structures; Symmetric
    exchange
Extensionist hypothesis, 4–6
  acquisition of syntax and, 37–38
  classificatory and descriptive
    kinship terms, 4–5
  family and, 35–46
  genetic fallacy, 5
  information processing mechanisms
    and, 37–38
  kinship terminology and, 35–38
  linguistic approach, 5
  semantic approach, 5
  social learning approach, 4
  stimulus generalization and, 37
  Trobriand case 39–46
  *See also* Linguistic models;
    Transformational analysis

*Famille souche*, 27–28
  *See also* Stem kindreds
Family, 1, 8–47, 49–51
  Adams' analytic scheme for, 26–27
  affective relations in, 28–33
  analytic priority of, 19

Bales-Longbaugh scoring system and, 30
*bilek*, 63–67
biology and kinship and, 33–35
comparative development, 56–58
competing theories and, 39
dyadic frame of reference and, 29–33
elementary form of, 53–55
eliciting frames and, 21–23
as ethnological construct, 28
ethnoscience and, 21n–22n
evidence against universality of, 24–25
explanatory value of, 29–30
extensionist hypothesis and, 35–46
*famille souche* and, 27–28
formal analysis and, 19
functions of, 22
household and, 19–46
incest and, 35
*jus in genetricem* and, 28
*jus in uxorem* and 28
matrilocal form of, 70–71
matrix of relational types and, 27
Murdock's definition of, 19
Nayar case, the, 24
nuclear form of, 54
Nuer social organization and, 22–23
role occupancy and, 28–29
stochastic processes and, 58–68
theories of kinship reckoning and, 19–20
Trobriand case and, 39–46
universality hypothesis, 23–24
*See also* Extensionist hypothesis; Transformational analysis
Fandango, 49
Father right, *see* Evolutionary stages
Filiation
alliance and, 130–35, 143–45
complementary, 70, 131–35, 136–38
definition, 69, 130
strategy rules and, 100–101
unilateral, 70
utrolateral, 66, 91
*See also* Alliance theory; Descent theory

Firestick father, 34
Fission
bride-price and, 81
descent groups and, 78–83
descent theory and, 78–83
*See also* Descent theory
Folk classification
information theory and, 297–309
*See also* Linguistic models
Folk taxa, *see* Linguistic models
Formal analysis, Chapter 13 (311–17)
componential accounts, 7
Davis-Warner approach and, 8
family and, 19
kinship terminologies and, 6–8
metalanguages and, 8
*See also* Componential analysis; Scalogram analysis; Transformational analysis; Trobriand kinship
French sociology, 2

Galton's problem, 181
*See also* Scalogram analysis
Genealogical charter, 78
*See also* Descent theory
Genealogical dimensions, 3–10
affinity, 6
bifurcation, 6
collaterality, 6
consanguinity, 3–4
decedence, 6
generation, 5–6
polarity, 6
relative age, 4–8
sex of relative, 3–4, 7–8
sex of speaker, 6
Genetic father, 34
Genetic mother, 34
Genetrix, 33–35
Genitor, 34
Gluckman hypothesis
alliance theory, 131
degree of lineality and, 82–87
description, 81–83
Leach, criticism of, 82–86
marriage stability and, 30–31

Graph theory, 151–53
asymmetric exchange models and,
159–64
mathematical structure of games
and, 100–101
matrices and digraphs, 159–60
paradigms and, 213–14
rule systems and, 100–101
score structures, 161–63
taxonomies and, 212–13
theorems for, 162–64
theory of sentiments and, 163
Groom service, 55–56
Group formation, 2–3, 8–14, 93–95
ideology and, 98–99
See also Descent groups; Descent
theory
Group marriage, see Evolutionary
stages

Head term, see Linguistic models
Homonyms in componential analysis,
199
Household
decision-oriented approach, 49–50,
52–53
definition of, 21
demographic constraints, 54
diachronic approach, 52–58
family and, 21–23
Fortes' approach, 53, 56
ideal types, 21
joint fraternal, 55–56
linear programming, 51–52
modal types, 21
Romney approach, 48
social learning and domestic cycle, 55
statistical approach, 48, 54–55
stochastic approach, 63–68
stochastic processes, 58–68
transformations and distinctive
features for, 67
See also Family
Hypergamy
descent groups and, 83–85
mathematical properties of, 153–55
residence and, 49

Hypogamy, 83

Ideal languages
biology and, 33–35
See also Biology and kinship
Incest, 117
elementary structures and, 117–19
family and, 35
Index, see Linguistic models
Indonesian case, the, 107–12
See also Alliance theory
Information processing, 314–15
analogy machines and, 314
descent theory and, 102–103
extensionist hypothesis and, 35–38
language acquisition and, 102
numerical machines and, 314
See also Information theory
Information theory, 279–309
actual entropy, 280, 291, 298–99
Aranda system, 284–91, 296
Australian systems and, 279, 281–82,
284, 297, 298
binary number system and, 293, 295
bits of information, 280, 292, 305,
308
comparative information measures,
289–91, 294–97
efficiency scales and, 298, 299
eliciting and, 303–5
ethnological theory and, 293
experimentation and, 301–7
genealogical queries and, 293–94
gradual uncertainty reduction and,
291–93, 302–305
information processing capacity,
300–309
Kariera system, 284–86, 291–92,
294–95
$\log_2$, 280–81, 298, 300–305, 308
marriage rules and, 279
maximum entropy, 280, 291, 298–99
Murngin, 297–300
native classifications and, 299–300
paradigms and, 300–301
recording processes and, 300
redundancy, 280, 291, 298–99

relative entropy, 280, 291, 298–99
search plans and, 308–309
section systems and, 281–84
span of perceptual dimensionality
  and, 305–307
taxonomies and, 303, 308
threshold effect and, 302–306, 308
twenty questions and, 291–94
*See also* Information processing
Inheritance, 9
"Inner Circle," 6
*See also* British social anthropology
Iroquois systems
  causal explanations and, 219–20
  criteria of structural adequacy and,
    221–33
  cross/parallel distinction in, 219,
    221–30
  developmental typology and, 220
  distinctive features of rules, 228–33
  Dravidian systems and, 233–42
  elder/younger age distinction in,
    224–28
  functional explanations and, 220
  generation-type classification in,
    221–25
  half-sibling rule of, 221
  Kay's formalization of, 232–33,
    244–45
  Lounsbury's analysis of, 231, 244–45
  merging rule in, 221–30
  Pospisil's analysis, 231
  principles of social organization and,
    219
  Romney notation and, 232, 244–45
  scalogram analysis and, 220–33
  threshold variables for, 221
  transformational analysis and,
    224–33
  transformation rule of, 224–25
  Tyler's analysis of, 242–46
  variation in, 219–20
  *See also* Alliance theory; Cross/
    parallel distinction; Dravidian
    systems; Kariera case; Scalogram
    analysis
Isolating systems, *see* Kinship
  terminology

Joking relationships, 70n

Kachin case
  asymmetric systems and, 122–27
  graph theory and, 159–61
Karadjeri type marriage, *see* Subsection
  systems
Kariera system
  information measures and, 281–86
  *See also* Alliance theory; Australian
    tribes; Cross/parallel distinction;
    Dravidian systems; Iroquois
    systems
Keys, *see* Linguistic models
Kinship terminology, 2, 6–13
  analysis of, 165–90
  basic member definitions, 267
  bifurcate merging, 10
  determinants of, 10–11
  Dravidian bifurcation and, 238
  extensionist hypothesis and, 35–38
  Hawaiian system, 3
  Iroquois systems of, 219–46
  isolating systems, 8
  primary kin types and, 171, 224
  relative products, 224–33
  Romney notation and, 232
  rules of extension, 267–69
  sociological and behavioral
    correlates, 11–12
  status change and reclassification,
    33–34
  Trobriand case, 39–46
  *See also* Biology and kinship;
    Classificatory and descriptive
    systems; Ethnogenealogical
    method; Extensionist hypothesis;
    Formal analysis; Iroquois systems;
    Omaha kinship systems;
    Trobriand kinship
Kinship terms
  Central Philippine systems, 207
  denotata, 93
  North American systems, 207
  significata, 93
  status change and reclassification,
    33–34

Kinship terms (*Cont'd*)
tree graphs for, 215
Trobriand case, 39–46
Kith, descent theory and, 87


Levirate, definition of, 252
Lexemes, *see* Linguistic models
Linear programming
decision theory and, 311–17
descent theory and, 90–92, 103–104
marriage and residence, 49–53
Lines of activation
ancestor-based groups and, 91–92
descent theory and, 87
Linguistic models, 5, 6–8, 191–217
contrast sets, 194
covert categories, 192, 211–12
decision processes and,
domain feature, 193
folk classifications and, 191–201
folk taxa, 196–201
head term, 193
index, 193
keys, 192–95
lexemes and, 191–94, 196–97
linguistic complementarity, 204–208
minimal classification events,
194–95
paradigms, 192, 194–98
paradigms, definition of, 195
perfect paradigms, 196–98
query-response models, 193–96
root feature, 193
segregates and, 191–92
single beginner, 193
taxonomies, 192–95, 209–11
tree measures, 193–94, 202
Trobriand case, 39–46
typologies, 192, 208–209
unique beginner, 193
*See also* Componential analysis;
Distinctive features;
Ethnogenealogical method;
Extensionist hypothesis;
Transformation analysis;
Trobriand kinship
Local lines, *see* Descent theory

Logical operators, *see* Componential
analysis
'Loose structure,'
descent groups and, 78–79
game theory and, 100–102
optation and, 81
selective advantage and, 80–81
*See also* Descent groups


Marriage
complex systems and, 250
elementary structures and, 250
Omaha systems and, 249–50
Purum case and, 268–76
stability and, 28–29
*See also* Alliance theory;
Asymmetric exchange; Australian
tribes; Dravidian systems;
Information theory; Iroquois
systems; Omaha systems;
Symmetric exchange
Marriage classes, *see* Australian tribes;
section systems
Mater, 35
Mathematical models, 154–64,
Chapter 13 (311–17)
difference equations, 156–58
differential equations, 152–55
graph theory, 151–52, 159–64
matrix algebra, 151
nonzero-sum games, 151–52
optimal lines, 152, 154
Pareto point, 153
statistical mechanics, 151
theory of games, 151
theory of groups of permutations, 151
*See also* Alliance theory; Stochastic
processes
Matriarchate, 9
*See also* Descent theory
Matrilateral cross-cousin marriage, *see*
Alliance theory; Asymmetric
exchange; Australian tribes;
section systems; Australian tribes;
subsection systems; Elementary
structures; Exchange
Mayu-Dama, 123, 131
*See also* Alliance theory

Metalanguages, social relations and, 94
Metaphors, in componential analysis, 159–60
Minimal classification event, *see* Linguistic models
Miwok systems
  distinctive features of, 250
  formal properties of, 249–50
  *See also* Asymmetric exchange; Omaha systems
Models
  alliance theory and, 129–49, 283–84
  complex systems and, 250
  concentric structures, 107–10
  conscious, 107
  Crow-Omaha systems and, 250
  descent theory and, 281–83
  diametric structures, 107–10
  elementary structures and, 250
  ideal types, 118–20
  linguistics and, 107
  mathematical relations and, 110–11
  mechanical and statistical, 115–20
  relation to theory, 120
  social structure and, 105–107
  unconscious, 107
  *See also* Alliance theory; Descent theory
Mother right, *see* Evolutionary explanations
Mourning terms, 169–70
  *See also* Distinctive features
Murdock marriages, 145
Murngin case, the
  information measures and, 297–300
  *See also* Alliance theory; Asymmetric exchange; Australian tribes; section systems

Natchez class system
  alternative solutions for, 157–58
  comparison with Kachin, 155–56
  difference equations and, 157
Nayar case, the
  affinity and, 136–37
  universality hypothesis (family) and, 23–28

Necronyms, 169–70
  *See also* Distinctive features
Nodal kindreds, descent theory and, 88
Nonbinary components, *see* Componential analysis
Noncommutative relational concepts, *see* Componential analysis
Nonorthogonal spaces, *see* Componential analysis

Occasional kin group, 71n
Omaha systems
  asymmetric exchange and, 267–76
  Crow-Omaha systems, asymmetric exchange and, 249–50
  descent theory principles and, 251–52
  determinants of, 247–48
  distinctive features of, 249–51
  formal properties of, 249–77
  historical reconstruction and, 256–59
  kin and residential groups as explanations for, 252–53
  lineal forms of classification, 261–62
  Miwok systems and, 249
  range reduction rules and, 262–76
  rank forms of classification, 261–62
  scalogram analysis of, 253–54
  skewing rules for, 255–56, 258–61
  transformation rules for, 255–60
Optimal lines, 152, 154
  *See also* Mathematical models
Organic solidarity, 15, 113
Orthogonal spaces, *see* Componential analysis

Paradigms
  asymmetrical paradigms, 214
  formal definitions for, 213–14
  graph theory and, 213
  information theory and, 300–301
  neutralization and, 214
  symmetrical paradigms, 214
  theorems for, 212
  *See also* Linguistic models
Parasitism, 151, 155
  *See also* Mathematical models

[364]  Subject Index

Parenté physique, 3
Parenté sociale, 3
Pareto point, 153
  See also Equilibrium states;
    Mathematical models
Pater, 34
Patriarchate, 9
  See also Descent theory
Pedimiento, 49, 52
Personal kindreds
  definition of, 89
  descent theory and, 86–87
  ethnogenealogical definition of,
    88–89
  range of, 87–89
  See also Descent groups; Descent
    theory
Physiological kinship, see Biology and
    kinship; Sociological parenthood
Political ideology, territorial
    organization and, 98–99
Polysemy, see Componential analysis
Prediction of naming, see
    Componential analysis
Primary kin types, see Distinctive
    features; Kinship terminology
Primitive promiscuity, see
    Evolutionary explanations
Psychological reality, see
    Componential analysis
Purum case, the
  graph theory and, 159–64
  sociological explanations for, 269–71,
    275–76
  transformation analysis and, 267–76

Quellenforschungen, 2
Query-response models, see Linguistic
    models

Redundant solutions, see
    Componential analysis
Relative products, see Kinship
    terminology
Research design, 10–12
  cross cultural files, 12–13
  sampling, 12

Residence
  compromise kin groups, 71
  descent theory and, 76–78
  lucrilocal, 56
  matrilocal, 67
  matrineolocal, 51
  neolocal, 67
  patrilocal, 67
  residential decisions, 49–53
  stochastic processes and, 58–68
  uxorilocal, 50
  virilocal, 49
  See also Descent groups; Descent
    theory; Stochastic processes;
    Trobriand case
Romney notational system, 289–91
  analysis of Iroquois, 232
  Purum analysis and, 274
  range reduction in Omaha and,
    262–67
  See also Componential analysis;
    Cross/parallel distinction;
    Household; Romney approach;
    Iroquois systems; Kinship
    terminology
Root feature, see Linguistic models
"Rubbish men," 99
  See also Descent theory
Rule systems, 49, 69–71, 73–83, 90–91,
    103–104
  as constraints, 100–101
  graph-theoretic characterization of,
    100–101
  move-defining, 101
  position-defining, 101–102
  probabilistic foundations of, 100
  residual rights, 133
  set-theoretic characterization of, 101

Scales
  analogy machines and, 314
  numerical machines and, 314
  preference, 103
  priorities of exchange, 95–97
Scalogram analysis, 174–81
  coefficient of reproducibility, 175,
    221–22, 253

examples of, 177–78, 222–23, 253–54
Iroquois systems and, 202–33
Omaha systems and, 253–60
ordinal measures and, 180
predictive properties of, 177–79,
   221–23, 255–56
scale types, 176, 222–23, 254
scale variables, 176, 221–23, 230–32,
   254
stability, 177
terminological equations and, 175,
   222–23, 253–54
test-retest reliability, 176
typology and, 179, 223, 251–54
unidimensionality, 176
universe of attributes, 175–76,
   221–30, 252–53
Section systems
   explanations of, 281–91
   Kay's theorem for Aranda type, 289–91
   *See also* Alliance theory; Aranda;
      Australian tribes; Dravidian
      systems; Kariera case; Murngin
      case; Njamal case
Segregates, *see* Linguistic models
Semantic differential, *see*
   Componential analysis
Semantic indeterminacy, *see*
   Componential analysis
Semantic transformations, *see*
   Componential analysis
Semological units, *see*
   Componential analysis
Sibs, *see* Descent theory
Single beginner, *see* Linguistic models
Sinhalese kindred, 148*n*
   *See also* Dravidian systems
Sociological parenthood, *see* Biology
   and kinship
Sororate, definition of, 248
Sortings, *see* Componential analysis
South Indian kinship, *see* Dravidian
   systems
Stem kindreds
   descent theory and, 88
   *See also Famille souche*
Stochastic processes, 58–68
   age grades and, 62

competence models and, 315
deterministic processes and, 315–16
family and household, 58–68
ground rules and, 316
Markov chains; definition, 59
Markov chains; equilibrium
   properties of, 63
Markov chains; limiting vectors,
   62, 66, 67
Markov chains; outcome states, 59–66
Markov chains; probability vectors,
   61, 62, 65
Markov chains; row vectors, 60, 61
Markov chains; transition
   probabilities, 59–61, 66
Markov chains; tree measures and
   matrices, 60–63, 65, 67
Mechanical and statistical processes
   and, 316–17
path rules and, 101
performance models and, 315
simulations, 68
simultaneous equations for, 66
strategy rules and, 316
Succession, definition, 9
Symmetric exchange, *see also*
   Australian tribes; section systems;
      Dravidian systems; Exchange;
      Iroquois systems; Kariera case
Synonymy, *see* Componential analysis


Taxonomies, 219–17
   axioms and theorems for, 209–13
   example of, 210
   extra-hierarchic relations, 211
   graph theory and, 212–13
   information theory and, 303–305
   multiple and interlocking hierarchies,
      211
   ontogenetic relations, 211
   path rules for, 213
   types of contrast in, 211
   *See also* Linguistic models
Teknonyms, 170
   *See also* Distinctive features
Theory of games, 311
   collaboration cases, 107

Theory of games (*Cont'd*)
  descent and, 152
  filiation and, 99
  ground rules, 68, 92, 98, 100, 102,
    153–59
  marital exchange and, 106–107
  recruitment and, 99–100
  residential processes and, 68
  strategy rules, 68, 92, 99, 100, 102,
    153–59
  utilities, 151–59
Transfer of rights
  descent theory, alliance theory and,
    114
  *in genetricem*, 29
  *in uxorem*, 29
  *See also* Descent theory
Transformations, in household analysis,
  66–67
Transformational analysis
  abstract explanation of, 168–70
  alpha rules, 173–74, 229–32
  basic member definitions, 267
  distinctive features and, 169, 171–74,
    226–29
  expansion rules, 167–68
  formalized theories and, 166–68
  formulation of rules, 166–74
  half-sibling rule, 225
  historical reconstruction and, 257–59
  Iroquois merging rules, 225–30
  Iroquois transformation rule, 225–28
  Omaha systems and, 254–60
  Purum case and, 267–76
  reduction rules, 167, 168, 169
  rewrite rules, 167, 224–33
  rules of extension, 267
  sex designators for, 224
  transformation rules, 167, 168, 169,
    171
  Trobriand case and, 39–46

Tree languages
  imperfect trees, 194
  Markov process and, 60
  semantics and, 191–93
  true (perfect) trees, 193–95
  *See also* Kinship terms; Linguistic
    models
Trobriand kinship
  concentric structures of, 107–108
  Leach-Lounsbury controversy, 39–46
  *See also* Epistemology of science,
    genetic fallacy; Extensionist
    hypothesis; Formal analysis;
    Kinship terminology; Linguistic
    models; Transformational analysis
Typology
  alliance theory and, 136, 145–48
  decision processes and, 102–103
  descent groups and, 82–85, 90–92
  of descent groups, 70–71
  descent rules and, 86
  Iroquois systems and, 219–46
  kinship terminologies, 6–7, 10
  linguistic models and, 191–93, 208–209
  Omaha classification and, 259–60
  ordinal measures and, 82
  *See also* Alliance theory;
    Epistemology of science;
    Scalogram analysis

Unique beginner, *see* Linguistic models
Universal grammars, 315
Universality hypothesis, family and,
  23–28

Wife-stealing, *see* Evolutionary
  explanations
Winnebago discrepancy, the, 107–11
  *See also* Alliance theory